Swerve
Dub Sex & Other Stories

Mark Hoyle

route

First published by Route in 2024
info@route-online.com
www.route-online.com

First Edition

Mark Hoyle asserts his moral right
to be identified as the author of this work

ISBN: 978-1-901927-93-1

Editors:
Ian Daley & Isabel Galán

Cover Design:
Golden

Printed by Books Factory

All rights reserved
No reproduction of this text without written permission

Dedicated to the memory of Patricia Hoyle (1932-1971)

And to Ellis, Stefan and Kelly

Contents

PART I: Turmoil
1: Beneath The Underneath — 11
2: Freefall — 22
3: Martin Lane — 30
4: Tommy — 38
5: Fallout — 47

PART II: Keeping Control
6: Vibrant Thigh — 55
7: Collective — 67
8: God's Gift — 77
9: Joy Division Close Up — 87
10: Substances — 101
11: Deeper — 110
12: To Hell With Poverty — 119

PART III: Scatter & Run
13: Karlos — 135
14: Wilderness — 148
15: Clubland — 162
16: Soul Open — 174
17: The Battle Of Whitworth Street West — 186
18: Streets In The Sky — 199

PART IV: And Here It Comes
19: Don't Trip On It — 215
20: Fire — 229
21: The Art Of Surprise — 238
22: Coming Up On Your Blind Side — 244
23: Push! — 253

24: A Touch Of Evil   261
25: Deutschland   270

PART V: Get This!
26: Funtime   291
27: Grip Of The Snarebeat   298
28: Two Eights Clash   307
29: Turn Into A Blur   314
30: The Ecstasy And The Agony   324
31: TV Eye   331
32: Overground   339
33: Martin Hannett And Me   350

PART VI: I Want
34: Time Of Life   365
35: Human   380
36: Endgame   392

Discography   403
Then…   407
Acknowledgements   411

Swerve or get hurt
The choice is yours
Grown up in the dirt you learned what I learned
And in this battle of nerves
They can hurt but never come first
Search for the right words
Search for the missing words
Swerve

PART I
Turmoil

Overleaf: Rhyl, 1971
(L to R) Ronnie McHale, MH, Mark McHale, Tony McHale
Photo courtesy of Tony McHale

1: Beneath The Underneath

Running and running and running. Hulme, Cheetham Hill, Ardwick, Plymouth Grove, Longsight, Salford... My mother's eyes were turned towards a future she could take no part in. As a state registered nurse, she understood how ill she was and how quickly and stealthily she had to move before the pain and the dark closed in and split us up.

I remember things from the early times, but not in order, and only through a small boy's filter. I have little to go on but I have known some things at least about Patricia Hoyle, my mother and saviour. There are stories from priests and nuns and friends' mothers. I've had glimpses of my care records, which are so difficult to read. And there are my first-hand, splintered memories, with fragments of people's faces and names, which help me to pick out the truth from the web of lies my mother spun in order to keep me safe for that little while longer.

I was born in a terraced house in Cornbrook Street, Old Trafford. That much is a matter of record. The facts stop there, though. For at least a short time, it seems my father and mother had tried to live together, a part of the invisible Irish diaspora; with him busy building Manchester while she tended to its sick.

I can see myself in the oxblood bricks of the Miles Platting walk-ups, tagging along with other people's kids in the rubble and the filth. Jumping from walls onto spring-filled mattresses until dark made the yellow street lights come on. Bruises unnoticed, cuts unkissed.

My mother is working in a nursing home on Smedley Lane, Cheetham Hill. I have my hair pulled by patients as I play with the Viking ship she bought me until it is crushed by the strong, blameless, childish hands of the grown-up psychiatric patients under her care.

She would go into hospital, and I would go and stay somewhere else, unofficial, a safety net of Irish women looking out for each other. I was one more child to stick on the settee, topping and tailing with Damien or Dermot or whoever was youngest. Who were these women? Kissing me on my forehead, eyes wet with pity in their damp flats, keeping the truth and me as far apart as possible. They had nothing themselves, and yet opened their hearts and homes to me, who had even less.

She'd have to go into hospital so often that sometimes I'd be placed with a foster family and moved to a new school far from where I knew: St. Chad's, St. Catherine's, St. Peter's, St. Paul's... always saints. I'd bite my lip and take the slaps from their resentful 'real' children, wetting the bed, living for the rolled-up tube of comics my mother would send. I kept myself to myself, lying silently on the floor, drawing Thor and The Sub-Mariner in my own little bubble. The minute she could, even though she was far too ill, she would discharge herself and get me back. It'd be another flat, another school, another part of inner-city Manchester.

I can see the night we left Miles Platting for the last time through salty eyes. I am in the back of a van as Lymouth Road gets smaller and smaller. There's shouting and screaming. My mother is running away from a world of violence and alcohol abuse. Frail and terminally ill, with a small child to make a life for, we arrive in Langley and move into a ground floor flat in Grisedale Drive. She tells me that my dad is dead.

Langley is a post-war overspill estate north of the city, built to house Mancunians displaced from the inner-city slums of Hulme, Moss Side and Harpurhey, which were being scraped away en masse to be replaced by labyrinthine crescents. Our redbrick, one-bedroom flat was part of a surge in low-cost housing that saw similar buildings spring up all over the country.

Some order happened for me when I was enrolled at St Mary's infant school on Wood Street. Aged six, I'd reached the age where I started to take things in, make some kind of sense of who we were, my mother and I, and how we lived. I was a filthy, shoeless thing, always hungry, and under no control.

My mother became really ill. Although I have memories of her standing up and walking, they have to be from an earlier time than this. I have no idea how she managed to feed me, or how she got hold of money for the basic things we needed. I just remember playing out until way after darkness fell, mainly alone, but sometimes tagging along uninvited with the other, cleaner kids. The crimes of Moors Murderers Brady and Hindley would have been fresh and painful to the people of Manchester, still nobody batted an eyelid at the dirt-encrusted Irish kid, dressed in his mother's blue tights, out on the freezing streets in the dead of night.

With nobody to look out for me, I roamed far and wide. It was inevitable that somebody would notice eventually. Someone like Mrs Moore. Two decades later I tracked down her daughter, Kathy Moore, and she was able to flesh out my mixed-up, child's version of how things were. Her mother told her a story of me turning up at the house she lived in, miles from our flat, a grubby, emaciated face at the ground-floor window. Her mother was a beautiful human being, a credit to her class. It was natural for her to feed, love and take an interest in me. As my story unfolded, she was able to guide me towards some help, without being taken away from my mother.

I understand now what my mother was up to – keeping me out of official council care as long as she could. I read in my care records a quote of her saying that she didn't want me to end up with the family she had left behind in Dublin because they were 'religion mad'. Although she had fled Ireland and its Catholic stranglehold, she did turn to religious people to help with her dire predicament. I was helped by many Catholic families, 'looking after their own', and this kept me out of children's homes for a year or two longer.

The Little Sisters of the Assumption were an order of Catholic nuns that would go out into the poorest communities, all over the world, and live amongst them, bringing expertise in nursing and teaching to those at the bottom of society's ladder. Like the missionaries of previous times, these selfless women donated their lives to those who had fallen through the cracks. Without the help of the Sisters, my life, and many other lives, would have been tragically different.

They cut quite a dash, to my childish eyes, as they rode their scooters up and down the hills of the estate, bringing relief and practical help to many below the breadline. They never pushed their beliefs on anybody, focussing instead on the practicalities of helping people through life. Despite my mother's misgivings about religious organisations, she allowed me to go to the local church, perhaps as a break for her. A brief few hours respite from an inquisitive kid asking question after question after question.

My mother managed to live longer than was expected. A note in my reports reveals that she was given two years to live in 1967. Three years later, in 1970, we moved further into the interior of the Langley estate to a ground floor maisonette, on Causey Drive. By now, I was in the second year of junior school and our new flat was only a short walk from my new school, Our Lady of the Assumption.

The Causey Drive flat had just one bedroom like other ones we had previously lived in. I had the bedroom and my mother slept in the living room. Although I remember playing and reading in my room, I only remember sleeping with her. She realised that the time was getting near so it is no surprise that she clung to every last minute with me, reading and chatting into the late night. She knew she would die while I was still a little boy, and the only way to get me through what lay ahead was for me to be bright and sharp and clever. She kept me close, nose to nose, teaching me to read and telling me stories. Not kid's books, but whatever she was reading... *The Pan Book of Horror Stories*, Dennis Wheatley, *The Reader's Digest*, and a book about flying saucers that I can still see the cover of. I can see her now if I want to... me and her, inches apart, reading to each other. We spent so much time together, us and nobody else, that I spoke in a bastardised Dublin brogue, mangled and hardened by the smashed glass Mancunian that I heard outside.

Of the few occasions I remember my mother standing up, one of them was when we took a bus ride to visit somebody she knew called Lillian. She lived in the park-keeper's house in Queen's Park, in nearby Heywood, and in my mind's eye we are a normal mother and son, just having a normal day out, so it must be from an earlier time. Another occasion was definitely from Causey Drive. We are together in the room she slept in, and as she passes a book to me she begins to shake and starts to look strange. She stands on a plate and, twisting, falls to the floor, still shaking. I run next door to our neighbour, Les Skinner, and she is taken to hospital, having suffered the first of several heart attacks.

Away from all this or, rather, running alongside it, the intensive attention I receive from my mum is starting to work. I develop a real love of reading. I devoured Enid Blyton's 'Dragon' series of children's books, and dived into a collection of *Goal* magazines, presumably donated by a kindly neighbour. Football was an important part of working-class life. Although we were desperately poor, I got my first Manchester City kit one Christmas, a red and black striped away one. I wore it until it fell off. Who paid for this? I may never know, but I suspect the unseen hand of the Little Sisters.

We were visited each day by Sister Ita. I loved her sky-blue scooter. I must have seen through her austere outward appearance as I remember sitting on her knee on one occasion and pulling her veil off, in a spirit of fun. Her hair was grey. Scary as she often was to me, she took it well. On Saturdays, I would go to the convent where she was based and spend hours cutting stamps off envelopes. I think this was linked to a charity appeal, but it seems just as likely that they were giving my mum some time to recharge.

We have other visitors. I am looked after by Kathy Moore. She washes me in the bath, and takes me places. From my child's viewpoint, she is just another grown-up, so it was a massive surprise to find out when I tracked her down later in life that she is only five years older than me.

Next to my mother's bed was the oxygen tank she needed to breathe. It was as tall as me, black and white, and when it needed changing, I had to bang on the wall to bring the neighbours to help. The faces of these people are etched into my consciousness... Les Skinner, dirty blond hair and his son with the same name. Joan McHale and her sons, Mark and Tony.

I started to make friends with Mark and Tony. The McHales were just a normal family, on the breadline like everybody else on Langley, and it was to their great credit that they didn't think twice about including me into their everyday life. The mother, Joan, would spend time with my mother, one of very few friends I can recall her having. I wonder what they talked about, the two of them? Did my mother confide in her as the days closed in? So much of my life is unknown. I know nothing of what she came from, or her life in Dublin before I was born.

The McHales would feed me, and even took me on holiday, the first I ever had, to a caravan park in Rhyl. Photographs on the beach and in their house are the only photos of me as a child I have ever seen, and give no clue to the turmoil that surrounded me. I seem pale and thin, but that's how everybody looked, as far as I can make out.

Things at home got more serious as my mother's health declined. Knowing that this is the last lap, she clings to me, we are the same person, almost. I can see the oxygen tank with its dangling rubber mask, the bedpan full of dark wee and tobacco, and her breathing as she slept. Up. Down. Up. Down. She reads to me when she's awake, but she sleeps a lot of the time. I play on the floor, oblivious to it all.

We didn't have a television but we had a radio, and I started to absorb what I heard. Just the hits of the day. 'Knock Three Times', 'Chirpy Chirpy Cheep Cheep', 'The Pushbike Song' by The Mixtures. Inane, nursery-rhyme songs; songs that could have been written for a child my age. I am transported back there whenever I am accidentally exposed to some of these tunes in a shop, or on television.

I was given a portable, Dansette-type record player by somebody. It looked like a typewriter, or a small suitcase. I can see myself now, loading up the stacking arm with the three records that I was given with it: 'Back Home' by The 1970 England World Cup squad, 'Little Arrows' by Leapy Lee, and a single by Clodagh Rodgers.

The reading at home was paying off. The classes at Assumption were streamed, with the brightest pupils on the 'top table' of four tables, working down to myself and other 'problem' children on the dreaded 'bottom table'. Despite the chaos of my home situation, I moved up through the class, ahead of many when it came to reading. Although quiet and reserved, I was encouraged by my teacher, Mr Hampson, and started to make progress, joining in with things. One good teacher can make all the difference. I came on leaps and bounds.

I was kept blissfully unaware of how bad things were with my mother. The Little Sisters carried out the essential tasks for me, but they had other people to look after too, and I was left without supervision a lot of the time. Freedom works both ways, and I had too much of it. I wandered far and wide, coming back late into the night, making everything worse without realising it. On one occasion, I ended up falling into a stream in some local woods a few miles away and came home full of cuts, soaking wet. I was in serious trouble and shortly after this, my mother was taken into hospital again. I linked her hospitalisation with me being bad, and blamed myself, believing my bad behaviour to be the catalyst of her decline.

Bleak though things were, I was a little boy with a little boy's interests. The 1969 Moon Landings had gripped the world, and like everyone, I was astronaut mad. I collected 'The Race Into Space' cards given away with PG Tips tea, immersed in a world of rockets and lunar modules. PG Tips also had a series of cards of Prehistoric Animals. I had begged, swapped and managed to collect 49 of the 50 cards in the series, and in my tiny world, nothing was more important than completing the set. Only number 50 evaded me: Australopithecus, the final card, and the link between man and ape. Standing straight-backed, naked arse on full display, a shocking thing for a young Catholic lad in such puritanical times. I had to have it.

On rainy days, of which there were many, we would go to school wearing wellington boots, changing into plimsolls as the day dried up, to play football or just run around the small concrete playground chasing our tails and each other. At the end of one rainy day, I was walking home, carrying my wellingtons, when I had an idea – I would steal what I needed. Surely the fiftieth card would soon be mine. I would be crowned King of the World without delay and be the envy of every other child on earth!

I must have thought that I was invisible when I snuck into the small Co-operative Society shop near my school. Making my blind, avaricious way to the tea section, I placed a packet of PG Tips into each boot, and turned to make my escape. Rough hands gripped me and I was bundled into the shop's guts as the red-faced shop manager screamed into my face.

'You thieving little bastard!'

I was in deep shit and started to cry next to a pile of boxes of cornflakes.

I was in no way a sophisticated criminal. I gave my correct name and address when asked, as a kind of damage limitation exercise. I was released, wet-eyed and blinking into the street, with the promise that my mother would be told. After the slowest walk home, I decided to tell her myself.

This is the only time I remember her hitting me, and in her weak, emaciated state, it couldn't possibly have been painful. She was lying down and could hardly have even connected. Nevertheless, I remember hurt and shame, and the knowledge that me letting her down was the worst of all possible things. Disappointment made her feeble blows feel like the vicious lashes of a cat-o'-nine-tails. Even now, when I bring back that day, I can feel pain that could not possibly have been real.

Around me, a network of help circled. Sister Ita and Kathy Moore would wash and feed me, keeping me from the clutches of Social Services. I continued to spend each night in bed with my mother, the two of us inches apart, her drinking in the last of the time left, keeping me close.

I can see now, her ever-present cigarette winking in the dark. She collected the tokens from inside the packs and I was given *The Park Drive Book of Football* as a present. I devoured anything to do with football, and, even with United's George Best on the cover, this really hit the spot. Rivalries between the two Manchester clubs took on a different form in those more innocent times, and some kids were even taken to City one week and to United the next. Either way, and because it came from her, I loved this book. She must have had to smoke hundreds and thousands of cigarettes to amass enough tokens to get it for me, advancing the emphysema that would eventually kill her. The irony of her destroying her lungs in order for me to have a book celebrating sport and good health is not lost on me. Smoking was normal, and rampant. Teachers, nurses, priests, everybody smoked. I even recall being examined by my doctor as his lit cigarette smouldered away in the ashtray on the desk in his consulting room.

My mother went into hospital and I was sent to stay at the house of a kind lady called Rita Stuart. She played the organ at a church in Salford. I remember being scared by the sound of the ship's horns in Salford docks, and running, terrified, into her big bed at the slightest groan of her bathroom plumbing. I remember songs on the radio at her house – 'Little White Bull' by Tommy Steele, 'Those Were the Days' by Mary Hopkin. Mrs Stuart had sons of her own, grown up by then, and I went to stay the odd weekend with her married son, Paul, and his wife, Pauline. His copy of *Bridge Over Troubled Water* by Simon and Garfunkel was probably the first record to leave an impression on me, sitting quietly with the sleeve on my lap, following the words to 'Baby Driver' with chewed fingers.

It must have been heartbreaking for the adults that took me in. I was the only one who didn't know the terrible future that lay ahead. The Stuarts kept a straight face, taking me to museums and listening to me prattling on about dinosaurs and astronauts. Young though I was, and shielded from the truth, I never detected any sadness from them as they let me get on with being a child for at least a little longer.

My mother was taken into hospital again, a different one. I had become used to visiting her at Crumpsall Hospital, not far from us in North Manchester, but this time she was admitted to Ancoats Hospital, a dark, forbidding Victorian edifice near the city centre, close to where we had lived in Miles Platting. I was taken to live in an unusual and temporary place, a day care centre in Rowrah Crescent on the other side of Langley. There must have been nowhere else to put me. I was the only child to live there.

The centre was a former police house, or rather two houses knocked through, with doors fitted to join the two together. It was heavily institutionalised, all graph-paper glass with school-type fittings and tables. Plastic cups and plates added to the prison-style atmosphere. I was under the care of full-time staff who lived in the house next door, in addition to other staff who would work shifts and sleep over. During the day it operated like a child care centre for working parents. Children of two and three years old would be dropped off in the morning by their parents and a different set of adults looked after them while I was at school. This must have been an improvised situation, as it seems unlikely and far from cost-effective to have one child looked after by five different adults who had to sleep there in a rota system.

It was December 1971 when my mother went into Ancoats Hospital, this much I know. Whether or not the adults around me knew how serious things were, I am encouraged to buy her a present for Christmas. I was taken to the city centre by Sister Ita. I can bring the day to mind as clearly as if it happened only yesterday. I was wearing shorts in the dark, Manchester cold. I can see exactly what part of Market Street we were on as she spat on a handkerchief and gave my freezing face a scrub, calling me every kind of mucky devil, and pulling me reluctantly into Lewis's store. I returned with a white satin headscarf for my mum, feeling grown up and proud of myself for choosing such a lovely present.

A few days later, I had wrapped the scarf and was waiting to be taken to see my mother. It was normally Sister Ita that took me, but on this occasion she was accompanied by Father Walsh. I knew him anyway, as he was a regular visitor to my school, which was staffed in part by other nuns from the Little Sisters of the Assumption. I was excited by Christmas, and the prospect of seeing my beloved mother. When she saw what I had bought her, she would be so happy.

I can remember the decorations, a tree, and a concertina of coloured paper hanging down from the light fitting in the middle of the room. I looked through the criss-crossed reinforced glass in the door, giddy and hyper, and bounced into the room. Nobody was smiling, though. I remember a few seconds of butterflies in the stomach, and a sense of something being not quite right. I was asked to sit down.

'Now, Mark...'

Still no smiles from anywhere. I was proudly gripping my mother's scarf. I had made a fine job of wrapping it.

'Now, Mark…'

No smiles from Father Walsh, although it didn't feel as though I was in trouble.

'Your Mammy has gone to Heaven…'

These words are the last thing I can remember. I am alone. I am nine years old.

My mother died on 20th December 1971. She was buried on Christmas Eve in a communal pauper's grave, along with four other people. She was 39 years old. I was not allowed to be present at the funeral, presumably to protect me, young as I was, from the harsh reality of it all. It was meant as a kindness.

With the help of Kathy Moore, 47 years later, I was able to trace my mother's grave. Number E-716. I stood inches away from her once more, my grown-up tears mixing with the Manchester rain, and I could say my goodbyes at last.

2: Freefall

I was lost without her. For so many intense years, it had been just my mother and me. As a self-preservation mechanism, I withdrew into myself even further. I had bad dreams, the like of which no child should have to live through. I would wake up, afraid and crying, with no idea where I was. I wet the bed every night. I have been told that I was virtually silent for the year after my mum died, and this is how I remember it.

Rowrah Crescent Day Centre was only meant to be a temporary place to live while my mum was in hospital, but I stayed there for a year and a half after she died, looked after by two residential care workers who would split the week into two shifts. I am sure that this was not the way things were planned. I had an entire pre-school play centre at my disposal, and I can see myself now, alone in the large playroom, reading and drawing on the cold, tiled floor. It was here that I had my first experience of playing music, plonking aimlessly on the out of tune upright piano they kept but never used.

Bringing me into the world of people proved to be a difficult task. There were many things I simply had no experience of, the kind of basic things that a child should have been taught. I couldn't use a knife and fork properly, and sitting at a table was something alien to me. Two members of staff had to sit on me to feed me scrambled egg. I had never seen such a thing, and fought with all my childish strength against my tormentors, my back arched like a frightened cat, kicking and screaming, spitting out this poison into their startled faces. My legs stung with every slap I received. In time, it seems, I settled down, and became close to the very people that had treated me with such force.

The two women whose job it was to look after me were very different from each other. They shared the same name, but it was spelled differently. Sheila F was the older of the two, and the strictest. With her hair scraped back into an austere bun, and large glasses, she scared me to death, although as the year progressed, and I became slightly more civilised, she proved to have a human side that wasn't apparent at first. She was a fervent Catholic and it seemed part of her personal remit to make sure that I followed her ways. I'd be taken to extra masses on special feast days and in the middle of the week. The fact that I understood little of the solemn, incense-filled rituals was irrelevant, a soul being a soul and all that. I was woken up in the early hours one time, to join her as she re-lived Christ's passion in the Garden of Gethsemane, praying all night as Good Friday approached. I passed on that one, and she didn't force the issue. Extreme as this seems, she meant well, and I hold no resentment for her, or her ways.

My other carer, Shelagh P, was entirely different. She, in contrast, had no religious agenda. She was young and, to my eyes, modern and energetic. I visited her parents' house with her, and in her room she introduced me to records by Cat Stevens, The Beatles and The Kinks.

Sheila F would send me to the shops near The Falcon pub to buy her cigarettes – 20 Peter Stuyvesant. As a reward for going to the shops, I was allowed to buy something for myself. I would always choose the popular songwords magazines, diving head-first into the latest copy of *Disco 45* or *Words*. Ever since I was first exposed to pop music, back in the world I shared with my mum, I was obsessed.

I stayed at the same school after my mother's death, Assumption Juniors, and there was a real improvement in my schoolwork. Being alone with a fierce reading habit was the making of me, as I believe she intended it to be. I moved up to the top table, and made a friend. Brian Logan was another boy of Irish descent who lived in a different part of Langley. I knew him when my mum was alive, and he actually met her in the last year of her life. At school we sat near each other, and I was even allowed to visit his house. His mum was always 'just about to make something to eat' whenever I arrived. His parents seemed young to me, and they had records, too! 'Papa Was A Rolling Stone' by The Temptations, and an album by The J. Geils Band. Brian was the first real friend I had, and one of few positives I can bring to mind from those dark times.

I was taken to visit a family in Stalybridge by my social worker, Mrs Ward. It seems the idea was for me to be fostered there, and as day visits became weekend visits, I was changing slightly, from a feral grief-damaged boy into someone with limited social skills. I remember playing football with the family's son, and though I was still in a raw mental state, it seems that some kind of small recovery was under way. I was even bought clothes to go on holiday with, although the holiday never actually happened, as the whole experiment came to an abrupt end when I was told I would not be joining this new family after all. The news was delivered to me in the same room in which I was told my mum had died, and I retreated within myself again, back inside my cocoon of books and the songs I heard on the radio... Slade, Hot Butter, The Stylistics, Johnny Nash. I adored Mott The Hoople's 'All the Young Dudes'. I used to sit alone in the day care centre with a little kid's crayon box, drawing Mott The Hoople, especially Ian Hunter, all sunglasses and corkscrew hair.

I remained alone in the play centre for most of the following year. The enforced solitude did wonders for my schoolwork. With little else to do but read, I lost myself in books, comics, and the radio. Shelagh P encouraged me, and her taste in music filtered down a little, although I found my own favourites too: T.Rex, The Sweet, David Bowie, and even more left-field, but still 'pop' artists such as Argent and The Move.

An under-14s Youth Club started in the play centre, one day per week, and although I was way too young, I sneaked downstairs and hung around in the background, being made a fuss of by the girls, and absorbing the Jackson 5 and Chi-Lites hits that they would dance to in formation. This popular soul music worked its magic on me. I began to broaden my musical horizons. It was chart stuff mainly, but I remained obsessed, still memorising songwords and happy to be left alone most of the time, listening to the radio, unconsciously soaking in songs and the way they twisted and turned and shaped my world.

I was taken to meet a new family in Chadderton, near Oldham. The Bradleys were an older couple, grey-haired and conservative, and were a world away from the previous adults in my life. They seemed nice enough. They had a son a year older than me, also called Mark. At first, all went fairly smoothly. Day visits became weekend visits, as is the way of such things, and although I remained at Assumption Juniors and had to get two buses to school each day, I was eventually fostered with them.

As the realities of taking on a high-maintenance child became apparent, things started to change. I was expected to call the mother 'Aunty', and I kicked against this. To me, my own mother was a perfect, sacred person. I worshipped the very thought of her and refused to call this woman 'Aunty'. She wasn't my mum's sister! With hindsight, I now believe that the family had fostered me for the wrong reasons, perhaps as company for their spoiled only son, or maybe to be seen as good people in their social circle. Either way, the novelty wore off fairly quickly for them, and trouble was on the horizon for me.

My bed-wetting continued, as did my nightmares, and while the staff in Rowrah Crescent probably weren't overjoyed to have to deal with stinking sheets every morning, they did their job in a professional manner, and knew they were dealing with a broken, nine-year-old child. The Bradleys, however, were unable to cope with me, and a unhappy period began.

I was subjected to cruel and unorthodox 'cures' for my problem. I was made to sleep with a rope tied around my waist, knotted against my spine, as apparently bed-wetting only happens when somebody sleeps on their back. The idea was that the feel of the tightly-knotted rope in my sleep would force me onto my side and stop it happening. It failed miserably, of course, leaving me feeling humiliated and embarrassed. Another 'cure', presumably sanctioned by a doctor, makes me shudder to remember it. I was forced to sleep on two metal grilles, with a sheet between them. This hated apparatus was plugged into the mains supply and featured an alarm, similar to handshake buzzers from joke shops. The device allowed water to pass through, but urine, being salty, completed the circuit, and the machine would snap me awake with a torturous buzzing. I hated it, and of course such pseudo-scientific nonsense was never going to work, serving only to make my growing sense of alienation even more pronounced. Eventually, my bed-wetting stopped on its own.

My namesake foster brother grew resentful of the cuckoo in the nest. He was treated very differently to me. I cannot say that I was cruelly treated by this family, but a two-tier way of living soon evolved. I was given only the basics, as far as clothing and birthday presents were concerned, whereas their biological son was spoiled rotten.

My bedroom was a Toblerone-shaped box room, large enough for a single bed and little else. I spent most of my time there. My foster brother and I were both given small mono cassette recorders, and I lost myself in a world of music, recording the charts each Sunday through the external hand-held microphone, keeping silent so no unwanted noises or voices crept in, cutting off the DJ's voice. I bought *Top of The Pops* and *Hot Hits* albums, compilations of cover versions by session musicians, pocket-money priced and crammed with inferior takes on the singles I actually wanted.

We were both allowed a weekly magazine. I chose *Disc*, which was probably a little old for me, and featured more grown-up stuff. For Christmas I got albums on tape that I played to death: *Aladdin Sane*, *Band on the Run*, and *Glitter* by Gary Glitter, whose double-drummer backing band really did it for me.

It was in these days that I first yearned to be a performer. I took my cassette recorder onto the nearby fields and recorded myself singing inside an echoey sewage pipe that all the local kids used to play in. 'See My Baby Jive' by Wizzard, 'The Groover' by T.Rex, and of course, David Bowie.

All children had to take an exam in the final year of primary school, the results of which could potentially change the way their lives would be shaped forever. The eleven-plus, as it was known, divided children into so-called 'academic' and 'practical' groups, with those who passed it going to grammar school, destined in theory to go on to university and become part of an educated elite, while those who failed went to secondary modern school and were steered towards more practical jobs, in engineering or manufacturing, for instance.

I took my eleven-plus while living with the Bradleys, and due to me being born in August, and being the youngest in the year, had passed aged 10. All the long hours that my mother had spent reading with me had paid off. My foster brother had failed his eleven-plus the year before, and my achievement caused even more of a distance between us. In order to appease his jealousy, he was given extra presents and pocket money, and I increasingly felt more of an outsider.

I started at Cardinal Langley Grammar School in 1973. I developed a degree of semi-independence, taking myself on two buses there and back every day. My red and black uniform was perceived as posh by pupils at the other local schools, who would frequently attack us on the way home. Nevertheless, I made friends at school and was allowed to go to Saturday afternoon discos in nearby Oldham. Two nightclubs, Baileys and The Cat's Whiskers, opened their doors to children of twelve and under. I went with my new friend, Andrew Flynn. It was love at first sight, I was overwhelmed. I was already immersed in music, but this sealed the deal.

I would take the bus to Oldham town centre, and on arrival I would hide my glasses behind the cistern in the public toilets. Girls were beginning to become interesting to me, and my thick-lensed National Health spectacles were the kiss of death, I felt. From one o'clock until five, I danced like only a twelve-year-old can. This early taste of daytime nightlife set me up for life. I loved it all. Swinging my arms under the strobe lighting, I had never heard music played so loud. The records played there were mainstream chart hits on the whole – Mud, Suzi Quatro, even 'Rock Around the Clock'(!) – but it was the soul music that had the biggest impact on me. Even through a child's distorted memory I can still hear such beauties as 'Love On A Mountain Top' by Robert Knight and 'Funky Street' by Arthur Conley. This tune would see the whole place clapping along with the verses, double time, and there was much diving onto the floor in childish emulation of the Northern soul scene, which, greatly diluted, had begun to chart in the form of 'Footsee' by Wigan's Chosen Few, and 'Skiing In The Snow' by Wigan's Ovation. My love of Northern soul started here, on these carefree Saturdays, dancing to forget my unhappy home life.

It was on one of these Saturdays that I was brought back to the Bradley's house by the police. It was hardly the crime of the century, and I think that it was meant as a 'short sharp shock' to nip things in the bud as far as my bad behaviour was concerned. I had stolen two books from a small shop on Yorkshire Street: *Slade in Flame*, the book version of the Slade film, and *That'll Be the Day*, the novel from which a current movie starring David Essex was based. I was not a thief as such, just a music-obsessed boy showing off, and must have stuck out a mile in my high-waisted baggy trousers and Northern soul inspired star jumper. I was, of course, caught straight away, and escorted to my foster parents in shame. Having the police round, in full view of the neighbours, was too much for this family, who'd had enough of me by now, I'm sure, and it seemed my card was marked from that moment.

It was another incident that sealed my fate, though, and I remain confused as to what actually happened. I was watching television on the settee with Mr Bradley. His wife was elsewhere, and we were alone. I was never close to him, and I feel that it was his wife's idea, rather than his, to invite a messed-up foster child into their home. His favouritism towards his real son was all too plain to see, although he had never displayed any really bad behaviour towards me. This day was different, though, and as I sat watching TV, I felt his hand upon my backside. I jumped up and, screaming at the top of my voice, ran away from him, knocking over a coffee table and spilling the drink that was on it. It was the only time that this, or anything like it, had happened to me. I have run the film in my head over and over again, and I remain convinced that this was the potential start of something horrible. Either way, it can be no coincidence that my time there was up the minute I resisted, and I was moved on straight away, after two years there.

I was placed with another family, in Whitworth, north of Rochdale. The father was a Church of England clergyman, and the family had several other children, all younger than me. I continued to attend Cardinal Langley, travelling an hour and a half each way to get to school. I felt isolated and alone there, spending most of my time in my room, once again soaking up pop radio. Frankie Valli's 'The Night' is one tune that I associate with my unhappy stay there. It is a beautiful record, uplifting with a gorgeous four-bar bass introduction. I encountered Kraftwerk, too, for the first time, as 'Autobahn' became a freak hit single. It was nothing more than a weird novelty record to me, and although I liked it, its revolutionary instrumentation and attitude went over my head.

This living arrangement proved to be a temporary one, and it may be that that was the idea all along. Having lived through so much upheaval and tragedy, I was unable to relate to these or any other people. I must have seemed a cold, withdrawn boy, and was simply not equipped to join somebody's family at the drop of a hat. I felt out of place in this semi-rural setting and never settled down. Before long, my social worker arrived with the news that I was to be placed in a children's home.

I was told that this was only to be a temporary measure, until a new family was found, but when I got there, the other children told me how things really were. I was laughed at when I told them that I was only going to be there for a few weeks. I had been in many children's homes before, when my mother was ill, but they were of the 'short-stay' variety. This one, I was informed by the other kids, was the end of the line.

With the realisation that I had been lied to, it hit me that this indeed was a long-stay facility. I began life at Martin Lane Children's Home.

3: Martin Lane

Martin Lane Children's Home was a custom-built facility several miles outside Rochdale. Everything was on an institutional scale, with a regime more suited to young offenders than a 'family' situation. Thirteen children were housed in separate male and female sections, with a bedroom in between them for the residential staff members looking after us. The staff would change shift on Sunday and Wednesday.

The children were made to work on a series of chores for an hour after mealtimes – peeling a huge bucket of potatoes each day, scrubbing pans, that sort of thing. We were told that such life skills were essential preparation for life after care, but in reality it was part of an elaborate control mechanism and a way of keeping the day filled with meaningless jobs so we could not cause trouble for the staff.

The whole life of the place was strictly regimented. I kicked against it from day one and didn't make life easy for myself by once again refusing to call them 'Aunty'. It was a small act of rebellion, but one I had no choice about. My mother was everything to me, and, in my messed-up eyes, they were pretending to be her sister!

After my mum died, as a keepsake I had been given a pair of her slippers (blue, size four) and a patent leather bag of hers. These had gone everywhere with me, forming a kind of shrine to her. I'd kept them safe for three years, but they were taken from me, never to be seen again. Techniques like this, and frequent slaps across the face, let me know who was in charge.

Everything I had to do was checked and re-checked, all part of the system of control that kept us afraid and compliant. A badly made bed was stripped to be re-done. I had to breathe into the nostrils of the staff to prove I had cleaned my teeth. After school my fingers would be sniffed to detect signs of smoking. Talking was not allowed during meals, or in the living room where limited television was watched. The smallest infringement of their rules would mean a slapped face. My strong Manchester accent set me apart from the other kids and staff, who chose to see me as 'too big for my boots'. My time here was bleak and unhappy from the first minute. I hated the place.

I shared a room/dormitory with three other boys. Two of them were brothers who had been abandoned as toddlers with their two sisters. There was no way that a family would foster four children, so the future looked bleak for them.

The third kid I will call 'Alec'. He was uncontrollable, at war with the world that had treated him so badly. Abandoned very young with his sister, he made everybody's lives difficult, just because he could. No amount of physical violence from the staff made the slightest difference to him. He would get up before our 6.45am wake-up time and piss the bed on purpose every day, fully awake, a weapon he used against the staff that he hated so much. He would destroy anything of anybody's, even things of his own. Each Christmas, all the boys were given Airfix kits, usually of World War Two bombers, and the finished models would be pinned above each child's bed. Alec would spitefully destroy these as a matter of course, especially if they seemed important to their owner. He would throw meals at staff members, not caring for his own well being or the inevitable punishment that would follow, and would initiate violent fights with staff and other children as a matter of course. He was so out of control that he was sent to a special school from Monday to Friday; a containment centre to all extents and purposes. He was always absconding from Martin Lane, and always on a Sunday, the day before he had to go to this residential school.

The school was Knowl View, and it's now known as the place where Cyril Smith MP abused children for many years. He was deeply involved in the home's organisation and wielded considerable power in Rochdale. He was a thoroughly corrupt man, and, shockingly, his abuse was ignored by the Liberal Party he represented, even after many complaints. Smith was given full access to these lost children, with keys and an office at Knowl View. I have no doubt in my own mind that 'Alec' suffered at his hands. You only had to know the child to know he was living through a personal hell. The abject fear he displayed when he had to return each Monday makes perfect sense now we know what happened there.

It was unheard of for a kid in care to have passed the eleven-plus exam, so I was used as a bit of a poster boy within social work circles. I stayed at the same school, even though it meant a journey of ninety minutes to get there. This was to be the saving of me, and gave me a life outside the home. It also meant that the strict rules at Martin Lane had an unusual side effect for me. Bedtime was 9pm, and the time between evening meal and bed was filled with jobs, baths for every child, and, for me, homework. I would pretend that I had more homework than I actually had in order to be on my own, away from the others. I hated being with the other kids and would give myself extra Spanish, French or maths, anything to get me through the day. During my time there, my schoolwork got better and better. The staff who were meant to check my work didn't know anything about what I was learning at school, so I was left to get on with it.

I would volunteer for everything at school in order to stay there that little bit longer. Football, drama, choir, anything to keep me away from my hated living situation. I took drum lessons, helped out with school plays, and started to make new friends.

David Coogan was one of the brightest kids in my class, and was part of a large family. His parents fostered children and, to their eternal credit, actually contacted the children's home and persuaded them to give me a little more freedom than I would have ordinarily have been allowed, making it possible for me to go to youth clubs and eventually even staying overnight at their house. I had never known a functional family before, and was greatly influenced by them. They would sit around a table to eat, and they were allowed to talk! They even seemed to like each other. They had a piano, and we were allowed to play records in the front room.

David's brother, Martin, was in the year above us, and was very popular at school. He played electric guitar using a pre-decimal sixpence as a plectrum, its serrated edges making a 'bowed' effect (he'd got the idea from Queen's Brian May). Despite our age difference, we became great friends. He turned me on to Be-Bop Deluxe, and we bonded over Bowie and Roxy Music.

David also had two younger brothers, Brendan and Stephen. I remember Stephen as a quiet boy, but I imagine he was soaking up every bit of his older brothers' performance skills. Both Martin and David were gifted impressionists, and would be cast in school plays as a matter of course. We would listen and re-listen to David's Monty Python albums, and I brought *Italians From Outer Space* by Alberto Y Lost Trios Paranoias, a Mancunian spoof rock outfit, which became a big favourite in their house.

Back in the kid's home, I finally taught myself to ride a bike, joylessly circling the high-fenced garden until I didn't fall off. I continued to immerse myself in music, but even the simple act of listening to records was strictly controlled by the staff. We had to pass a test to be allowed to use the record player in the dining room – basic stuff like making sure the records weren't being scratched and that they were put away correctly afterwards. Even having passed this test, there was little to play. There was Bay City Rollers, The Stylistics *Greatest Hits* and David Essex's *All the Fun of the Fair* album. The one saving grace was *K-Tel's Story of Pop*, a double compilation with such delights as the Faces, Sly and the Family Stone, and Desmond Dekker's 'Israelites' nestling amongst The Everly Brothers and Chris Montez's 'Let's Dance'. I took solace in 'I'm Going Home' by Ten Years After.

I continued to keep up with the music papers at school. A small group of my classmates became interested in music and copies of *Disc* and *Melody Maker* were passed around. I was aware of 10cc, Bowie and Cockney Rebel, artists I had liked since being fostered in Chadderton, but things were about to get very interesting, both in music and in society as a whole. It was while I was in care that the first rumblings of change were starting to happen as music prepared to move from the progressive era – top heavy and self-important – to the DIY, no frills approach that preceded punk.

My social worker, Mrs Daybank, came to see me at the home. She visited me occasionally, but his time it felt different. She had brought my care records with her. I wasn't allowed to read them all, but together we went over some things that had been hidden from me up until then. My mother, it seems, had constructed a simplified version of our life when she was finally forced to engage with the authorities, and this edited account had erased my father from history altogether. My mother had told me that my father had died, presumably to provide a simple answer to an ever-inquisitive kid and no doubt to keep me safe. Mrs Daybank told me that my father was very much alive and had traced me through Social Services.

His name was Thomas Kilfeather. I could remember asking my mum about her maiden name, and she told me that it was Howard. After her death, it turned out that she had never been married, and had lived and died as Patricia Hoyle. Why did she pick Howard? Was this the name of another partner? Why did she make up the story of my father not being alive, instead of another, less upsetting lie? I was shell-shocked and thrown into confusion by the fact that my mum had lied to me about him. I had put her on a pedestal as someone who could do no wrong. My world was turned inside out.

It was explained that my father was not a complete stranger to me after all. He had visited my mum and me in Langley, but I had known him as Uncle Tommy. I did remember this, as he had brought a Thorntons Easter egg with my name on it in icing, a rare luxury in those hand-to-mouth days. I could recall the chocolate egg far better than the man himself though. I was told that he was to visit me here in Rochdale in a matter of weeks. I struggled to take it all in.

Eventually, the day came, and he turned up smelling of drink and cigarettes. He was clean-shaven and wore a blue three-piece suit with a thin raincoat and trilby hat. I did indeed recall him from earlier in my childhood, albeit in a mixed-up way. He seemed kind of old fashioned to me, but he had clearly made an effort for our strange reunion and was overcome by the whole experience. Our meeting was brief, but I remember there were tears on both sides. I was left in a confused state by this new turn of events.

At the children's home, I was treated as something of an unusual case. The fact that I went to grammar school looked good for them and my social work team. For a child to be reunited with a family member was another great result for them, so my father turning up out of the blue like that suited everybody.

I started to visit him on Saturdays, to test the water. He still lived in the Miles Platting area of Manchester, near the city centre, an hour and a half away from my Martin Lane prison. I hated that place so much that I would have jumped at the chance to spend any amount of time away from it, but as it turned out, the two of us got on fairly well, in a cautious way. These Saturday visits only lasted about six hours, and it was easy to get through the day, especially as at least three of those hours were spent in the Nelson pub – or 'Pat McDonagh's' as he called it – near Victoria Mansions on Oldham Road.

Each visit followed the same pattern. I would arrive at noon, and after he had filled in his Spot the Ball and Pools forms, we would walk down Oldham Road and then Oldham Street until we got to the Woolworths department store in Piccadilly. He would spit through his nostril into the gutter as I pretended he wasn't with me. We would stock up on ingredients for a basic stew that would last the week, getting reheated every day after he came back from work. We'd then walk back and spend the rest of the day in the Nelson, he drinking pint after pint of thick bitter as I nursed a cola. I was a bit of a novelty for the other, almost exclusively Irish, drinkers, and through them became good at pool and darts.

The flat itself, on Lymouth Road, was the one I remembered being driven away from, crying, as a small child. It was a redbrick, ground-floor flat with two bedrooms, and was in a dirty and neglected condition, my dad having lived alone there for many years. He worked as a 'ganger' on building sites, and would be picked up early in the morning, then would go straight to the pub after work, where he would stay until closing time. He was, by any sense of the word, an alcoholic.

After a period of visiting on Saturdays, I began to stay for weekends. To my father's credit, he cleared out the spare room and decorated it to the best of his abilities. He got me an old Bakelite radio, which, although looking like something from a film about the Second World War, became my link to a world of music, and I spent many hours lost in crap pop and Saturday rock programmes.

I forgive him everything now, of course, but he was in no way equipped to look after me. This suited me fine, as after years of repression and institutional life, I was free to do what I wanted. He began to stay in the pub for the whole of Saturday, leaving me alone, and would come back in the early hours, falling around, pissed. As far as I was concerned, anything was better than the children's home, and I made the most of my independence.

I began to stay for longer during school holidays. It was a weird period. He couldn't break the habits of a lifetime, and spent nearly all the time at work or in the pub, but I was happy enough, either lost in music or investigating the city centre. With a friend from school, I wandered around town, playing pool in the Oldham Street cafes, coming back after dark to an empty flat, listening to the first germs of punk infecting the radio schedules.

Back in the children's home, I was left to my own devices to some extent. I continued to read the music papers and was curious about the change in the music world they were reporting. I was 14 and couldn't have been a more perfect age for punk music to invade my consciousness. In my life so far, I'd retreated inside music as a way of keeping myself safe, and because of this, I was open to everything that punk had to throw at me. Precocious and hurting for something to call my own, with a knowledge of music far beyond my years, what came next was mine.

A new staff member started work at the home and I became friendly with her daughter, Shane, who was a few years older than me. We sometimes got the same bus; her from college, me from school. She was a massive Bowie fan, and as punk started to break out everywhere, she was part of the first wave of sharp young kids to pick up on what was happening.

Rochdale, with the best will in the world, is something of a cultural backwater, and with her dyed hair and recently taken-in drainpipe trousers, she stood out a mile. I found her incredibly stylish and brave, and developed a huge crush on her, despite her being way out of my league and age group. She knew all about the new bands I had become so interested in, and showed me her copy of Buzzcocks' *Spiral Scratch* on the bus. I'd been reading about all this, and here it was, in my hand. Shane was a real pioneer, in at the start of this musical and cultural revolution, and she told me about her underage nights at The Ranch Bar and Pips in Manchester.

My weekend and school holiday visits to my dad had been continuing to everybody's satisfaction, and after a case conference involving social workers, care staff, teachers (but not me!), I went to live in Lymouth Road with him, full time.

I was driven to my dad's flat by my social worker, and a new life began. Being under the control of others for so long had left me institutionalised. Ever since I first appeared on the radar of Social Services, somebody else had been in charge of every aspect of the way I lived: when I got up, when I went to bed, what I did, what I ate, who I was allowed to see, everything. All this was to end in the space of a day, and after so long as a prisoner, I was free.

4: Tommy

Miles Platting was going through significant changes. Many of the flats surrounding the one we lived in were boarded up and ready for demolition, but my father stayed doggedly on as the neighbourhood disintegrated. The empty dwellings were destroyed by gangs made up of the children of the few families that remained. Water tanks were stolen and the flooding of the flats on the upper levels meant that the remaining residents' lives were a complete misery. It was a slum. Whenever I got a lift home from school by a parent of one of my friends, I would get them to drop me off far away from where I actually lived. 'I'll be alright here,' I'd tell them and walk the rest of the way.

My dad continued the same routine he always had: work, pub, home, sleep. Ever since my mother took me away from him, all he had done is work on building sites then go straight to the pub the minute he finished work. My arrival caused massive upheaval for him and he struggled to adjust. He carried around a lot of guilt for not having been part of my life. He would get tearful and emotional when drunk, saying how he had let me down.

I was coming up to my last year at grammar school and was working towards my O-levels. His education was a practical one and his job as a building site worker was a long way away from the kind of things I was studying. I watched him struggle whenever he tried writing anything down. When he saw me with French and Spanish homework, he would be reminded of the distance between us. We were different on every level. He had a thick Sligo accent, I had a strong Manchester twang. Even talking to me must have made him think of the wasted time that we never had. His sense of alienation must have grown and festered during these months. I understood that our lives had been very different. It didn't matter to me, but it mattered a lot to him.

Although he still managed to keep his job going, his functional alcoholism was becoming less and less functional. He became resentful and started to spend more time away from the flat. On one occasion he'd been away for two days when I walked in to Collyhurst police station to report him missing. The kindly desk sergeant, hearing of another Irish building worker who had not come home all weekend, told me to wait at home until he arrived. He was right; back he came on the Monday night, dishevelled and still pissed.

After a short time of us living together in Miles Platting, he was offered a two-bedroom house a little further out from the city centre in nearby Newton Heath. It was newly built and seemed like a palace after the last place. Hot water! Radiators! There was even a tiny garden for us to ignore. It should have been a fresh start for us both, but we remained virtual strangers.

Shortly after moving into the new house, I was woken in the middle of the night by crashing noises and found him in my room. Convinced that something dark and terrible was about to happen, I jumped out of bed and screamed at him at the top of my voice. This made no difference, and he came further into my room. I was properly scared by now, but I had no need to be. In his drunken state, and having so recently moved into this new house, he had got mixed up between my room and the toilet. I went from being afraid, to amused, to pitiful all within a matter of seconds.

Poor Tommy. Left with a hole in his life for so many years, drinking was the only way he knew how to deal with it. I never mentioned this incident to him, there seemed little point, and we settled into a routine of hardly seeing each other. Things were civil enough between us, and I was determined to never be sent back into council care, so I put up with his behaviour for as long as I could, ignoring him falling around the house in the early hours, swearing his head off, raging against the life he was so guilty about having ruined, or having had ruined for him. To his credit, he always left some pocket money, and there was always beans on toast at home to supplement the free dinners I had at school, but to all extents and purposes I was bringing myself up. This suited me fine.

I took to my new-found freedom like a fish to water. Things were different now that I was allowed to do whatever I wanted. I had my own door key and no restrictions on what time I had to be back. I was ready to let music take over. I found other music fans at school, often older, and would read their music papers from cover to cover. Punk was on the ascendant. Like a football fan who lives many miles from his team, but slavishly follows their results and reads everything they can about them, I was a teenage punk obsessive, devouring everything I could.

My dad could never have known how important that second-hand Bakelite radio was to become to me. It was a window to another world. I would listen to BBC Manchester's *Saturday Rock* programme and was able to hear the new bands I had been reading about. I became aware of Radio 1's John Peel. Peel was starting to include bands like The Damned, Sex Pistols and Buzzcocks, alongside more traditional fare that had dominated musical life for years – the old wave 'dinosaur' acts like Led Zeppelin, Pink Floyd, and Derek and the Dominoes. Such bloated superstars existed on a plane above us mere mortals. I felt no kinship with them at all.

Much was written about the need to return to a grass roots scene. Punk music was meant to be experienced live, and living where I did put me right in the loop, with loads of brilliant gigs practically on my doorstep. I couldn't have been in a better place to get swept up in the optimism and breath of fresh air that punk brought to Manchester. I was like a greyhound in a trap that was about to be released.

While I was in Rochdale Authority care I had been allowed to attend the under-14s disco nights at Middleton Civic Hall. This was through the intervention of David Coogan's father and mother, who as foster parents themselves were perceived to be 'safe' people for me to be around. It was a square-shaped, modern no-frills kind of a place with a mezzanine bar for over-18s. This separate bar area meant that younger kids like myself were allowed in, as long as we kept to the main concert hall.

Middleton has always been a violent place, and the 1970s were violent times. Underage drinking was rife, a rite of passage almost, and rivalries between different districts and different football supporters meant that things would kick off for the slightest reason, or for no reason at all. Fights between schools were common enough during the daytime, and it was a nailed-on certainty that punk, already thought of as a violent subculture, would bring out the worst in the local youth. It was for that reason that we were chaperoned by David's older brother Martin when, on 14th May 1977, we went to see The Damned and The Adverts at Middleton Civic Hall. I was excited to be going out anywhere, and the threat of danger made things even more exciting. This was to be my first exposure to live music as far as I was concerned. I had seen a Rochdale glam rock band called Shabby Tiger at a local disco while I was fostered in Whitworth some years before, but their sub-Sweet posturing did nothing for me. This, however, was to be a different kettle of fish altogether.

We made the short journey from David and Martin's house on foot in the still light evening, turning up at Middleton Civic Hall with open ears and minds. A motley collection of inquisitive souls snaked around the venue, queuing to get in. Regulars from the under-14s nights in star jumpers and patch-pocket, high-waistband flares, milled around causing trouble, and a smattering of hippyish twenty-somethings smelling of patchouli oil looked snobbily down on them. Denim-clad rockers, kaftan-wearing hippies and thirty-something beer monsters mingled in amongst the first of the Manchester youth to take punk to their hearts.

For most of the several hundred people there that night it was their first encounter with the shock of the new. The Damned had a strong sense of the visual, and several of the young punks had taken the slicked-back ghoulishness of singer Dave Vanian as a template. They were far from the majority, though, the crowd was a strange mix of ages and tribes. Denim, double-denim, monkey boots and greasy long hair for the boys, and the odd full-length leather coat from lovers of the Northern soul scene.

The first band on were a covers band called Déjà Vu. They actually featured a sixth former from my school. He was a friend of Martin Coogan's. It was clear that he, along with his bandmates, had yet to be touched by the changes afoot in the world of music. Their plodding, workmanlike versions of Rolling Stones and Beatles songs did nothing for me. Versions of Be Bop Deluxe's 'Fair Exchange' and 'Ships In The Night' made Martin happy, but it was all somewhat underwhelming.

The opening band's equipment was taken away and the stage was cleared for the real support act. As the hall filled up, I stood slightly to the left of the centre of the stage waiting for what was to come next. I was all eyes, taking in this strange and wonderful atmosphere. Roadies came and switched on amplifiers at both sides of the stage, and an eternity seemed to pass before four scruffy, leather-clad figures walked on.

A thin, curly haired man gripped the microphone stand slightly to my right, staring out into the middle distance, as the drummer tested his kit briefly and the other members gave their instruments a quick blast. I could feel the air move. This was twice as loud as the previous band, and I was at once shocked by the volume and overwhelmed by the coiled malevolence coming off them all. This was The Adverts. The darkened stage erupted in a flash of light and everything exploded.

'ONE CHORD WONDERS!!!!'

TV Smith's voice filled the room.

'ONE, TWO, THREE, FOUR!!!'

I was gripped. All around me the tightly-packed crowd surged closer to the action, knocking people flying. To my left, bassist Gaye Advert stared into the distance, chewing gum in a nonchalant, couldn't care less way. Wearing a black leather jacket, swamped by her bass, she oozed charisma. Pale complexion, panda-eyed with smudged mascara, she was compelling and beautiful, her fingers descending down the E string following the simplest of sequences.

TV Smith, stage centre, was also unlike anything I had experienced before. He fizzed with energy, eyes on stalks, wrapping himself up in his microphone cable in a natural, non-theatrical kind of way. The advertising for the Damned/Adverts tour made much of both band's limited musical talent, using the strapline 'The Damned can now play three chords, The Adverts can play one… Come and hear all four at… (insert venue name).' This gave a totally false impression of what was going on, as both bands knew exactly what they were doing. The Adverts were using stop/start techniques on songs like 'On The Roof' and 'Bombsite Boy'. After this blistering baptism, I was hooked, big time, and as the encore ended (a repeated 'One Chord Wonders') I knew what I wanted. To be a part of all this.

I hardly had time to recover from this life-changing onslaught when it was time for The Damned. The difference between both groups' approach was huge. To my teenage ears and eyes, they were totally different animals. TV Smith's issue-based lyrics really spoke to me, and The Adverts' passionate performances were less about fashion and trivial fun than many of their contemporaries. The Damned bounded on to a hail of spitting and fighting, and although I liked them well enough, it was clear that they were something of a 'good time' band. I just didn't believe in them, they were too theatrical. Brian James cut an enigmatic figure, but his guitar histrionics seemed based in the past to my young ears. I was drawn to the new music, not this celebration of the past, albeit speeded up. They covered The Stooges 'I Feel Alright', and although things got good and messy, and a good time was had by all, it was The Adverts that had won me over.

The contrast between The Adverts and The Damned helped reveal to me what it was I was looking for in the new music. This was further strengthened at my second gig when I returned to Middleton to see The Jam on their *In The City* tour. I was struck with a sense of mistrust once again. Although they were a high-powered, tightly rehearsed three-piece, and the hall was going crazy for them, something didn't ring true. For a start, they dressed in matching mod suits and would jump in the air in a hard to believe, over-practised fashion. They played fast and hard, but with an eye towards the fashions of the generation that preceded them. Paul Weller was a skilled songwriter, no doubt about that, but apart from enjoying the energy of it all, I remained untouched. They sped through their album, displaying a fine understanding of the past, but didn't seem to be part of the future. The fact that they played the theme from *Batman*, and it was received with such enthusiasm by the adoring crowd, told me everything I needed to know. Where was the real stuff that I craved so desperately? Further exposure to bands like The Rezillos and The Drones over the course of the year confirmed my stance.

The Electric Circus was the epicentre of Manchester's growing punk scene and was walking distance from where I lived. I had the good fortune to be a part of the crowd there on two very different occasions. My first visit to see my beloved Adverts was a revelation. I met Martin Coogan and his friend Phil outside the venue. Phil had taken to calling himself 'Elvis Dead' for the evening, an antagonistic punky joke in the wake of Elvis Presley's recent demise. There was a sense of 'Year Zero' about everything, and anything from the dark cultural void before punk was fair game. Johnny Rotten himself had famously scrawled 'I hate…' on a Pink Floyd t-shirt, and we sneeringly dismissed the 'dinosaurs' that our revolution had swept away.

It was a bright summer's Sunday evening and a healthy queue had started to gather on Collyhurst Street. Once again, all human life was there, or so it seemed. Inquisitive long-hairs, kids my age, and everything in between. I was far too young to be there, but I was tall enough to get away with it, and attitudes were relaxed with things like age restrictions and fire regulations. Promoters would employ a 'rubber wall' approach for the more popular shows. I tried to look old, and with fingers, toes and eyes crossed, they let me in. Result!

First up were The Slugs. I hadn't heard of them before, and there was a buzz going around those of us that weren't in the know that this could be the Pistols in disguise. Having been banned from so many shows by local councils, Sex Pistols had played a series of secret gigs under the name The Spots (Sex Pistols On Tour Secretly), and expectations were high. No such luck, though, The Slugs were indeed The Slugs. I find it hard to recall what they were like, so busy was I taking the atmosphere in. The people, the dangerous, scruffy building, the sweat dripping walls, all of it.

999, the next band, were much more like the real deal. Loud and frantic, colourful and fast. I knew their singles, 'I'm Alive' and 'Nasty

Nasty', and they turned in a good performance, winning lots of new friends amongst the lively audience. I was struck by how high the voice of singer Nick Cash was. Part of being a punk was turning against what had gone before, and this type of high-register singing had been employed by a thousand heavy metal singers in the pre-punk days, and had been (along with extensive guitar solos) consigned to the bin of history. 999 pulled it off, though, and reclaimed it in style.

The Adverts followed and I felt like an invited guest. I watched from the balcony. I'd been transfixed the first time I saw them, but that was my first gig ever, so I could have been caught up in the euphoria of the moment. I shouldn't have worried. The Adverts had grown in confidence and skill. At their Middleton gig supporting The Damned, they seemed fragile as well as powerful, and Gaye Advert's size and determination brought out people's protective side. They weren't the sort of band to jump up and down or run around the stage, their approach was more intense and concentrated, somehow turned in on itself. The Electric Circus show was a masterclass of coiled tension. 'Bored Teenagers', 'New Church', 'Quickstep', and of course 'One Chord Wonders' went past in a blur of frenzied confidence. I fucking loved it.

I was back at The Electric Circus the following week. The Boys were the advertised band, and their cancellation gave me my first taste of what a relatively empty gig felt like. It seemed like everybody but me and my friend Kevin had been tipped off. Far from being disappointed, I felt even more special to be one of a handful of punks in attendance and was a bit less intimidated than I had been at the previous week's Adverts show. Exciting though that was, it was scary too, and that edginess was not in evidence here. Support band, The Accelerators, were older and had one foot in the world before punk. Basically, it was twelve-bar rock played fast. It washed over me.

Manchester's V2 finished things off, all make-up and glam poses. They had sprung out of the Bowie/Pips scene and took their appearance very seriously. It might have been the empty venue, or the trivial nature of V2's image-based approach, but it went over my little head. I craved the real, and this wasn't it.

The Electric Circus didn't last long, and I didn't go again, but my appetite for live music had been brought to life in a massive way. All I wanted was more of it. I soon got another dose free of charge back at Middleton Civic Hall courtesy of Granada TV who were filming an episode of *So It Goes* there, with Mink DeVille, XTC and the Tom Robinson Band on the bill. Tony Wilson, the man behind *So It Goes*, was well known already as a regular presenter of local news and current affairs, but to us he was intrinsically linked to punk after bringing us the Sex Pistols' 'Get off your arse' debut on his show. His championing of new bands on Granada's *What's On* made him the public face of all things punk, and being too young to be fashionably nonchalant about such matters, I was impressed to see such a high-profile character amongst us. He seemed a decent guy, too, happy enough to chat and sign his name for those who asked him. I was not an autograph hunter, but he found time to talk to me and my friend Kev about the bands we liked – Buzzcocks in particular – something he didn't really have to do. This encounter meant a lot, and served as further proof of punk as a great leveller. Despite my tender years, I felt included in this strange revolution.

5: Fallout

After seeing The Adverts in Middleton, many of those present reacted to their Damascene-type conversion by rushing away to take in their trousers and cut their shoulder-length hair. For me, the whole idea of punk was that it was something that you did for yourself. 'Quickstep', the B-side to The Advert's 'One Chord Wonders', was a kind of mission statement, with its 'See what punks can do!' refrain. I could shut my eyes and see them doing it that night, almost daring me to follow their lead. Having had such an unusual life, nobody else could talk about the things I'd lived through. Who would speak for me? The answer to that question was staring me in the face each day as I looked in the mirror.

I'd started to hang around with some musical kids at school. While I was in the children's home, I had made it my business to volunteer for all kinds of extra activities, many of them based in music. I had taken drum lessons for a while, studying the book *Buddy Rich's Modern Interpretation of Snare Drum Rudiments* with a view to playing orchestral percussion. I took to it like a duck to water, and spent many rainy lunchtimes avoiding outdoor activities, jamming along with the older kids, providing simple backbeats for Beatles, Who and even Black Sabbath tunes. I was a real sponge, taking everything in, and learning to express myself on guitar and bass along the way, too. I started to write poems and song lyrics, something that I would never stop doing. From this time onwards, songwriting became a crucial part of my life.

I didn't have a guitar of my own, but I picked up enough technique from watching Martin Coogan to express myself to some extent, so I began to put words and tunes together. When an instrument was to hand, I found that I could lose myself for hours trying to become better. If there wasn't a guitar around, I'd still make up songs by writing lyrics and simply imagining the fretboard. Using a barre chord based around the E shape, I could invent little song sequences in my mind to put into practice later. This skill, born out of poverty and a lack of equipment, using the sound and rhythm of my own footsteps, broke the back of the writing process for me. I could have ideas while I was miles away from any instrument and write songs in my head.

Life at home had become increasingly strained. The pattern of my dad's work/drink/sleep lifestyle carried on as before. He would vanish for days on end, coming back drunk, and subjecting me to horrible verbal and psychological abuse. I would laugh to myself at the string of foul but inventive swear words he brought into play ('Ya fucking, bastarding, cunting twat, ya!') but in reality, it wasn't funny in the slightest. In front of me was a man racked with guilt and pain, in the grip of a full-blown alcohol addiction, who would frequently become over-emotional and angry. Things started to feel dangerous and I grew scared of him.

He started to drink at home as well as the pub. The living room cabinet was filled with over-strength barley wine and Special Brew in bottles. It was inevitable that it would all come to a head eventually. One night, his frustration reached its peak, and he lashed out at me on the stairs, hitting me several times around the head before slamming the door on his way out. This was seen by neighbours through the uncurtained hall window. After he left the house, they came round, asking if I needed them to help, or to call the police or Social Services. They would have heard him screaming and shouting quite often, but it would have sounded more menacing this time. For my part, I was deeply embarrassed by being in need of their help, and played things down, saying, unconvincingly, that everything was alright. Nothing could have been further from the truth. It was two days before he came home.

I carried on as before, and lost myself in music, both live and on record. My beloved Adverts first LP, *Crossing the Red Sea with The Adverts*, came out in February 1978. I had been waiting for it for ages, and by this time knew their set backwards in my head. In March I was at Virgin Records on Lever Street for the launch of *Another Music in a Different Kitchen*, the new Buzzcocks album, who had now signed to United Artists, a major label. The UA publicity drive was in full effect and the release was accompanied by the letting off of hundreds of helium-filled balloons. The idea was that the finders of these balloons would receive an album, badge and sticker, all wrapped in a Malcolm Garrett-designed carrier bag. I grabbed one before it had even had a chance to take off. When the album arrived, I played it until the needle of my record player wore out. I loved Buzzcocks, and saw them many times as their career exploded.

A Buzzcocks show in Middleton shortly after the album release introduced me to The Slits, who were supporting for the whole of their tour. They were a frantic, full-speed breath of fresh air. I was smitten again. They didn't give a shit! This was what I wanted. Anarchy personified, all scary hair and confrontation. The sight of Ari Up and Viv Albertine invading the stage during the extended drum break from Buzzcocks' 'Moving Away From The Pulsebeat' was spectacular.

This was an amazing time, as punk gave way to a more cerebral approach. Howard Devoto had been a game changer for me and, like many others, I couldn't wait to see what he would do after he left Buzzcocks. He had debuted his new band, Magazine, at the closing weekend of The Electric Circus, and although the two-day event had been recorded by Virgin, their three-song set had not made it on to *Short Circuit*, the ten-inch mini album documenting the Circus' last days. Plenty of good stuff had made the cut, though, and this underrated release gave many people their first taste of Joy Division (Warsaw on the night) and The Fall, whose two tracks 'Last Orders' and 'Stepping Out' pointed to a new future, one I had been waiting for. The Fall spoke in my accent and were angular and strange, looking forwards. I listened to their debut Peel session growl abrasively out from my Bakelite radio. Guitarist Martin Bramah's left-handed, spidery, spiralling melody lines sounding like something from another planet.

Magazine's debut album, *Real Life*, came out round about the same time as *Short Circuit* and it did not disappoint. I had been well into Bowie and Roxy Music in pre-punk days, and was more than ready for Magazine's lush, keyboard-enhanced take on things. In wilful opposition to what people expected of the creator of *Spiral Scratch*,

Howard Devoto had bravely employed Dave Formula's synth textures and was not afraid to slow things right down on such songs as 'Burst'. Barry Adamson's twisted funk basslines were prominent and thickened by use of chorus and distortion, and John McGeogh's guitar inventions took the whole genre kicking and screaming into the future. I loved the sleeve, too, by Linder Sterling. It spoke of a tribal strangeness, all disembodied heads and weirdly beautiful piercing eyes. *Real Life* opened many minds, mine in particular.

I continued to mess about with guitars whenever I could. I was passionate and heavy handed and was often breaking guitar strings. If I broke a string and could not afford a new set, I'd simply have to find a new way to get to the note I wanted. This led to my love of unusual, weird open chords, the type you're never taught about by traditional guitar teachers. The guitarists that I was starting to love were moving in similar areas: John McKay from the Banshees, Magazine's John McGeogh, Martin Bramah from The Fall, all ground-breaking musicians with a real sense of space and intelligence.

Previously, rock music was often about force and reinforcing the low end with bottom-heavy power chords. These innovators took the opposite approach, leaving the bottom end to the bass guitar and drums. This created a base to sprinkle beautiful stripped down melodies in and around the rhythm section's firm foundation. This was a brave approach, displaying a lack of ego that put the song first. If the song only needed a one, or two note sequence, then so be it.

I found that I had a natural feel for bass guitar. Learning to play bass while singing gave me a great sense of pleasure and achievement.

I started a Saturday job in Dolcis shoe shop on Market Street, which gave me enough money to really get stuck in to the music scene. School had finished for me now, I only had to go in for the actual O-level exams themselves, so I was able to take extra shifts in the shop to pay for my social life. I was out as often as possible, either at clubs or gigs. I was enjoying working in the centre of Manchester, and made some new friends at Dolcis. One lad, Iain, who was a year or two older than me, was the owner of a Honda Dream 250cc motorbike. He would pack his spare helmet for me to use and we would go out clubbing together to Pips or to gigs at Rafters.

My dad and I had become virtual strangers. We operated almost in shifts. When I was out, he would be in, and vice versa. On the occasions that we were in the house together, and I was not in my room, he would fall asleep in a drunken haze in front of the TV, drowning out whatever was on with loud snoring, sending me running to my safe space. My bedroom was spartan, unpainted, and contained little more than a bed, a radio, and a small portable record player. I would spend hours here with the door shut, just me and John Peel against the world.

One Saturday I stayed out overnight myself, going back to the house of a girl that I had met at Pips. My friend Iain had ended up with her friend, and after saying our goodbyes to them, he gave me a lift home, dropping me off at my dad's in a flurry of motorbike engine noise. It was Sunday evening by then, and my dad was clearly the worst for wear after the weekend's hard drinking.

The abuse started the minute I closed the front door. Calling me every name under the sun, he let fly with a stream of hatred that must have been always there, just under the surface. I was 'too fucking good for the likes of me' and 'a stuck up little cunt' and everything in between.

He advanced towards me, fists clenched with a look on his face I hadn't seen before: other-worldly, staring into the middle distance, looking at me and straight through me at the same time. He connected with my head, sending my glasses flying across the room. I was taken aback by the amount of pain he had inflicted. I dropped to the floor to find my glasses. He came at me again as I cowered beneath him and more blows rained down. I didn't recognise this man. His face was a mask of hatred and wasted opportunity. It seemed that I was paying the price for everything that had ever happened to him.

I stood up, bleeding, and made my way towards the door, protecting my face with my arm. He came again, but this time I hit him squarely on the right jaw as he pulled his arm back. This surprised him enough for me to reach the door. Slamming it behind me, I was gone. I take no pride in my retaliation, but I was being battered by a fully-grown, pissed-up man, and there was no other way for me to escape.

I had a friend called Ged, not too far away. He wasn't a close friend, but when I turned up at his door that night, shaken and covered in blood, his mother sprung straight into action, cleaning up my wounds, feeding me and putting me in the spare room. I have known such people at various times in my life, and here was another angel, helping a messed-up kid, no questions asked. Throughout my childhood, even in the middle of the most appalling events, I found reasons to have faith in human beings. Teachers, nuns, other children's parents, help came from many places, and these fine people, acting for no personal gain, did much to balance out the cruelty and pain.

I woke up in a strange bedroom with a sore face. Things were different now. There was no way that I was going back to my dad's. I was scared of being put back into council care again, so it was with a heavy heart that I picked up the phone and rang my social worker, Mrs Daybank. My childhood had never really started, but now, without any shadow of a doubt, it was already over.

PART II
Keeping Control

Overleaf: Vibrant Thigh, Rochdale Tropical Club
(L to R) Martin Coogan, Mark Iveson, MH, Andy Hannay
Photo courtesy of Mark Iveson

6: Vibrant Thigh

Although I was officially under the care of Social Services, the first places I lived after things kicked-off with my dad were found for me by the school. Like so many other things in my life, I have my mother to thank for this turn of events. By teaching me to read, and to lose myself in books, she led me to grammar school where I became useful to Social Services. I was due to start A-levels at Cardinal Langley's sixth form. For a child to progress to university (as was planned for me) after such a disastrous start was unheard of, and was great PR for the authorities. I am convinced that it was this that swung the deal and I escaped being re-incarcerated by the skin of my teeth. My social worker was able to argue that I should be allowed a bit of latitude.

The first people to help were the De La Salle Brothers, who taught me at Cardinal Langley. They had links to the local community and placed me with various families for a few weeks at a time. I must have been a terrible house guest. I'd fall in at all hours, pissed after a night out at Pips, or a gig at Rafters, and disrupt the lives of these poor people who took me in, overstaying my welcome everywhere I stayed.

I was too fond of my new-found freedom to have any regard for the way these families lived. They would soon lose patience with me, meaning that I'd have to move on. This happened again and again. I lived briefly with a family next door to school, there was also a short stay in Castleton, Rochdale, living in the house of an ex-pupil who had joined the army, leaving his house unoccupied. Brief stays with the families of school friends Susan Abbott and Colette McKenzie added to the ever-growing number of places I lived.

I was becoming fairly proficient on guitar, bass and drums, picking up tricks from jamming at school, and was ready to begin making my own music. I had started playing bass with a couple of lads from school, nothing very serious, just messing about at weekends. We rehearsed at the house of John Clift. His father was a doctor. They were a large family, with an outbuilding some distance away from the house where we could make a bit of noise. John was older than me, and was a talented guitarist. He wrote his own songs, but we mainly cut our teeth on covers. We would play enthusiastic versions of 'I Don't Care' by The Ramones, 'Substitute' by The Who (although this was because of the raucous Sex Pistols version), 'The Wind Cries Mary' by Jimi Hendrix, and The Velvet Underground's 'I'll Be Your Mirror'. The Velvets were just another band as far as I was concerned, and although I was aware of Bowie's love of them, and his cover of 'White Light/White Heat', I was yet to understand their importance. It was John who turned me on to this major musical influence.

On drums was Mike (Vince) Handley, a pretty quiet lad from my class at school. Softly-spoken and somewhat reserved, he brought an untutored enthusiasm to the proceedings. It was Vince who named our little band Vibrant Thigh. The name stuck. Neither I nor Vince had any instruments, so we would make full use of John's well-equipped practise room. I was happy to lose myself in the sheer joy of making a loud noise with my two friends, forgetting the horrors of my home life for a while at least.

Young though I was, I was becoming quite a regular face in Manchester's live music venues, barging into conversations with people far older than me – barely shaving but full of opinions. Punk had taught me that reverence for the past was the first great mistake. I must have been quite a novelty to my elders, this fresh-faced kid, giving out chapter and verse about the way things should be, dividing the world into 'great' and 'shit' like some barometer of right and wrong. I was filled with verve and self-belief. As a product of punk's great levelling, I was the equal of anybody. This was what the revolution taught me. Anybody can do anything. We are all equal. End of.

I was fond of mooching around Manchester's Underground Market, in particular Discount Records, one of several record stalls frequented by punky kids like myself. I bought the first PiL single there, and '(White Man) In Hammersmith Palais' by The Clash. I was drawn to the back wall, which, like Virgin Records on Lever Street, had a healthy and intriguing 'Musicians Wanted' noticeboard. It was through an advert in this shop that I came to know Steve Murray. We talked on the phone and he invited me to see his band Fast Cars at Band on the Wall, a venue in the centre of Manchester. It was raucous and exciting, and although I didn't end up playing with them, I had made some new friends.

Steve was an energetic, upful person, and I was impressed that his band had supported Joy Division and Ed Banger and the Nosebleeds, amongst other luminaries. They played a full speed, tuneful brand of powerful punky pop, as their Buzzcocks-influenced name suggests. I told him about my fledgling band, probably exaggerating about how ready we were to play, and he told me about an organisation where different bands helped each other with equipment and put on gigs at Band on the Wall. I was invited down to one of their meetings.

The Manchester Musicians' Collective took its inspiration from a similar, more jazz-based group that had sprung up in London. The southern version leaned heavily towards improvisation, and it attracted left-field experimental musicians before changes in the musical landscape enticed performers from the more 'out there' end of punk, such as ATV. Fiercely left-wing, the ethos of the Collective was based on equality and the helping of people without a voice to express themselves musically. This way of thinking struck a chord with musicians in Manchester and fed into the Year Zero feeling brought about by the arrival of punk.

Manchester's version was, like its southern counterpart, expected to cater for the experimental/improvisational scene, and featured performers from that background, notably Trevor Wishart and Hallé percussionist Dick Witts. Launching in 1977, however, it meant the weekly meetings at North West Arts on King Street were soon attended by the more outward looking and inquisitive of the new groups. The Fall's first performance took place at a Collective meeting, with the tallest members, Mark Smith and Martin Bramah, having to play bent over because of the venue's low roof.

The Collective received a £410 grant from North West Arts to help with rehearsal space hire and transport. This marked the first time that the organisation had officially supported 'rock' music, and pointed to the way that music in Manchester was developing. Meetings moved to the Sawyers Arms pub on Deansgate, and gradually more of the new bands started to attend. Joy Division, A Certain Ratio, The Manchester Mekon and Mick Hucknall's Frantic Elevators took an active role in those early days.

Once the Collective started putting nights on at Band on the Wall, a scene began to develop organically. It was against this backdrop that I started to get involved. Even as a spotty teenager, the encouragement that I received from everybody concerned with the Collective did wonders for my confidence. The reception I got from my elders and betters made me even more sure of what I wanted to do with my life. Here was the embodiment of the punk ethic in action as far as I could see. Anyone could do anything, from a 16-year-old novice like me, to an experienced professional like, say, Dick Witts, who was an accomplished classical musician and TV presenter. After a life without encouragement, I felt welcomed and valued for perhaps the first time.

The meetings were chaired in an informal way by Louise Alderman and Frank Ewart of The Manchester Mekon. The egalitarian nature of proceedings meant that the regular Tuesday night residency at Band on the Wall would sometimes feature wildly inappropriate combinations of bands from differing ends of the musical spectrum, put together simply because it was their turn. All were equal here, from the likes of Ian Curtis and Rob Gretton to little old me.

I started to go regularly to the Collective nights. Although I'd had a few chats with Dick Witts, and found him to be encouraging and supportive, I was in no way prepared for the impact his band The Passage had on me the first time I saw them. The Passage had been formed by Dick and Tony Friel, who had recently left The Fall. I had been keeping my eye on The Fall since their earliest outings, and Tony's forceful and strident basslines were a large part of what I liked about them. I'd been introduced to Tony by Frank Ewart, and was struck by his confidence and the way he seemed to have an opinion on everything. I was a bit of a wide-eyed kid, to be fair, but I wasn't the only one swept up by the guy's personality. Funny as fuck, too. The band, though, was something else.

For a start, there was no guitar. There was a lot of innovative new music happening at the time, but all the bands I'd seen had kept to the traditional line-up of drums/bass/guitars and vocals. The Passage turned all this on its head. Instead of using a traditional 'rock' kit, Dick Witts drew upon his background in the Hallé Orchestra, and his setup looked alien. He used two snares for God's sake. Sitting low, behind an unusual collection of percussion instruments, his left hand snaked out across an array of differently tuned tom-toms. He even held his sticks like a classical musician, balanced between his fingers as opposed to the vice-like death grip employed by almost everybody else I'd seen.

Tony Friel wore his bass high and drove the songs from the bottom up, as had previously been hinted at during his time with The Fall. It is not much of a leap from The Fall's 'Last Orders' to The Passage's 'New Kind of Love'. The Passage used a twin lead-vocal approach to great effect, with Dick and Tony sharing vocal duties in a 'call and response' fashion, especially on the groundbreaking 'Love Song'. This song, more than any other, encapsulates what made The Passage so different to everybody else.

The whole thing about The Passage, from lyrics to line-up, was stridently anti-sexist, but not in a preachy way. The world was changing fast, and here was a group that taught by example. Lorraine Hilton's horror film organ playing was swirling, spooky and textural, it came across as intelligent, feminine even, and made me re-adjust, trying to find new coordinates in an attempt to get a handle on the lack of guitar histrionics.

Another regular at the Collective meetings was Steve Solamar of Spherical Objects. Previously the DJ at The Electric Circus (and a member of the mysterious Slugs), he radiated an edgy presence on stage, with shaky, high vocals, and something alien about his charismatic delivery. Thin and wiry, he reminded me of Brian Eno or Howard Devoto; very intense, uncomfortable to watch. Steve also ran Object Records. It was a label set up to release Spherical Objects records, but it soon began to give a voice to other acts, including The Passage.

At one meeting, Steve announced that he wanted contributions for a projected album of Collective bands to be released on Object. I handed in a rough tape made at a Vibrant Thigh rehearsal that contained just one song. I talked the talk, it has to be said, and as we were all equal, I managed to convince the meeting that it was my band's turn for a gig at one of the Collective nights at Band on the Wall. It worked and soon enough I saw my band's name on flyers alongside the likes of Joy Division and A Certain Ratio.

The first Vibrant Thigh gig, and therefore the first time I stepped out onto a stage in earnest, took place on 30th January 1979. I was 16 years and 5 months old. The 'your turn' democracy of the way gigs were given out had us paired with hairy retro rockers, Virginia Wolf, which meant we would be playing to a smattering of backward-looking dinosaur rock fans, brought by the 'main' band from wherever they came from. I was more excited and scared than I had ever been.

We had agreed to use Virginia Wolf's equipment, nominally to make changeovers faster, but this masked the fact that we didn't actually have our own gear, apart from John Clift's battered hand-me-down amps and ramshackle drum kit, which in all likelihood wouldn't have survived the four-mile journey from his house. Our live debut coincided with a bus strike, which meant that most of our friends were unable to attend. Not that we had many friends. In fact, most of the people from school that would have been interested wouldn't have been allowed into town at such a tender age, so we played to a decidedly small and friendless audience. Collective regulars, Louise Alderman, Frank Ewart and a few other bands were there every week, but apart from them, and the four or five school friends that had made it, this historic day was witnessed by very few people.

I looked out, catching my reflection in the mirrors at the back of the venue, and even though I was only playing to a few clumps of freezing humanity in a virtually empty club, it felt right. There was no time to get big-headed or to dwell on what had happened though, as I had to do a stint on the door, taking the 70p admission fees, and doubling up as a ticket giver and cloakroom assistant. I had entered the world of live music and it was far from glamorous, but I got a real buzz.

Vibrant Thigh had started as a kind of joke band, a school-based thing, and school for me was something I was very much leaving behind. Since splitting with my dad and living semi-independently, my attendance had nosedived. I felt I was a world away from such childish things. Eventually, I stopped going in altogether, as the contrast between my new-found freedom and the rules and regulations of school became too much. I turned my back on it and, with a few notable exceptions, left my contemporaries behind. John Clift and Vince Handley were never as keen as I was on the whole band thing, apart from jamming, and they disappeared from my life like so many others at this time.

Bouncing from one family home to another, living my life in clubs and venues and turning up at all hours of the night with no consideration for the generous people who were kind enough to put me up was not a sustainable proposition. A solution came from an unexpected quarter, the father of Liam O'Dea, a boy in my class. Liam's dad had several children at the school and had some involvement there. I suspect he must have been asked by the De La Salle Brothers if he knew of any accommodation I could be placed in. Liam's dad was an insurance agent, travelling door to door, and on his travels he got wind of a house to let near the centre of Middleton on Middleton View. Being a pillar of the community, he was able to smooth talk the owners to rent it to me.

I was still under the care of Social Services which meant that I had my rent and utility bills paid directly, so I couldn't mess that side of things up, plus I was given an allowance for food and other basics. It was an arrangement that had been tried out before with girls that had become pregnant at 15 and 16, but this was the first time that they had tried it with a young male like me.

It was soon revealed that this magnanimous gesture of Liam O'Dea's dad was connected to the living arrangements of an elder son, Ged. I don't remember particularly 'choosing' Ged as a house mate, but he moved in not long after I did. He was a strange fish. The black sheep of his own large family, he had lived a little, despite being only in his early twenties. He was something of a soulboy at heart, and had one foot in the world of Northern soul. He'd been to Wigan Casino, but was in no way a regular. He was, however, full of stories about his experiences, and the brilliant music that sprung from the Northern scene. It was a scene that was fuelled by speed.

The mid- to late-seventies saw a rise in barbiturate and amphetamine use amongst working-class Northern males. Chemist break-ins were rife, as drug-fuelled young men went in search of the elusive 'Dangerous Drugs Act' cabinet. Many local characters got caught up in this, and Ged had kind of existed on the fringes of this shady world, mainly by going to school with some of them.

Apparently, during his early club experiences, it was popular to abuse a nasal decongestant called Benzedrex. It came in inhaler form and determined thrill seekers would crush the case and chew the lint-type contents, which apparently contained a stimulant called propylhexedrine. I never tried this, of course, being of a younger generation, but Ged even knowing about such things spoke volumes about the difference between us, in age, in lifestyle and life experiences. Although I do think he exaggerated his tales of Northern soul all-nighters and the attendant lifestyle to impress me, he did point me towards some decent music, like Marvin Gaye and Isaac Hayes, even if this was cancelled out by endless Santana and John McLaughlin.

At one of the regular Sawyers Arms meetings I was told by Steve Solamar that Vibrant Thigh had made the cut for the Object compilation album. Many of my friends' bands had been selected, too. Picture Chords, for example, were an improvisational two-piece guitar and synth unit, and had only submitted their tape at the last minute for a laugh, feeling themselves too 'lo-fi' and 'out there' for inclusion. It was also to feature more established bands like Steve Murray's Fast Cars, and Fireplace, who had recently supported Magazine. For all my punk rhetoric and nonchalant exterior, to be making a record was unbelievably exciting, and when Steve Solamar told me I would be going to Revolution, in Cheadle Hulme, a *real* studio, I could scarcely believe my ears.

With John Clift and Vince Handley no longer in my life, I was badly in need of a band. Ged played guitar, so he was in, and I met a drummer called Andy Hannay when I visited a jam night at St. Dominic Savio's school youth club with David Coogan. We rehearsed a song I'd written called 'Wooden Gangsters', a spirited attack on violent youth, heavily influenced in structure by John Cooper Clarke's 'Suspended Sentence'.

I kept the name Vibrant Thigh as it was the name on the tape submitted to Steve and I didn't want to confuse the issue or rock the boat. So it was a Vibrant Thigh line-up that was just a few weeks old that set off for Revolution Studios to record my song. It was hard to believe that I was on my way to a real recording studio. At this point, the very thought of there being a record with me on it was straight from the realms of fantasy. I had dreamed of making and releasing a record for as long as I could remember, even if the mechanics of doing so remained an untouchable mystery. And now, without really understanding what went on there, I was to enter a studio for the first time.

The surreal aspect of all this was reinforced by the fact that we were travelling to Cheadle Hulme by bus, and we were going to be using the studio's own instruments and amplifiers. Only Ged had brought his own Kimbara Stratocaster copy, which although it was his pride and joy, would bounce out of tune at the slightest rumour of vigorous strumming. So it was that we showed up for this momentous day almost empty-handed.

I had only seen a studio before on television, or on album sleeves, so even a relatively modest setup like Revolution impressed the hell out of me. I felt at home straight away. Subdued lighting, soundproofed walls, and through the control-room window I could see banks of lights and expensive-looking equipment. I didn't have a clue what any of it did, but I knew I was in a special place.

We weren't invited into the control room, instead we were ushered into the adjacent playing room and helped to set up by Andy, the studio owner. After a quick level check, we played the 1 minute 42 seconds of 'Wooden Gangsters' twice through, all three of us in the same room. This was enough for the silhouettes of Steve Solamar and Andy Mac that we could see in the control room window. My lead and backing vocals went down in a similar breakneck fashion, and, with all this done, we were thanked and ushered towards the front door.

We weren't invited to take part in the mixing process. We wouldn't have known what was going on in any case. Instead, we retreated to a nearby pub, with two of us not even of legal drinking age, and sat there, changed forever.

A photo shoot was arranged at Band on the Wall with *NME* photographer Kevin Cummins, who was meant to have been taking individual shots of each of the bands. Unfortunately for all of us, some delay meant that he only had time to do a huge group shot outside the venue of all the musicians featured on the album which was to be called *A Manchester Collection*.

When I moved into my new rented house, having no furniture or bedding, or any of life's basics, I had been given a small amount of money to start me off. I had never had any amount of money before, and although it was only a few hundred pounds, it would have really helped. Ged, however, had other ideas. To be fair, I was a willing playmate, and it felt good splashing my cash around with my new, older friend.

And what a day we had! We took a taxi into the centre of Manchester, where we ensconced ourselves in the poolroom of the Cork and Screw on Oxford Road and I dutifully shelled out for a heavy afternoon session. I was then talked into paying for new clothes for Ged, a slap-up meal, and, as my finances dwindled, it was suggested that we take a taxi to Moss Side to buy some draw.

Although the late sixties had seen a drug-filled counterculture emerge, and it was common knowledge that the music of The Beatles, Stones, Jimi Hendrix (amongst others) were built upon a firm foundation of drug use, society at large had not come into contact with wholesale drug use. Penalties for possession of cannabis, and particularly possession with intent to supply, were extreme, so I had butterflies in my stomach as the black cab took us to Moss Side's 'front', a place that represented the great unknown.

We got out at the corner of Princess Road and Moss Lane East, under the shadow of the massive Harp lager brewery, and entered another world. Stepping through a small crowd of surly youth into Seymour & Story's bookies, we were separated and surrounded by intimidating groups of small-time dealers, getting up close and personal, shouting right into my face.

'Charas!'

'Black 'ash!'

The whole bookies seemed to be full of street dealers, young and old, hustling like fuck. It was hard to believe that any legitimate gambling was taking place at all, as a barrage of barked offers and commands bewildered and confused me. As an intimidated sixteen-year-old I must have seemed like a gift from heaven, so obviously out of my depth, but a tall Rastaman, clearly a person of some standing with the people here, took charge and I spent thirty quid – half the average UK weekly wage – on three sticks of pliable green-tinged, black oily resin, wrapped in silver paper. Ged was taken to the other side of the room, and with money he'd 'borrowed' from me, was sold a tenner deal of 'formula'.

It turned out that what Ged had been palmed off with was psychoactively useless. It must have been his Carlos Santana moustache. There were no such hiccups with what I'd bought though. I assume that the amounts were on the small side, but there was nothing at all wrong with the quality of the Indian 'charas' that I had been sold. I didn't smoke, so I chewed one of the sticks into a fine mush and swallowed.

We returned to Oxford Road for more drinks in The Salisbury as the draw I had eaten began to take effect. We flagged down a cab to take us home and by the time our taxi got back to the house we shared, the world was a very different place. I'd managed to not be sick for the duration of the journey, but was coming up strong now. I had no reference points for the way I was feeling, as queasiness gave way to light-headed euphoria.

I had immersed myself in drug-based music for years, and was well acquainted with the counterculture, from reading and films, but it was a wonderful surprise that first time to experience the effect that being stoned had on music, both listening to it and playing it. I swam in the sounds. Stereo effects seemed to come from all sides at once. Marvin

Gaye's *What's Going On* album, Penetration's *Moving Targets*, the Pistols and the newly released *Live at the Witch Trials* album by The Fall. Everything seemed to come alive for me.

A part of my innocence was lost forever, that much was true, but as I lost myself in hours of playing guitar, I thought that this was a fair exchange. Innocence, I felt, was overrated. Safe in my own space, I ate what was left and played my guitar as the neighbours knocked furiously on the wall. Things had changed.

I was summoned to the Sawyers Arms one Saturday afternoon to collect my freshly-minted copy of *A Manchester Collection*. After a long wait, a motley crew of musicians left the comfort of the pub and formed an orderly queue outside a suspicious-looking minivan parked on the nearest side street, where Steve Solamar gave two copies to each of us. Being the only Vibrant Thigh member present, I ended up with Andy and Ged's copies as well as my own.

Grinning from ear to ear, I went back into the pub to examine my album. The cover featured Kevin Cummins's photo of us all outside Band on the Wall. It looked great. The back sleeve was a different matter altogether. Where there should have been the never-taken individual band shots, there was something that looked like it had been cobbled together by an enthusiastic eight-year-old in about ten minutes. Our band name had been abbreviated to 'Vib. Thigh' and written in shaky, comedic lettering. The rest of the groups hadn't fared any better.

None of this, however, detracted from the magic of the day. There it was, my name in the brackets after the song title on the label. Even though I was well versed in the punk ideal of anyone being able to do anything, I felt ten feet tall and a part of something far bigger than myself. I wasn't sure exactly what it was, but it was definitely something worth being a part of.

7: Collective

Ged's pattern of spending my money continued for a short while but, thankfully, after a couple of months of living with him, he moved out. I had never received any contributions for rent or bills, and this would prove to make things difficult for me. I buried my head in the sand as far as my responsibilities were concerned. Having my own place meant that I would find myself with a living room full of sleeping youth most weekends, and would even use the place for band rehearsals, with full drum kit, all of which was bringing me ever nearer to my inevitable eviction.

I soon found myself with another 'lodger', this time a member of another Collective band, Rare Device. He was several years older than me, a pattern that seemed to repeat itself as far as my friends were concerned. His name was Jeff Bridges.

Jeff had been one of the first people that I had got to know at the Collective meetings. His band stood out from their contemporaries in several ways. Their guitarist Brendan Chesterton had an unusual style, using his fingers as opposed to a plectrum. He reminded me a little of John McKay of Siouxie and the Banshees. Being slightly older than me, they had one foot in the twilight world before punk, and their cover of 'White Rabbit' led me to investigate Jefferson Airplane and other music from that era, something my punk purism had kept me from doing.

Jeff had a style of his own, kind of punky, but psychedelic-looking, with paisley scarves and Roger McGuinn-style tinted round sunglasses, whilst still retaining the harder edges of punk. I liked him immensely, and could see a huge future for him in music. He was a skilled and charismatic frontman, and well connected. I was impressed that he would regularly visit Pete Shelley in Gorton where he lived in a terraced house with Jeff's friend, Carol. He always knew lots of people wherever we went. We'd be at all the best gigs together, The Russell Club, Band on the Wall, De Ville's, everywhere. Jeff introduced me to many amazing musicians and artists at these gigs. People seemed to love Jeff.

Along with their bass player, Mark Ellis, Jeff, Brendan and I would drink in Auld Reekie, a subterranean hangout beneath Market Street in central Manchester, or one of the many Yates's Wine Lodges scattered around the city, getting drunk fast and easily on their famous Blobs, made with hot water, sugar and Australian white wine. Jeff even took me to a side bar in Manchester's glitzy Midland Hotel. We must have stood out a mile in such posh surroundings, dressed down in punky charity shop clothes, and me being so obviously underage, but our confidence saw us through.

Jeff was nothing if not unpredictable. He once did a runner from a café on Newton Street, forcing me to follow him, with no warning at all. Things turned out alright as we collapsed in Stevenson Square, laughing, but we could have easily ended up with a beating (or worse). Instant justice for delinquents was the order of the day.

Jeff only stayed with me in Middleton for a short time, but being included by him and his older friends gave me a boost of self-belief, something I was hardly lacking in to begin with.

With Ged off the scene, a new Vibrant Thigh line-up had evolved. Andy Hannay, who had played on 'Wooden Gangsters', was slightly younger than me but had been playing for years in school bands and was a brilliant, unique drummer, even at such a young age. His brother, Chris, replaced me on bass guitar, leaving me to concentrate on vocals. Having brothers on bass and drums was a brilliant move. They had learned their instruments together, and had already spent thousands of hours becoming a fine rhythm section. They possessed an almost psychic sense of understanding, and together they provided an exciting foundation on which to build my songs.

Their friend, Mark Iveson, joined on keyboards. A lot of the music that I was influenced by at the time, like Magazine and XTC, had built upon punk's energy by adding keyboard textures, so I was excited to be able to expand the band's sound with the arrival of Mark. These were the early days of affordable synthesizers. Mark got the most out of his monophonic Elka synth by judicious use of primitive echo and delay effects. Being able to only play one note at a time had its own benefits and led to him coming up with some beautiful keyboard earworms. He was also a fine pianist, and would underlay chords on electric piano that added an extra layer of sophistication.

The line-up was completed by Martin Coogan on guitar. I'd known Martin for several years as I had spent a lot of time at his house as a friend of his brother, David. Even though Martin was a couple of years older than me, we had always got on really well. Alongside the usual Beatles and Stones, he had immersed himself in the world of Bowie, Roxy Music and Sparks, all of whom I also loved, and he introduced me to his beloved Be Bop Deluxe, who, apart from the minor hit, 'Ships in the Night', had not been on my radar.

Martin was already a skilled guitarist when I first met him. He'd reached out beyond himself to learn some pretty complicated stuff note for note. He would effortlessly rattle off tricky solos from the likes of Bill Nelson and Queen's Brian May on his Jedson Telecaster, as we younger kids gawped on in admiration. It was Martin who had taught me how to play barre chords, which in turn led me to begin writing different kinds of songs. Martin had reacted well to the new music, and had been with me at my first visit to The Electric Circus, and the eye-opening Damned/Adverts show that for me had started the ball rolling. I was delighted to have him on board.

With the line-up complete, it was time for some adventures. First of all, we needed a place to rehearse. I'd tried having Andy Hannay round to my house, but the noise was bringing me grief from the neighbours. I had put the word around, and we were eventually able to practise in All Saints and Martyrs church hall in Langley. This was down to a remarkable man, Jim Allen. He was a fiercely committed socialist, and went out of his way to help young people.

Our rehearsals were very productive; having good musicians involved was paying off. Previously, playing bass as well as singing meant that I was doing both things half as well as I could be. I'd have to look at where my fingers were on the fretboard to see where I was, often mid-way through a vocal line. Many lyrical gems were cut in half as I moved my head away from the microphone to check my fingers were in the right place. It also affected the kind of melodies I was actually writing, as things had to be kept simple when I was doing both jobs.

Freed from bass duties, my singing became stronger and more adventurous, and the new members' musicality meant that the songs were becoming a lot more musical. Martin is a great tunesmith, and he and Mark Iveson introduced light and shade to the proceedings. Chris and Andy took things to the next level rhythmically, introducing unusual time signatures and a jazz/funk element to the bottom end that underpinned the 'rockier' side of things, making it that bit more interesting.

Chris and Andy's unspoken, brotherly understanding meant they took to this messed-up funk approach like two ducks to water. The songs were coming and our sound building. Mark Iveson's futuristic low rumbling synth introduction to 'Walking Away' and his staccato hook lines to 'Sacred Heart' and 'Targets' were every bit as catchy as the vocal lines, and stayed in the head long after the songs themselves had finished. Songs like 'No Romance' were drenched in syncopated dance rhythms, as Martin and Mark's overlaid electronics pointed our sound towards the future. I was allowed the space to grow as a singer, and gradually we began to chisel out a sound of our own.

Due to the existence of the Musicians' Collective, getting gigs was a relatively easy process. The regular Band on the Wall nights were one thing, but just meeting other bands and making friends led to opportunities to play. At the weekly meetings, there was no such thing as taking a register of names or the paying of 'subs', it was more of a social occasion with a group of musicians talking and getting to know each other. We gathered in a raised mezzanine-type area to one side of the Sawyers Arms, overlooking the main pub itself, while below us, the pub's regulars were carrying on as normal. After the main business was dealt with, small groups would split off and friendships were formed. We would decide on whose equipment would be used, sharing backline and drum kits. This meant for faster changeovers as well as giving bands without their own gear an opportunity to play.

Being so close to the epicentre of what was going on musically in Manchester was a wonderful stroke of luck, both for the music I was making, and the music that was going on around me. The scene in Manchester was on the up, much of it due to the efforts of the Collective. Several of the bands had made real progress, both in their music and in the amount of attention they were getting. The Fall were one band that I had been close to throughout their early phase, and I felt a personal sense of pleasure to see them break through nationally, and even internationally.

Joy Division were firm advocates of the Collective. Ian Curtis and manager Rob Gretton attended meetings with some regularity, and although their career was starting to take off, they were down to earth and happy to chat with anybody, myself included. Rob did most of the talking, Ian was polite and softly spoken, a complete contrast to his on-stage persona. I had been aware of Warsaw in the Electric Circus days, but didn't see them live. I had bought the Virgin Records *Short Circuit* compilation containing their song 'At A Later Date', recorded live during the final closing weekend of the club, and although it was forceful enough, it seemed to me to be somewhat old-fashioned sounding compared to the genuine strides made by The Fall on the same release. To me, The Fall spoke of the future, and spoke of it in my accent, whereas Warsaw, whilst not looking backwards at all, spoke of the present at best.

The first gig under their new name was at Pips, but I didn't go to that one, although I had been practically living there at the time. The first time I saw them was at Band on the Wall, and they still had one foot in the musical world that they had occupied as Warsaw. The songs were fast and rocky, more full-on than those which came after. I left wondering what all the fuss was about. In October 1978, however, they were to record 'Digital' and 'Glass' with Martin Hannett, and this led to a complete rethink of their sound. They created more space, putting the drums and bass at the front of the mix, leaving room for the guitars to be used as punctuation, and for Ian Curtis's voice to become more 'musical', as opposed to fighting against a wall of sound.

As Joy Division got better, and more well known, there was much behind the scenes wrangling to be on the same bill as them at the Collective's Tuesday night Band on the Wall gigs. I didn't quite manage it with the new line up of Vibrant Thigh, I missed out by just one week; we were booked to play with Slight Seconds and Cindy and the Virgins on 6th March, Joy Division were paired with Fireplace for the following Tuesday.

This was my second gig, but it was the first time for the rest of the band, so they were filled with an extra level of nerves. Martin and Mark Iveson had the use of their parents' cars so they drove themselves there. Andy and Chris were dropped off by their ultra-helpful father, who, as a self-employed electrician, had his own work van. I travelled in on the number 17 bus. We assembled at around five o'clock and surveyed the scene.

Band on the Wall, on the north side of the centre, was a musical landmark in the city. It got its unusual name in 1937 when the charismatic landlord Ernie Tyson placed the stage on the wall, which the bands had to climb up to to play on. It became a popular hang out for American GIs during the war, many of whom were stationed in the North West. Their presence – and spending power – caused much resentment amongst the local male population and it became known as a rough and violent place to go. Prostitution was rife, and fighting would break out frequently. The whole area maintained that kind of reputation.

Three decades later, the venue still had a run-down look. Any paintwork that had originally been white was coated with a veneer of nicotine. The archaic-looking lamps, dotted around the walls, looked like they had been bought in a job lot from a specialist in Victorian railway equipment. Pictures of jazz musicians looked down on to the small stage, reinforcing the point that every other night of the week, jazz ruled.

Sitting around one small table were an assorted group of hairy, rocky looking folk, all denim and badges. This was Cindy and the Virgins, about who I knew nothing. Sitting around another table, looking moody and serious, were Slight Seconds, who I knew a little from Collective meetings, and had seen play before. They had formerly been called The Elite, and had supported Joy Division. There were things in common between the two bands. Both were the polar opposite of how bands were supposed to act. Introspective, shy even. No talking between numbers, simple stop/start dynamics, and a similar sense of economy within the music. I liked them a lot, and was delighted to be sharing a bill with them. Musically, they used the traditional line-up of drums, guitar, bass and vocals. Singer/guitarist, Kevin Eden, had a naturally sparse approach to his guitar playing, leaving the powerful drum and bass of Peter Hibbert and Mike Shaw to carry the empty sections, which would be punctuated by slabs of chewed-up melody in the space where there were no vocals.

They started their set with a 37-second long piece called '…And', involving the whole band at full pelt, all impassioned vocals and urgent, busy drums. Just as the audience were fully engaged with this loud and intense piece of music, everything would stop dead apart from the bass, which started immediately with the throbbing introduction to 'Puppet On A String', arguably their most compelling song. It was a brilliant way to start.

Vibrant Thigh were on second, sandwiched between Slight Seconds and the ultimately forgettable straight rock of Cindy and the Virgins. We lacked the stagecraft of Slight Seconds, who were a step or two ahead of us in their development. Image-wise, we were something of a mixed bag. Crammed at the back of a stage already crowded with equipment, Andy and Chris stood close to each other, heavy on eye contact and deep in concentration. Wearing 'normal' working clothes, they formed a band within a band, feeding off each other, almost to the exclusion of everything outside their little bubble. Mark Iveson, dressed in jeans and t-shirt, occupied a space slightly more forward, behind his electric piano and synth set-up.

Our front line, as it were, consisted of me and Martin, flanking left and right at the front of the stage. Martin would add backing vocals to some songs, and the two of us worked well together, both having similar speaking voices, tonally. We would harmonise on songs like 'Breaking Down', stretching the long notes and playing to our strengths. Martin had evolved a style of his own on guitar as he began to experiment with phaser and distortion pedals, and, coupled with Mark's synth lines, it made for a suitably futuristic noise.

It was Martin's influence that had led to an influx of several 'faces' from Pips, and the Bowie/Roxy scene. Collective nights, although high on musical treats, were low on glamour, and to see heavily made-up and overdressed people in the audience alongside the usual Collective scruffies made for an amusing contrast. Not that I could see anything in great detail, though, as I surveyed the sparse crowd in front of me. Teenage vanity had made me brave the world without my much-needed glasses, putting things into a soft focus. From where I was standing, everybody looked beautiful.

I was back at Band on the Wall for the Joy Division gig the following Tuesday. Anticipation for the show was high as many people had been reading about the band but were yet to see them. The place filled up as support band Fireplace set the tone with their keyboard-led songs reminiscent of Magazine's recent output.

It was a band in transition that I saw that night. Older songs like 'They Walked In Line' were sprinkled amongst the likes of 'Shadowplay', 'She's Lost Control' and 'The Only Mistake'. Steven Morris's use of the new Synare 3 electronic drum synth made everybody's ears prick up, and showed that the band had come a startlingly long way in a short time. Gone was the low-end onslaught of their previous, rockier incarnation, replaced by a new, modern, forward-looking unit. Ian Curtis was more exciting to watch in a smaller, narrower venue. With less space to move sideways, he was forced to operate within a small area, centre stage, which intensified his presence greatly, and from just a few feet away, he seemed possessed. Now I got it.

The release of 'Wooden Gangsters' on *A Manchester Collection* had made things much more real for me in the world of music. The album featured in alternative charts in the *NME* and *Sounds*, and was positively reviewed by Paul Morley. It was being featured on John Peel's Radio 1 show. Up until now, my belief in the punk ethic of 'anybody can do anything' was heartfelt, but purely theoretical. Now I had proof. All those lonely nights listening to John Peel, all those days spent with my head stuck in music papers, and now I was a part of this mysterious world. On ground level, my band was getting mentioned in fanzines, too, like *City Fun* and the Collective's own *Keeping Control*. These were my people, and it felt good to a kid who had never belonged anywhere until now.

As the Collective became better known, other Collectives started up in satellite towns surrounding the city, notably Burnley, where a band called The Not Sensibles had created one, which led to gig exchanges between the two organisations. The Stiffs from Blackburn had been played on John Peel's show but wanted to take the next step up and play to bigger audiences in bigger places, so they connected. Gradually, a network of 'gig swaps' began to happen, as well as tip-offs of places bands had played in their own towns. Places like The Lamp Room, some 35 miles away in Blackburn, where Vibrant Thigh got booked to play.

Martin and I spent the morning cramming the Coogan family car with equipment. We waited for the Hannays' work van to join us before heading north in a loose convoy through gentle farmland and rolling hills. Mark Iveson travelled separately. Mark was a self-contained unit, retaining full control over his set up and travelling arrangements.

When we got to the town, we stopped to ask for directions several times, not fully understanding the rich Lancashire accent that answered us but we were too polite to say so. Blackburn, although relatively close to Manchester, seemed like another world to me; different, but familiar. Its rows of compact houses put me in mind of Rochdale, or Oldham, or any of the working mill towns that I knew, but something about the accent made it impossible to forget that I was seriously out of my comfort zone. We eventually arrived at a tiny pub on a steep, hilly street of two-up, two-down terraced houses.

Getting our gear upstairs reinforced the unglamorous nature of it all. We were sharing a bill with Rare Device, and both bands got stuck in to the heavy lifting. Living with Jeff Bridges meant that I was close to Rare Device and I spent more time with Jeff and Brendan than with my own band members. Nevertheless, there was a sense of the special occasion about the day, with us playing outside Manchester for the first time. Soundchecks, such as they were, went quickly, leaving us to start drinking a little too early as we waited for the good people of Blackburn to arrive.

Several hours, and several drinks later, it was time for action. Rare Device played first, and if anything, benefited from the cramped and intimate venue. The scruffy upper room had no stage, so the bands were on the same level as the audience. Jeff was a natural. Lost in himself, eyes closed, gripping the microphone stand for dear life, he oozed vulnerability, as Brendan's weird, finger driven guitar lines filled the room. I loved it.

By the time we were due to go on, the place had filled up a little, although this was largely down to interested musicians from the area, rather than masses of Blackburn's 'civilian' population. We kept it punky and direct on the whole, Martin and I inches from the front row, close enough to see the whites of their eyes. Songs like 'No Romance' filled the room with a blended wash of Martin's effected guitar and Mark's bass synth noises, as Chris and Andy nailed things down, but it was the more intense material like 'Walking Away' and 'Breaking Down' that really made the place shake.

Powerful as they were, those songs weren't the only thing that made the walls of The Lamp Room shake that night. In the silence between songs, I moved forward towards the microphone to impart some words of wisdom, only to be drowned out by the noise of a goods train – endless carriages long – bringing a little of the San Francisco earthquake to the night's proceedings. Lamps swung, lights flickered, and eyes rolled as I waited for the noise to stop. Comedy gold, but no amount of strangeness could detract from the specialness of the day. We had played our first out of town gig, and survived.

8: God's Gift

The novelty of the honeymoon period of my freedom had given way to a harsh and often lonely reality. When the parties were over, I was left as alone as I had ever been, trying to make sense of it all. I ignored my problems, like any self-respecting wild child would. The red letters would arrive and remain unopened for a while before being thrown away.

A blast from the past occurred when I met up with Brian Logan again. He had been my best friend for a while although we had drifted apart since. Brian was as touched by the new music as I was, so we started to go to gigs together, following the likes of The Fall and A Certain Ratio. It was a real honour and a piece of luck to catch these bands so early, and as they progressed from small venues like Band on the Wall and Cyprus Tavern, we were there to see them grow.

Brian lived quite near to my flat, and I would often visit his house. Mr and Mrs Logan would have remembered me from when I used to play with their son in Asssumption Juniors and would have been affected by the death of my mother. Now, as a young man, I was always welcome, and the frequent snacks and bowls of soup would still mysteriously appear whenever I did, subtly presented to minimise my embarrassment.

Brian and our friends Paddy Matthews and John Stefaniuk would come with me to some mind-blowing gigs. Magazine, The Human League, Stiff Little Fingers, everybody who was anybody played at Hulme's Russell Club, renamed The Factory for these nights, and we would practically live there, getting in some real states along the way. We lost one of our number after a particularly messy Cure gig. Robert Smith, all cropped spiky hair, led his three-piece through a mesmerising set of songs from their debut *Three Imaginary Boys* album. We eventually found our fallen comrade asleep amongst the debris at the foot of Charles Barry Crescent, the intimidating concrete edifice next door to the club. Par for the course, really.

My friends and I had become very fond of mind-altering substances of one sort or another. Nothing too heavy, but the parties at mine could be crazy. I became a frequent visitor to Moss Side, visiting the little Alex pub, or Seymour and Story's bookies, where I would be treated pretty well for a naive outsider. Every now and again, I'd be palmed off with some homemade fakery, but on the whole, what I was sold was what it was supposed to be and did the job it was supposed to do. Gradually, I began to meet other dealers closer to home, and began to sample other types of draw.

It seemed that the types of solid 'resin' available at the time had a lot to do with politics, in a strange way. We were treated to the finest black from Nepal and Afghanistan, and a whole range of different coloured (red, blond, dark) varieties from the Lebanon. This seemed to be a direct result of the UK's military presence in such places, often as part of an international peacekeeping force. Soldiers topped up their income by bringing bits home to sell.

There has always been a degree of cross-pollination between the worlds of music and drug sales, with dealers enjoying the company of musicians, and musicians just loving to sample their wares. This was as true in jazz-era America as it is today and will always be. It was certainly the way things worked in Manchester in the seventies. I was now moving more in 'druggy' circles, and although it was undoubtedly a murky world, I came to no real harm, and made some good friends.

Money wasn't always necessary in the pursuit of altered states. Late summer and early autumn saw an annual explosion of psilocybin mushrooms all over the North of England. Middleton and its surrounding countryside was fertile ground. Each day, the grass verges, bowling greens and school playing fields would become spotted with the white heads of liberty cap mushrooms, and I could pick more than enough for everyone in no time.

I had been heavily influenced by psychedelic culture for years, and although punks were nominally against all that had gone before, we made an exception when it came to drugs. I, for one, jumped in off the top diving board and would put my little brain through its paces at the slightest excuse, taking far too much, far too often. And sometimes with drink, too, which could be a far more dangerous activity. Middleton, with its roughneck reputation, was one of the worst areas for alcohol-fuelled, post-pub fighting.

One night I was out with Brian and Paddy Matthews. We had been at the Olde Boar's Head in Middleton, drinking pint after pint of Webster's bitter. Of the three of us, I was by far the worst for wear, slurring my words and stumbling around. All the pubs closed their doors at eleven o'clock, which meant that the drunken troublemakers spilled out into the open-plan town centre all at the same time. We headed for Tommy's chippy, which was a hotspot for gangs of drunken males finishing off a night's drinking with a fish supper and some ultraviolence. I'd like to think it was my hair, recently dyed a fetching shade of dirty blond/bluey green that singled me out for attention that particular night, but in reality it could have been anyone, for any reason.

Angry words led in seconds to a real altercation. There was a lot of shouting and then a bang. I'd been hit on the head and separated from my friends. I collapsed to the floor and curled into a ball as my assailants, grown men in their late twenties, kicked me repeatedly as I lay on the floor. I don't remember much, but I do remember thinking that my time was up and that I would not get up from this. I protected my face and offered no resistance. Mercifully, the anaesthetic effect of so much alcohol delayed any real pain.

My bruises subsided, and thankfully no lasting serious physical damage had occurred. The real damage, of course, was psychological. In the cold light of the following day, I was more disgusted than hurt. Such violence was not exclusive to Middleton, but the whole episode played a large part in me wanting to go out into the world and leave this backwater behind.

I would travel into Manchester most Tuesdays for the Band on the Wall Collective nights. One Tuesday I went in for a Hunt Saboteurs benefit show featuring The Knives, a band slightly outside our circle. I knew the sax player, Stalwart, but on the whole, although there were many Collective members present, the make up of the audience was older and more overtly political. I had come in from Middleton on a number 17 bus, which meant getting off just before Swan Street on the north side of the city. I went directly to the venue.

Inside Band on the Wall, people were somewhat subdued. Five minutes walk away on Oldham Street, there had been an horrific fire at Woolworths that afternoon, with several people killed. The true horror of the day's events were only just sinking in. It was a shock to find out that such a terrible tragedy had happened so close to my world. Music aside, the whole area had played a huge role in my childhood, and Woolworths itself was part of my Saturday ritual in those fragile early days of getting to know my dad again after years of estrangement. A few years earlier, and with a different set of circumstances, it could have been me and him there, trapped in a doomed department store.

It was all too easy to imagine the chaos and panic in the subterranean food hall we used to visit, situated one floor below ground in a basement served by just two escalators. There were 500 people in the building at the time of the fire, 10 of whom lost their lives. I can't have been the only person to feel a sense of empathy and kinship with those unfortunate people. It really could have been any of us.

The centre of Manchester had served as a backdrop to my life since I was a small child, and the months following the fire were no different. There was music to make, fun to be had, and things to be done. I continued to be a creature of the inner city. It was hard, however, to not feel a shiver when passing through Piccadilly.

Although we got on well enough as a group, the members of Vibrant Thigh were not close friends as such. Only me and Martin Coogan would socialise together, and within that framework we had differing tastes in music; Martin being drawn to the more electronic side of things (The Human League, The Normal etc) and was somewhat resistant to the scratchier, more abrasive sounds that I was enjoying at the time, like Gang of Four or The Pop Group.

Apart from rehearsals and gigs, I would never see Mark Iveson. Although we got on pretty well, we couldn't be described as close. Chris and Andy formed a little group within a group and kept themselves to themselves. Both of them were always trying to stretch their playing, which would take them into 'jazzier' areas. Chris in particular had great admiration for bass players like Jaco Pastorius and Stanley Clarke, and it was difficult sometimes to get him to keep things simple. Their father was totally supportive of his sons, and we would be dropped off at gigs in a 'Hannay Electricians' van, too young and inexperienced to find this at all embarrassing.

We started to rehearse in central Manchester, at a warehouse in the Knott Mill area belonging to Tony Davidson. Many other notable bands practised there, including Frantic Elevators, Joy Division, Buzzcocks and The Fall. It felt good to be mixing with other bands after our previous isolation. Tony Davidson took to us, promising to release an album on his TJM label, home of V2 and The Distractions, but this all came to nothing.

We improved as a band and started to get better gigs as our reputation grew. People responded to us, too. We played to enthusiastic audiences both in Manchester and further afield in places like Rochdale's Tropical Club. Fanzines liked us, and it was rewarding to see the same people coming to gigs as we built up a modest following.

We played Collective nights with such luminaries as Slight Seconds, Crispy Ambulance and Picture Chords, and became allies and friends with some amazing people. God's Gift, for example, who stood head and shoulders above most trivial, pop-type bands. Singer Steve Edwards, a psychiatric nurse at Prestwich Hospital, was one of the most compelling frontmen of his time. Over simple, driving basslines, and Mo Tucker-esque rhythms, he stood stock-still and deadpanned his cynical poetry against a barrage of atonal distorted guitar. I was immediately attracted to his accent, which was harsh Mancunian like my own. He was a natural, no doubt about it. People would be reminded of John Lydon, or Mark Smith, but he carried around his own urchin-type intensity, more like the kid out of *Kes* than anybody in the field of music. I have seen God's Gift empty a room, and irritate their audience so much that glasses were thrown, but I loved them. To be in the same room as they powered through 'Discipline' or 'There Is No God' was a profoundly unsettling experience.

I managed to get us a gig at The Factory. Although I was a regular there, we had never been invited to play. It was one of the quieter Thursday nights and most Russell Club/Factory regulars would have been saving their money for the Joy Division gig taking place the day after ours. Nevertheless, we managed to half-fill the place, and made ourselves some new fans. Having our name on Factory flyers alongside the likes of The Cure and The Pretenders didn't do our reputation any harm.

I was back the next night as a punter to watch Joy Division and returned to see many other bands on the bill. I checked out Echo & the Bunnymen supporting The Fall. The 'Echo' in their name referred to the drum machine they used. Their drum machine-driven psychedelic tinged pop made them a lot of friends. One look at Ian McCulloch staring out at the Russell Club audience, all big black pupils, wearing a check shirt, told me all I needed to know about the band's future prospects.

There was quite a lot of cross-pollination between the musicians of Manchester and Liverpool. Much has been made of the rivalry between the two cities, but on a musical level, there was always a great deal of mutual respect. We would follow the Liverpool scene almost as closely as our own. I watched The Teardrop Explodes and Wah! Heat as they developed, often in tiny venues like De Ville's, inches away from the slightly raised dancefloor, close enough to see the steam rising under the too-hot lights. The early Teardrop Explodes singles 'Sleeping Gas' and 'Bouncing Babies' on Zoo records were big tunes on my side of the M62, and the druggy beauty of 'All I Am Is Loving You', thrown away on the B-side of 'Bouncing Babies', made it one of the year's most compelling songs. It slows time down to a standstill as Julian Cope's deadpan delivery weaves in and out of echo-swamped, ice-cream van keyboards and guitar. I'm full of admiration for singing bass players, the way they have to think in two directions. Julian Cope was a delight, his bass playing going in one direction, while his vocal melodies went in another. Not easy, not easy at all.

I had a soft spot for Big in Japan, featuring the charismatic Jayne Casey. I loved their debut EP, especially the sublime 'Nothing Special'. The line-up of this band contained Bill Drummond, Holly Johnson, Budgie and Ian Broudie, but it was Jayne Casey who fascinated me the most. She was a friend of Jeff Bridges. Jeff seemed to be as well connected with the Liverpool bands as he was with the Manchester scene.

Both Manchester and Liverpool fell under the umbrella of the Granada TV region, and were therefore exposed to *What's On*, fronted by Tony Wilson. Appearances on the show by Margi Clarke, under her early alias 'Margox', made her an easily identifiable figure, and she would be a regular sight at Factory events, both as an audience member and even as a performer. Upfront and punky as she was, she was an actress, and this was more fiction, unlike another rising Liverpool personality that made the 35-mile journey on the M62 from time to time, Pete Burns.

I remember the impact of Pete and his girlfriend falling around the upstairs bar of the Russell Club at a Factory night. It wasn't even one of his own gigs, but it was definitely Pete Burns (and his entourage) that I remember about the night. His band, Nightmares In Wax, had played there previously and, although I hadn't seen them, some of my friends had said that the singer was 'well out there'. Their small party made up for lack of numbers with sheer attitude. Very Scouse, very loud and very intimidating, they were seriously pissed, knocking drinks over and smashing glasses without a care in the world. They stood out a mile with their colourful clothes and make-up, a sharp contrast to the massed grey overcoats of the Factory regulars. Pete Burns's girlfriend wore a 'Beat me, Bite me, Whip me, Fuck me' dress, and was a terrifying prospect, tottering away on very high heels.

Superficially, this was a variation of the fashions on view at Manchester's Pips club, albeit that little bit darker. Less vain, less easy on the eye, and prepared to look challenging and ugly in the cause of provocation. Not in the slightest bit dainty, the two of them looked as if they would snap you in half as soon as look at you. Both sported huge, upwardly pointing hair, the result of a full can of hairspray each, at least.

Orchestral Manoeuvres in the Dark were another Liverpool band that I was exposed to at the Factory nights, playing early in the evening on a bill with Joy Division and A Certain Ratio. We had heard that Factory were to release a single by a new, electronic-based Liverpool band, and, even in a half-full Russell Club, they made an impression. Things had been moving in this direction for some time, and while the likes of The Normal and The Human League were on my radar, their electronica was still perceived as 'difficult' to listen to. OMD, however, were charming and tuneful, shy even. The A-side of their Factory single 'Electricity' certainly made a few heads stop and listen, but for me, the flipside, 'Almost', was the real treasure. Slow and mournful, with a lush, unforgettable synth melody. It stayed in my head for days.

Even though I'd been living a somewhat free and chaotic life, I was still under council care and would be until my 18th birthday. I continued to have periodic meetings with my social worker Kath Daybank. She decided that something had to be done about my living situation to give me a sense of security for the next phase of my life. She'd realised that the arrangement organised by Ged's dad, which saw me accumulating debt and problems with the neighbours, was far from satisfactory and needed to change. The families that had helped me initially by giving me a short-term place to stay were all kind people, but I was simply not equipped to slip effortlessly into somebody else's family structure. That much had been proved over and over. Mrs Daybank decided I needed to have a flat of my own and had convinced the powers that be to give me the tenancy of a one-bedroom flat in Middleton's Hollin estate at a weekly rent of £7.61. A series of safety nets were put into place, like getting money for electricity and gas deducted at source before I got anywhere near it, and having my rent paid directly to the council.

I went to see my flat, all empty and echoey, with its tiled floor. I had virtually nothing, but even with no possessions, it felt good to be beholden to no one. Money was found, via Mrs Daybank, for cheap carpets to be fitted, and a cooker was sourced from Social Services, along with a second-hand bed and some bedding and various pots and pans, of which I had none. A small amount of money was made available for me to brighten up and personalise the place. With Brian in tow, I spent £58 on floor cushions and a print of Picasso's *Guernica* from Lewis's department store in Manchester, the very place I had bought my mother's scarf from just eight years before. So much had happened since then, and sitting in the taxi on the way back to my new home, it felt like I was turning bad memories into good, and that a positive new phase of my life was starting.

Worn out after a long day, Brian took one cushion, and I took the other. I put the Virgin Records *Front Line Volume One* reggae compilation on my wardrobe-sized radiogram and breathed a sigh of relief. At last, I lived somewhere.

Vibrant Thigh headlined a benefit gig for the Deeply Vale Festival at Band on the Wall, which got us an invite to play at the festival itself. As our van descended into the valley, I was plunged headfirst into a strange and alien world that looked half refugee camp, half medieval battleground. Tents with signs offering LSD and Afghani black for sale mingled with healthy food stalls, and everywhere you looked, feral, scruffy, happy children. This was a major eye-opener for me. It was a head-on collision with the counterculture that I'd known about but was yet to properly experience.

Punks, hippies, bikers, Rastas and everything in between gathered in the hills outside Rochdale and stayed for weeks. In front of my teenage eyes, a society in microcosm had taken residence in the outskirts of the very town that had treated me so badly as a child in care. This beautiful valley had transformed itself into a sprawling mini-city, populated by people that you simply did not see anywhere else. Who were these strange folk? How did they live? What was in that cup of tea?

The whole caboodle was entirely free. Money was the enemy here, and naive as this may sound, it kind of worked. The prime movers were the traveller community, families that had dropped out from mainstream society years ago and had become mobile, moving around the country in convoys of garishly painted and mechanically suspect vehicles. Having celebrated the solstice at Stonehenge in June, they would hit Wales in early summer as the first psilocybin mushrooms popped their cheeky little heads above ground, before ending up in the Lancashire hills.

They led by example. There was free food served from steaming bowls of meatless stew to anyone and everyone. They built tepee encampments and campfires for their dirty-faced, half-naked kids to dance around. In a quiet, unpreachy way, they showed city dwellers like me that there was an underground way of living. Idealism reigned supreme.

The bill was amazing: The Fall, Misty in Roots, The Ruts, Spizzenergi, ATV. The previous year had seen Steve Hillage's head music attract a 20,000 crowd, so I was equal parts nervous and excited out of my tiny mind. Manchester Mekon's 'The Cake Shop Device' floated over this biblical scene as midnight approached and it was showtime for Vibrant Thigh.

We were probably a little too clean looking for most of the audience, but thousands watched and listened. A group of third-wave 'punks', more about fashion than revolution, crowded the stage beneath my feet and subjected me to the most disgusting barrage of spitting I had seen since the days of The Adverts or Ultravox! at Middleton Civic Hall. It was everywhere, dripping off the microphone stand as I dodged and weaved. Hadn't they got the memo? Nobody had ever thought that this was cool! We bravely got through our set, the final notes of 'Sacred Heart' ringing round the valley.

Instead of going home with everybody else, I decided to stay. No tent, no money, no nothing, but I ended up wringing every ounce of pleasure out of this amazing place. Misty in Roots were a revelation. I had passed their van before they played, clouds of weed smoke billowing out of the rear door, and had no idea of the impact they would have on me. They came on early in the morning, and their mournful, slow-paced music entered my heart.

9: Joy Division Close Up

My time at Cardinal Langley was coming to an end. I was nominally enrolled in their sixth form to do A-levels but there was clearly no future in that. The contrast between school life and the life I was leading was simply too great. The idea of me getting up in the morning after a late-night party, putting on my school uniform and heading to class was a non-starter. It was obvious that I had little in common with people of my own age, who still had the luxury of passing from childhood to adulthood in a less abrupt fashion. Most of the people in school seemed childish to me. Something had to give, and before the new term started in September I officially dropped out of Cardinal Langley and enrolled in St. John's College, a more adult environment in the shadow of Granada Studios in central Manchester.

Living on my own was a massive challenge for me. In the few years since I'd left the children's home I had learned very little about how to live. I had been taught to iron my school clothes and carry out mundane domestic tasks, but I had no idea of budgeting or cooking, or any of the practical skills that I might need to get by. I made it up as I went along, but I was much more interested in being part of Manchester's musical community and had little time for anything else.

My flat became something of a party-central. Once again I had no idea of how much of an impact my noisy late-night sessions were having on my neighbours, many of whom were on the elderly side. As most of the parties took place after we'd come back from gigs at places like Rafters or The Factory nights at the Russell Club, it would be early in the morning when they started, scaring the other residents half to death as they cowered behind their doors, fearful of everything, but especially the drunken punky types that would invade my flat to carry on partying into the early hours.

Most of my friends still lived with their parents, so my front room floor would be populated with three or four pissed young men most weekends, causing all kinds of chaos. The walkways outside would be covered in shaving foam, as messy play fights inspired by The Phantom Flan Flinger from *Tiswas* broke out in the early hours. Eggs would be thrown everywhere, and the terrified neighbours would find pools of vomit and the occasional sleeping reveller dead to the world in the communal stairwell. I was, without doubt, the worst neighbour in the world. I knew no better. This, however, was of no consequence to the powers that be, who brought out the big guns in the form of letters threatening eviction. Such threats meant nothing to me, and I continued to bury my head in the metaphorical sand like some punky ostrich.

As the band continued to make headway, I continued to make new friends. One night I was working on the door with Dick Witts at a Collective Band on the Wall night when two young musicians came to find out about what we were doing and how we could help their bands. I had met them briefly before in Middleton, they were Mark Burgess and Dave Fielding who were from two separate bands, Years and The Cliches. Both were a few years older than me. They were unsure about the Collective, seeing it as cliquey and self-serving. This was very possibly true, but I told them that by making myself an 'insider', I made it work to my advantage.

Despite Dave and Mark's reservations about the Musicians' Collective, they seemed to quite like Vibrant Thigh and started to come to some of our gigs. They came to see us play at Salford University with The Hoax one night. Instead of staying with my band and getting a lift home in the van, I ended up walking back into town with Dave and Mark instead, chatting and putting the world to rights.

Dave was a quiet, artistic lad, who lived with his parents, brothers and sister Diane on Stanycliffe Lane, near to where I had gone to school. I'd known Diane for some time. Dave was keeping himself busy with his band, Years, playing covers and some originals around local pubs. A traditional type of three-piece, they consisted of Dave on guitar, his mate Sid on drums, and another very shy-seeming but charismatic bass player called Reg.

Dave and Reg were something of a double act. They played gigs around the north Manchester venues, and as a result felt a little left out of the Manchester scene. This developed an 'us against the world' vibe about what they were doing. They had released their own independent single, 'Come Dancing', recorded at Cargo Studios in Rochdale. I was impressed by them.

They had passed through Rochdale College's Art Foundation course and had good take on new music. We enjoyed a lot of the same new bands. The Psychedelic Furs' 'Sister Europe' was a favourite of Dave's when it came out. We bonded over The Undertones and even The Dead Kennedys' early singles. Dave became a regular visitor to my flat, just hanging out, listening to John Peel together, smoking weed.

I was also a regular visitor to the Fielding household. The first Christmas after I'd met Dave, I was all ready to just batten down the hatches and wait until it was all over. No family, no presents, no company, nothing. Things were looking less than festive when suddenly there was a tapping at the door. Dave had come to take me to the family home to spend Christmas with them. I tried to protest, but he was having none of it. I was whisked away to share Christmas with a lovely group of people. Large families often have extra friends round at times like this, and it probably wasn't that unusual to them, but for me it was the most wonderful unexpected kindness.

The Cliches were a direct result of Mark Burgess's exposure to the first wave of punk. Mark had loved music since he was a kid, with a particular fondness for the likes of T.Rex, Bowie and Sparks, but it was punk that had galvanised him into action. He had even hitched his way to Huddersfield on Christmas Day 1977 to attend the legendary Sex Pistols show at Ivanhoe's in support of the children of striking firemen. I took to him straight away, he was obviously a skilled player and a brilliant frontman. He only lived a short walk from my flat, and we would spend many afternoons together, listening to records in his bedroom. Once again, I brought out the protective side of things as far as Mark's mum was concerned. She would always make sure I was okay for snacks and, on occasions, she'd pack me off with parcels of food, or, one time, a catering size tin of coffee that just happened to be 'going spare'.

Mark and I shared a lot of musical influences. The Pistols, obviously, had got under everybody's skin, but he had also been at some of the same Middleton Civic Hall gigs that I had. The Adverts had touched his heart in the same way that they had touched mine, and the Middleton show by Ultravox! had affected him greatly. It was magnificent, to be fair, a real eye-opener, with glimpses of how punk would progress with the addition of keyboard textures and a real intelligence. The unforgettable strobe-lit barrage of 'Artificial Life', with John Foxx's thousand-yard staring beyond the spitting front row, other-worldly and unbothered. Such a brilliant frontman, and a major influence on both of us. Mark went to see Ultravox! as often as he could, and their Eno-produced debut album was never off my radiogram.

We watched PiL's game-changing *Old Grey Whistle Test* appearance together at my flat. It was a direct descendent of Lydon's 'Get off your arse' call to arms appearance on Tony Wilson's *So It Goes* and every bit as important, albeit in a different way. Keith Levine prowled around, alternating between attacking, air-raid siren type synths and his own unique empty guitar style. Wobble's bass anchored it all down from a seated position, arrogantly aware of the power of it all. John Lydon shone that night, absolutely owning the whole performance.

Mark's friend, Tony Skinkis, was another character that I had a lot of time for. Again, he was a few years older than me, and seemed to be a very practical type of person with his own van. He had a flat on Rochdale Road that was a popular meeting up/hanging out place. I was something of a novelty with these more experienced, slightly more mature people. With my friends Brian and Paddy, I was busy getting the most out of life, and the states we would get in were a source of great amusement to them all.

I spent a lot of time at Tony's listening to music. 'King and Country' by Television Personalities, 'Einstein on the Beach' by Philip Glass, and *The Image Has Cracked*, the debut album by ATV. ATV were already on my radar. Singer Mark Perry had been very important to me (and thousands of others) and was a bona fide hero of the revolution. His fanzine *Sniffin' Glue* had inspired many others, both in the UK and further afield, to start their own small, DIY publications. From the highlands of Scotland to the tip of Cornwall, fans of the new music created their own, alternative network of cheaply-printed fanzines, and it was to these that we turned to find stuff out. One called *Sideburns* printed a drawing of three chord diagrams (A, E and G) with the words 'This is a chord. This is another. This is a third. Now form a band.' Their 'anybody can do it' approach inspired many to do exactly that.

ATV seemed to have a foot in both the old and the new worlds. The cultural apartheid that prevailed between punks and hippies meant nothing to them, and they travelled the country with anarcho-drop outs Here and Now, teaching by example at events like Deeply Vale Festival that to be 'anti-state' was more than a matter of mere dress code. This was all well and good, but it was the music itself that won me over and led me to trust their rhetoric.

'Action Time Vision' is one of *the* great punk singles, anthemic and powerfully produced, and there is evidence of real intelligence and skill on *The Image Has Cracked*'s other highlights. 'Nasty Little Lonely', for instance, goes from vulnerable and understated to all out attack in a display of control that points the way towards the future while still being unashamedly human.

It is the album's opener, though, 'Alternatives' that did it for me. Constructed from different lo-fi live performances, it sees Mark Perry invite the audience onto the stage in an open mic situation. Things degenerate throughout the track's nine minutes as the open mic session is hijacked by right-wing skinheads, leading to Perry's angry outburst, 'I love all you people, but I hate it when you act like stupid idiots, because that's when they grind you DOWN!' Putting this sprawling, simplistic experimental piece as the first track on the album was a brave thing to do and served as a statement of intent, two fingers to the traditional way of putting an album together.

I first met Siobhan at a Collective meeting. She was an unusual person, very much a product of the Rochdale punk/art scene centred around the college's art foundation course. She was attractive and fashionable, with dyed red hair and a style of her own. Her band, Jerking In Braille, had yet to play live, but had started to get involved with the Collective, looking for a way forward. The band contained Siobhan on guitar, her friend Jane on drums and two men, Mark and Jason, on voice and bass guitar respectively.

Siobhan had a serious devotion to live music. Living some miles outside Rochdale, it took a great deal of effort and planning for her to get to gigs in Manchester. I started to bump into her at the Factory at some of the better shows, and enjoyed chatting with her. She was funny and well-informed, and would record gigs on a primitive mono cassette player that would be hidden in her bag, always unchecked by door staff. She had a great collection of self-made bootlegs featuring the likes of The Fall, Magazine and Echo & the Bunnymen. Terrible quality, as you might expect, but all capturing brilliant performances. My kind of person, I thought.

At a Vibrant Thigh gig at Birch Community Centre in Rusholme, where we were billed with fellow Collective bands Undercovermen and The Enigma, the audience head count was precisely four: Siobhan and the three other members of her band were the only paying customers. To underline the absurdity of it all, I jumped off stage mid-set and went to shake the hands of everybody in the hall. It was this, I think, that broke the ice properly, and before long Siobhan became my first serious girlfriend. I had taken a few girls out previously, but these were mere teenage flings, and apart from basic attraction, I would have little or nothing in common with any of them. Siobhan was the first girl to live in the same world as me and care about the same things that I cared about, which was, of course, mainly music.

Like me, she was an only child and independent in her outlook. I had become used to being the most clued in of my friends when it came to music so it was unusual to find a person with the same enthusiastic zeal for finding new bands. Siobhan introduced me to some real obscurities, often wonderful records that I wouldn't have known about without her influence. Fad Gadget's 'Back to Nature', Lemon Kittens (featuring Danielle Dax), and 'In The Quiet of My Room' by Ada Wilson, an overlooked classic – effortlessly strange and uniquely English sounding. It was very rare indeed to meet a person with such good taste in music.

We would go to Pips together, the two of us sharing a love of Bowie, as well as more ground-level music of the type we would encounter at live events in Manchester. Just being with Siobhan showed me another side to things, gentle small things that I had never had in my life before.

Vibrant Thigh continued to improve, and the gigs kept coming. The Collective was developing into a valuable and worthwhile endeavour, and as word spread, press attention for many of the bands grew and opportunities to travel further afield opened up. A follow-up album to *A Manchester Collection* was planned, this time on the Collective's own MMC label, and we headed into Cargo Studios in Rochdale to record 'Walking Away' and four other tunes with studio owner, John Brierley. Many of my favourite records from this era were made at Cargo. John Peel was said to play anything that had 'Recorded at Cargo' on the sleeve, and had released records by Tractor (produced by John Brierley) on his own Dandelion Records label in the early seventies.

I was mostly impressed that I was recording in the same studio where The Fall had recorded their latest album, *Dragnet*. I was aware of some of the songs that would end up on the album for quite a while, having seen them develop through various line-up changes. Songs like 'Put Away' and 'Before The Moon Falls' had been part of the set for some time, but it was a very different Fall that came to make *Dragnet*. Karl Burns and Martin Bramah's sharp, angular proficiency had been one of the highlights of their debut album, but they'd moved on and a new band had emerged. Marc Riley moved from bass to guitar, and Steve Hanley and Craig Scanlon from Staff 9 joined on bass and guitar. I had seen Staff 9 at Band on the Wall and thought they were 'a bit Fall-y', so were a good fit. New drummer Mike Leigh couldn't have been more different to Karl if he tried. He came from rockabilly band, Rocking Ricky and the Velvet Collars, and had a sloppier, but more human approach.

It was the production that makes *Dragnet* such a brave and special album. Mark Smith claimed that Cargo were so appalled by producer

Grant Showbiz's commercially suicidal mix that they wanted the studio's name removed from the album's credits. In an era that saw many bands lose their integrity as they glimpsed possible success, The Fall did the polar opposite. I loved them for it.

Another reason I was so happy to be working at Cargo was that it was where the first Gang of Four single had been recorded. 'Damaged Goods' and 'Armalite Rifle' were a great influence, and it is fair to say that Andy Gill's approach showed me that textured feedback has a wonderful life of its own. 'Love Like Anthrax', the third track on the EP, cemented Cargo into musical history forever – the studio's advertising leaflet is recited on one side of the mix as a distraction technique in the manner of The Velvet Underground's 'The Gift'. Brilliant.

This was only the second time I had been in a studio, and the first time that I had observed and taken part in the mixing process. We were quickly invited to record again too, this time for a session on Manchester's independent radio station, Piccadilly Radio, at Oldham's Pennine Studios, where Joy Division's *Ideal For Living* EP was recorded. We were to be featured in a series of sessions for a programme called *Transmission* presented by Mark Radcliffe. We were in good company, with Wah! Heat, A Certain Ratio, Joy Division and The Diagram Brothers also being featured.

The whole process did the band good, and the better gigs kept coming. We played for Rock Against Racism alongside Factory reggae band X-O-Dus at the West Indian Centre on Carmoor Road in Moss Side, and played a Collective benefit at The Mayflower with Scritti Politti. Their drummer, Tom Morley, had a different approach to most drummers I had seen. He seemed to come from the world of dub, as opposed to rock, and was not afraid to employ things like xylophones and weird bits of metal in an attempt to create something new. Scritti Politti championed musical independence and were approachable and helpful to young bands by explaining the mechanics and costs of releasing records on their own label. We soaked it up.

We were booked to play Derby Hall in Bury, a beautiful Victorian neo-classical building designed by the same architect responsible for the circular reading room at the British Museum. It was used for theatre and classical concerts as well as being a 'rock' venue. The organising and promoting of shows at Derby Hall was done by an energetic and well-liked guy called Adrian Mealing. Adrian was a friend of Mark Burgess and Dave Fielding, and had put their bands The Cliches and Years on there, attracting a decent crowd for such new and relatively unknown bands.

Bury, only eleven miles from Manchester, was somewhat suspicious of the big city on its doorstep, retaining its insularity with a mistrust of all things Mancunian. As the owner of a Manchester accent, I was as much on my guard in places like Bury as I would have been in, say, Liverpool, where anti-Manc trouble had ruined things for several of my friends on visits to Eric's. When Vibrant Thigh took to the stage there was very much a sense of 'Come on, show us what you can do, then' from the assembled throng.

In other ways, Bury had a lot going for it. There seemed to be a real interest in new music in the town; there was Vibes Records, an independent record shop, plus it had its own *Violent Times* fanzine. Unfortunately, as often seemed to be the case in more provincial places, it also had its pockets of retro punk fashionistas and a sizeable skinhead population; big fish in a little pool, intent on trouble and resentful of outsiders.

Shortly after we'd played there, I went back on April Fool's Day with a few friends to see A Certain Ratio, who were an ongoing revelation. I had been into ACR since they were a drummerless noise-based battle of nerves, sending half the audience into angry irritation and the other half into stunned admiration. Songs like 'Crippled Child' and the set-closing 'Genotype/Phenotype' would antagonise some listeners into throwing missiles as Peter Terrell's electronically generated insect swarms – already too loud for comfort – went on for just that little bit too long. The addition of drummer Donald Johnson was a masterstroke. I was at the first Manchester gig to feature him, and the sense of shock was palpable. Funky and tight, but with all the abrasiveness and white noise of their early confrontational shows, it was something completely new.

It was this enhanced version of the band that was on view that night in Bury. From the off, there was a sense of unease. A small group of local skinheads, with a particularly obnoxious ringleader, made a show of intimidating dancing in the centre of the hall, bumping into people on purpose and spilling drinks everywhere. It was as if they were hell-bent on disrupting the gig just because it featured 'outsiders' playing music they perceived as 'arty'. We had encountered a similar vibe when Vibrant Thigh had played, and the same idiots probably disrupted anything outside their comfort zone. With severe number-one haircuts and oversized demob suits, A Certain Ratio looked very different to the norm, and it was dangerous to stand out like that in the satellite towns. Such individuality could lead to a good kicking.

The band were ace. Simon Topping and Martin Moscrop doubled up on tuned cowbell and duetted on spooky, atonal trumpet parts, bringing layers of depth to the songs on their recent *The Graveyard and the Ballroom* release. I loved it, but the shock of the new seemed only to wind up the closed-minded regulars. There was trouble and fighting outside. Like sitting ducks in the taxi rank, several of my friends were attacked for no reason at all.

The following week we headed back to Bury for a Factory showcase gig featuring Joy Division, Section 25 and Minny Pops. Tickets were £1.00, or £1.25 on the door. Some of us had picked them up in advance, so no worries for us. We met at my flat for a bit of a pre-gig session, the normal procedure, really; weed and tunes before getting a bus to the venue. It was a Tuesday night so we had to wait for Brian to get out of work before heading off, which meant it was well into the early evening before we got there.

We were meeting Mark Burgess, Dave Fielding and Reg Smithies at Derby Hall. The three of them were starting to spend more time in each other's company. They were moving towards playing together and were at the 'going to gigs together and bonding' stage. They were all good company, and I'd been enjoying seeing some great bands at the Russell Club and other places with them, including the times they came to Vibrant Thigh gigs, which I greatly approved of.

When we got to the venue, there were signs up informing us that the gig had sold out. This was no surprise as Joy Division's star was in the ascendant, and their frequently repeated second John Peel session of a few months earlier had won them loads of new fans. Mark, luckily, used his charm on promoter Adrian Mealing, who let him, Dave and Reg in on the condition that they help with the collecting of glasses after the show.

With my friends Brian and Paddy, I'd seen Joy Division several times, and at each gig they seemed more at home with their new-found, dynamics-led sound. There was heightened tension at these shows as the band's fanbase grew, as if the creeping malevolence of the music was seeping out into the audience. Fights were commonplace at Joy Division gigs, I even witnessed Peter Hook leave the Russell Club stage, swinging his bass as a weapon in response to violence from idiots at the front.

Their groundbreaking appearance on *Granada Reports* showed a subtlety and control to a world hungry for something new. The release of *Unknown Pleasures* brought larger, more expectant crowds, piling more pressure on Ian Curtis, who, unbeknown to most people, was battling his advancing epilepsy as the band's gruelling workload added to his stress. The band's live shows were coloured by a weird sense of unease and a gathering storm of violence as Ian's seizures became more and more pronounced. Things were coming to a head.

The 400 capacity hall was filling up to unreasonable levels. I have heard that the actual head count was nearer to 600, with favours been called in, and people being sneaked in everywhere. Of course, the local disruptive skinheads that we had encountered at previous gigs were out in force, as were pockets of Mancunian Perry Boys that had started to be seen at Joy Division shows of late. They took their name from the Fred Perry sportswear that they wore. They favoured eye-covering flick fringes. Waiting for a night bus at Piccadilly had become an ordeal in recent months as they would gather in large groups, picking off anyone they deemed strange for a dose of ultraviolence. I knew to keep well clear, as several of my more outlandish friends had been attacked on their way back from Pips. They seemed like Anthony Burgess's *Clockwork Orange* 'droogs' brought to life, frighteningly young, hunting in hyena-like packs, cowardly and merciless.

With all of us inside the venue, I got a drink from the bar and made my way to the front of the stage as Minny Pops shuffled on with no announcements or preamble. Factory bands had in common a kind of reserve, a shyness even, and these recent Factory signings certainly gave off an aloof nonchalance. Under muted lighting, the slow, hypnotic drum machine and synths swept around the hall as several moody-looking Dutch guys stood stock still, staring the growing audience out. They lulled everyone into a false sense of security. The calm before the coming storm.

After Minny Pops, I stayed where I was, slightly to the left of centre stage, almost at the front. Following a quick changeover, it was time for Section 25, a recent addition to the Factory roster. They started with a drum and bass-heavy pulsing sound, thuddingly low, reminiscent of the kind of areas that PiL had been moving into. People, on the whole, seemed appreciative and the first few songs brought a smattering of applause. It was sparse and forceful, and certainly very Factory-sounding. Then, things got really strange as A Certain Ratio's Simon Topping joined them on stage. What was going on? The band broke into a meandering, overlong piece, with Topping providing obscure echo-drenched vocals in the manner of ACR's 'Feltch'. The sound engineer caught his voice and, using long delay settings, bounced it around the hall, making a confusing swell. At the conclusion of this workout, another figure joined the assembled musicians and confusion started to descend upon the watching crowd, who were expecting a straightforward night's entertainment.

Not many people in the audience knew that it was Alan Hempsall, of Crispy Ambulance, who had taken his position at the microphone as the assembled 'Factory All Stars' launched into another tune, which I later found out was Section 25's 'Girls Don't Count', only with Alan taking over the vocal duties. I was, unlike many of the Bury audience, familiar with Crispy Ambulance. Vibrant Thigh had played Collective nights with them at Band on the Wall, and I had bought their pre-Factory single 'Cradle To The Grave' which showed off their sense of discipline and showcased the singer's baritone croon.

The mood of the assembled watchers was beginning to change. Things were running late, and the evening's entertainment so far had been challenging, to say the least. The weird supergroup ground to an end. Next, Joy Division walked on to a relieved cheer, and after what seemed like ages, launched into 'Love Will Tear Us Apart', an unreleased song that had aired on their last John Peel session. At this point, disgruntled murmurings started to travel around the audience. 'That isn't Ian Curtis!!' shouted one unhappy punter, and of course they were right. Alan Hempsall's low register vocals suited the song perfectly, but united the local contingent of hard-to-please skinheads into one betrayed mass. It was as if they had only come along to be disappointed, and the air was alive with catcalls. A Curtis-less 'Digital' followed and the atmosphere got worse as parts of the audience got the feeling that they had been cheated.

The song ended, and to everybody's relief, Ian Curtis walked on. He looked pale and withdrawn, but then again, he always did. Unknown to me, and to the assembled crowd, he had attempted to take his own life with an overdose of phenobarbitone only a day before. Peter Hook, in hindsight, has said that the gig should not have taken place.

There was another long pause before the band started on a synth-heavy version of new song 'Decades'. Ian Curtis, eyes shut, was lost in the music, but after this and the following song, 'The Eternal', it seemed like it was all too much for him, and he left the stage again.

This was the last straw for many of the negative elements present, and offended booing broke out in the hall, especially behind me, and slightly to my right. It was the obnoxious ringleader and his crew who were the epicentre of trouble when I had been here before. I planned an escape route in case any fighting broke out and turned my attention back to the stage, where Section 25's Vinnie Cassidy, along with Simon Topping, Alan Hempsall and the rest of Joy Division had started a sprawling jam version of the Velvet Underground's 'Sister Ray'.

It only took a slight change in atmosphere for things to turn nasty. A pint glass was thrown from the place the shaven-headed troublemaker was standing with his cronies, and this started off a chain reaction of thrown bottles, as clumps of hand-to-hand combat broke out simultaneously in different parts of the room. All hell broke loose. This was real Wild West stuff. I took cover, making myself invisible, flat to the wall. I watched the Joy Division roadies leap into action, fighting back the troublemakers with fists and microphone stands as Rob Gretton entered the fray, trying to protect the band's gear, and steaming into things himself to considerable effect.

The lights came on and revealed that the place was wrecked. Chairs, blood, broken glass and shaken people littered the hall. Mark, Dave and Reg's commitment to clean up the empty glasses at the end of the show was now comically redundant. There was plenty of glass, but it was all smashed. Splintered pint pots, broken spectacles, and the remains of Derby Hall's elaborate chandelier sparkled amongst pools of blood. I was okay, and so were my friends, but this was the worse violence I had ever seen at a music event. I was shaken up in a big way.

I found Mark, Dave and Reg, who were taking refuge backstage. Mark actually talked to Ian Curtis, who mentioned their upcoming American tour. He apparently seemed distant and sad, although following a night like that, I think that anybody would be.

There would be only three more Joy Division performances after that one, and five weeks later, on 18th May, Ian Curtis was found at the family home having taken his own life. He was 23 years old.

10: Substances

Martin Coogan had previously played guitar for an ad-hoc group which drew its members from the Pips scene, including John Richmond and Stefan Korab. They had named themselves Dollars in Drag after a Bowie bootleg. They once played an afternoon show at my school, starting with Roxy Music's 'Remake/Remodel', working through a set that included 'Rebel Rebel', 'The Jean Genie' and some other Bowie tunes. When I got an invitation to a party in the Bury area from one of their group of friends, I was expecting a very glam affair.

It turned out to be a regular type of house party that started tamely enough. I got chatting to a nice man, somewhat older than myself, but we were getting on well and after a few drinks had gone down, he asked me if I fancied some speed. I was more than curious. I'd been drawn to speed mainly through what I knew about London's amphetamine-driven 'mod' scene. I had discovered Do-Do bronchial tablets, which contained ephedrine, and although they made me very sick in return for very little buzz, they were a step in the right direction. Mixed with alcohol, they left me in a right mess. I had also sampled the popular slimming pills called chalkies (Tenuate Dospan), and although they were a further step in the right direction, they left me messed up in the same way that the experiments with Do-Dos had done. Both were entry level stimulants. This guy, however, was something of a Wigan Casino veteran, and the pills he offered me were a popular choice with the Northern soul heads.

I was given six yellow tablets which, I was told, were called Filon. These contained Fenbutrazate, an appetite-suppressing chemical, which worked by speeding up the body's metabolism, burning off excess weight. The side effects of this tinkering were exactly what the doctor (hadn't!) ordered. I felt elated. I was filled with a boundless energy I had never experienced before. This was great! I was suddenly very self-assured and talked long into the early hours, holding court with people much older and more experienced than myself. The drug is listed as a psychostimulant, and that's exactly what it was. It seemed that every aspect of my personality had been boosted.

This new feeling was exactly what I had been waiting for. Music sounded sharper and clearer, I lost myself in it, dancing for hours in a bubble of self-contained happiness, filled with unlimited energy. Dripping in sweat, and with butterflies in my stomach, the night went by in a haze of Bowie and soul tunes, as good-looking boys and girls with pupils like black circles danced until the early morning light around me. I was an instant convert.

I had, of course, no idea about the downside of stimulant use at this point. For now, all I wanted to know about was how I could get to that psychological place again. I didn't have long to wait.

John Mather was a tall, blond drummer, again slightly older than me, who shared a flat with his girlfriend, Diane, near the centre of Middleton. He had played with Bury punk band, The Reducers. We all liked him and would spend time together in his flat, smoking weed and listening to all kinds of diverse music. One weekend, John had acquired some 'uppers', as he called them, and offered me some. This was very different to the clean, euphoric Filon high that I had enjoyed so much at the party. This was amphetamine sulphate, a home-made, illegal concoction that could vary in quality and 'dirtiness', being completely unregulated. It came in powder form, and was sniffed nasally, chopped into lines of caustic, burning nastiness.

I entered a different world of energy and clarity. Sleep was unthinkable. All of us were brought closer together as friends by this shared new experience. The disgusting taste was nothing to me, a badge of honour, even, as the changes to my state of mind outweighed the bad side. Music, again, came through to me with a clarity and force I had never experienced before. I felt a sense of purpose totally new to me. When I got back to my flat, still full of this new and exciting feeling, I was no longer afraid to be on my own in the same way as I had been before. All I needed was my guitar and this new way of being. I had, unfortunately, found my poison.

The second Collective album, *Unzipping The Abstract*, featured Vibrant Thigh's song 'Walking Away'. The release of the album had helped things along nicely for us and we were booked to play Deeply Vale Festival for the second time. I was excited to be part of the whole thing, not just to be playing. Siobhan had brought a tent and we were in it for the long haul. The original festivals at Deeply Vale had lasted weeks and weeks, so who knew what could happen?

The festival had been forced to change venue after a protest campaign from lovers of peace and quiet in the local area. Pressure from local councillors had forced the organisers to move the event to a place called Pickup Bank in the windswept hills above Darwen. Although not as beautiful as the natural valley of the previous festivals, the new site had a twisted charm of its own, nestled high in the hills overlooking the twinkling lights of the satanic mills and satellite towns below. The bill included The Fall, The Distractions, and, bravely, The Ruts, who were to perform as a three-piece a mere couple of weeks after the death of their singer, Malcolm Owen, from a heroin overdose. The Ruts, along with Misty in Roots (with whom they had shared a label, People Unite) were great friends to the festival, and it was to be an emotional day, both for them and for the many friends that Malcolm had made amongst us.

From the start, I realised that things were noticeably different from the other site, with a distinct lack of the peace and love vibes that had been so prevalent before. More bikers, more punks, more glue, less children. The change in site had demoralised many of the idealistic free spirits that had made the previous festivals so special. This time things felt more urban, with more people going home at the end of each day, as opposed to staying for the duration.

We took to the stage in the early evening. It felt good to be playing in the open air as a small crowd gathered. We played well enough, and went down okay, but if felt slightly less magical than the previous year's experience. The Distractions were playing directly after us, and as they started their set, Siobhan and I found a group of friendly bikers who welcomed us warmly. They sold us eight blotters of acid with the yin and yang symbol printed on them. Enough for all of us!

Reading about the LSD scene in the late sixties had made us all very acid-curious. I dutifully swallowed one. The Distractions set went by in a flurry of anticipation as things started to slowly happen. This was a different feeling to mushrooms; more physical and decidedly more visual. I swallowed my butterflies and prepared for The Fall. Something about the combination of the grimy hills, the towns of Lancashire below, the creeping malevolence that seemed to be descending upon the site, and of course, the super-strength LSD that I had taken, made for a perfect Fall show.

The set was mainly taken from their *Grotesque* album, which contained the marvellously observant Lancastrian anthem, 'English Scheme' – 'They talk of Chile while driving through Haslingden!'. This was not amongst the delights on offer on this occasion, but sprawling renditions of 'Gramme Friday', 'The North Will Rise Again', and '2nd Dark Age' were tailor-made for the dangerous and spooky surroundings. The trip bent time and I retreated to a safe place until I had been turned inside out and back again as the haunted rockabilly of 'Fiery Jack' looped around my head.

I had long known that I would be leaving care when I reached eighteen. I had been looking forward to the magical day since the start of my teens, but the closer the day came, the more that looked to be a juvenile fantasy. Living the way I did, with financial support from Social Services and mixing with older friends who themselves lived in relative stability, was an artificial situation which led me to bury my head in the sand about the realities of my unusual home life until the very last minute.

August came, and with it, my birthday. My social worker, Kath Daybank, had employed something of a hands-off approach with me in this last year. It had been quite a few months since I had seen her. Taking a handful of ten pence pieces to the phone box in the centre of Hollin Estate, I rang Dunsterville House, the local government office where Middleton's social work team were based. I was told that I couldn't be put through to Kath. After years of her involvement, she had been moved on to another vulnerable child. After all the emotional and life-changing events we had navigated together, I was never to see her again. It was that abrupt.

I called down to the offices in person, and it was explained to me that I was no longer under the care of them, or for that matter, anybody else. All financial support was to stop, too, and I was responsible for rent, bills, clothing, everything. Reeling from the shock of it all, I was told to go to the local Job Centre as I had to find my own money to live on. I was truly on my own now, real cold turkey.

Middleton's Job Centre was a harsh and depressing place, with resentful staff behind protective glass and a real air of despair wherever you looked. At this point in 1980, there were about one and a half million people in the UK looking for work, and although vacancies did exist, it was definitely an unhealthy time for the world of employment opportunities. I scoured the boards, my eyes flicking past factory work and shop assistant vacancies that held no appeal. Then one caught my eye: 'Carver wanted. No experience necessary as on the job training will be given.'

I needed something now, and working with wood appealed to me more than anything else on offer. I imagined myself having a hidden natural talent for carpentry, making beautiful furniture or rocking horses for needy children. Taking the card to the relevant window, I was told that the making of fine furniture was the last thing that I would be doing, if, indeed I was lucky enough to get the job. The carving referred to was the carving of breadcrumb-covered legs of ham at Lewis's department store, a place I knew well for other, more emotional reasons.

An interview was arranged at the store. I turned up and was told there and then that I had got the job. I was to start at 8.30am the following Monday, working on the 'ham on the bone' department on the noisy ground floor food hall. I had entered the grown-up world of work. Slicing ham, all day, every day. My immediate boss was a Polish gentleman called Peter who had been there for over 30 years. He told me that if I applied myself, I could easily achieve the position he held. I was horrified, and after being shown how to slice ham thin enough to see through, I started what, in Peter's eyes, was potentially the first day of many decades of the same mind-numbing task.

From the off, I didn't care. I would give needy-looking old ladies twice as much as they asked for, for the same money, and kept myself fed by eating as much as I could when nobody was looking. Although I hated every minute of it, and resented having to wear the obligatory white coat and air hostess-style hat, I did manage to get myself there every day.

We who worked in the food hall were at the bottom of the food chain. Covered in grease, I would gawp dreamily at the elegant girls from the nearby make-up counter, invisible to their mascara'd eyes. My friend, Shan Hira, visited me one lunchtime. Shan was the drummer of Collective band, Bathroom, and he knew me as a musician. Being seen by him in these circumstances embarrassed me. I was a singer and simply not cut out for this sort of thing.

I did try to fit in to some extent and made an effort with the other staff. One night after going to The Shakespeare pub next door straight from work, a number of other Lewis's employees ended up back at mine. It was horrible. I felt alone and isolated as they invaded my safe space. My bed was commandeered by two of them and I was left to sleep on my living room floor with strangers who simply saw me as a weird novelty. These people were not my people.

Vibrant Thigh were pared up with fellow Collective bands Units and IQ Zero for a series of gigs in Manchester and places out of town, swapping top billing each time. Due to my friendship with a man called Chris Brierley, one of the out of town gigs was in the windswept, forbidding hills above Rochdale at Buckley Hall Young Offenders Institution.

I had become friendly with Chris at Factory nights at the Russell Club. He lived outside Rochdale and, as his route in took him through Middleton, he would give a lift to me and Mick Duffy from IQ Zero. Mick was studying at De La Salle Teacher Training College in Hopwood, and had just started writing for the *NME* as a freelancer. Chris was part way through a sociology degree, with a particular focus on youth culture, and had found a wealth of raw material for his dissertation by studying me and my friends as we carved out an alternate existence of sorts, away from the mainstream. He also taught a fortnightly literacy class at Buckley Hall Prison.

Buckley Hall catered for the 16 to 18 age group, young lads who had mainly been convicted of non-violent offences, although it housed many dangerous young men at the start of their prison 'career'. Every other Friday saw the visit of outside agencies, like church groups or alcohol awareness workers, who would give a talk in a bid to change these young men's behaviour. Chris had somehow persuaded the prison authorities that it would be a good idea to hold a three-band gig featuring ourselves, IQ Zero and Units instead of the usual worthy but dull lectures.

Before getting picked up from home, something had made me think it was a great idea to eat sixty magic mushrooms. New crops appeared every day in the fields around where I lived, and I had stocked up. This was something of a departure for me as I would usually trip with friends, as part of a shared experience, but I had always been something of a loner and so began to embark on solo adventures.

Things started to get weird when we arrived at the prison gates, where a wide-eyed bunch of miscreants were escorted from two transit vans into the prison's reception area to be searched by a posse of mean-looking officers. I had bought a wonderful oversized yellow woollen jumper from an antique clothes stall on Bridge Street, and although I thought I looked a million dollars, it was the worst thing in the world to wear when you are coming up on mushrooms. I was drenched in sweat as a series of doors were locked behind us with a scary clang.

We were ushered in to meet the governor and his intimidating staff. We were expected to have tea and biscuits as if everything was normal, but my beach-ball pupils and soaking wet hair were giving the game away. It was all I could do to stop myself from collapsing with laughter. Chris Brierley managed to pull off some kind of damage limitation exercise, keeping me, for the best part, out of trouble in front of the prison staff.

Units played first. Their singer George had a certain Freddie Garrity charm about him, and an ear for a catchy tune. Their Buzzcocks-type pop kicked things off well enough, but it was the appearance of IQ Zero that really turned things into an all-out weird-fest. They had a penchant for dressing up in brightly coloured costumes; retina-burning neon green and orange nylon custom-made jumpsuits, somewhere between an American football kit and the kind of thing that a Marvel superhero would wear. The shoulders of these garish outfits were padded like those of the Sugar Puffs Honey Monster. As they took to the makeshift stage, I was a gibbering mess.

Psilocybin and anything is a recipe for uncontrollable laughter, but this was beyond the pale. Locked inside a correctional facility, in an altered state, their Devo/XTC hybrid brought me to my knees as they hurtled through their quirky set. How I got through it all is beyond me. As their *Manchester Collection* track 'I Must Obey' transformed itself into 'I Masturbate' before my very ears, I was liquid. Peaking, it was time for our set and my Johnny Cash at San Quentin moment.

Time stretched in every direction and although it seemed like ages before we took to the stage, it could only have been a matter of minutes before we launched into our first song, 'Sacred Heart'. It sounded great! The tiled, echoey walls of the canteen-cum-association room threw my words back at me, and looking out, flanked by the heaviest-looking prison guards imaginable, I saw two hundred of Rochdale's finest car thieves, shoplifters and assorted other wrong 'uns absolutely loving it. Admittedly, the alternative was being locked up in their cells, but hey, at this point, I would take what I could get, and so, it seemed would they. To leave their seats would have meant a beating, for sure, but somehow they showed their appreciation by swaying back and forth, heads nodding. As each song ended, a deafening roar rang around the place as voices both deep and yet-to-break yelled for all they were worth.

It probably had little to do with the music, and everything to do with this being a rare chance to let off some steam, but to me, tripping balls, it was a magic moment up there with the best of them. I hung onto the microphone stand for dear life until the final song, a funk-fuelled instrumental called 'One of Its Legs'. All I did on this tune was dance around, worrying a cowbell to within an inch of its life, but, having got to the end of the set, I was elated, and threw myself into the task with gusto.

Phew! We'd done it. The prisoners filed out, and after more tea and biscuits with the governor and his henchmen, we were released into the world outside, to live another day. My mental state had stabilised somewhat by the time I was dropped off at home, hardly daring to believe that all of this had actually happened.

11: Deeper

My studies had naturally come to end when I was forced to enter the world of work to support myself after Social Services pulled the plug on me. I was to make a triumphant return to St. John's College though when Vibrant Thigh were booked to play a gig at what was now my alma mater. We were supporting Hawkwind's Nik Turner and his band Inner City Unit, which brought out an audience not seen by these eyes since the excesses of the original Deeply Vale. Hippies of every stripe mingled with our regular small following. It wasn't our kind of crowd, but we managed to win over a large number of them, turning the initial apathy into a sea of bobbing heads.

Though we didn't know it at the time, this was to be the last act of this incarnation of Vibrant Thigh. Our drummer Andy had started working for his dad as an electrician. Shortly after the gig he informed us that he was leaving the band. It was all amicable enough. Andy's brother Chris remained as our bass player, but there was a sense that the writing was on the wall. Before we could figure out how to replace Andy, there was a pressing matter of an imminent gig in Leeds as part of the triple header with Units and IQ Zero that I was in no mood to cancel, band or no band. The gig had to happen. It had been organised by legendary Leeds promoter John Keenan, as was nearly everything interesting in Leeds at the time. He was the man behind the Queens Hall Futurama festival which had attracted thousands of people to see the likes of Public Image Limited, Hawkwind and Joy Division the year before. I didn't want to be seen by John as someone who cancelled shows at short notice.

I'd been spending a lot of time with Mark Burgess and Dave Fielding and I felt closer to them that I did my own bandmates. With the Leeds gig on my mind, I had a light bulb moment and suddenly I was brimming with ideas. I thought that I could make something good out of it. I just knew that, even with very little time to prepare, Mark and Dave would rise to the occasion. It had all the hallmarks of a great adventure.

I'd had a few low-key jams with Dave, much to the displeasure of my neighbours, and I liked his guitar style. I'd been impressed with Mark's musicianship from the off, singing bass players always had my respect. I called for Dave at his parent's house and outlined my plan. The gig was only a matter of days away, but to Dave's credit, he jumped right in. I was barely eighteen, and annoyingly full of myself, but Dave was open-minded enough to take such a young upstart seriously.

With Dave on board, together we called for Mark at his family home on Hollin Estate. We got stuck in straight away. I showed Dave and Mark my basic ideas and we jammed them into some kind of shape. With no microphone, I just approximated the kind of thing I would be doing. I didn't have lyrics as the songs were coming together for the very first time there in the room, but it was wonderful to hear these two musicians get a grip on what I was trying to put over. We created the backbone of a whole new thing there and then in Mark's bedroom. In the space of a day, we had created something special out of thin air. It was exhilarating to have pulled it off, and to be gigging in a new city, with new people, playing songs that hadn't even existed a day earlier. This was what punk was supposed to be like!

The gig itself was billed as an Object Records night. The venue, Brannigans, was the place to play in that city, in the same way that Manchester had The Russell Club/Factory or Liverpool had Eric's. We arrived for soundcheck to be met with the sight of some local skinheads deep into the first part of an evening's solvent abuse in the street outside. Unorthodox, to be sure, but nothing was going to faze us. Scary-looking as they were, they turned out to be as harmless as kittens. Positively friendly, even. Backstage we met up with a pal of Dave's who was studying at Leeds University and had come along to support his old mate. He was another Dave, Dave Gedge, a Middleton lad. The two Daves, along with Years drummer, Chris 'Sid' Seddon, had been in a band together at Hollin High School called Sen as far back as 1974.

The time came for us to do our stuff, and we dutifully took to the small stage, me on guitar and vocals, being flanked by Dave on guitar and Mark on bass. Things went by in a blur, but the small crowd of dubious-looking Yorkshire punks seemed to love it, even the glueheads we had met earlier. The atmosphere was electric. After playing the songs that we had sketched out in Mark's bedroom, I put Mark on the spot by diving behind IQ Zero's drum kit, leaving him to take over singing duties as I clattered away on the kit. Completely off the cuff, Mark sang and played anything that came into his head. He was brilliant, of course. Back in the dressing room I told Mark that I knew he'd be fine. It was the first time that Mark and Dave had played together. It would not be the last.

Things were coming to a natural end with Siobhan. As I was psychologically moving away from all things Middleton, Siobhan seemed to be becoming a closer part of things there, growing more friendly with Middleton people just as I was outgrowing them. It was inevitable that things were going to change.

I had met a girl called Alison some months before at Band on the Wall. She had come to give a bit of support to Spurtz, a Musicians' Collective band that she was friends with. I liked Spurtz. Musically, they were deliberately lo-fi, shambolic even. Singer Andy Wilson would wear a dress and Corky, the diminutive female band leader, looked too young to be so well informed politically, but wrote lyrics dealing with sexual politics in a non-preachy and fun way. They inhabited the same world as The Slits, I suppose, anarchic and irreverent.

Alison was an unusual person, and there was something brave about the way she carried herself. Small and very tidy, she dressed differently to the people she knew, almost a wartime look, and was not afraid to be different in a classy and understated way. The first time I saw her was when we had driven into the Deeply Vale festival. I saw her walking down a dirt path, alone. She stood out in complete contrast to the denim-clad hairies that were making their own way to the action. Her tidiness and short bobbed hair, held in place with a spotted hairband, seemed so out of place. I must admit, I felt a level of protectiveness towards her. Apart from seeing her on our way in, I hadn't bumped into her at the festival itself, but I met her at Rafters in the weeks after. It turned out that she lived not far from the festival site, in Bury, and had just been popping her head in to have a look. She had good taste in music, being fond of The Pop Group and recent Factory releases. Before long we both realised that we liked each other. We started going out together, and this caused quite a lot of bad feeling with Siobhan's new friends, which served to strengthen my resolve to leave that restrictive town behind.

Once things settled down we had a lot of fun. I enjoyed being with her friends, who were bright folk. We even ended up going to the same barber, and emerged with matching shaven-necked demob type haircuts. Alison showed me a cosmopolitanism that was missing from my life before, and for a while, we were inseparable.

This was in sharp contrast to my life at work. Despite being seen as the resident freak, I continued to make efforts and even attended a staff Christmas 'do', held in the ornate ballroom in the upper part of the store. This was their highlight of the year, but was undoubtedly the lowlight of mine. I kept myself to myself, getting slowly drunk, watching my fellow workers cover themselves in dust and cigarette ends doing the 'sitting on the floor' dance to the Gap Band's 'Oops Upside Your Head'. I knew that something had to give,

The top floor of Lewis's had been transformed into the obligatory Winter Wonderland, as it did every year. Elves, fake snow and the usual trappings were a hit with the younger children, and queues to meet Santa started as soon as the store opened. In the week after the Christmas party, the elderly man employed to be Father Christmas had come into work, changed into his red and white costume and false beard, settled down into his chair and dropped dead, having suffered a massive heart attack. I am not superstitious, but when Santa Claus dies on the job, the rule book goes out of the window – omens were at play and I knew in my heart that I had to get out of this cursed place.

As things turned out, I would be leaving sooner than I thought. Vibrant Thigh had been booked as support to Bow Wow Wow at Manchester Polytechnic on 16th December. All eyes were on Malcolm McClaren and the first thing he had become involved with since the Sex Pistols. The Sex Pistols had changed the world for everyone, and the nation was waiting to see what McClaren would do next. Bow Wow Wow were fronted by a highly sexualised 14-year-old singer called Annabella Lwin, backed by a tribal drum and bass section lifted from the original Adam and the Ants line up. The whole concept had been thought about, incorporating home taping and cassette culture which was deeply troubling to the profits of the record industry – their debut single 'C30, C60, C90, Go!' was a cassette-only call to arms. They announced that they would be using up-and-coming bands local to each show as support acts. In Manchester, Vibrant Thigh were the chosen ones.

We'd been told that we had to be at the venue in the late afternoon, which meant leaving my ham carving duties a few hours early. I spoke with my supervisor and explained that I could make up for it by working extra hours another day. I was turned down flat and was forced to make, for the first time in my life, a choice that comes to many. Music or work? I spontaneously advised my supervisor to 'stuff your job, then'.

I went to the staff room, dumped my hated, white food-preparation coat, and skipped out of there like a happy lamb, making my way across town to do what I had been put on earth to do. I met my band in time for soundcheck and didn't even mention my enforced choice to the others. I had already left Lewis's, and that shitty job, far behind. Work versus music? No contest!

We had decided not to replace Andy with another drummer, but to recruit a friend of mine, Craig (Cooey) Cooper as a drum machine operator to fulfil the few gigs that we had coming up. His job was simple: switch our Roland Dr. Rhythm off and on, and stand there, looking handsome and moody.

The gig was ace. Our drummerless new look certainly resonated with the way things were going at the time. We had to start the drum machine and then join in by ear, as best we could. Scientific, it most certainly was not. Futuristic acts like The Human League and Orchestral Manoeuvres in the Dark were gaining attention everywhere, and we had a secret weapon to unleash, too. Martin, ever the electronics genius, had invented an effects pedal that he called the 'Vomiting Cat'. It was basically little more than an on/off switch that made sustained notes sweep off and on. It made our closing cover of Donna Summer's 'I Feel Love' a throbbing, genre-crossing beast of a thing. We felt like the future.

After our show, I headed up to the balcony overlooking the stage with Cooey and Martin to catch the end of the Bow Wow Wow set. For their second encore, they had to repeat their mini-album *Your Cassette Pet* release almost in its entirety, due to a lack of songs, but nobody seemed to mind. We surveyed the scene below us. With one voice, the audience were shouting not for the band, but for the manager. 'Malcolm, Malcolm, Malcolm.'

Martin had started a degree course at Salford University and had moved into university accommodation at the old Salford Racecourse complex at Castle Irwell. His life was moving in a different direction, and, although we remained close and I would visit him, he was finding new friends the same way that I was. By hanging around with Dave Fielding and Mark Burgess more, and being into slightly different music, I was moving away from Martin and the rest of the band. My growing interest in recreational drugs also set me apart from everyone else, who were the total opposite to me where such things were concerned.

After the triumph of the Bow Wow Wow support, we played a gig at De Ville's. Without the adrenalin surge of playing to a packed house, it became clear to me that since Andy had left, I wasn't enjoying the music as much. The drummerless Vibrant Thigh was more heavily synth-based, and Martin's innovative experiments with guitar effects made his guitar sound like a synth anyway. Drum machines in our price range were primitive and unconvincing, and I felt, if I was being honest with myself, that we were a long way from the exciting, edgy group we used to be when Andy was playing drums.

Nevertheless, it was a surprise when I was visited one night by Martin and Mark with Krzysztof Korab, the cousin of Stefan Korab from Dollars in Drag. He and Martin had been playing together, and he told me that he didn't want to be in Vibrant Thigh anymore. He wanted to start a new band with Krzysztof, who played synth. I knew that Vibrant Thigh had run its course, but still felt a sense of deep sadness. This band had taken the place of a family in many ways over the last few years. So with Christmas upon us, always a bleak time for me, I found myself without a band and a job. Merry Christmas to me.

With the New Year comes new opportunities, and they did for me, at least in the world of work. It arrived from a friend called Sue Davies in the unlikely setting of a Fall gig at Rafters. I'd first met Sue at Pips. She worked at a clothes shop in town called Roxy that specialised in copycat designs of the latest trends. It was *the* place to go for the legions of Bowie and Roxy Music fans that would copy their idol's every image change. Working there afforded Sue a level of celebrity amongst the clones that would look upon the shop as some kind of temple of vanity, a place that understood their infatuations, celebrate them even. Sue, of course, was no part of this. She was an ex-punk, and even though she worked in the peacock world of clothes sales, she subscribed to the anti-vanity school of thought, wearing mainly black, with dyed black hair. She was an impressive character, supremely confident, petite and easy to talk to. She was a popular and well-connected figure in the Manchester music scene. Although she was attractive in so many ways, we kept things platonic, which led to our friendship being deeper, somehow.

Sue was from Prestwich, home of The Fall, and had been around the various versions of the band as they had started to make an impact on the world. One night she was out with Karl Burns and introduced me. It seems strange for someone like me, a product of punk's anti-star way of thinking, but being introduced to Karl left me a little speechless and shy. *Live at the Witch Trials* was vitally important to me, and Karl's magnificent drumming was a large part of what had dragged me in. I had memorised every last beat, every hi-hat hiss, every snare roll, and here, standing in front of me, was the man who had created it.

At the Fall gig at Rafters, Sue told me that there was to be a vacancy at Roxy, as a member of staff – a budding actress called Joanne Whalley – was leaving. Sue told me I should turn up and have a word with the shop owner, Lloyd.

I was taken on straight away, starting the following week. I found myself at the centre of a specialised scene that was the most important thing in the world to a small, devoted group of music fans. Lloyd was a sharp cookie when it came to knowing what his customers wanted, and would keep ahead of things by following the music and style orientated magazines, then getting the clothes that they featured (or near-identical copies) on the racks of his shop in time for the weekend invasion of eager fashionistas. This was the era of Tubeway Army and Japan, and Lloyd's versions of David Sylvian's trousers or Gary Numan's jackets would fly out of the shop in huge numbers. Fans of Roxy Music and Bowie would strip the shelves of the pleated trousers sported by Bowie on the live *Stage* album, or Ferry-esque dinner jackets, and mimic their idols in the specialist 'Roxy' room at Pips at night. It used to amuse me to see large numbers of so-called 'individuals' dressed identically in Pips on the more popular weekend nights, having bought their costumes from me that very afternoon.

I was less extreme in my taste in clothes than my customers. Hairwise, I favoured the short, back and sides with a floppy fringe approach, and although I dyed it dark, I was moving towards a simpler, almost Second World War look. I had taken to finding massive suits in charity shops, and, along with others in Manchester, enjoyed the demob look, popularised in a small way by A Certain Ratio and the other Factory bands. As the world went all extrovert and pretentious as the New Romantic look was foisted upon a gullible and fickle public, I went in the other direction, veering towards the simplicity of the muted grey and darker tones of another era. I didn't mind selling these peacocks their gear, though, and I had a lot of fun working there with Sue, and manager, Elly.

A delegation from *The Face* magazine arrived to see what all the fuss was about, sending photographer Kevin Cummins to immortalise the shop and all that went on there. I was snapped amongst the rows of tartan bondage trousers, decidedly dressed down in a second-hand overcoat and charity shop scarf, a stark contrast to our clothes-horse clientele.

The manager, Elly, was Lloyd's partner. She was from a previous alternative generation, being about ten years older than me. She and her contemporaries had seen it all before in the earlier part of the seventies, and had some very wise words for me about amphetamines in particular. Her generation hated speed with a vengeance. The slogan 'Speed Kills', so often seen in counterculture publications like *IT* or *The Fabulous Furry Freak Brothers* comics by Gilbert Sheldon, had been taken to heart by this age group, who had seen first-hand many casualties. I, of course, was just starting to dabble in these areas and was upfront about it. Elly warned me off in no uncertain terms, but to no avail. I was in no mood to listen to such negativity, and could only see the good points of this lifestyle that I had recently discovered. I countered her warnings with a shrug and carried on regardless.

12: To Hell With Poverty

Upstairs from me, in an identical flat, lived a girl my age called Sammy. We had a lot in common, she had passed through the care system after a similarly chaotic childhood and even knew some of the same social workers that had worked with me when I was younger. She was a real force of nature, outspoken, outrageous and beautiful. She cultivated a 'hard as nails' image and was known to be able to handle herself in the Moss Side after-hours club scene, where female on female violence was rife. In reality, like me, she was just another vulnerable child, forced to grow up too early. We got on like a house on fire.

Sammy was well liked in the reggae and jazz funk community in Moss Side, which led to me getting treated well by the regulars at blues parties and suchlike just because I was a friend of hers. It was through Sammy that I met Essy, an older man that she had been seeing for a while, off and on. Essy was in his late twenties, which seemed like another world to the teenage me. He would take us to Moss Side's front, where just a few years previously I had bought my first weed. Things were different with Essy, though. Just being seen in his company afforded me a layer of protection that was missing during my earlier, solo visits.

We would breeze into The Reno and The Nile clubs in the early hours of the morning and would get no trouble, whatever state we were in. The Reno concentrated on soul and R'n'B. The DJ, Persian, played smooth US dance friendly stuff like 'Searching' by Change or even mainstream artists like George Benson. The Nile, upstairs, was where you got to hear the deeper, darker dubbier tunes. I took it all in, sitting in the semi-darkness, making notes for my musical future. Essy was clearly a man of importance in this world. Although him acting flash and throwing his money around in a conspicuous show of wealth was largely for Sammy's benefit, the trickle down effect of this was that none of us wanted for anything.

Afterwards we'd go back to Sammy's. Essy was a great person to be around. A musician himself (he played sax), he turned me on to music I hadn't heard before, like 'House Is Not A Home' by One Blood (and its bouncing dub flipside) and introduced me to the best of the UK jazz/funk acts that were starting to come through, like Freeze and Olympic Runners.

One night at one of these post-Reno sessions Essy turned to me with a question.

'You punks like a bit of speed, don't you?'

I was new to the world of amphetamines, of course, having only sampled speed for the first time recently, but, not wanting to seem naive, I answered in the affirmative. Within no time I had been talked into accepting five ounces of insanely pure speed on credit. I think a large part of this 'generous' offer was about impressing Sammy, but either way, I left her flat having agreed to take it off Essy's hands. He delivered it to my flat a couple of days later.

My credit from Essy extended to £500. The speed he'd given me could retail for over £2000. With no idea of what to do next, I turned to the only person I knew who might possibly be able to help me, John Mather, who had recently introduced me to speed. Working backwards, I asked him to introduce me to the person that he had bought it from, a person I'll refer to as 'P'.

On the face of it, P was a decent enough character, notwithstanding his role in the seedy world of retail drug sales. We came to an arrangement that he would take three ounces off my hands, leaving me to get rid of the other two. I didn't have any scales, so he *kindly* came round and weighed things out for me before disappearing into the night, leaving me with 56 grammes to do with as I wanted. The retail price of speed, at ground level, was £15 a gramme, so I felt optimistic enough about being able to pay Essy back for my part of the split.

Unfortunately, I proved to be the world's worst dealer. My main problem was being too trusting of people. I would often guess amounts, always to the benefit of the recipient, or would give people my large(ish) bag of chemicals, saying, 'Just go to the toilets and take yours out, and give me the bag back when you've finished.' I would give credit whenever I was asked, which was never paid back, and with my growing personal use, it was only a matter of time before the entire batch was gone. Still, I had made sure I'd saved Essy's £200, so I was alright there. I arranged to meet Essy, with P, so that we could pay back what we owed.

At the meet, P swore blind that it was him that had taken the two ounces, and me that owed him for the rest. I couldn't believe such treachery, and gibbered in disbelief, like a wronged child. Unfortunately, or maybe because he sensed my vulnerability, Essy chose to believe P. He took the £200 pounds I had brought to the meeting, but I had no way of getting the rest. I was in big trouble.

Things came to a head a week later. Essy turned up at Roxy, and, standing near to the Stolen From Ivor shop opposite, beckoned me to come out. Gone was the Mr Nice Guy, flashing his cash at the Reno. Gone was the fellow musician, showing me new music I hadn't heard before. Gone was my innocence. This was serious. Taking me to one side, slightly out of sight of the door, he punched me in the face. Blood poured out of me.

'I want my fucking money!!'

Violence in the vicinity of the shop proved to be the last straw for Lloyd. I had been increasingly erratic at work, turning up late several times. Although I thought things were alright with Lloyd, in reality people were getting pretty pissed off with me and my druggy ways. It came as no real surprise when I was given my marching orders that day.

In one fell swoop, I was unemployed and scared. I was in debt to a very bad man and entered a period of fear, always looking over my shoulder for the worst to happen. Essy knew where I lived. I expected a violent house call at any minute. I tried to be at my flat as little as possible, and would overstay my welcome at John Mather's flat, crashing on the settee that little bit too often. I had no idea what to do next, and felt more cornered and alone than I had ever felt.

A letter arrived from a friend of my dad called Vera. I used to see her around a little bit when I lived with him. Her letter informed me that my dad was ill and he'd been admitted to a nursing home in nearby

Moston. She told me that he wanted me to visit him. Things were obviously far from good between us, and I was wrapped up in what was going on in my own life, but decided I should make the effort and look for some kind of peace.

I had no idea of how ill my father was, and was told nothing by the nursing home staff, even though they knew I was his estranged son. The visit was odd. There were long, uncomfortable silences. He told me that he and Vera had become close in recent times and before he was admitted into hospital he was spending most of his time at her house. This meant that his place was not being used. He gave me the keys to the house we used to share in Newton Heath.

My dad had inadvertently given me the escape route that I so desperately needed. I began to live there. Being in a different part of town, and not having a job to go into, I was that little bit harder to find. This made me feel a touch safer, although the fear never really went away. I would suffer from anxiety attacks, seeing people that looked like Essy everywhere. It was never him, of course. Gradually, I started to relax a little. By finally being out of Middleton and much nearer to my beloved city centre, I let myself believe that I had left my troubles behind and looked forward to a new phase of my life.

I turned, as ever, to music to carry me on. Alan Wise offered me a support slot to Orange Juice at Rafters, which felt like quite a coup. I had been taken to meet Alan a year earlier by a mutual friend, Ged Duffy. Alan was involved in lots of the more interesting shows in Manchester. I tried to talk him into putting on a double header of Joy Division and The Fall at Middleton Civic Hall so that we could grab the third support slot. This, alas, came to nothing, but I had spent the afternoon at his office, using his phones, making him laugh and generally amusing him. I presume this was why, a year later, he offered me the support slot at Rafters.

Rafters was one of my favourite clubs. It was a low-roofed, long, cellar venue, and when it was full it had an atmosphere all of its own. I'd been many times but had never played there. I put together a one-off show using musicians that I had only just met, in the same way that I did for the one-off gig in Leeds with Mark and Dave. This time I recruited a 16-year-old drummer called Ken and a young saxophonist called Nicky Reilly. I played bass and sang.

I had something of a natural aversion to saxophones, at least outside the framework of soul and reggae. So many bands used them as a soloing instrument rather than as a textural device and would insert a sax solo just to kind of pad things out. Although I had always loved the heavily treated saxophone work that Bowie had brought to parts of his *Low* album, it would take something special and unusual for me to let one near anything I was involved with. What Nicky did was exactly that, taking things in a different direction to anything else I had been involved with.

Nicky was no ordinary sax player. He had adapted a Watkins Copycat echo unit to achieve some dubby effects. This primitive machine dated back to the early sixties and was popularised by the likes of Hank Marvin and The Shadows. It utilised ¼ inch tape, a recording head and several playback heads to create delay and repeat effects in a human, non-scientific way. Nicky had extended the length of these repeats almost to infinity by bypassing the erasing part of things with judicious use of humble clear sticky tape. It sounded huge. I loved the random factor involved with massive delay times, it coloured the entire venue as it bounced back from the far wall as I was singing. Things sounded different every time, and I found I was duetting with myself in new and unplanned ways.

With this secret weapon, and my voice being mangled in a similar way by the sound engineer's Roland Space echo, I decided that less is more as far as the other instruments were concerned. I had Ken doing simple, drum-roll-free rhythms and I kept my basslines sparse and empty. I wish somebody had recorded the set that night. Who knows, perhaps somebody did?

When Orange Juice came on, Edwyn Collins looked about twelve years old. He led his band efficiently enough through a set of trebley twee love songs, but they seemed remarkably straight and backwards-looking to me. The future was to be weird, and I was to be a part of it.

Our hastily prepared show had worked and, in coming up with new lyrics on the spot, I had the starting points for several new songs. Alan Wise was pleased and actually paid me twenty pounds more than he had originally offered me. I was a happy bunny.

After the show, I popped into a take-away near the venue with Alison. As I was leaving, I took the food but left my bag containing my effects pedals and the drum machine on the shop's counter. Luckily for me, two young citizens who had been at the show and were behind me in the queue did the decent thing and chased me down Oxford Road to return it. I was moved by their honesty, they could have just kept it and I would have been none the wiser. One of these considerate young men was Terry Egan. The other was Lee Pickering.

It couldn't have been a better time for Lee to come into my life. Sue Davies had previously introduced us in Roxy, and I'd introduced Lee to some of the faster business that Essy had lumbered me with. He was, like me, a product of Manchester's inner city, and we had lots in common, not least of all our accents. Lee spoke just like me. We bonded as friends in no time.

Lee lived with Terry and another friend, Tony France, in the notorious Turkey Lane flats in nearby Harpurhey, where music was very much the order of the day. Terry's band, Beach Red, had supported the recently formed New Order on some of their early dates, and Tony was the singer in Stockholm Monsters, who were signed to Factory and were part of Tony Wilson's inner circle. They also contained Shan Hira and his sister, Lita, who as part of Spurtz had played with Vibrant Thigh some years previously, in particular at Deeply Vale and as part of the bill with Scritti Politti at The Mayflower.

All in all, we had loads of friends in common, and had come through the Manchester punk finishing school of Electric Circus/Rafters/Russell Club, being present at the same gigs even before meeting each other. Lee played bass, and we jammed together in his room after gigs, staying up all night, making every minute of every hour count. Having come to the end of one phase of my life, musically and in every other way, my friendship with Lee helped me start to rebuild in the Manchester summer.

We were together that July watching *Top of The Pops* as The Specials' 'Ghost Town' captured perfectly the mood of the nation's youth. If ever a song had spoken on behalf of the many, it was this one. Lee had turned up clutching a copy of Gang of Four's 'To Hell With Poverty', which itself carried a powerful call to arms message. We hammered that record. Its dirty guitar and rumbling bassline spoke to me, but The Specials had taken their tune to the heart of the mainstream, reaching number one just as rioting was breaking out in Toxteth. This had followed earlier civil unrest in Brixton and St. Paul's in Bristol, and as their 'people getting angry' refrain rang in our ears, we hot-footed it down to Moss Side where things were starting to kick off.

A crowd of hundreds had besieged Moss Side police station, with windows broken and police vehicles being set on fire. Heavily tooled-up reinforcements arrived in force, leading to one unfortunate officer getting shot in the leg with a crossbow bolt. The whole area became a scene of mayhem. Lee was friendly with Muppet, the singer from Armed Force, and we watched the action from the balcony of his flat near Moss Side precinct, high above the carnage below, a ballet of pincer movements and burning cars, like so many fighting ants. People getting angry.

Lee had a great ear for the weirder, more immersive kind of sounds coming through from labels like 4AD and Rough Trade. He had a thing for Chrome's *Half Machine Lip Moves* and I came to love its hallucinogenic power. Cabaret Voltaire's seminal albums *Mix Up* and *The Voice of America* would soundtrack our post-club sessions, and when their *Red Mecca* album was released it was constantly on his record deck. I had been into Wire since punk days, but Lee introduced me to the various members' spin-off projects. Dome, featuring Bruce Gilbert and Graham Lewis provided trippy accompaniment to many altered states, as did singer Colin Newman's *A-Z* and *Provisionally Entitled The Singing Fish*.

Playing bass round at Lee's had given me an appetite to play bass again more seriously. I kept an eye on the musician's wanted noticeboard at Virgin Records shop on Lever Street and spotted one that read 'Bass Player wanted for Ludus' or words to that effect. Ludus, and their charismatic singer, Linder Sterling, had been on my radar since the early punk days. She was a pioneer of the punk scene in Manchester, and her collage-based artwork was highly influential. It was Linder who created the brilliant 'disembodied heads' cover artwork for Magazine's *Real Life* album; Malcolm Garrett's sleeve for Buzzcocks' 'Orgasm Addict' featured Linder's disturbing image of a naked woman with an iron for a head and teeth for nipples. She designed the legendary 'menstrual egg timer' for Factory Records, which was given its own catalogue number (FAC 8) but never went into production.

The starting point for the music Linder made was unusual and jazz based, off to one side and defiantly female. This was exactly the sort of thing I wanted to be involved in. I wasted no time in calling the number scrawled at the bottom of the ad. My call was answered by Richard Boon, Buzzcocks' manager and head honcho at New Hormones Records. The label had already sealed its place in cultural history by releasing *Spiral Scratch*, the Martin Hannett-produced Buzzcocks masterpiece that had started the whole UK independent scene back in 1977. Further releases by Eric Random and The Tiller Boys had cemented their impeccable credentials. They seemed to be about artistic integrity, as opposed to commercial success. I was a frequent attendee at their Beach Club nights, so when Richard turned out to be a really nice guy, I was delighted. I was invited up to the office for a chat, and it was arranged that I should meet Linder and guitarist Ian Devine at their practise room at the back of the Rialto cinema in Lower Broughton. The place had something of a Factory Records history, as both A Certain Ratio and Joy Division had rehearsed there.

I had bought the latest Ludus release, *Pickpocket*, and had admired its packaging. The attention to detail was amazing, a six-track cassette-only release in its own bespoke plastic bag, with wonderful photos of Linder by Birrer in a limited edition booklet. The music was great, too, an unusual blend of jazzy stop/start rhythms and angular guitar. It was a little complicated for me so I was extremely nervous as I got off the bus for my audition. I was reaching well out of my comfort zone, musically, but I must have done something right as Linder invited me to her flat in Whalley Range to go over some more songs.

When I got to the flat on Mayfield Road, not far from Alexandra Park, Linder and Ian had set a couple of amps up in a spare bedroom. I was told to sit on the bed and was shown the bass parts to the six songs on *Pickpocket* in the space of an hour or so. My head was reeling. These people were real musicians. Ian in particular was flying around his fretboard, knocking out complicated jazzy runs that really called my bluff. I had done some homework on 'Patient' and 'Hugo Blanco', and knew them pretty well, so I was pleased when these were the first couple to be looked at. I was a little star struck at first. To hear Linder singing without a microphone, just inches away, was an incredible experience for me, and it was all I could do to concentrate on what I was doing. I came out in goosebumps.

There were two gigs coming up in the weeks ahead, one large, one small. Just as I was getting anxious about it all, the smaller one, a warm-up date in London, was cancelled. The remaining show was only a few weeks away and would be in the largest indoor venue I had ever been in, let alone played. Gulp.

Stafford Bingley Hall was a 10,000 capacity shed-type affair. Just thinking about the size of the place was scaring me to death. The one and a half rehearsals that we'd had so far had gone okay, but I still felt painfully out of my depth. I set about going over the songs at home endlessly, staying up for days, practising until my fingers could take no more.

The event was the third Futurama festival, organised by John Keenan from Leeds. He had assembled quite a bill over two days, a Who's Who of everybody relevant in alternative music at the time: Gang of Four, Bauhaus, 23 Skidoo, and that was just the Saturday. We were to play on the Sunday at 6pm, several hours before headliners Simple Minds and Bow Wow Wow. My bottom lip was physically wobbling at the scale of it all. I slept very little in the week leading up to the festival.

I took Lee along with me for moral support on the day. The band met up at the New Hormones office and crammed everyone, plus Lee and Richard Boon, into what felt like an incredibly small van. In no time at all we were at this enormous cattle shed, and in no time after that I found myself on stage with my stomach churning, suffering badly with the temporary amnesia that hits so often in such situations.

Things started well with 'Patient'. I was on top of that one. Linder wanted me to use her short scale Fender bass so that it was easy to move around the fretboard quickly and smoothly, and it really suited the fluid nature of the music. I hadn't met the drummer, Graham 'Dids' Dowdall, before, so it was quite an experience to hear the songs fleshed out so brilliantly, with flailing arms and twisted metal percussion as Linder shrieked 'Anaesthetise! Anaesthetise!'. She really was brilliant.

'Hugo Blanco' went well, but I was caught out once or twice by some of the more stop/start songs like 'The Fool' and 'Mutilate'. With more rehearsal, I could have nailed them, but their tricky, jazzy arrangements were just at the outer limits of what I could do. I was relieved to reach the end of the set without too much collateral damage. Heart beating, nineteen to the dozen, I found Lee and we melted into the crowd to check out Martin Bramah's Blue Orchids, who were incandescent and strangely beautiful, as always.

I was asked for my autograph whilst having a piss at the grim aluminium urinals. The same chap also asked Lee for his, which stopped my head getting too big, but I was as happy as Larry, and as we stowed away on an organised coach to Manchester, I knew that I wanted more of the same, as soon and as often as possible. Unfortunately, the week after, I received a note from Linder. It contained my split of the fee and a short message thanking me, but explaining that my services would no longer be required.

Oh well. It wasn't to be with me and Ludus, but the experience had fired me up. It was time to turn my attention to the next thing. I had some songs inside me that were burning to come out. I knuckled down to a creative period of songwriting. Something had changed in me, over the last few years in particular, and while it was certainly true that I carried emotional scars, I had also stumbled across a way to deal with them. I found the self-belief to write about my real feelings in an honest way.

Some of the early Vibrant Thigh songs contained lyrical input from Ged O'Dea, but I never felt comfortable singing someone else's words.

With my own life experiences, I was not short of ideas and things to write about. I had always worked well with other people, but it was usually the case that I would get songs into shape first before letting anybody else near them.

As far as collaborators went, I knew that I wanted Lee as part of the setup I was creating, but he hadn't been playing bass for very long. He would only mess about with his Gibson in his bedroom, jamming along with his beloved Cabaret Voltaire or Wire in the small hours after being out at a club in town. I could see the potential in him, and knew that he would be the perfect person to play with, even if he couldn't see it himself. It would simply be a case of keeping him on board while he became better at bass. We continued with jamming sessions in his flat, laying the foundations for the future.

I had started to spend some time in Didsbury with a small group of friends that I had met through the Musicians' Collective. Gina, Patti and Donna were collectively known as The Liggers, and had a track on the *Unzipping The Abstract* album alongside Vibrant Thigh. They had also done a John Peel session, so they were making waves. It was Gina that I saw most of. She was upbeat, full of positive energy and a lot of fun to be around. She was also a friend of Frank Ewart so we'd spend time at 'Mekon House', a second floor flat on Burton Road that Frank shared with his Manchester Mekon bandmates, Louise Alderman and Chris Griffin.

Frank had set up a primitive 4-track recording facility in one of the spare bedrooms at the flat. He was brilliant at getting the most out of the setup, despite the challenging conditions. Soundproofing was achieved by use of mattresses and egg boxes on the walls. Frank would bring his reel-to-reel down to gigs occasionally, too. He had recorded some cracking Fall gigs, when they still had early songs like 'Hey Fascist!' and 'Dresden Dolls' in the set.

I used to enjoy going round there, just hanging out, getting stoned and meeting the other musicians that would pass through. Amazingly, Frank had been recording his own band there. The Manchester Mekon were a six-piece unit, containing such esoteric instruments as flute and mellotron, in addition to the more expected drums, bass and guitars. It was a miracle that they could all fit in Frank's tiny recording room, but somehow he managed it. Most of the Mekon's output was instrumental but on one of my visits I was asked to contribute a vocal to a track. I dutifully came up with the goods, an impromptu stream-of-consciousness, everything coming out all at once.

I talked Frank into letting me record some of my own songs. This material was more coherent and worked out. I wanted to play all the instruments myself, so we set about doing exactly that in the most basic way imaginable. I had brought two songs to the session and proceeded to lay down drum tracks for both of them on the rickety Mekon kit. I recorded two different four-minute rhythm parts, then added bass, then guitar, all 'freehand' as it were. If the initial drum take was sloppy, none of the other parts would have worked, so I kept things very simple. As I added my vocals, I knew that there was a future for these deeply personal songs.

The first song, 'Doubt', was a moody, dark, slowly paced piece, dealing with the loss of my mother. It found me feeling pretty sorry for myself, interrogating a seemingly absent God.

> Well, I don't like questions
> But I have got one
> Why can't you raise my mother
> Like you did your son?

The second song, 'The Manchester Irish', concerned my father. My limited memories of him and his life were tainted by the breakdown of us living together, but this song evokes an earlier time, a time of Whit Walks and the wider Irish experience.

> Green clothing at the Easter parade
> Red faces from anger and alcohol
> Safe ghetto, you keep to your own kind
> The Manchester Irish, my father was one of them.

It was as if I had stumbled upon something so powerful and emotionally raw that I would have to learn to use it in a controlled and measured way. The one thing I did know was that I wanted to deal in fact, not fiction. Truth, not lies.

I now had a two-song demo of real worth, to further my cause. Slowly, I was emerging from the fog of the past with the tools I needed to move forward. It was time to take things up a notch. I decided to move (back) to Hulme.

PART III
Scatter & Run

Overleaf: At Turkey Lane flats, Harpurhey
Photo by Terry Egan

13: Karlos

Hulme was in my blood. I was born on Cornbrook Street, facing the notorious Spinners pub on the border of Hulme/Old Trafford. More recently I'd spent many formative nights at the Russell Club in the heart of Hulme. These nights usually ended up at a party in one of the crescents or at a session in somebody's flat there. It was a place unlike any other.

The crescents had been built to replace the crumbling and overcrowded terraced housing that I'd been born in, which had been demolished in the slum clearances of central Manchester in the sixties. They consisted of four massive blocks of flats constructed from pre-fabricated concrete, designed by the architects Hugh Wilson and J. Lewis Womersley, who were also responsible for the brutalist Manchester Arndale Centre. Inspired by the grand crescents of Georgian London and Bath, the Hulme cresents were named after four major architects of the Georgian era: Robert Adam, John Nash, William Kent and Charles Barry.

The high-minded vision was to create a modern, utopian urban living environment, but it was obvious soon after the first wave of families moved there in 1972 that there was no way that this type of housing was going to work in the way it was meant to. The initial families that moved in still held a strong bond to the communities they had been uprooted from, so there were social problems from the off. Design faults led to cockroaches and mice infesting parts of the estate, the ill-thought out heating system led to condensation problems, and there was a distinct lack of facilities for children. This cocktail of discontent led to a new housing policy coming into play, encouraging students, single people and younger first-time tenants to rent these flats.

By the late seventies, the very nature of the place had entirely changed. Artists and musicians could make as much noise as they wanted and had the freedom to set up workspaces and studios in the 'not fit for purpose' dwellings. It was, after all, better than letting them remain empty. The council, and the new influx of residents, knew that the crescents would not last forever so the normal rules of tenancy began to fall by the wayside. Full-band rehearsals, organised all-night reggae 'bluesies', and even recording studios began to spring up in the three- and four-bedroom living spaces. Some families stayed-on, leading to a sharp divide between the people that had moved into the area after the demolition of their terraced houses and the interlopers.

In addition to the artistic community, the council used it as something of a debtor's retreat estate. You could go to the council housing office in Moss Side precinct and walk out with the keys to a three-bedroom crescent flat that very day, whatever kind of mess you had made of any previous tenancy. Hell, they even gave you a decorating grant. Two hundred pounds, half paid there and then, the other half paid after the overworked tenancy officer had seen a tin of paint and a brush in your hallway when he made a two-minute visit.

The situation suited me down to the ground. I signed up for a three-bedroom flat. Mad as my life had been so far, it was about to get a whole lot madder.

The flat, on the first floor of Charles Barry Crescent, was in my name, but I was soon to be joined by one of Hulme's many larger than life characters, Sarah Keynes, or 'Lady Sarah' as she was known to Manchester's ever expanding alternative community. Sarah existed on the fringes of the Factory scene, and it was at the Factory that I had first seen her perform with her band Elti-Fits, a band that also contained Karl Burns on drums, a detail that had made me pay attention that little bit more. Elti-Fits had a certain credibility about them, having recorded a John Peel session and played at one of Peel's live roadshows at Manchester Polytechnic. They also played at the Zoo Meets Factory Half-Way festival in Leigh, and at Stuff The Superstars festival at Manchester's Mayflower club, which also had incendiary performances by Joy Division and The Fall.

Their music was abrasive and unwelcoming at first listen. It featured a very different drumming style to that employed by Karl on *Live At The Witch Trials*. Rather than supply a backbeat on its own, Karl would follow Sarah's vocals syllable by syllable, leading to a disjointed and staccato sound, most obvious on a track like 'Letter Box', which featured on both their Peel session and on their single on Worthing Street Records. Sarah's theatrical style of singing echoed singers like Lene Lovich, which, coupled with Karl's mathematical approach, put the band into XTC territory. They were a little too unbelievable and untrustworthy for my tastes, but an interesting proposition, nonetheless.

As a person, Sarah stood out a mile against Hulme's urban greyness. Her posh accent led to her acquiring the Lady Sarah nickname, although she probably wasn't quite as posh as she seemed. As far as I was concerned, she could have been from another planet. I had little experience of people from different class backgrounds, so even if she was exaggerating her upbringing somewhat, it certainly worked on me and many other working-class people that she encountered. Sarah was possessed of supreme self-belief, and definitely cultivated an air of otherness that served her well in this strange and upside-down world. She wore vintage dresses and immaculate make-up against a backdrop of downbeat, overcoat-wearing Factory regulars and their dressed-down female companions.

Sarah moved effortlessly between worlds, equally at home with the estate's 'intellectuals' (who had largely moved to Manchester to study and dropped out) and the likes of me and my friends, true products of the inner-city. Like many 'posh' inhabitants of Hulme, Sarah loved slumming it, and dived in to the estate's nefarious underworld. Nothing too serious, just helping people get what they might need, and taking a portion out for herself. A handling charge, if you will.

Sarah also had strong links to the city's black community. This was reflected in her music taste, which was eclectic and often rather excellent. We hammered the *Heavyweight Dub Champion* album by Scientist along with albums by Slave and Funkadelic, but the stand-out was Prince Far I's *Under Heavy Manners*, playful and serious at the same time, with Far I's deep commanding voice ringing around the crescents at full volume through our open window, educating the neighbours.

I had previously become friends with Ex-Spherical Objects keyboard player, Duncan Prestbury, and his girlfriend, Claire. They lived in Whalley Range, and knew Lady Sarah. Through them I met another of their friends, a psychology student from London called Francesca. Fran was popular, eccentric and outgoing with a taste for amphetamines and having fun that mirrored my own. I was pretty taken by her and after hanging out a few times I arranged to meet her at an ACR gig at the Ardri, which was going to be a belter.

I had taken a great deal of pleasure at the way A Certain Ratio had progressed into a weird, funk-influenced left-field outfit. They aimed for the feet, but excited the head, too, with the almost mathematical precision of 'Forced Laugh' or 'Loss' from their album *To Each*.

This gig, however, featured material from their second album, *Sextet*, and it was startling to see how far they had progressed. They had taken the strangeness and abrasive noise, and welded it to an impossible-to-resist funk sensibility. Equal parts Tangerine Dream and Bootsy Collins, the whole gig was a celebration of this unlikely new formula they had created for themselves. It was a genuine treat to be there. Support was from Swamp Children containing Ann Quigley, who had painted the weird collage on the Ratio's *To Each* sleeve, and Martin Moscrop's involvement with both groups gave the event a 'family affair' feel. With the throbbing bass of 'Knife Slits Water' ringing in our heads, we made our way together back to Fran's flat in William Kent Crescent.

We talked into the night, and as is the way of such things, we ended up together, enjoying a no-strings one-night stand, as natural as anything. Morning came along, and as the day broke and the light shone on the walls of Fran's room, I could see her half-hearted attempts at brightening things up with assorted posters, flyers and photographs. Nothing too unusual: a Russell Club poster, a live action Iggy Pop photograph, a university timetable. Suddenly my eye was drawn to a strip of photo booth images blu-tacked to the wall. It was Fran, mugging for the camera with her arms draped around a curly-haired, swarthy looking individual that I had encountered elsewhere. It was Karl Burns.

Shit! Shit! Shit! I had seen how hard he hits those drums of his, and when Fran told me that, yes, they were seeing each other, and yes, he would be back from playing a US tour with The Fall in the near future, I could only imagine that my face would become part of his percussion setup if and when things came out. Nice one, Mark.

My next act was inspired by an audacious move made by my old friends Mark Burgess and Dave Fielding. After their baptism of fire at our gig in Leeds, it seemed inevitable that The Cliches and Years would combine into a new band, and this was exactly what happened.

I was on my own mission, living my life closer to the city centre, but I kept up with news from Middleton, and things had really been coming together for them. Still nameless and drummerless, they had recorded some basic ideas on a ghettoblaster and sent it to John Peel. They received an encouraging reply, saying that if they were to do a proper studio recording, he'd be keen to hear it. The three of them set about selling everything they had (apart from guitars and amps!) in order to book some studio time at Cargo in Rochdale. Using a stand-in drummer called Scoffer, recruited from the local heavy metal/cabaret scene, they recorded three songs. Instead of posting their tape (and risking it being added to Peel's legendary pile of a thousand cassettes), they decided to turn up at Broadcasting House and give it to him in person.

Peel loved it, and even in their raw, embryonic state, he offered them a session, which in turn, led to them being signed to Virgin Publishing and CBS Records within days of it going out. They were now The Chameleons. This was astounding to me, and served to reinforce my belief in punk's first commandment. It was true, anything is possible.

I decided to follow in the footsteps of my Chameleon friends. I had belief in what I was doing, and I knew that if I could only get heard, then I would surely be offered a session on the show. London it was then, and armed with the recording I had made at Frank Ewart's flat, I shuffled onto a coach at Chorlton Street bus station.

I was to stay with Alison. Even though her moving to London had marked the beginning of the end for us as a couple, she was happy enough for me to stay with her for a while, semi-platonically, in her student flat off the Holloway Road. I was left to my own devices while she went to her lectures, so I investigated Camden, browsing the vintage clothes and record shops, excited but invisible.

Fortune had smiled upon me with the timing of my London trip. It coincided with a Fall show at nearby North London Polytechnic. No other group had resonated so strongly with me, and I had, by now, followed the band through various incarnations and had met several members. I felt like more than just a punter and was fascinated to see the band outside the area that had spawned them.

The group now included two drummers, with Paul Hanley and Karl joining forces to devastating effect. Starting with 'Fiery Jack', it took four or five songs for the live mix to start making sense in the echoey canteen-like hall. One minute it was all drums, the next minute a locust swarm of guitars would swell up, drowning out everything else. Far from detracting from my love of things, this unplanned deconstruction was perfect, finding a brand new, dubby, Krautrock-y sound by accident.

This was the first time I had seen any band in London, and it being The Fall only made things even more special. The set was largely made up of new songs, although some material from their recent release *Slates* was aired, in particular a sprawling version of 'Middle Mass' which marked the turning point in the proceedings as far as the sound engineer went. Something suddenly clicked, making the next song, 'Fantastic Life', a thing of pulsing beauty, with both drummers sitting on top of the mix alongside Mark Smith's sneering, accusatory vocals… 'And people tend to let you down/ it's a swine.'

It might have been the fact that I started to live in the same world as Karl Burns, but I simply could not take my eyes off him. Already my favourite drummer, he and Paul Hanley were so much more than just a lethal double drummer combination, they had reinvented drumming itself, and had come up with something as far removed from traditional rock drumming as Mark's vocals were from those of a 'standard' rock singer. It seemed like The Fall were playing for me alone that night. I felt that there was no way that the rest of the respectably-sized crowd could possibly have understood the intricacies of what was going on. Drenched in North Mancunian drug slang, and informed by Northern soul and the kind of life I had been living thus far, I felt party to a deeper understanding, and even felt a responsibility to pick up the baton and run with it.

I took the final song, 'Prole Art Threat', as a call to arms. I was myself one of those very proles. Once again, The Fall had shown me not only that I could create something unique and wonderful, but that it was my absolute duty to do so. The next evening, I set out to negotiate the tube system and deliver the goods into John Peel's sweaty, and hopefully grateful, palm.

Reinforced by Mancunian amphetamines, I marched into Broadcasting House reception as if I belonged there and greeted the receptionist with a jaunty, 'Hello, Mark Hoyle to see John Peel', as if it was the most natural thing in the world for a scruffy teenager with dilated pupils to be asking such a thing. I must have come across as not too dangerous, or perhaps the BBC staff were used to such occurrences. Either way, I was treated very politely and urged to wait for Peel in a nearby seating area. To my total surprise, in he walked. I knew that Mark and Dave had managed to see him, but somewhere in the back of my mind I felt that I would be really, really lucky to get a similar result.

Nevertheless, and to his eternal credit, John was fine about me just turning up and took me to his nearby parked car, where, after I explained that I had been in Vibrant Thigh, he listened to a portion of the first song, 'Doubt'. Although I had played all the instruments myself, I told him that it was the work of a band called Love Like Napalm. He loved it, and said that he'd be in touch soon. Result! I skipped away from the car like a pools winner, barely able to believe what had just happened. With the promise of a future Peel session, I made my way back to Alison's, and from there, back to Manchester, invigorated and in some disbelief that my scheme had actually worked. I'd better get cracking.

Fran had taken a bedsit on Range Road in Whalley Range, the centre of Manchester's red-light district and the very picture of seediness. Any lone female had to run the gauntlet of kerb-crawling men, who were incredibly persistent. It was quite the contrast to the kind of society that these grand Victorian houses were originally built for. Lee Pickering and I called round to see Fran, only to find that Karl Burns was there. Fran and I had put our little fling behind us by this time, and it remained forever unmentioned. Despite everything, things weren't too weird at all.

We soon started to see more of Karl, becoming friends. Before long we were being included by Karl in future musical plans, which I found incredibly flattering. He had a top floor flat in Old Lansdowne Road in Didsbury, and I became part of the furniture there, sleeping, albeit infrequently, on the settee between speed-fuelled bouts of film watching. Being able to watch whatever film we wanted whenever we wanted was something of a novelty, and we would dissect *The Man Who Fell To Earth* again and again, along with *Apocalypse Now*, a big favourite of Karl's due to its content being heavy on drugs and war, two of Karl's favourite things.

It would be fair to say that both Lee and I were impressed with Karl and the world he moved in. Aside from his duties with The Fall, he had played with an early incarnation of The Associates, and had some brilliant stories from his recent brief period as the drummer in Public Image Limited. It seemed that John Lydon had taken to him. Karl told us about Lydon's charismatic bravery when faced with danger from the general public. Apparently, trouble would follow him around, and there was always someone that wanted to have a go in pubs and clubs. Lydon would face down troublemakers just by sheer force of character. That thousand-yard stare that had changed a whole nation in a few seconds on *So It Goes* was no less powerful in real life, it seemed, and Karl regaled us with tales of Irish workmen, hell-bent on a good scrap, backing down under the force of the former Mr Rotten's withering gaze and razor-sharp, piss-taking humour.

All these connections added to Karl's growing reputation as a drummer, and various admirers came calling. Living nearby in Clyde Road was a Northern Irish band called Victim who had relocated to the

UK, picking up a Mancunian drummer called Mike Joyce along the way. I knew Mike from his earlier band, The Hoax. He was a total Karl fan. We saw a lot of him as he would visit often with demos for Karl to give his opinion on. Karl would bask in the attention, and then take the piss mercilessly. We both felt that Mike was better than the music he was playing with Victim and that he would move on to better things, but in the meantime Karl was happy to shoot the breeze and hold court to such an attentive audience, like some dark, bug-eyed guru.

Karl was unlike anybody I had encountered. Although he had a mother and family in the background, he, like me, existed as a self-contained unit, instantly mobile, with the very minimum of baggage. Apart from a couple of Sven Hassel paperbacks, a video player, a record player and a few albums, he owned virtually nothing. Clothes-wise, Karl only owned what he stood up in. Black jeans, a few t-shirts and a leather jacket, all of which would remain unchanged and unwashed for weeks, slept in and drenched in chemically induced night sweats. Everything was about the art.

We would spend every hour of every day dividing the world into 'Good' and 'Shit', something I had done a lot of before. All the time, we were moving nearer to making this music that we knew we were going to make. Karl had firm ideas about what we would *not* be like. He came up with a brilliant name for our project that was short, sharp and memorable, like Karl's drumming. 'Dub Sex'. I liked it.

Karl would rehearse with The Fall in their Ancoats practise room, and when everybody had gone home and the coast was clear, I'd join him, using Lee's bass through Steve Hanley's amp. I was nervous to be pushed in the deep end with my absolute favourite drummer, but I had belief in what I was writing, and Karl's enthusiasm for my ideas made that belief even stronger. He was full of it, and I was ready to listen and learn. He had a wealth of experience, and although he had a reputation as a bit of a nutcase, when it came to music, his heart was pure, and to hear him taking my songs seriously made me believe in myself even more.

Karl had clocked that I was putting a lot of anger and force into my bass playing, which led to me putting less input into the singing side of things. This led, in his opinion, to me doing both things half as well as I could be doing them. I knew this already, of course. Lee took over on bass, freeing me up to turn my full attention to guitar and vocals. I came to develop a style that would bring out the best of both worlds, leaving things empty where the vocals were, and punctuating the gaps with slabs of fierce, distorted guitar, reinforcing Karl's genius drum patterns. I was changed forever as a musician and a singer from the experience.

At his core, Karl had an absolute love of, and belief in, the power of music. He didn't care about clothes, possessions, appearance, where he lived, none of it. Money was only important in a hand-to-mouth way (that is, to buy the necessary chemicals) and he bounced around the world, concerned only with making brilliant music and being in the altered state required for such a mission. I learnt so much from being part of a setup with him. He was a natural, no doubt about it. Martin Bramah tells of when Karl got on a kit for the first time, and it was love at first sight, but let nobody assume that Karl hadn't worked at it. He had cut his teeth with hard-working heavy metal bands, all tricky time signatures and complicated structures, and to overcome the guitarist's volumes and egos, had developed a style so violent and hard-hitting that he hardly needed miking up. He told me that rule one was 'Twat it!', and he did exactly that. There was method in his apparent madness. Sound engineers knew where they were with such a definite and loud signal coming through the desk, and would be left slack-jawed at his skill and power. Karl was a total one-off.

Spending so much time at Karl's flat was something of a baptism of fire for me. It was a very intense thing to be hothoused by such a full-on character. I had given myself totally to music in my own way, but here was somebody that simply did not stop, even for sleep breaks. When sleep breaks actually did come, they hit him hard and nothing could wake him. I have seen him come crashing to a halt mid-sentence and proceed to remain comatose through a six-hour, full volume mixing session on many occasions, when the last drops of his seemingly boundless energy had finally been used up.

Karl had his fingers in a lot of pies. Alongside his work with The Fall and what he was doing with me and Lee, he and Duncan Prestbury, along with a bass player called Jimmy Carter (from Manchester Musicians' Collective band FT Index) had combined forces to release a single on Illuminated Records, known for releasing, amongst others, 23 Skidoo, DAF and 400 Blows. The single 'Running Away'/'The Last Sunset' couldn't have been further away from the sort of stuff that Karl and I were doing, or for that matter The Fall's uncompromising and challenging noise. The presence of Duncan's musicality, coupled with a listener-friendly production hinted at possible mainstream acceptance, and they were even invited to record a session for Capitol Radio in London. Things fizzled out after the single's release but for a short time, The Future Primitives seemed to be making headway in a different world.

We continued to be part of the furniture up in Ancoats. The early method of sneaking into The Fall's room after everybody had gone home had been improved on somewhat, as Karl had befriended the staff there, and they couldn't do enough for us. The studio, Decibelle, set up by the ever-so-French Philippe Delcloque, housed a 16-track recording facility in addition to the rehearsal rooms we had been stealthily using. The chief engineer, Jan Dzaran, was a huge Fall fan. Before too long, Jan became a useful ally, and was more than happy to use the studio's downtime to record us. Gratis, of course.

Even though Lee was a full part of what we were doing, I played bass on these recordings. Duncan Prestbury joined us, supplying tasty organ and a snarling synth line to a new, untitled piece that Karl and I had created upstairs in The Fall's room. Vocal-less and full-paced, it pointed to new directions, like some mutant child of Captain Beefheart and 'My Sharona', with Karl's staccato beat pushing me to the limits of my ability. Together with one of my songs, 'It's Only Natural', we had a decent starting point for our fledgling group.

Enticed by Karl, poor Jan would throw himself into endless re-mixes until his head exploded. Keeping up with Karl's amphetamine use was a job in itself, and I felt sorry for this friendly, laid-back man, thrown into chemical excesses he never wanted or needed. Soz.

Also using Decibelle at this time was a three-piece, funk influenced outfit called Freak Party, whose first demo had been recorded by Jan at around the same time that we were using the studio. Freak Party had Andy Rourke on bass, Johnny Marr on guitar and Simon Wolstencroft on drums. There was talk of Johnny having an audition with Psychedelic Furs. One mad night saw Karl and Simon doing a double drummer thing, with Andy on bass, Johnny on guitar and me on organ.

Trying to start a group in the midst of such chaos was always going to prove next to impossible. It had been built upon Karl's charisma, with me and Lee, the sorcerer's apprentices, caught up in his slipstream. Psychologically speaking, I was stretching myself far too thinly, hallucinating through lack of sleep and scarcely able to make sense of this crazy world I found myself in. It was hard not to feel a touch of imposter syndrome with Karl. Anybody would. He was louder and more skilful than any drummer I had ever known, and with me singing as well as playing, having to concentrate on both things at the same time sometimes stopped me from being able to join Karl when he went into full flight. Lee, on the other hand, was coming along in leaps and bounds on the bass, and having been hothoused by Karl, was developing his own style, a world away from standard ways of counting and song construction. The two of them were gelling into quite a rhythm section.

We had 'ideas', rather than songs, and the extremist nature of the way we all lived meant that we couldn't, or didn't, do these ideas justice and turn them into finished tunes. Karl was getting called away for Fall duty more and more, and, frankly, things were in a bit of a mess when a letter came from the BBC's Chris Lycett, offering Love Like Napalm (consisting of me, me and me) a John Peel session. Things were in such disarray that we couldn't possibly have done it. We all felt the same way, and turned the offer down.

Even though it was such an important thing to let go, not doing the session didn't seem to affect me deeply. The joy I'd felt when Peel turned up at Broadcasting House had been burnt out. It was as if my true feelings were being suppressed by the chemicals and the lifestyle, leaving me curiously numb.

Things had more or less run their course for our fledgling group. Karl and Lee took a flat together in Glebelands Road in Prestwich, next door to Mark Smith and his girlfriend Kay Carroll, who was also The Fall's manager. I visited them shortly after they moved in. Although we were all fine with each other, things felt distant and different somehow. I had no bad feelings and I had learned loads from our experience. I was now even more fired up to get things moving, and set about planning my next step.

14: Wilderness

My flat in Charles Barry Crescent had become a bit of a mad house. As I'd been spending a lot of time at Karl's flat in Didsbury, I'd taken my eye off the ball somewhat as far as my flatshare with Sarah went. Like many of Hulme's wanderers, she lived in the now, with little concern for the long-term consequences of the way she lived, or the lives of the people she encountered. It was a case of easy come, easy go.

Sarah would get regular visits from various restaurant workers, who, after finishing their shifts at about 1am, would drop by to pick up a bit of weed, and stay to socialise until the early morning. I quite enjoyed this upside-down social life at first, with people I already knew, but as the frequency of these visits increased, and I was forced to endure the company of strangers, the novelty wore off.

One night when I came back exhausted and in need of sleep after a weekend with Karl, the scene that met me looked like a cross between the aftermath of a party and a burglary. There was a sea of crushed cans and spilled drinks, records were thrown everywhere, and the balcony door was wide open, with the curtains blowing in the wind. My room, like the others, had no lock on it, and as I opened my door slightly, an overwhelming smell of heat and sweat hit me like a solid wall. I cautiously pushed the door open to find a strange man asleep in my bed, fully clothed and still wearing mud-covered boots.

Things started to go missing from my room too. Karl and I, along with Lee, had made a fascinating new friend at Decibelle Studios. Pete had been blind since childhood, and following a government retraining scheme had become a piano tuner. Pete was an accomplished drummer, too, so music was a huge part of his life anyway. After he tuned the studio piano one day, we went back to his flat in nearby Miles Platting, where he gave us a sizeable bag of low-grade cuttings from his weed plants. It was weak, and barely psychoactive, but there was lots of it. I hid my portion in an obscure corner of my room, behind some books, for emergency use. When I returned from another Didsbury weekend I perhaps should not have been surprised to find that it had gone. Sarah had been moving more and more in opiate-loving circles, and whether it was her or one of her cronies that had stolen it was neither here nor there to me. The flat felt tainted, and the writing was on the wall from that moment on.

Heroin seemed to be gaining a foothold everywhere I went. Rochdale, Langley, Moss Side, wherever I looked there seemed to be more and more people in its filthy grip. Good people too, who a year previously had been enjoying life with perhaps the help of a little weed, or no drugs at all, were now getting sucked into the cycle of addiction and the resulting life of crime that it inevitably brought with it. Break-ins were rife and news of someone's death from heroin filtered in with alarming regularity.

With this epidemic arriving in my flat, it was time for me to move on. It had only taken me an afternoon to get the flat so I'd be able to get another one just as quickly in the future if the need arose.

My first port of call was Rochdale to link up with Cooey and Glynnis, two music lovers that I hadn't seen for a while – Cooey had operated the Vibrant Thigh drum machine for our final two gigs. Heroin was working its way into this community too, but these people were prepared to meet it head on.

A mutual friend of ours had developed the mother of all smack addictions over the preceding few years and had tried all manner of methods to get clean. Try as he might, being surrounded by the stuff wherever he went wasn't helping his genuine desire to put heroin behind him. The only thing for it was the absolute, no mercy, cold turkey method. To pull something like that off successfully, it had to be done far from home, where, when temptation raised its ugly unwanted head, nothing could be done about it.

Glynnis had an inspired idea. She was close to the core group of people that had organised the Deeply Vale festivals, including John Ord Clarke, who was something of a legend amongst those in the know. John had retreated to the Scottish Lowlands, a mere four-hour drive away, and it sounded like the ideal place for our toxic friend to detoxify. John's nearest neighbours were Tibetan Buddhist monks at the Kagyu Samye Ling Monastery somewhere in the next valley, and we all felt reasonably confident that they hadn't yet taken to smack dealing to supplement their income the way that their Buckfast-peddling Christian counterparts had done. Our increasingly sweaty friend could scream, kick, promise, cajole and lie through his teeth as much as he wanted, he wouldn't be able to get anything.

It came to pass that one Sunday night, Cooey, Glynnis and I, along with Glynnis's driver friend, Dave, came to the rescue of our addicted friend. It was dark for almost the whole journey and, knowing what lay ahead of him, our patient was as depressed as I've ever seen anyone. He was seriously withdrawing. He had been dealing to feed his habit, and with it always being nearby, he had been caning it, building up a massive tolerance.

It was a real King Lear storm of a night when we piled out of Dave's transit.

'Yeah, use the other caravan,' said John Ord Clarke. 'No sweat.' Second nature to help a sufferer.

It turned out that he hated smack as much as I did. A similar epidemic had happened in 1970, doing the same damage to a different bunch of friends as was repeated with mine. Deaths, lost opportunities, broken families. It could have been my friends he was telling me about. I had the chance to express my gratitude to him for putting something in place that had shaped my life in such a positive way. Deeply Vale had its dreamlike aspects, but it was born of a fierce urban reality, and my experience reflected exactly that. Other festivals seemed to offer distraction, unicorning the badness of the world away in an escapist haze. We went the other way. Our turn-on was confrontation. In the music, in our politics, in our cities and towns, dancing on the hills over Satanic Lancashire.

I learned that John had been an integral part of the inspirational team of anti-establishment heroes that combined to make it all happen at Deeply Vale, and was one of the more vocal in their dealings with the council when they came out in opposition to the festival. So much so that he ended up running for council office himself, and getting voted in. It must have put the fear of God into his fellow councillors to have to treat this unusual man as an equal. He was the first person I had ever seen to have a dotted line and scissors tattooed on his neck, with the words 'Cut Here' underneath.

When the Deeply Vale adventure had run its course, after being chased from pillar to post by hostile, local political alliances, John washed his hands of the whole affair and went to live in a caravan next to a stream, completely off-grid, without electricity, gas or any of the basics that we all took for granted.

And off-grid was exactly what our friend needed. If you can't score, you can't reset the clocks back to 000. Eventually, the body cleans the toxin out of the system, which is, of course, when the real battle begins, as it is the psychological grip that defines and enslaves you. For now, though, the help of a beautiful man in a beautiful place, together with the love of some close friends, led to a cleaned-up version of our unnamed wanderer landing back on earth to go, at least for now, about his life.

Cooey and Glynnis were inseparable as a couple. Although Cooey had his own place, he invariably would be found where Glynnis was, which meant that his other residence was empty more or less all of the time. It was no skin off anybody's nose for me to stay there so, as it suited my current situation, this is exactly what I did. Hulme had been full-on for the last year, so I welcomed the opportunity to recharge my batteries.

The house was a crumbling two-up, two-down terrace, situated on Manchester Road in Castleton, the main thoroughfare between Manchester and Rochdale. Castleton itself is not to be confused with the Derbyshire beauty spot overlooked by Mam Tor, and widely regarded as one of Derbyshire's most visitable and pleasant villages. This Castleton was a mesh of mills and low-grade housing for the people who would have worked in them, and Cooey's place was at the lowest end of things.

Devoid of hot water, and condemned for demolition in the not too distant future, the entire block was like a historical reconstruction. The only toilet was an outside one, and mould covered the damp walls in huge patches. I woke up one morning to see a frog crossing the floor of the living room in which I slept, the other rooms being unfit for human habitation. I had lived in some rough places as a child, but this was off the scale.

A nominal rent of two pounds was supposed to be paid to the local shop (which was condemned as well), but this was never paid by me, and never asked for by the kindly woman who had lived most of her life in the area and worked in the shop forever. Instead, she offered me credit, and this kindness kept me from starvation more than once.

I had only a few friends in the area. I would visit Biggles, a well-known music lover and local character in nearby Ashfield Valley, an estate often compared to Hulme in its failure as a housing project. I also got to know Andy Schemet of local heroes Accident On The East Lancs, whose 'We Want It Legalised' single was a huge favourite amongst the Deeply Vale people, me included. But mainly I kept myself to myself, writing and playing my guitar, which was one of the few material possessions I had brought with me.

I was, to all extents and purposes, lost. But, as low as I was, just when I thought that I couldn't fall a whole lot lower, I very nearly did.

On a visit to Langley with another acquaintance, Billy, we had ended up at the house of a local draw dealer, also called Mark. This character had an owl tethered on a perch in the living room and would feed it slices of sparrow and mouse that he had shot with an air rifle. He would go hunting on nearby Bowlee Fields in the early mornings to see what he could find, and sit there with bloody fingers, feeding the bird as if everything was perfectly normal.

He offered me some heroin, smoked on a piece of tinfoil.

'Yeah, go on then,' I meekly responded, despite everything I felt about this despicable drug – the drug that had driven me out of my own flat and was wreaking havoc all across the north of England. This is how it gets its claws in, preying on the despondent.

It couldn't have been much, as smack users are not known for their generosity, but it felt as if I had been hit on the back of my head with a shovel. I was instantly sick and entered a numbing void, like being underwater. I hated it. Looking around, I hated these people, too. There they were, sliding down into their comfy chairs, as happy as Larry to welcome this nothingness. Never mind the crime, dishonesty and broken lives that I knew heroin brought with it, it was the feeling itself, so celebrated by smack users as some kind of religious experience that I hated. It was vile.

I couldn't wait for the effects to wear off. I left just as soon as I could, knocking up a friend called Debbie in nearby Millbeck Court. I stayed on her sofa for a little while. She said that she had never seen me like that, and I agreed. This was shit. It was clear to me that my tastes in fun and people lay at the opposite side of the drug spectrum. With speed, life was faster, more productive, and brought me into contact with witty, creative people, or so I reasoned. I thought about my namesake, up all night feeding animal corpses to his owl in an opiate haze, and knew which way my bread was buttered. I had been right all along.

I went to see Mark Burgess. He was still living on the Hollin Estate with his mum, a short walk from my first flat. Mark opened the door and we went up to his bedroom. It'd been a while since we'd seen each other. We played a few records and Mark told me a little of what had been going on, although, lacking any real experience of life in the fast lane of the music industry, much of it went over my head.

'Check this out, Mark…'

Showing me a legal looking wedge of paper, we laughed at the scope of the arrangement the band had agreed to, outlining the fact that the record company's rights extended to parts of the universe that hadn't yet been discovered! This was indeed a whole new ball game.

Things had been going astronomically well for Mark and his band. They had been swept up in a wave of excitement and action, the likes of which all of us used to dream about as music-obsessed teenagers just a short time ago. Recording at good studios, interviews in the music papers, Radio 1 sessions, all of it. In the space of a few short months, everything had started to happen for them. The pace of things must have left them reeling.

For my part, I had little to report. My own rather aimless wandering made a stark contrast to the progress that Mark, Dave and Reg had made, and a real friend like Mark must have found it a little upsetting to see that I hadn't been looking after myself very well lately. His arm reached out.

'Here y'are, Mark.'

I hadn't asked, but here was Mark slipping a fiver into my hand. I had thought that I wasn't looking too bad, and that I was coming across alright, but this was somebody that had known me for a while and could see the changes in me. He could see that I wasn't on a good path.

It was as if I was in some kind of bubble, one step removed from real emotional experiences. His simple act of kindness made me think long and hard about the direction my life had been taking. I was a little embarrassed to be so obviously in need of charity, but at the same time, I knew that I could make things change.

As I was leaving, Mark gave me a copy of the debut Chameleons single 'In Shreds'/'Less Than Human', released by Epic records, who had won the bidding frenzy started by the band's Peel session. When I got it home I couldn't believe my ears. This was amazing! From the very first beat of John Lever's drum intro, I was hooked. The breakneck-paced tom-tom work is joined several bars later by Reg and Dave's guitars, which had evolved into a mesh of power and swirling beauty. The two of them had always had a psychic understanding, but this was something else as the full tonal register was brought into play, either by the notes they were playing or the notes your brain imagined in the gaps they left in between.

Mark's vocals were nothing short of brilliant, conveying isolation and yearning at the same time as being a great, uplifting single. I was so proud. Proud of my friends, proud of the city that had spawned us all, and grateful beyond belief to have been lucky enough to have been exposed to the influences that led to such a stone-cold classic of a record being made at all. Lost though I was, hearing 'In Shreds' spurred me on to find the right people and make my own dent on the world of music that I loved so much.

This couldn't happen while I was living where I was. I needed to be back in the thick of it, communing and interacting with other musicians. Many of the bands that I knew from the Musicians' Collective were based in and around Didsbury, and it was there that I decided to move to. I had been generating tiny amounts of money by being someone who would get hold of what people needed, and adding a small amount on to the price for my trouble. It was a very hand-to-mouth existence, but it gave me the beginnings of an escape plan. On visits to South Manchester, and to Didsbury in particular, I had been surprised at how many flats there were advertised in newsagent's windows, often available to move into with just one week's rent changing hands. Miraculously, I managed to hang onto what amounted to two week's rent, and within an hour of seeing an advert in a paper shop on Lapwing Lane, I had moved into a tiny room at the top of a house on Clyde Road.

Twenty quid a week got me one room, sharing a bathroom and tiny kitchenette with various nomadic folk, invariably 'just passing through' until something better came along. The room opposite mine was occupied by one of the most illusive and legendary characters of the Mancunian punk scene, Dave (a.k.a 'Woody') from The Worst.

The Worst embodied the very essence of what punk should have been about, and never ruined their reputation with anything as mainstream as, well, actually recording their music. They were the purest distillation of all that was lo-fi and street level. They were, whichever way you looked at it, the real thing. I never saw them, but knew about them from older, first off the block punks like Denise Shaw. Unable, or rather, unwilling to play even slightly, their sets would degenerate into a state of collapse and ranting. One night, at Chorlton Oaks, they stopped mid-performance to give the hapless Dave a spiky haircut! Performance art without ever trying to be, they were in at the very start, counting John McGeoch and Siouxsie Sioux amongst their many inner circle fans.

They were managed by Steve Shy, of *Shy Talk* fanzine, and played in Ireland and at Birmingham Barbarella's with Buzzcocks, who took them under their protective wing. They were the Manchester punk band that nobody had ever heard. No recordings exist, although rumours of a live bootleg are part of our oral folklore.

Dave was very much a game-of-two-halves kind of person. He was as nice as pie in the daytime, when he would come into my room for a chat and a brew, and to avoid our landlord, Mr Hussain. At night time, he was a different proposition altogether. Everyone kept their door locked when he came rolling in, shouting and screaming and hurting himself, falling around, destroying furniture and attacking any person unfortunate to get in his way.

The life of a hard drinker is one of constant poverty, and Dave was certainly a hard drinker. He was trapped in that age-old cycle of drink/sleep/repeat, and every penny he could beg, steal or long-term borrow went towards getting pissed to block out whatever demonic reality he was running away from. It was a real shame to see. Dave's Dr Jekyll side was as placid as a lamb, but his Mr Hyde side was something you wouldn't wish on anybody.

Moving to Didsbury had its positive aspects, too. I was near to many musicians. Frank Ewart of The Manchester Mekon was a great ally during this time, and I was always welcome at his studio/flat, where I'd pass the time hanging out with other Collective alumni, like Bathroom Renovations and Spurtz.

Factory Records had opened a new club on Whitworth Street West. It was a natural extension of the scene that had started at The Russell Club, when Factory had used a pre-existing club to put on Factory nights. At the end of the day, though, The Russell Club was owned by Don Tonay, and it had its own downbeat, scruffy atmosphere. This new venture, to be called the Haçienda, was to be a different beast altogether. Inspired by visits to clubs like Danceteria and Paradise Garage on their jaunts to the USA, New Order and the rest of the Factory inner circle had wanted to bring a little of that frenetic Hispanic dance scene home with them, and commissioned Ben Kelly to design a cathedral-scale club space.

I knew this end of town well. Tony Davidson's rehearsal rooms were nearby, and the whole area was a gloomy hangover from the

Victorian industrial period. Mills, rope works, and doomy, stained former workplaces dominated the landscape. A former boat showroom called International Marine dominated a corner block, and it was here that Wilson and co. had decided to build their temple.

I wasn't there on the opening night, where ESG's already empty funk would have bounced around the cavernous walls. Famously, compère Bernard Manning returned his fee, saying, 'Give up now while you've got the chance.' It was, to say the least, a work in progress.

It was a few months later when I first went. I had met up with Paul Copp, a friend from ex-Collective band, Picture Chords, and his girlfriend, Sandy. They were going one Saturday night so I tagged along. It was a weird experience to be going as a punter to something that I already felt emotionally involved with. I had been a part of all the steps that had led to here, The Electric Circus, Rafters, The Russell Club, and here I was, going through the front door like everybody else. I even paid in!

It was quite a sight to behold. It was barely more than half full and the empty spaces served to show off Ben Kelly's startling design to great effect. Bollards, reflective cat's eyes, and embossed metal panelling made it unlike anywhere I had seen before. Everything had been considered, from the colour scheme (Pigeon Blue, Poppy, RAF Blue, Signal Red) to the 'Use Hearing Protection' sign outside the DJ box.

The music veered towards the well-known, there was chart singles by the likes of Yazoo or Soft Cell alongside dance hits like 'Don't Make Me Wait' by Peech Boys, or Patrice Rushen's 'Forget Me Nots'. The sound was better on the upstairs balcony, where you were at the same level as the suspended speakers, and it was here that I met Lee Pickering for the first time in a while. He wasted no time in mercilessly taking the piss out of my extremely short new haircut, saying that it looked as if I had been sectioned. It was weirdly appropriate bumping into Lee here as I was mad keen for him to get involved with making music with me again. There were other friends there, too. Ged Duffy and his mate Slim were working there, having been a part of the furniture at Rafters and The Russell Club Factory nights. The Haçienda acted as a magnet for the lost souls, who, like me, had been fired up by punk's early promise. After spinning around in North Manchester for what seemed like a long time in the wilderness, living inside my own head, it was nice to not be so lonely. It was brilliant to feel I was back with my own people again.

I began to get close to a young man from Blackburn called Martin. He was a couple of years older than me and had spent some time working on the oil rigs in Scotland. We shared a love of the direction that music was going in at the time. He had the money to dive into the wealth of new electronic, synth-based soul that was starting to emerge from the States, and he kindly let me tag along on exciting record-buying missions at Spin Inn on Cross Street.

On import day, the tiny shop would be full of the cream of the city's DJs, making their minds up about a tune within a few bars, and greedily ghosting it away to be pulled out as a secret weapon when the time was right. Competition was rife, as hard to find Disconet remixes and unmarked white labels would attract price tags of twenty pounds or more, unheard of amounts for a 12-inch single.

The main Haçienda resident DJ at this time was our friend, Hewan Clarke, who had cut his teeth playing jazz-funk at the Reno and Fevers. His playlists reflected the changes slowly taking place. Gradually, the Roy Ayres and Herbie Hancock tunes were getting infiltrated by large, synth-washed productions by Sharon Redd and D-Train. The arrival of 'Planet Rock' by Afrika Bambaataa was a game changer, and illustrated perfectly the lack of snobbery in the scene. Mixing Kraftwerk's spartan Eurotech with a black street sensibility seemed odd to many, but was perfectly natural and a thing of great beauty to those with open ears.

Hewan introduced me to the majestic 'Holland Tunnel Dive' by impLOG. It was released in 1980, a strange little masterpiece from New York's 'No Wave' movement. Made by Don Christensen, it consists of a muffled spoken list of what is wrong with the narrator's life, obscured by distortion over a primitive, Cabaret Voltaire-esque drum machine pattern. It gathers intensity gradually and is overtaken by what sounds like an approaching train that achieves speaker-splitting levels of volume before reverting to the bleak first part again.

The noise (actually a drill) is just too loud, and goes on for just too long, making the listener doubt their own senses. In a club, it seems like the roof is falling in, and the illusion of collapse is taken to the very last possible second, before, on its second pass, it gives way to a saxophone theme so uplifting and happy that you doubt that you had ever got so scared by the record's suicidal early sections. I have seen dancers run for cover, confused by this hyper-intense whirring sound, as their club/drug experience goes seriously wrong for them, only to be brought back from the brink by the redemptive qualities of the dual sax break, which seems as happy as the Laurel and Hardy theme after the bleakness of all that led up to it. Absolute genius.

I ended up spending loads of my time at the Haçienda. After my first night, I never had to pay in again, but I think that was the case for most people. It was open every night, more or less, and Martin and I would turn up for the last hour or two, watching our breath as we exhaled in the freezing cavernous space that was built to accommodate 1650 punters but was attracting more like 50-100 on the quiet midweek nights. It was like having a club of our own. The staff were all friends, I hardly drank at all, so it was totally affordable. They were losing money hand over fist, but keeping the place open for the likes of me and my friends was the remit. It was always meant to be more of a place to be than a commercial venue, there was talk of rehearsal facilities and all manner of café bar/hangout space ideas.

Their gig booking policy was inventive and wide reaching, being bankrolled by New Order's record-sales money, and this led to many risks being taken as far as who played there went. Not every venue could boast that William Burroughs had appeared there, as he did at Psychic TV's Final Academy event. That opening year saw gigs by Defunkt, The Birthday Party, J. Walter Negro & the Loose Jointz and many more. All free, all spellbinding.

It wasn't all about the Haçienda, I was still going to other clubs. On one fateful night, I was invited to a party after a particularly messy evening at Legends, where a fledgling rock scene was emerging. Legends was in many ways the spiritual successor to Pips, with its accent on extreme fashion and harder edged dance-based alternative stuff like Killing Joke, The Cure, Bauhaus and the like. The smell of hairspray and leather-enhanced perspiration was overpowering, but the girls (and boys) were visions of beauty, and it was good for the soul if not always the ears to be in the midst of it.

The party I'd been invited to was on Great Western Street, in Moss Side. By a strange turn of events, there were two parties on the same road that night and I ended up at the wrong one. The one I had turned up at was thrown by three girls from Leeds who had recently moved to Manchester to study. Ever my charming self, by the morning, after staying up all night shooting the breeze, I was invited to move into a vacant room that they wanted to rent out. I was lonely in my Didsbury bedsit so I jumped at the chance to live with such a lively bunch of people.

I slung my few belongings into a carrier bag and moved in that very week, happy to be nearer to my beloved inner city, and ready to immerse myself fully in what was going down. So began my time with Wendy, Julie and Jane. The four of us lived as platonic housemates, drinking in all the delights that my city had to offer.

Living at Great Western Street suited me down to the ground. Unlike other times when I had shared my living space with other people, we all got on well. The four of us settled into a pattern of living that I had never experienced before. We would put money into a collective pot for food and essentials, and take it in turns to cook and share household jobs. It was as near to a 'family' kind of life as I had ever been, and it smoothed a few of my rough edges off in a way that had been tried before by various previous foster families to no avail.

Jane, Wendy and Julie were quite a feisty trio who would bring any party to life. Younger than me, but informed by the same rebellious streak, they were well known in Leeds punk circles. Wendy had been going out with Nev, the drummer from second wave Leeds punk band Abrasive Wheels, and for a while, we were beset with leather-clad house guests most weekends, drinking to oblivion and flattening their mohicans as they slept where they fell. I would chuckle to myself at the thought of how much these late-to-the-party rentapunks had missed the point, choosing the trivial, fashion-obsessed dressing-up angle over the real sense of personal and political change that lay at the core of it all. Gradually, their visits became rarer as my three housemates settled into the Manchester scene.

It was amusing to see the effect that my new friends had on the male population of our corner of Manchester. Jane, Wendy and Julie had a fierce sense of style, and were beautiful in different ways, as well as being witty. The house was never short of visitors, as a parade of potential suitors would show up, bearing gifts with a cheery 'I was just passing...'. Being the platonic housemate meant I would have all manner of hopefuls wanting to be my best friend in order to visit more often. We'd give them marks out of ten, ridiculing their transparent approach and weary chat-up lines. It felt good to be included as an honorary member of this girl gang. To think that it all started with me turning up at the wrong party!

15: Clubland

My social life was back on track and once again I was lucky to be well placed to enjoy another fertile period of the Manchester social scene. New clubs and venues were starting to spring up across the city. Through a friend called Hazel, I was invited to meet John Kennedy, a larger-than-life character who had persuaded somebody with more money than sense to invest in his vision of an exclusive, decadent playspace – something that crossed the 'up for anything' mood of the times with a cooler edge, and the best underground DJs that Manchester had to offer. In a tip of the hat to John's love of Christopher Isherwood's Germanic chic – which had been brought to life for so many in the 1972 film *Cabaret* – it was to be called Berlin.

Berlin was situated just off Deansgate, on Bridge Street, and had, in a previous incarnation, been a boutique called Edwardia, owned jointly by Manchester United's George Best and Manchester City's Mike Summerbee. In the late sixties, this part of the city was amongst the most fashionable places to be seen, and the shop regularly attracted gangs of girls who would hang around all day in the hope of a glimpse of their idol. This ritual was fictionalised in the classic 1973 movie *The Lovers*, starring Richard Beckinsale and Paula Wilcox, which itself presents an interesting time capsule of early seventies Manchester life.

By the time John Kennedy opened the club, the area was slightly more downmarket, although it retained its reputation as a place to shop, with several vintage clothing stores nearby, notably the Carl Twigg shop that I called into on my way home from St. John's College some years earlier. The club was well situated in relation to the gay culture that it sprung out of. It was a two-fingered salute to Manchester's Chief Constable, the religious homophobe James Anderton, who had brought the full power of the law down upon those he considered to be 'swirling in a human cesspit of their own making'. He employed methods of entrapment to catch and prosecute gay men in a savage and prolonged pogrom.

A real nasty piece of work. He targeted sex workers and closed down bookshops in a flurry of 'heaven sent' evangelism.

It was in this climate that Berlin and other, more exclusively gay venues, were forced to operate. Bars like New York New York and The Thompsons Arms were well established hangouts, but the scene was split up all over the city. There was Dickens on Oldham Street for the more outrageous; Manhattan Sound on Spring Gardens, which was more relaxed; and around the Deansgate area there was a selection of clubs and bars which gave the whole area a friendly, but exciting veneer. Bernard Slingsby's Bernard's Bar and Exit were situated at this end of town, as was the rather more hardcore Hero's, which would attract a fiercely hedonistic leather-loving crowd, enticed by the company and the far-sighted musical policy of DJ Les Cockell.

DJs like Les Cockell brought a Northern soul influence to the new dance orientated direction in electro music that was sweeping through Manchester's gay (and gay friendly) community. The parallels were obvious. Yearning, love-orientated emotional songwriting, a love of endurance-enhancing drugs and all-night partying, a sense of 'this only belongs to us', and the refining of beats to a beautiful, bass drum-driven simplicity. It was against this sonic backdrop that Berlin first opened its doors as a more intelligent alternative to the cavernous Haçienda.

I got on well with John and he offered me a job as a glass collector, which was the easiest job in the world. John's staff budget would be spread around amongst various friends of ours, and the whole operation was little more than a chance for John to have his friends near him on his great adventure. He had the respect and trust of many people in many different areas of Manchester nightlife. He had the knack of being at the centre of things, time and time again.

Johnny Marr and Andrew Berry had been DJing together at Exit, and while attendances were modest, the people that did go there were very much 'inner circle' as far as Manchester and its music were concerned. John was aware of the high regard that Andrew was held in, so brought him to Berlin to be the club's main regular DJ. Tunes like Klein & M.B.O.'s 'Dirty Talk' and Stone's 'Girl I Like The Way

That You Move' would be sprinkled amongst better known dancefloor fillers. Almost from the opening night – attended by John's London mates, Spandau Ballet, to a distinct lack of excitement from the hard to impress Manchester crowd – Berlin was a place for those in the know to relax in.

We ran it into the ground, or rather John did. With money behind him, life was just one long party for us all. We'd shut at two after the last punters had left, and that was when it really got going. It was the lock-in to end all lock-ins. Fuelled by high quality Mancunian amphetamines, all the staff and selected lucky punters would party hard until daybreak came around, rinsing the place for free drinks and emerging, blinking into the morning sun, as John would use the club money to take everyone for breakfast at one of the city's posher hotels. From there, we would go to John's flat in Didsbury and frequently carry things on until it was time to go back to open the club up again. Good times.

At one lock-in we were entertained by Malcolm McClaren & The World's Famous Supreme Team. They had been at the Haçienda that night and after finishing their appearance they arrived with us just as we were closing. Phone calls ahead meant that we were ready for everyone and everything, and it turned into a masterclass of energetic hip-hop. Armed only with several copies of their 'Buffalo Gals' 12-inch and a whole load of attitude, they took the roof off the place, to an audience of maybe twenty friends and barstaff. There was a lot of snobbery around dance music, and McClaren himself invoked a great deal of mistrust amongst purists of many persuasions, being seen as something of a dilettante, moving from one scene to another for his own ends. All this might well be true, but the after-show that The World's Famous Supreme Team pulled out of the bag that night was astonishing.

Trevor Horn's production on 'Buffalo Gals' is a weird one, and when it was released, it stood out as both unusual and useful to aspiring DJs everywhere. It split beats, music and vocals into two separate and distinct sides of the mix, with drums, for instance on the right, and a naked a capella vocal on the other side. In a club, this led to all kinds of sensory trickery, as the force of Horn's Fairlight drum sounds would jump out at you from different sides of the building, with only a split second's delay.

It was a remarkable time in my city, and remarkable times produce remarkable people. One such soul was Anthony Behrendt, who had a lot going on. He had developed a unique and skilful guitar style, informed by funk and soul, but embracing the better and more thoughtful rock-based approach coming from the likes of Killing Joke or Magazine. He was something of a lone wolf and had evolved a way of performing; just him on his own, layering seriously dirty slap bass or heavily effected guitar over pre-prepared drum and basslines using a Tascam 4-track Portastudio. His confidence knew no bounds, and he had a way of being able to talk people into doing what he wanted, whilst at the same time leaving them believing that it was their idea in the first place.

In a world where unemployment was almost a default setting, Anthony had gone straight from school to work at an engineering firm and brought this sense of discipline to the music he made and the life he led. I liked his work ethic and was impressed that he had convinced the organisers at Legends to allow him to punctuate their formulaic night's programming with one of his solo workouts, and even more impressed when he included Byrne and Eno's 'The Jezebel Spirit', and a version of ACR's mighty 'Knife Slits Water' as part of the proceedings. It was clear that we were destined to become friends, which is exactly what we became and together we made the most of a city full of life.

Anthony had been asked by Mick Ward of The Suns of Arqa to assemble an ad-hoc pick-up band to accompany the legendary reggae singer Prince Far I at Band on the Wall. Anthony invited me to come along and get involved, on guitar or percussion. I was a huge Prince Far I fan but for whatever reason, something stopped me. A lack of confidence? A disbelief that something thrown together so haphazardly could work with no rehearsal? Either way, I passed on the invitation and then kicked myself hard when the gig was a great success. The show was recorded for a live album release which included such wonders as 'Throw Away Your Guns' and 'Foggy Road'. It was one that got away. I would have loved to have been part of things for that show. Damn.

As Christmas got nearer, I was headhunted by Martin Davies's housemate, Steve Shoreman, who had been tasked with finding a new glass collector for the Haçienda. I had been part of the furniture there, plus a lot of my friends were working there either as bar staff or on the crewing side of things, so it was the most natural thing in the world for me to join them. On 10th December, at a Grandmaster Flash and the Furious Five gig, I started work at the Haçienda.

I worked downstairs, mainly, in the Gay Traitor bar. Tony Wilson, a Cambridge graduate himself, had a long-standing fascination with the case of the Cambridge Five, a network of well-connected British spies, who in the 1960s were revealed to have been passing sensitive information to the USSR for decades. Photos of Anthony Blunt adorned the walls, he being the traitor that had inspired the whole theme. It was a sanctuary within the club for those in the know, and although it got good and busy for an hour or two on Saturdays or for well-attended gig nights, on the whole it was a refuge from the normal punters that, even on popular nights, did not show up in enough numbers to make the cavernous upstairs space look full.

As befitted its name, the Gay Traitor was a gay-friendly bar. Not exclusively gay, but open to fun-loving folk of all persuasions, and refreshingly free of any traces of the anti-straight feeling that could sometimes be felt in more hardcore clubs. Of course, every single day we opened was another massive two-fingered salute to the medieval demagogue James Anderton. Our very make up, staff-wise, proclaimed our intent. Bar manager, Gerry, was an older, wiser character, paternal, even. He was a well-known figure in Mancunian gay life, and was loved by many in the clubs and bars like Hero's and Bernard's Bar. He was a lovely man, living a quiet life in the sticks with his dog by day, and bringing his arched eyebrowed calm to the city's barflies by night. Me being straight was neither here nor there to him. He took me under his wing and encouraged me to bring in compilation tapes to play in the bar. On quieter nights it was a joy to hear the likes of Manicured Noise's 'Faith', or Wire's 'Outdoor Miner' ringing around the echoey walls.

My other cohorts were a long-standing couple, Glenn and Brendon. Again, I was treated as a loved colleague and friend by the two of them and by the fourth member of our little group, Karen Routledge. I loved working with these people. It was party-central, and so much fun to be at the epicentre. After the full-on mayhem of the Grandmaster Flash gig, and working flat out over Christmas and New Year, I had proved myself as a hard worker and somebody who could be relied on in a high-pressure situation. Many nights were poorly attended, but the weekend club nights would see an ocean of drinkers, five deep at the bar, screaming for attention and waving banknotes for hours at a time. It wasn't for everybody but it was clear that I was somebody who didn't mind getting stuck in, so I was invited to do more shifts, and was soon working every night.

Working at Berlin had made me nocturnal, and working in the Haçienda consolidated this pattern of upside down days, putting me in a different place to my housemates, who were doing their best to take their studies seriously. I would stay up for days on end, squeezing every last drop out of life, immersing myself in music, following my shifts at the Haçienda with some hardcore all-back-to-mine action. Even the most dedicated hedonist would have raised an eyebrow at my lifestyle at this time, and I felt that it would be best if I left Wendy, Jane and Julie to their own devices. We remained the best of friends, but I was on the hunt for a room or flat somewhere within a brisk walking distance of the city centre.

I didn't have to look very far. Calling in to Manchester Polytechnic on Oxford Road, I spied a noticeboard with 'Room to Let' advertisements on it. They were presumably aimed at students, but what the hell. I jotted down the first phone number I saw and arranged to go round for a look that evening.

The flat was in Arnesby Walk, which was built at the same time as Moss Side precinct and was of the same design as the flat in Gretney Walk from which I had watched the 1981 riots unfold. This was perfect for me, and even though I was probably not what my new landlords expected, I put my money down and moved in straight away, swinging a carrier bag containing my few possessions behind me. The couple who lived there, Nigel and Krysia, were happy enough to have someone renting their spare room, which was just doing nothing, and I was delighted to find out that they were also involved in music and had their own band.

The band in question had evolved from The Performing Ferret Band, who had moved from the south of England to relocate in Manchester. I was aware of them through John Peel, who had championed their lo-fi eccentricity and encouraged them the way he did with so many others. They had now changed their name to The Floating Adults. They held full-on band rehearsals, drum kit and all, in the living room of the flat. One time when they were setting up they introduced me to their bass player, Cathy Brooks. I shyly said 'Hello' and retreated to my room, letting the music wash over me for an hour or two before setting off for work.

Of course, the word 'work' is perhaps a little strong for what I was getting paid for. Weekend nights would see me running around like a mad thing, collecting glasses and generally keeping on top of things downstairs, but it was like a private party for me and my friends on the quieter midweek nights. I was one lucky bunny to be exposed to so much brilliant music whilst getting paid for the pleasure.

I wasn't always downstairs in the building's guts in the Gay Traitor. I would be deployed upstairs to work the live gigs, which was hardly a chore for me. I was spoiled by exposure to the best and most relevant acts that the UK (and the US) had to offer. From soundcheck to final encore, I was engrossed, making mental notes that would serve me well when it came time to make my own moves. I tried to organise my workload so that I could catch the whole set of whoever was playing, which I'd manage if it was quiet enough. In just my first few months I was there for Kurtis Blow, New Order, The Chameleons, Fad Gadget, Divine, JoBoxers, The Birthday Party, Virgin Prunes, Eurythmics and the third Smiths gig.

The Smiths had developed out of the band Freak Party, who I had jammed with at Decibelle Studios in Ancoats. They were singerless at that time, but I was impressed by Andy Rourke and Johnny Marr's musicality and wondered in which direction they would take things, particularly now that Funky Si Wolstencroft had been replaced by Mike Joyce. I had missed their first show supporting Blue Rondo à la Turk at The Ritz – organised by John Kennedy and featuring Dale Hibbert from Musicians' Collective band Bathroom Renovations on bass – but the week before the Haçienda show I had been dragged down to Manhattan Sound by my friend Martin to catch their second gig, this time with Andy Rourke on bass. I was fairly underwhelmed. Overloud guitar rang confusingly around the small underground space and singer Morrissey seemed wrapped up in himself, all closed eyes, somewhat reticent to connect with the audience, who were close enough to smell. The antics of the spare 'dancer' James Maker turned things into something of a private joke, and the set ended with some wild antics from Morrissey. Saying goodbye to Tony Wilson, and a few other Factory types who had been invited by Smiths manager Joe Moss to see what all the fuss was about, I jumped in a taxi and headed for wherever I could find some soul to balance things out.

The Haçienda had booked The Smiths and my old mates The Chameleons as part of a month-long programme of rising local bands on four consecutive Fridays. The first night featured The Kray Twins (featuring Bob Dickinson, briefly a member of Magazine, and co-writer of the brilliant 'Motorcade'). The second night saw a performance by James, with Gavan Whelan (who I knew from the Didsbury/Musicians' Collective set) on drums. The third show featured The Chameleons and Foreign Press. I was kept busy downstairs in the Gay Traitor for most of the night, but it was good to say hello to everybody at soundcheck time, and the very fact that they were playing here was testament to the progress they had been making.

Foreign Press had played with Vibrant Thigh at De Ville's, and their singer, Ralph, was a well-liked figure around town. They were, unfortunately, very standard and backward looking. I managed to catch a large part of The Chameleons set, and it was clear that all their hard work was starting to pay off. Opening with the anthemic 'Paper Tigers', they sounded tight and confident. Mark made a few jokes about the Haçienda's perceived 'coolness', saying that he should have had a haircut, which went down well with their fans. I could tell that they had started to attract something of a following, largely from the satellite towns to the north of Manchester, who identified with the band's anti-fashion approach and saw them as separate from the more critically acclaimed Factory groups. It was enjoyable, but I couldn't give their set my full attention, with work stuff to do. I was able to tell Dave and Mark how happy I was for them before they left, and it was genuinely true. I really was.

The Smiths played the final showcase night in a double header with Factory funk band 52nd Street. Once again, I was mainly downstairs and only popped up for a while. I hadn't been overly impressed the previous week at Manhattan Sound, and although they sounded more coherent and musical, their set largely washed over me. Tellingly though, both The Chameleons and The Smiths gigs were fuller than the other showcase nights, and seemed to attract a slightly different clientele than what we saw at the weekends. This crowd was made up of students and music lovers informed by John Peel and the weekly music press, as much in search of the next big thing as of a good night out with their friends.

My own personal musical education wasn't just limited to gig nights. From nine o'clock when the club opened, I'd have the pleasure of a (more or less) private set from Hewan Clarke, Greg Wilson or whoever was on that night. Even elder statesman of Manchester soul Mike Shaft had his day in the sun. These early hours were when Hewan would be slightly more open-minded in his approach, and I'd get to hear loads of new releases that revealed a real, but subtle change in the UK and US soul scene. Synthesisers had started to become more affordable to people and this change was reflected in the shape of the newer stuff that would creep into our consciousness. Records like Sharon Redd's 'Can You Handle It' and 'Beat The Street' on the Prelude label, especially when deconstructed by Shep Pettibone and thrown around this echoey former boat showroom. The emptiness of the sparsely populated nights would add another layer of weirdness to almost everything we heard. The sound of a record like D-Train's 'You're The One for Me' bouncing around and catching up with itself in a confusion of accidental delay was a revelation. Something was changing and these synth-tinged pop tunes filtered down, influencing many musicians of different genres. New Order, for instance, could see which way the wind was blowing very early on. Cabaret Voltaire also took notice and changed direction, incorporating cleaner sounds and the thud of the electro bass drum into their *Double Vision*-era body of work.

One of the perks of the job was a free taxi home, but as I lived so close, I'd invariably use it to dive off elsewhere, to an impromptu party or to visit my friend Martin in Didsbury, who had the same nocturnal habits as me and would always be up for an all-night session. Although he didn't work in any particular club, he took his DJing seriously, and was still spending a king's ransom on records each week. All-nighters with Martin were a real education and complemented the rest of my musical life perfectly.

Most of the staff at the club had other things going on. I would walk home sometimes with Pete, a diminutive, somewhat eccentric character from Salisbury, who was working on his first novel. He lived alone in a massive four-bedroomed flat in Charles Barry Crescent, using only one room, and we would plan our respective futures, sure of good fortune. People like Pete and Stirling and Sean and a whole collection of earnest and optimistic young artists and musicians were, like me, financing their first artistic baby steps by working at the Haçienda. I enjoyed being part of it all, and the work wasn't particularly difficult.

I would much rather be at work, to be perfectly honest, taking in the music and spending time with my co-workers than in my tiny room in Arnesby Walk. Once again, it proved too difficult to share a flat with people who kept totally different hours to me, and before long I was sat in front of another housing officer, signing up for a two-bedroom flat just for myself. My new place was on Boundary Lane in Hulme, opposite the infamous Salmon cabs. A twenty-four hour taxi place on the face of it, it also housed the only all-night shop for miles, where, if you were known, you could pick up decent weed and out-of-hours alcohol, along with the chocolate and Rizla papers you had originally come in for. An unremarkable-looking door led to a gambling room, and in this dangerous atmosphere, with the beautiful aroma of curry goat or rice and peas filling the air, a different side of life existed. I met all kinds of people there, night dwellers all. People like me, having finished for the night at one club or another in town, drug dealers, working girls, and the gum-chewing legions of speed-fuelled kids, up all night in search of a party. Any old party.

Music-wise, I had been feeling ready to get back in the saddle for some time, and I had got to know one of my fellow glass collectors quite well over the quieter periods when there was little to do except talk music and make plans. His name was Colin Seddon, and he was part of Biting Tongues, a well-respected jazz-influenced outfit that had been on my radar for several years. They had recorded an album for Richard Boon's New Hormones label although financial problems meant its eventual release was via another label, Paragon. The album, *Libreville*, was a fascinating, tribal-sounding, left-field affair. Clever horn arrangements and strange noises weaved in and out of a fluid and sometimes complicated rhythm section. I was put in mind of the kind of things coming out of Bristol at this time.

By pure chance Biting Tongues were on the lookout for a new bass player and Colin invited me for an audition. I was excited by the proposition. I had a lot of time for the work of The Pop Group and Maximum Joy, and it felt to me that Biting Tongues were mining a similar seam. My frequent chats with Colin had revealed him to have a wide and eclectic taste in music, and he was a nice guy, too. Ludus were very much known to him, as both bands operated from within a kind of South Manchester circle of intelligent musicians that had taken root in the wasteland cleared by punk all that time ago, and I think that it was my Ludus connection that had got me invited.

The audition was important to me so I spent some time preparing for it, getting used to the tape of *Libreville* I had been given. Songs like 'First Use All The G's' and 'Aair Care' were groove-based, but you could tell that these people could really play. Several of the tracks were in unusual time signatures and displayed a jazzy sensibility that was somewhat alien to what I had been doing with Karl Burns and Lee Pickering, for instance, so I was nervous when I turned up at Colin's flat in Didsbury one Sunday afternoon. I was, if truth be told, a little worse for wear, having worked at the Haçienda the night before and stayed up all night practising until the morning. As a result, I may have tried a little too hard to impress. I could feel myself adding little frills and stylistic tricks that cluttered up the fluidity of the songs. Colin, ever the gentleman, let me down gently, and we continued to be friends and co-workers, just as before.

Similar to when I was let go by Ludus, the experience of trying out for Biting Tongues had the effect of inching me closer to making music under my own control. I was fired up again, and I would spend hours long into the early morning playing guitar, and generally being the world's worst neighbour (again). Gradually, these sessions started to produce results. In what felt like no time at all, I had dusted off the cobwebs and started to construct songs again.

16: Soul Open

I could hardly believe it when I was told that my beloved Curtis Mayfield was to appear at the Haçienda. I wasted no time in booking the night off. I would normally watch live acts from the side of the stage, or from the mixing desk, but for this gig I just wanted to be part of the crowd, with no distractions. I wanted to look Curtis Mayfield in the eye while he sang to me.

I stood in the crowd as the anticipation built waiting for the great man to take to the stage. The tiny red and green standby lights on the group's equipment told us that we didn't have long to wait and then bang, they were there. The first thing that struck me was the size and make-up of the band. For all my love of the great soul artists, I hadn't seen many up to this point. I had been hungrily devouring live music for years now but had yet to experience anything like this. There were horns, extra vocals, percussion and, centre stage, small in stature but carrying all the warmth and authority of a trusted friend, stood Curtis Mayfield! The whole place erupted in a wave of love and gratitude, and we were off.

The band included Mayfield's own son amongst their number and was as tight and proficient as you would expect. I felt like I was in the presence of greatness. Like every other person there, I was convinced Curtis was singing to me, and me alone. I had expected a run through of his life's work, and was always going to enjoy hearing the big hits, what I was less prepared for, however, was the sheer charisma and believability of the man.

Caught in the beam of two spotlights that bounced off the polished metal parts of his guitar, he came across as an unassuming, avuncular figure. He seemed like an elder statesman from an earlier, purer time, even though he was only in his early forties. His trademark smooth falsetto was every bit as compelling as when I had first heard his unmistakable voice on those early Impressions records, and if anybody had any doubts, they were gone within seconds of hearing him sing.

'People Get Ready' and 'It's All Right' have their own place in people's hearts, but for me, the absolute highlight of the night was a sprawling, extended 'Move On Up'. Percussion led and taken at pace, disciplined horns punched and punctuated Mayfield's beautiful and impassioned lead vocal, high pitched and trustable. Frenzied congas took the song away from the relentless backbeat and brought it back again just when it seemed to melt into something else entirely. Fifteen, perhaps twenty minutes went by, I was so wrapped up in the song that time had no meaning. Suddenly, in mid-flight, it was over as abruptly as it had begun. There was a split second of silence that followed the song's ending, followed by the roar of one-and-a-half thousand voices, elevated and filled with joy. Wonderful.

I have always had love for a wide range of musical styles. In fact, spending too much time on one sends me running towards another. Taking some Chi-Lites or Chairmen of the Board to balance out the effects of Einstürzende Neubauten or Crass. Seeking refuge in the sweet Dennis Bovell-produced Lover's Rock of Janet Kay, or the sublime vocals of Johnny Nash or Ken Boothe when my head has had its fill of independent angst. Everything counts, if it's real. Everything.

Soul is in the ear of the beholder, and you can find it anywhere and everywhere. To hear another person being carried away beyond all caring, transported by the power of music to a pure and special place, is one of the most fulfilling experiences there is. It enters your heart and makes it sing. It makes it so that nothing else is good enough. Make me cry, or stay on the pile. These are stupid, trivial times.

It may have been a reaction to being bombarded with false emotion in the Haçienda, night after night, as the world was filled with identikit dance tunes trying to emulate the early breakthrough of UK and US electro, but something didn't sit right with me. I needed more truth, more honesty, more wild abandon and, most of all, more songs. I wasn't alone in this yearning. I had become friendly with a fellow Haçienda worker called Aubrey, and would go back to his Hulme crescent flat after work and have my ears opened to the real beauty of Northern soul.

Aubrey was a bright and upful individual, originally from Bury, who had cared passionately about music in the same way as me for most of his life. He was the driving force behind the Bury fanzine *Violent Times*, which was produced in small numbers but mixed music, art and thoughts on literature and society into a readable and cohesive whole. Like me, Aubrey's musical tastes were spread across genres and it became a matter of pride for us to introduce each other to new things that would blow the other one's head off. I brought the reggae and funk to the table, and he would scour the all-nighters for obscure Northern surprises, head stuck in the wooden record boxes that ringed the pop-up events he attended in the Lancashire satellite towns where soul was king, and always will be.

We would work at the club from eight until about three in the morning, then follow this up with a ritual cleansing session, washing out the club tunes with the holiest and most incandescent soul we could find. Aubrey would sellotape wads of tissue paper around both knees and spread talcum powder on the tiled floor of his flat to make for smoother slides and never-ending turns as song-based masterpieces took me from zero to the highest heights in the space of two minutes or so. 'Panic' by Reparata and the Delrons, 'Your Autumn of Tomorrow' by The Crow, 'Turnin' My Heartbeat Up' by The M.V.P.'s, we hammered the life out of anything that made us love it. It wasn't just the obscurities, we also showed love to some of the truly brilliant records that crossed over to mainstream appeal. 'Here I Go Again' by Archie Bell & The Drells, or Judy Street's 'What' would nestle amongst Aubrey's white label obscurities. The song was everything.

I learnt so much during these sessions about how to express myself in the space of a few minutes: trimming songs down to their component parts, leaving only those sections that actually took the listener somewhere. My groundwork in the youth clubs of Langley had given me the vocabulary and listening skills to really feel and understand the songwriter's craft, and I immersed myself in the pain and unrequited love pouring out of these wonderful records, a willing victim, thrown into feeling every emotion felt by these genius songwriters, and left heartbroken and spent by singer after brilliant singer.

Things got a bit much for Aubrey at his shared flat. His two flatmates, Frankie and Teresa, both worked at the Haçienda themselves and kept the same upside-down hours, but it was our all-night mayhem that finally tipped the scales. We decided that it would be in everybody's best interests (apart from my neighbours!) that Aubrey moved in with me at the Boundary Lane flat. What seemed like fifteen million boxes of brilliant records moved in with him, and we wasted no time in filling the previously placid flatblock with music.

We had so much in common, and not just extremist tunes. I developed a love for BBC Radio 4, falling in and out of sleep with the reassuring dulcet tones of the presenter's standard received English in the background. I would take in odd facts in my sleep and not know how I came by them, really obscure stuff like Benin's main export (cotton and cashew nuts) or Idi Amin's fourth wife (Nalongo Madina). Knowledge is power, they say. We both had a deep love of reading, too, and after staying up all night, we would scour Manchester's many second-hand shops, coming back laden with vinyl and paperbacks to devour at will. Our tastes in literature were similar but different, and it was good to turn each other on to our respective favourite things. Kurt Vonnegut, John Pilger, Anthony Burgess and, especially, William Burroughs.

Aubrey had one foot in the dark and mysterious world of Throbbing Gristle, having been present at some of the group's most incendiary performances. Deliberately hard work, their confrontational and sonically torturous approach led many to see them as pretentious and superficial, but when they resonated with people, they really resonated. Their imprint, and the impact of Genesis P-Orridge's project Psychic TV, has informed and helped shape the artistic mindset of many of those exposed to it all, and Aubrey was very much a case in point. I was less convinced myself, but had been at the Haçienda for the Psychic TV 'Final Academy' and can testify to the overwhelming weirdness of the whole event and its effect on those that opened themselves to it. The strangeness of Burroughs and John Giorno performing that night was infectious.

This mixture of all things made for an interesting balance around the flat. For every bouncing Northern soul floorfiller, there would be a ritualistic marimba workout by Arthur Lyman, for every Harold Melvin & the Blue Notes B-side, a Monte Cazazza dirge. I would hole up in my room, working my way through *Cities of the Red Night* as strange and unsettling sounds drifted in, educating and frightening me in equal measure.

Our flat became a party-central for various members of Haçienda staff and hangers-on. After the club closed, they would head for ours to debrief with something less repetitive and weirder than the music we had been hearing at work. Early Cabaret Voltaire, Cupol, or the head curdling mischief of The Residents would balance out Eno's ambient works, or the electronic/classical collisions of Tomita or Wendy Carlos. All human life was here, somewhere or other. These were unusual times for everyone. It felt like robbery to work until the early hours and not have any time for your own fun, so a kind of alternative scene evolved for us all, aided and abetted by premium quality fast drugs.

In the midst of all this madness, I started to crystallise my ideas and shape the impact of what was going on around me into something more articulate. For all my interest in the avant-garde, it was songs that did it for me – well-crafted songwriting, from Motown to Studio One, and I was, by now, aching to express myself in words and music. I was surrounded by creative people, and had a strong sense of 'now is the time'. I worked hard on my lyrics, and several songs started to emerge.

My friend Anthony Behrendt was in the process of setting up a studio in Robert Adam Crescent, to be called Jerusalem. At this early stage it was pretty basic, recording onto a four-track Portastudio, but he had a good sized mixing desk which meant that a decent drum sound was achievable. I began to think that his whole set-up could help me with what I wanted to do. In addition to this, I had met up with Lee and Karl there. We started seeing each other a lot at the Haçienda, where everybody bumped into everybody, which led us to spending time together again. Any tension that had come between us quickly evaporated as we enjoyed the start of a new scene springing up around Jerusalem.

Lee had got more confident as a bass player and had been making his own Portastudio recordings at his flat. One tune called 'Blood Drinkers' featured my flatmate Aubrey on ghostly, impromptu vocals, and Karl out of his comfort zone on guitar. As a statement of intent, it worked excellently, always threatening to come into sharp focus, but retreating into a mysterious blur as quickly as it had materialised.

The Fall's driver Henry Cowell and Karl would inhabit Lee's Moss Side flat, bringing extra chaos to an already chaotic situation. We were all fairly hardcore, but these two were Olympic standard. It was a wonder that anything creative could ever come out of such extremist hedonism, but somehow it did. I witnessed The Fall's guitarist Craig Scanlon and bassist Steve Hanley spend an afternoon with Karl, knocking song ideas into shape. This was a special enough occasion, as The Fall rarely rehearsed in a traditional manner, but as the spidery guitar parts of 'Garden' filtered through the thin walls, I knew that something special was afoot. Even just keeping time without a drum kit, Karl's brilliance shone through, and to hear the early stages of this and the superb 'Smile' was mesmerizing.

A few weeks later, I was out in town with Lee and Henry, having afternoon drinks in a downstairs bar called Horts in St. Ann's Square. I always carried my small address book with me, and for some reason got a spontaneous urge to ring the nursing home my dad was in for an update. I left Lee and Henry drinking and made my way to the phone boxes near to the Hidden Gem church, armed with some ten pence pieces. After establishing that I was his son, I was told that he had died nearly a year before, and that without any contact details for me, there was no way of letting me know.

As the initial shock subsided, I was surprised by how untouched and numb I felt by this revelation. I had made my peace with him when I had visited him in the hospital a few years earlier, but, living as I did, one step removed from my deepest feelings, the news of his death just bounced off me.

Returning to Horts bar, I told Lee and Henry, but played it down somewhat, saying that, 'We were never that close anyway.' In some senses, that was true, but in my own mind, I knew that there was more to it than that. I had spent a large part of my life believing that he had died when I was a child, and the brief period of us living together had ended in violence and pain. Nevertheless, he was my father. I left my friends in town, and made my way home with mixed-up thoughts about my dad bouncing around in my head. I was now the orphan that I had always believed myself to be.

A new glass collector had started at the Haçienda called Mike Hutton. I'd known him by sight for quite a while, having spotted him at gigs and around Hulme. He lived in the flats on Bonsall Street with his dog, Zero, a beautiful Dalmatian, and like me, had been attending musical events and clubs for years despite being far too young to be allowed in officially. Tony Wilson had given him a note to show to the Russell Club doormen, explaining that Mike, despite his baby face, was old enough to be admitted. Now Mike was working for Tony in his club, alongside me and several of the original Factory crowd.

We all took to Mike, and before long he was part of our lives. The time was right for several artistic worlds to collide, and in Hulme we were given the space and freedom to do pretty well what we wanted. Mike's flat was a work of art in itself, with banks of television sets tuned to nothingness, illuminating an array of found street objects and garish, naive paintings. He had a taste for the same kind of weirdness as Lee and Karl, and we would lose hours and days, our senses sharpened by fierce uppers and black microdot acid, immersed in The Residents' *Third Reich and Roll* album or their 'Duck Stab' EP and even more left-field fare.

Mike's girlfriend, Jackie, shared a flat in William Kent Crescent with a clothes designer and fashion graduate called Catherine. She was from Hazel Grove, near Stockport, and had known some of the more interesting people that had been part of that town's punk and post-punk scene, like Paul Morley and Joanne Whalley, whose job I had taken over several years earlier at Roxy.

Catherine was small, with striking, cyclamen-dyed hair, and, being skilled in that direction, she used to make her own clothes, which gave her a look all of her own; plain fabrics and pencil skirts of an almost wartime simplicity. She was something of a self-contained unit, like me, although her friendship with her next-door neighbour, Michelle, would see her go out with Michelle's wider group of friends to Berlin, the club where I used to work. She had even ended up going on a scooter run with them but found the laddishness not to her liking.

I started to visit Catherine as a friend, and, as ever, music was at the heart of everything. We bonded over a shared appreciation of the better guitar-based music around at the time, stuff like Echo & the Bunnymen, The Comsat Angels and The Psychedelic Furs, and she had a good ear for decent US soul and funk, arrived at, like many, by hearing David Bowie's *Young Americans* and *Station To Station*, then working backwards.

Hulme had its own arthouse cinema, The Aaben, something of a trailblazer, and the only place to see films outside the mainstream at this point, and we'd go there to watch classics like *The Boys From Brazil* and *The Tin Drum*, getting closer, but all the time keeping our growing relationship under wraps. It wasn't anybody else's business, but the amount of time I was spending at Catherine's flat must have made things obvious to our friends if they had given it any thought.

We saw a lot of Michelle next door. Once again, we had friends in common, in particular Lita Hira from Spurtz and Stockholm Monsters. Her boyfriend, Ian Brown, was part of a scooter-loving crowd who frequented Berlin and other city centre hangouts. We got on well, the two of us being informed and kick-started by punk, and I already knew some of his other friends, (Skinhead) Rob Powell and Ste Cresser.

I kept my Boundary Lane flat on, but spending more time at Catherine's turned in to moving in there, to all extents and purposes. By now, we had 'gone public' and settled into a fairly intense period where it was just the two of us. We'd go out to the local White Horse pub or to clubs in town, but were always together, even in a crowd.

Catherine's civilising influence was rubbing off on me. With no experience in such matters, I marvelled as she brought her eye for taste to the flat. Jackie had moved into Mike Hutton's flat by now, and I got involved in re-decorating Catherine's place with her, picking paint colours and having them mixed in a shop, a totally new experience for me. It was good to be not too crazy for once.

We'd get visits from Dave Fielding and his girlfriend, Julie. He had moved to Cheetham Hill, and although Hulme scared him, he'd brave the concrete to come and see me. It was good to show him that I was living a more stable lifestyle. The Chameleons were taking off in a massive way by now, especially in the US, and Dave was frequently away, but the four of us had some magical days together. We trekked over to Alexandra Park for the Moss Side Carnival to see our friend, Kwasi, who was performing with Sword of Jah Mouth, one of Manchester's rising reggae bands. They were dark, religious and mournful, and I was reminded of the impact that Misty In Roots had on me the first time I saw them at Deeply Vale. As their set progressed, local youths started to move en masse through the crowd, hitting people and snatching bags. Even the weather became moody as the whole carnival atmosphere evaporated. I felt it myself, but Dave took it to heart, reinforcing his fear of Hulme and Moss Side even further.

Next door to Catherine, plans were underway for Michelle's 21st birthday party. I helped Ian and Skinhead Rob move some furniture into Catherine's in the daytime, and afterwards, we flopped down on the settee for a hard-earned rest. I hadn't known Ian for very long. He worked for the DHSS, and had only just moved, semi-officially into Michelle's. I think that his crowd saw Haçienda workers as somewhat aloof, but we got on fine, and had some musical taste in common, although I was neither here nor there about Generation X, who Ian absolutely loved.

Once the party was in full flight, Catherine and I were lucky enough to have a place of respite next door, and would take occasional breaks from the action to recharge our batteries, pacing ourselves. It was just as well, as the music was full on from minute one. Northern soul, ska and punk tunes shook the prefab flats, and to be honest, it sounded just as loud in Catherine's flat.

Much later, after the clubs had shut, the party's attendance was swelled by well-meaning gatecrashers of every description, and things were in full swing. Ian and Skinhead Rob sauntered over to me.

'Eh, Mark. Do you know where we can get some draw from?'

It seemed important and, to Ian and Rob, it was. Soul legend Geno Washington, in Manchester to perform, had been dragged down to Hulme post-show by a friend of Ian's who was part of Geno's road crew. He wanted to buy some weed.

'The Front, Ian...' I replied. I referred to the row of shops in the shadow of the Harp lager brewery on Princess Road, just along from the Nile and Reno clubs.

After asking almost everybody else, a mission was embarked upon, and within the half hour, Mr Washington had what he wanted, and Hulme's reputation as a den of iniquity remained intact.

The stabilising influence of having somebody in my life made for a productive time, music-wise. I was writing in a more coherent and fluid manner, and unlike other previous bursts of activity, I was writing some songs I was feeling happy with. Songs like 'Play Street', 'Snapper' and 'Deny It' started to emerge and moved me that little bit nearer to formulating some kind of a plan on the music front. I had been enjoying working at the Haçienda, but despite being immersed in music of all kinds nearly every night of the week, I wasn't getting any nearer to where I wanted to be. For a start, I was spending as much as I earned on speed to get me in the right frame of mind to do the job in the first place, and nobody could keep up such an unsustainable lifestyle for long. Something had to change so that I could find my way back on the right path. Music was calling me and I knew in my heart of hearts that it was time for a job change. I had grown tired of the triviality and superficiality of club life, and it was high time I put some proper work into expressing myself and making the music that I knew was inside. I hatched a plan.

Leaving the Haçienda behind, I took a job in a place called Paramount Book Exchange in the Shudehill area of Manchester. The shop operated under a wide remit. Students would sell textbooks there, and it was well known that the owner, Paul, would buy anything, no questions asked which meant that the most brazen of the city's shoplifting community would be in many times per week with a wide and diverse collection of newly released hardbacks, safe in the knowledge that they would receive hard cash for whatever they brought in. Not much hard cash, to be fair, as my employer would pay as little as possible for something he could later re-sell for decent money. He would encourage widows to bring their late husband's book collections down, only to offer a small amount, knowing that a grieving person would be in no position to drive any kind of a hard bargain. I would see him in these situations, offering, say, twenty or thirty pounds for a complete set of the *Encyclopedia Britannica*, worth about a thousand, as the late owner's wife would stand wet-eyed at how life had turned out.

Chief Constable James Anderton's holy war on the gay community included bookshops, which meant the world of gay literature and magazines was, to some extent, covert and secretive. Paramount became known amongst the community as a place where gay and trans magazines could be quietly obtained. Paul would hike the price up by many hundred percent, knowing that they were nearly impossible to obtain discretely anywhere else. 'Contact' magazines were another of his many rackets; extracting twelve pounds out of desperate and lonely customers in exchange for a photocopied fanzine style booklet, all blacked-out eyes and lovelessness, like an advert-splattered London phone box in book form.

The main person being exploited, however, was most certainly me. I would work from seven in the morning until seven at night, with no dinner break. The owner would buy a round of sandwiches for us, but this was so that the work didn't have to stop for anything as unproductive as a lunch hour. These marathon shifts were possible because we could claim benefit while we worked there. We'd take the morning off to sign on.

I would return home dusty and dishevelled, and deeply disappointed with the slimy world I was forced to inhabit. I took solace from the fact that I was not in it for the long haul; I had started this job with a clear motive in mind. I intended to work there until I had saved enough money to record the latest batch of songs that I had been writing. I would pay for everything myself, and be in total control of how things were shaped. This, I felt, would be the way forward.

17: The Battle Of Whitworth Street West

Anthony Behrendt's Jerusalem studio was based at 127 Robert Adam Crescent. Anthony was just one of a number of forward-thinking people prepared to put these large, multi-roomed dwellings to another use. The flats lent themselves admirably to conversion to small-scale recording studios, the chipboard inner walls were easy to cut and shape, and the insertion of a window between the control room and the recording room was relatively simple to achieve. The smaller bedrooms proved ideal as isolated vocal booths, or sterile rooms for placing speakers and to record guitar parts ambiently at differing distances to create a textured and complex mesh. The main benefit of these crescent flats, though, was that you could make as much noise as you wanted at more or less any time of day or night.

We recorded through a mixing desk onto a Tascam 4-track Portastudio. Judicious use of bouncing down tracks would open up this seemingly limited set-up, and we were able to build things up, layering multiple vocal lines and thickening guitar parts, simply by planning ahead and working out how to get the most of the limited number of tracks available to us. Anthony worked out how to create backwards guitar parts by turning the tape over and counting backwards from the place the chord needed to be. As Portastudios used standard cassette tapes, this was something of an imprecise science, nevertheless, it led to a very human sound, not tied metronomically to any kind of click track, but free, and impossible to do the same way twice. This technique taught me to think differently about the space within my songs.

I had been working hard to amass enough money to pay Anthony properly and had a firm plan of action. I would play drums myself and invite Lee down to play bass on some songs that I had been kicking into shape over the preceding months. I would then layer guitars, vocals and extraneous noises over the top, stretching Anthony's four tracks into many more. Each overdub would lead to a slight depreciation in sound quality, but I was all in favour of this, and welcomed the abrasive, lo-fi edge that working at ground level brought to the music. The UK music scene was awash with polished, opportunistic wannabees, desperate to achieve chart success. Clean was everywhere, and I was happy to stand against the likes of Aztec Camera and Frankie Goes To Hollywood, supplying a gritty truth to counter the fiction and soulless drivel being lionised almost everywhere else.

We worked fast and before long we had versions of 'Deny It', 'On The Beach' and an instrumental called 'Basketcase'. Although these songs were to live and die in a very short time, some techniques that we chanced upon in making them would turn out to be very useful. For example, on 'Deny It' I employed a 'bending all the strings at once' trick, born out of wanting to use tremolo effects without having a tremolo arm on my guitar. Necessity really is the mother of invention.

I had played everything except bass on these tunes, but they had gone so well that we decided to take things up a notch. We set out to assemble a band, and for this we needed a drummer. Karl, although a large part of our lives socially, was fully committed to being part of The Fall through one of their most productive and exciting periods thus far. We needed a drummer with the same kind of impact and skill, and luckily, Lee knew the very person. Guy Ainsworth had a hard-hitting and rigid style, but with the ability and assuredness to fill the gaps between the beats with well thought out fills. Guy had many strings to his bow, he'd worked as a model and at this point was running his own screen-printing business as well as being a busy musician. He lived in Didsbury. I liked him from the very first minute I met him, and in no time at all, we had gelled as a unit and were ready to record some more of our songs, once again at Anthony's.

Lyrically, I seemed to have had a lot to get out of my system. New songs like 'Aim For The Face' found me looking back over my turbulent past, trying to make sense of the cause and effect nature of violence and a broken childhood.

>   Mouth pour crap like rain
>   I heard it again today

> We live in a dangerous age
> And some of us have grown up strange
> Aim for the face!
>
> Children play
> Educational games
> That's how the foundations are laid
> Behave how your parents behave
> How your parents behave
> How your parents behave
> Aim for the Face!

Built over a drum and vocal introduction, this, and several of the songs screamed with unresolved pain. Having found a voice, it was as if there was a backlog of hurt to get out of my system. Lee and Guy made for a rock-solid rhythm section, which left me the freedom to express myself honestly and truthfully for the first time in a long time. It felt good, and the more we played together, the better we got. We approached Anthony and began a phase of recording that would produce, amongst other things, 'Yonkers'.

The song itself had started life as a Portastudio recording that Lee had made at his flat in Didsbury which featured his bass playing pushed heavily to the foreground. His writing style was refreshingly unlike any other I had encountered, and, having taught himself song structure, was free of the traps that over-taught musicians were prone to fall into. Vocal-less, it featured disembodied American voices taken from a US religious radio show, cut up and reassembled into a scary collage. I added spooky tremolo guitar parts over Guy's forceful, strident drum patterns. When we played it, the taped radio voices would appear at slightly different places each time, which would make for a tense and human feel, and would frequently catch me out. It all added to the weirdness.

Emboldened by good reactions to our first recordings, it was time to play live. Anthony was doing the sound for a benefit night in aid of the striking miners, and he invited us to play at it. The miners were in the middle of the biggest and most important political action to have happened in my lifetime; their strike was about more than just a collision between conflicting economic beliefs, it was all-out war, waged upon a series of communities and the industry that kept them alive. Margaret Thatcher and her Conservative government had put themselves up against the power of the unions in an ideological fight to the death, and the implications for all of us were truly dire. It was a no-brainer for us to be part of the fight, and an honour to be invited. In addition, the benefit was to take place at Manchester's Lesser Free Trade Hall. It was the Sex Pistols historic appearance there that had kicked the Mancunian punk scene into existence back in 1976. Spiritually, it felt the perfect venue for a band like ours to make our debut. In many ways, we were the musical and cultural descendants of the people who had their minds blown that night.

We arrived in the late afternoon, set up and soundchecked, with Anthony swapping his studio head for a stint as our live engineer. Anthony really understood where we were coming from. Never one to shy away from extremism, he accentuated the weirder aspects of our sound, making a meal of Lee's tape inserts, and it was looking good for the actual performance later in the evening. Unluckily for us, the event ran late, with speeches from activists and striking miners from Agecroft Colliery taking up all of the allotted time so we never got to play that night, which was a shame, as we sounded great in soundcheck and were more than ready to add to this beautiful building's rich history. We threw what money we had into the buckets that were being passed round and chalked the whole thing down to experience.

Our actual live debut was just around the corner though. Anthony had the idea of a day-long mini festival, partly to raise funds for his new studio, and partly to act as a showcase for some of the bands that had recorded there. There was a healthy scene springing up, with bands like Cry I, Fistfunk, My American Wife and ourselves gravitating towards Robert Adam Crescent as Jerusalem began to take shape.

The idea was that ten bands would play two songs each at the Tropicana, a garish, plastic palm tree-strewn dance club off Oxford Road. Largely known as a rather cheesy disco with all the trimmings, it wasn't used much for live music. I'd certainly never been there before.

We'd kept the name Dub Sex almost unconsciously. There were no shortlists or anything. It was short and sharp and felt right, and with both me and Lee involved, it seemed like something of a continuation from the promising start we had made with Karl a few years earlier.

We had cheekily prepared a three-song medley of 'Aim For The Face', 'Play Street' and 'On The Beach', and although we were only going to be playing for less than ten minutes, it became the most important thing on earth to me. I found myself physically affected sometimes when I remembered that it was coming up. Half panic attack and half pure joy. We'd rehearse at Anthony's in the daytimes, and make it our business to go out spreading the word and selling the twenty or so tickets that each band got instead of a fee. It felt good to be part of something born at ground level in Hulme.

The day came, and as everyone was sharing the same backline, there was minimal carrying and lifting. We taxied it to Lee's flat to prepare mentally away from the multi-band mayhem, arriving minutes before we were due to go on, wired and oblivious to everything else.

Guy's drum intro to 'Aim For The Face' started, all tension and tightly controlled hi-hats, and blinking like a rabbit in headlights, I sang my first line as the singer of Dub Sex.

It was over as soon as it had begun. No talking between songs, no thank yous, no nothing. There was a sharp intake of breath as our last song came to an abrupt stop, and we were gone.

In the Tropicana dressing room, I slumped onto a settee, still wearing my guitar, now minus two strings. I had only been on stage for eight minutes or so, but I was soaked to the bone.

The door burst open. It was blond Mikey Eastwood, from Factory band Lavolta Lakota, who was grinning from ear to ear in a most un-Factorylike way.

'Fucking 'ell, Mark! You're a bit of a dark horse, aren't you?'

It felt great.

We followed up our Tropicana debut with another gig organised by Anthony, this time at the Sir Henry Royce pub in Hulme. Normally filled with loud domino players from Hulme's West Indian community,

Anthony had talked the landlord into letting him put on local bands on one of the quieter weekday nights. We had expanded the set a little, adding two newer songs, 'Snapper' and 'Kristallnacht', but I ended up using an unfamiliar guitar, borrowed from Metal Monkey Machine, who were sharing the bill with us. It was altogether too bassy and rocky for my style, and I came away feeling frustrated by the whole experience. Equipment was a problem for me as my lifestyle and low income meant I was always desperately poor.

We were friends with an energetic young chap called Barry Sutton. Barry was a Fall obsessive (and sometime roadie) from Liverpool, and would see the band as often as he could, travelling around the North West and frequently making the trip to Manchester to catch them in their home environment. It was on one of these jaunts that he'd ended up at Lee's flat, and heard the music that we'd been making.

Barry was quite a face around Liverpool, and told us of a forthcoming cassette compilation being put together by Jeremy Lewis of Inevitable Records, home of Wah! Heat and It's Immaterial. He said he'd pass our tape on and put in a good word for us. Several weeks later, Lee was contacted by the label with the good news that our track 'Yonkers' was to be included on *Two Points To Tonka*, on an offshoot of theirs called Son of Inevitable, alongside such wonders as 'Decimal Food' by Glam Tardis and 'Stereo Bad Printing' by Barry's own unit, the wonderfully named Marshmallow Overcoat.

It was an inauspicious start, but we all felt good about it. We decided that being associated with a non-Manchester label added an extra layer of intrigue, and to celebrate, Guy screen printed a small run of t-shirts, the first to ever feature the Dub Sex name. We definitely existed now.

Unfortunately, while I was making good progress with the music, my personal life had become chaotic and fractured. Hulme had its benefits in a lot of ways, easy access to rehearsal space and the possibility of making noise amongst them, but the downside of all that was that anybody living there was surrounded by an all-pervading drug culture. This was, of course, true of many neglected working-class estates, but Hulme, having being left to its own devices for so long, had attracted dealers and customers from everywhere. It became easier to obtain psychoactive chemicals than it was to buy a bottle of milk. My predilection for amphetamines meant that I was a valued client for many of the Hulme dealers, who would open avenues of credit that kept me ensnared.

To be fair, I was a willing victim, and counted these people as my friends. It was just the way things were. I blame nobody for anything, though my excesses were driving a wedge between me and my band. I would stay awake for days, and turn up for practises in a less than inspirational state. I would never have any money, and would try to operate as a musician with a series of borrowed guitars, stretching the patience of all who knew me, including Lee and Guy, who were growing sick of me turning up unprepared, with no instrument to play.

Things had not been right between Catherine and me either. We had been living an intense lifestyle, just the two of us, for some time now, and as my musical life grew I was spending more time with Lee and Guy, and at Anthony's studio. Catherine, on the other hand, had very little with which to fill her time and the distance between us grew bigger.

I didn't exactly help things by frequently disappearing to Langley whenever I had any money, to join my North Manchester friends in weekend-long sessions. I would try to involve Catherine at first, bringing her along and encouraging her to join us in our copious drug use, but this misguided attempt at inclusion backfired badly. It was the worst possible thing for her already fragile mental state.

Things came to a head after a particularly stretched weekend when Catherine, hallucinating after days of sleep deprivation, entered an unreachable place and ended up hitting me across the back of my head with a half-full bottle of Ben Shaws cream soda. Even at this point, shell-shocked and bleeding profusely, I was more concerned for Catherine than I was for myself. It was all my fault that her mental health had got into such a terrible mess, and I knew that there was no way back from here for us.

After a taxi ride to Manchester Royal Infirmary, I found myself lying on my front, still unable to shut up, a mixture of nerves and chemicals.

'How long have you been a doctor, then? Do you like Manchester?'

Trivialities poured out of me as I wriggled, hampering all attempts to stitch me up. I must have been a nightmare patient.

Catherine gave up her flat shortly afterwards and moved back into her mother's house in Hazel Grove. I forgave her instantly and totally for her violent moment, understanding that it was our lifestyle that had led us there. We both didn't want to be together any more. Things had been like that for a long time, if we were to be honest. We went our separate ways. Once again, I put it down to experience.

Our friend Tommy Richardson had taken an interest in what we were doing ever since we had started using Jerusalem to rehearse. He DJ'd an 'alternative' night at Wigan Pier, and at De Ville's, where he played more soulful fare, like Evelyn King and Phyllis Nelson. He also lived opposite the newly opened International Club, and knowing the promoter Roger Eagle, had alerted us to the possibility of getting a gig there. Roger had made a success of Eric's club in Liverpool, during the punk years, and even earlier had been a pioneer here in Manchester, building up a reputation as a Northern soul DJ at The Twisted Wheel, and the freakier Magic Village. He had brought the likes of John Lee Hooker, Captain Beefheart and Ann Peebles to Manchester.

Roger agreed to put us on with Levellers, a new band containing Mike Fawcett, one of the late-night visitors to my first Hulme flat with Lady Sarah. The gig was sparsely attended, being a midweek local band thing, but it gave us an opportunity to add a couple of songs, including 'Basketcase', to our still short set. I was once again plagued with equipment problems, which stretched the patience of my bandmates that little bit more. My constant poverty – caused, of course, by my own lifestyle – meant that I had no spare guitar, and when accidents occurred, like string breakages, I would have no backup plan. On this occasion, I made a meal of things, becoming even more violent with my instrument, covering up my wildly out of tune guitar by scraping it against the microphone stand, concentrating more on performing as a singer. The extra showmanship paid off, and several audience members complimented us on our anger and verve, but the writing was definitely on the wall.

Back at Tommy's, a less than serious game of Risk had been embarked upon by Tommy, Lee and Guy, but I took no part in it. My attention was elsewhere. Amongst the audience for the gig was my ex-housemate, Jane, one of the three Leeds girls that I'd shared a house with at Great Western Street in Moss Side. Jane had ended up back at Tommy's too.

The chaotic lifestyle I had been leading was no good at all for keeping medical appointments, and I had neglected to return to Manchester Royal Infirmary to have my stitches removed. I was well overdue, and as Jane had started (but not completed) the first part of a nursing course, I let her cut and remove them. No sterilisation procedures were followed, of course, she just snipped them with Tommy's kitchen scissors and pulled them out.

Mercifully, no infection followed, but something about the tactile nature of this ad hoc operation brought us closer together than we had ever been as friends, and by the end of that week, despite it having been the last thing on both of our minds, we had become a couple.

I called round to my previous house on Great Western Street that I'd shared with Wendy, Julie and Jane opposite Alvino's Pattie and Dumplin shop. It was only a social visit, but I found that things had changed. Joanne, Wendy's older sister and the owner of the house, had moved back in after travelling around India along with another slightly older friend of hers, an artist and potter called Dave Priestley. Wendy still lived there, and it turned out that there was a spare room going. As I was a friend anyway, I could move in straight away without having to pay any money up front, and this is exactly what I did. Joanne was fine about waiting for the paperwork to get sorted and gave me a rent book to take down to Manchester Town Hall to get the process started. It seemed like a good time for a new start of sorts.

Jane nominally had her own room in a shared house in Chorlton, but was something of a fixture in the Great Western Street house anyway, being Wendy's best friend. It was the most natural thing in the world for Jane to be around all the time, and to be honest, she felt more at home there anyway. So began another phase in the house that held so many memories. We were all slightly older, and the dynamics of the house were different, but it felt like the right thing to do.

Even though it had only been a few years since I had lived there, the very nature of Moss Side itself was changing fast, and a darker phase of the area's history was just beginning. Moss Side had become a magnet for out-of-town drug purchasers, who would buy large amounts to take back to the satellite towns surrounding Manchester, and in some cases even further afield. The sheer amount of money changing hands meant that rival groups of dealers would be fighting over control of the markets, and the streets around Moss Side precinct, previously the site of the 1981 riots, were awash with local youth on mountain bikes, working in shifts to cover the influx of consumers from as far away as Leeds or the Midlands. A palpable sense of rising danger could be felt as the youth of the area began to feel untouchable.

I bumbled along regardless and put myself in some very scary situations. I would regularly end up in a blues on nearby Broadfield Road, always on my own, and always too engrossed in the trouser flapping bass end of the wonderful music I heard there to even stop for a minute and consider the danger I was supposed to be in. Violently loud, and shaking the foundations of the terraced house it was held in, the tunes were nonetheless sweet and enticing, soulful vocals over genius basslines. I would turn up in the early hours of the morning, and never once encounter any trouble. I feel there was a sense of double bluff at work. A sort of 'If this lone white guy just turns up dancing at 4am without a care in the world, then he must be some kind of badass' mentality. I wasn't, of course, but either way, I was a regular at Broadfield Road and other illegal gatherings, and I was always left alone.

Jane had left her previous partner in order for us to be together, leaving her ex, 'P', in a devastated state. The devastation turned to hatred – directed against me, of course – in a very short time. For a month or so he had been stalking me and carrying out a campaign of harassment against me and Jane. He would park his motorbike outside her house, and knock us up in the early hours of the morning, pleading and crying with her to take him back. He made it his life's work to bombard us with endless phone calls, threatening to have me badly hurt, or even killed for ruining his life in such a manner. He was in the early stages of a vicious and life-ruining heroin problem and had some dodgy friends. Smack addicts need money so desperately that such threats have to be taken relatively seriously, although, in my heart of hearts, I felt that he was too unstable and incompetent to arrange anything bad. My mistake.

Things were to come to a head in spectacular fashion at a gig at Manchester's Venue, a seedy club on Whitworth Street West, situated almost exactly between the Haçienda and The Ritz.

The previous live appearances that we had made were short, 'blink and you'll miss it' affairs, with us playing short sets of perhaps four songs and the instrumental 'On The Beach'. It was all over as soon as people had started getting into it. For this night at the Venue, we had added some more songs, making it more of a full set. I was nervous and had been awake for days, worrying about everything, and growing in excitement as the day got nearer.

When the day of the show came around, I was in a right state. Days of sleep deprivation had brought a trippy, cartoony edge to my already poor vision, and I was suffering auditory hallucinations that made me jump in fright at the slightest noise. In short, between the death threats and the stagefright, I was a complete ball of anxiety. Little did I know that P had organised a small group of wreckers to do me some real violence, and to disrupt the gig. Paid for, I can only presume, with promises of class As, they infiltrated the decent-sized audience and waited for the right time to strike.

The gig creaked with a sense of unease and malevolence from the moment we walked into the place. The show was brilliant, musically. If anything, my self-induced mental state lent a strange and compelling edge. We kicked off with 'Aim For The Face', and sped through a set that also contained 'Snapper', another song dealing with violence. Lee's taped inserts brought an otherworldly edge to the dense instrumental parts, and he and Guy played out of their skins, welding into a fierce and dynamic rhythm section. We left the stage to roars of surprised applause as our instruments were feeding back over the disembodied cut up voices coming from the tape player.

We had asked Dave Haslam of *Debris* fanzine to DJ for the night. As the confusion of our exit morphed into his first record, a group of shady-looking lads surrounded me, fronted by P, who, feeling confident in the presence of his henchmen, punched me square in the face, sending my glasses flying across the dancefloor. I was now more or less blind, having to negotiate my sleep-deprived tripped out state as well as my normal myopia. Flailing madly, and connecting only with thin air, I soaked up the blows for what seemed like a very long time indeed. Suddenly, from out of the darkness came Karl Burns, swinging a chair against my tormentors, and connecting with P with a stomach-churning thud. His weasely hit-squad scattered to the four winds. I had seen nothing like it since the night of Joy Division's Derby Hall riot. Glasses smashing, tables getting overturned, blood all over people's clothes, a real scene of carnage.

It was touching to know that so many of my friends were looking out for me, and without their loyal intervention, I could have been very seriously hurt. The nightmare ended with Anthony Behrendt throwing P horizontally out of the club doors with a sickening noise as he skidded down Whitworth Street West, bouncing like a skimmed stone on a still lake. Dave Haslam spoke to me about it later, saying that the atmosphere of evil had seeped right into everything. He seemed genuinely affected by it all. He wasn't alone. I still wake up in a cold sweat dreaming about it, even now.

The madness and bad feeling thrown up by the events at the Venue proved to be the straw that broke the camel's back as far as this incarnation of Dub Sex was concerned. Exciting though it was, and as good as the music had sounded, chaos seemed to follow me around. Although there was no big 'Right, that's it!' moment, we didn't see each other for a few weeks, and it was an unspoken truth that we weren't going to carry on. Lee continued to improve musically, both on his own and with Karl, when his Fall duties allowed, and Guy threw himself into his screen printing, as well as drumming for a number of projects. We all remained friends, but it was definitely time for me to lick my wounds and have a rethink.

I continued to write lyrics and take advantage of any recording opportunities that came my way. I experimented with new ways of texturing my vocals, and was lucky enough to meet up with an open-minded young musician called Matt Wand. At his home studio in Flixton, I was encouraged to make the most of his multi-track recording facilities where I hit upon a new technique; I put down the main vocal line first, and then, as near perfectly as I could, sang the same thing, one octave above, and then one octave below, thickening and giving extra depth to the lead vocal. This led me to take the same technique and use it in slightly different ways. I layered soft breathy vocals on top of the same line screamed at the top of my voice, or juxtaposed a perfectly clean voice on top of the same line through a distortion pedal. I began to understand my voice's strong points, and how to blend the harsh and the beautiful into one cohesive whole. Vocals are the thing upon which a song will stand or fall, and are the entry point to any given song. A good vocal leads the listener in, and can repel the listener within a few seconds just as easily. I learnt lots from being given the space to try things out with Matt, it marked the point in which I really started to believe in myself as a singer.

18: Streets In The Sky

Jane inhabited a different world to me in many ways. When we were housemates, she was part of a trio of female friends, new to Manchester and excited to be in a city so full of opportunity and things to do. Two years of living here, however, had added a certain hardness to her gentle personality, and she had got to know some rather interesting characters.

We would visit her friend Ralph in Chorlton, who lived off the grid as far as the authorities went. He claimed no benefits, paid no rent, and would talk of his total self-contained independence with pride. There would always be a little weed around the place, and Ralph had invented a machine that used a wire filament to instantly heat cannabis oil, which led to much mellow contemplation around his kitchen table.

He lived with Jan, the engineer at Decibelle who Karl had pushed to the limits of his mental endurance some years earlier. All such things were forgotten now, and we would spend time with the two of them, and with Ralph's third housemate, Dave, a somewhat hippyish sound engineer and musician who Jane had known for some years.

Dave Rumney was something of a loner outside this domestic set-up. He rarely went to gigs or clubs when he wasn't doing the live sound, and led an almost monastic life, smoking weed and playing his guitar. Music-wise, he had a soft spot for Bowie and the Velvet Underground, but also an ear for slow, controlled music, especially Leonard Cohen. Punk-wise, he had a lot of time for The Fall and Blue Orchids, but it was Wire that really got him, although he never really progressed beyond their first two albums, *Pink Flag* and *Chairs Missing*. Still, at least we had that in common.

He existed on benefits and had pared down his lifestyle accordingly, living off cheap vegetable stews and spending as little money as possible. He did, however, have a spare acoustic guitar, and gradually, after a few visits, I felt comfortable enough to play it. This led to us going into another room away from the household, where I discovered that he was fairly proficient, certainly enough to be of use as a second, backup guitarist.

The two of us would start to meet up, with me showing him round some of the songs I had been writing, and him fleshing out the general sound with extra guitar parts. As our rehearsals progressed, we started to gel as a guitar duo. It was good to have that extra textural support, especially when I was singing, and before long, songs like 'Look Away', 'Voice of Reason' and 'Splintered' started to emerge in skeletal form.

It felt like a good time to move back into Hulme and take advantage of the opportunities there. We took over two three-bedroomed flats on the top floor of Charles Barry Crescent. I lived in one with Jane, and Dave shared the one next door with Martin Bramah, who was in the process of assembling his post Blue Orchids project, Thirst.

I had admired Martin's music since I was a teenage Fall fan. I was fairly pre-disposed to listening to anything that he did with Una Baines in Blue Orchids with a favourable ear, the two of them having been so central to the early Fall. I was on board from the very first time I heard their brilliant singles 'The Flood' and 'Work'. I wore out my copy of their John Peel session, which effortlessly yielded one of my favourite Orchids songs, 'A Year With No Head'. Karl Burns later introduced me to their manager Gywn, and I ended up as a regular visitor to their house in Chorlton, shooting the breeze and taking mental notes as the band got ready for the release of their debut album, *The Greatest Hit (Money Mountain)*.

Of all of that year's albums, the Orchids flawed masterpiece sits on its own, head and shoulders above most of its contemporaries. It harks back to the *Pebbles* and *Nuggets* US garage compilations that had so much influence of the sound of the early Fall. Una's organ is high in the mix, a staple, rather than an embellishment of the whole sound, and Martin's voice is a thing of real beauty; half-spoken, half sung, always perfectly natural and believable. Stood there, left-handed, lanky and thin, I have lost all sense of where I was while absorbed in an Orchids show.

In an almost unbelievable turn of events, I saw them backing Velvets chanteuse Nico at Manchester University. The larger than life

Manchester promoter, Alan Wise, who had put me on at Rafters with Orange Juice, had recently become involved with Nico and he saw it as his mission to take control of her career, so ravaged by heroin and its attendant lifestyle, and turn things around for her.

Post Velvet Underground, her solo albums, especially *The Marble Index*, had gained her a reputation for dark, druggy soundscapes. Mournful and harmonium driven, she existed in a parallel world. Nico seemed to invent her own way of dealing with timing, melody and space. Her music had more to do with medieval high church solemnity than the trivial world of rock in which it found itself. Not an easy thing for Alan Wise to sell, but he was a driven man, and proceeded to try and create a world that Nico could thrive in.

First things first, he had to address Nico's long established heroin habit, and set about registering her in a methadone programme. Moving to Manchester unfortunately meant that her poison of choice was never too far away. She, and certainly Alan, entered into this course of action in good faith, but a junkie's hands are always tied, so to speak, and she would fall back into scoring street drugs time and time again.

Alan had the inspired idea to introduce her to the Blue Orchids. For a short but wonderful period, Una Baines, Martin Bramah and the other Orchids served as her backing band and partners in crime. The shows would open with a Blue Orchids set, and this was when they were arguably at their very best. Una's organ evoked the garagey swirl of Question Mark and the Mysterians as much as Nico's own emotional drone, but the insistent drum and bass pulse behind it made it impossible to ignore. They opened with 'Tighten My Belt', vocal-less and stark, like a druggy Booker T. & the M.G.'s, and the die was cast. Nico followed them, seated and solo for her neo-classical sounding, mournful pieces until the spell was broken by the Blue Orchids joining her again for versions of the rockier Velvets classics like 'Waiting For the Man'. Unforgettable.

I watched spellbound as the show hit Manchester University, never taking my eyes off her, giving myself to the music as it ebbed and swelled like something organic. The final clanging of Martin's guitar chords meant it was time to snap back to earth once more. Grabbing Lee, I flashed my pass and hurtled at full speed down the labyrinth of corridors behind the stage, eager to tell Martin how good it had been. Turning a corner, I smashed into Nico's leather trousered and much-punctured leg, knocking her flying onto the floor.

'I-D-I-O-T!' in a familiar Germanic voice echoed around the tiled corridor.

Living next door to each other in Charles Barry Crescent, Martin and I would spend a lot of time just hanging out, playing guitar, and trying out bits of songs on each other. It was a great privilege to be there as Martin perfected songs like 'The Unknown' and 'Crystal Kiss'.

The flatblock we lived in was a real hive of activity. Noise being no problem, various bands and musicians had made it their base. Inca Babies, Vee VV, Tools You Can Trust and Edward Barton had all chosen to live and work there, and in a bedroom just a few doors down from us, a young (Guy Called) Gerald Simpson was starting to experiment with a squelchy synth-driven sound. It was a great time to be alive.

The jewel in the crown of the Hulme scene was undoubtedly The Kitchen. Situated just ten doors down from where I lived in one of the bigger flats that were built over the communal stairwell, The Kitchen started life as an eight-track recording facility. Its owner, Jamie Nicholson, was from a very different background to me, but we got on like a house on fire. His father was an airline pilot, and he was entitled to cut-price flights until his twenty-fifth birthday, therefore he was well travelled in a way that opportunity had never led me to. He had been to some amazing places; Brazil, Africa, the Far East. I was drawn to his worldliness. He in turn knew nothing of the kind of life that I had lived. As people, we had a lot to learn from each other, up there on the fifth floor of a doomed housing project. I got the feeling that Jamie came to Manchester to experience a reality that was absent from the life he had known growing up, and he caught me at a time when I was just starting to articulate my own story. I felt good and safe in his company, and sensed that The Kitchen was a place that I could make music in.

Jamie's studio was a comparatively expensively fitted out operation. A healthy scene had sprung up there. I got to know several people who were cutting their teeth at The Kitchen. Danny Evans and Devon Shaw were regular faces. Devon was a force of nature, enthusiastic and full of life. I was thinking ahead about getting more musicians involved in what I was doing, and a demo to play to any potential drummers or bass players would be more than useful. I decided to record simple versions of the songs I had been working out with Dave Rumney, with Jamie engineering.

I played drums myself, using a hexagonal Simmons electronic kit, adding bass and guitar, to which Dave would overdub his lead parts. As the session progressed, it was apparent that a change was happening in what I was doing. The tracks sounded like nothing I had heard before, and when it came to me adding my vocals, a new controlled voice had emerged. Soulful and self-assured, it possessed a confidence that had been lacking in anything I had done previously. We all felt it, and raised our game accordingly. Jamie in particular understood that we were present at the birth of something good, and from this minute on, he was totally on my side.

Jamie had some brilliant ideas about how to treat my voice, and I would extend the longer notes by repeating several of the same lines on another track, and then blending the two together, as seamlessly as possible. This worked especially well with falsetto notes, and it led to me making a feature of the higher end of my vocal range. Clever placing of these 'ghost' vocals made them seem endless. It was a technique that I took and made my own. I emerged with a two-track demo that coupled 'Splintered' with 'Voice of Reason'. It sounded great, and as well as further cementing my musical relationship with Dave, I now had something to play to potential band members when I found them.

Despite the deprivation and poverty that, admittedly, was a part of the lives of all the people that lived in Hulme, it became my playground and I never had so much fun. I was spending more of my time with Karl, and, with The Fall being in the ascendant, doors of many kinds opened for us. Drugs on credit, parties all the time, rehearsal places that were happy to let us destroy their instruments, the world was indeed oyster-shaped. Karl seemed to be forgiven everything, a one man blagging machine, steamrolling through life like an out of control tank, living only for the next crazy experience before being called back to Fall duty, either touring or recording. This, of course, was his real life, and running around Hulme just filled the gaps before the next big Fall thing. It was a brilliant time for all of us.

We kept upside-down hours, as was usual in the amphetamine subculture that we inhabited. From dark until light, the sleeping estate belonged to a different population, one that co-existed, unseen by those who didn't know where to look. It seemed like it belonged to us, and us alone. Everybody knew who Karl was, and because of The Fall's high profile, and frequent John Peel plays, most people assumed that he was making good money. I never saw him with any substantial wads, but his behaviour, which was getting madder and madder, would be tolerated by dealers, who could smell solvency a mile away, or so they thought.

One such unfortunate was 'T', who lived in the flimsier, cockroach-attracting flats on nearby Bonsall Street. He was, like many of his age group, a massive John Lydon fan. His life revolved around his adoration of the Sex Pistols and the effect that the punk revolution had on him several years earlier. Karl, of course, had passed through the ranks of Public Image Limited, which made him, in T's eyes, some kind of punk saint. Karl would stretch the limits of this adoration to within snapping distance.

T's main income stream was the making of bespoke stained-glass framed pictures, although he supplemented this with the selling of rather potent Afghani black cannabis resin, of which we were inordinately fond. He led a peaceful enough existence, working on his stained glass as his (very expensive) pedigree cat looked on, and was doing exactly that when we called round in the early hours, both of us sporting big black pupils and fizzing with kinetic energy.

As he opened the front door, his cat, some rare kind of Siamese, shot through the tiniest of spaces into the black Hulme night. We were ushered into the front room, where I accidentally stood on his latest stained-glass creation, a commission for a clothes shop in the centre of Manchester. It had already been paid for, but now lay in splintered pieces beneath my size ten boot. T's girlfriend went out to hunt for the unfortunate moggy, swearing under her breath. Within a matter of minutes, we had ruined this poor man's day and cost him hundreds of pounds. Incredibly, Karl's reputation saw us through. We left with a healthy deal of black to be paid for at some unspecified future date, leaving a trail of chaos in our wake. This was by no means a rare occurrence. Karl's bullish charisma was his secret weapon when employed on the right person. I was frequently left slack-jawed at the sheer cheek of the guy, he was totally without shame and would then fuck off abroad on Fall business leaving a trail of promises behind him for the rest of us to clear up.

We spent a hilarious day near the university, busking Elvis Presley classics like 'Rock-A-Hula Baby' and 'Suspicious Minds', terrifying the students in their own comfort zone. One drum, one guitar and two tabs of windowpane acid. If anybody had been vulgar enough to actually throw any money at us, we would have thrown it back, but the sight of two unkempt tripping maniacs mainly made our would-be benefactors cross the road with the distinct look of abject fear in their eyes, so it never came up.

We had the misfortune to walk unwittingly into a full-scale police bust on one of our nocturnal adventures. These occasions were far from rare, as there were dealers of every size and persuasion wherever you cared to look, and the sound of somebody's door going through was as much a part of the aural landscape as birdsong would be to a country village. Nevertheless, we had no inkling of what was going on behind the fifth-floor Charles Barry Crescent door when we knocked on it, sometime after midnight.

The door was opened by a friendly enough young man, scruffy and unshaven. I didn't know him, but it wasn't unusual for a customer to be asked 'just get the door for us, would you?' in such a situation. The person who lived there was not a close friend or anything, just one of many residents who had chosen to supplement their income with a little chemical retail operation. Nothing too big, just enough for him to cover his own needs. I had been before, and the speed was okay, if not wonderful. The place was something of a last resort, to be honest.

I was ushered into the front room, where the whole scenario became painfully clear to the two of us. The subject of our late night call had been placed with his hands up against the wall of his own living room, and was undergoing a thorough body search as four undercover police officers went around the flat, turning things over and generally making their presence felt.

Shit! What had we walked into here? Even though we hardly knew this poor unfortunate soul, we were in his dwelling, and therefore could presumably be in the same amount of trouble as he was. Possession with intent to supply was no laughing matter, and my stomach went queasy at the thought of being incarcerated, especially in such unfair circumstances.

I had asked the person who had opened the door if the object of their raid was at home, like an idiot, and whether or not he had anything in. It looked like my big mouth had got me into trouble again, and as the police separated Karl and me, taking us into different rooms, the realisation hit me that things were potentially even worse than I had at first thought. My coat pockets were a drug squad officer's dream. An eighth of an ounce of Lebanese weed, partly finished wraps and other drug paraphernalia nestled in the depths of my charity shop overcoat. Surely I was in the deepest of deep shit.

It was then that my guardian angel, or someone like her, intervened. The plain-clothed policeman removed my coat and threw it into a corner of the room, saying 'Right, let's see what we have here, then...' in an anachronistic Dixon of Dock Green voice. He then ignored the coat while subjecting me to a comprehensive, but fruitless body search. I could have kissed him. Finding nothing, he instructed me to put my coat back on and get out of here, fast, and think myself lucky. I did exactly that, and thought myself a very lucky bunny indeed.

Karl's experience was longer, but no less surreal. He had about his person a business card that had lay undisturbed in his back pocket since The Fall's last visit to America. It was given to him by a company called Fantasy Factory, the name of which had sent the police into overdrive. You could practically hear their squeals of delight as they dreamt ahead of promotion, thinking they had accidentally unearthed another huge acid factory, along the lines of the celebrated Operation Julie, based in Wales, which had made massive headlines in the late seventies.

It didn't take long for things to be cleared up. The company in question specialised in converting American video tapes to UK formats like VHS and Betamax, and were not, as PC Wrong supposed, corruptors of British youth after all. It took a few hours but Karl turned up at my flat highly amused. We spent the rest of the night toasting the recruitment policies of Greater Manchester Police with the lump of Red Leb, so kindly returned to me by my unwitting plain-clothed new best friend. I had never believed much in the luck of the Irish before, for obvious reasons, but I undoubtedly had a rub of the green that night in deepest, darkest, dangerous, hilarious Hulme.

Away from these adventures, there was a serious side to the way we were living our lives. Karl was one of the most driven and dedicated musicians I have ever met, and for all his extremism when it came to his lifestyle choices, his devotion to his craft was absolute. From the very first time we played together, it was obvious that he was something special. He took me under his wing at a time when his style was just turning into something that belonged to him, and him alone, accelerating The Fall from the song-based outfit of their earlier material, into a brave, uncompromising, mathematical thing. They seemed to belong to the past as well as the future, and inhabited a place all of their own, head and shoulders above their contemporaries. The majestic, sprawling 'Hexen Definitive/Strife Knot' pointed the way and would stretch itself into different lengths and shapes each time it was played, a bastard child of 'Spectre Vs. Rector' from their earlier days. Traditional ideas of song length were trashed as the likes of 'Garden' and 'Smile' frequently broke the ten-minute barrier. Karl brought home a live mixing desk tape from Switzerland with an unreleased song called 'Backdrop'. It exemplifies perfectly the way they were going. It shuns convention completely, stopping and starting in sections more akin to a play than a song, all underpinned by the most rigid and disciplined drumming you could ever wish to be exposed to.

It is difficult to trace the origin of Karl's drumming style by merely focussing on the kind of music he liked. His tastes were strangely mainstream. He had spent time in various heavy metal bands, pre-Fall, and always had time for Deep Purple and Black Sabbath, but was drawn to simple, metronomic drumming of many different types. We spent a lot of time listening to the B-52s, whose rhythm section Karl really enjoyed, and old soul records, Booker T. & the M.G.'s in particular. What really floated his boat though was classic period Roxy Music, and the drumming of Paul Thompson. I can hear the similarities in their two styles, economical and hard hitting, ego-less. Both drummers were hard hitters, and unless you had heard Karl from just a couple of feet away it would be hard to explain how different he was from anybody else. I have never heard anybody louder who still retained a deftness of touch and an innate musicality. Just brilliant.

Apart from teaching me loads about stagecraft, and how to make the most of my strong points, Karl did me the favour of introducing me to two people who would help me along my musical path. It was no secret that I was on the lookout for a decent new guitar, and Karl had heard that a friend of his had bought a job lot of musical equipment, including a red and black Fender Bullet guitar that seemed to be just what I was looking for. Karl took me round to the Hulme flat of Andy Cadman that he shared with his brother, Roger.

The Cadman brothers were part of a large Wythenshawe family. They lived in a three-bedroom flat in Bonsall Street, at the end nearest to the university, close to Oxford Road. These dwellings had more of a traditional feel to them, with several residents having lived in the area for most of their lives, a world away from the anarchic goings on a few hundred yards away in the other direction where the flats in the crescents were being modified into recording studios and clandestine party spaces left, right and centre. Their flat was comfortable and more of a home than I had been used to visiting on the estate, and it was a refreshing change to encounter some civilisation there amongst the madness that prevailed almost everywhere else in my life.

Roger worked for a car leasing company. He was very close to his brother Andy, who worked as a barber in Levenshulme as well as having something of an unofficial salon at home. Both of them were huge music lovers, and it turned out that we had a lot of friends in common from music and the twilight world that surrounded it. Their flat was a hive of activity and the brothers were a source of encouragement and support for many of their musician friends, many of whom I had met before in earlier times. Andy and Roger were mates with a new band called The Weeds who contained both Andrew Berry, who I had known since his days DJing at Berlin, and (Funky) Simon Wolstencroft, who I had met years before at Decibelle Studios, jamming with him, Johnny Marr and Andy Rourke in their pre-Smiths outfit, Freak Party. It was unusual for me to feel so at home anywhere, but something about Andy and Roger, and the scene that was springing up around their flat, relaxed me straight away and I knew I was with my own kind of people.

Roger was a few years older than me and a thousand times more sensible. He had worked since school, and consequently was organised in a way that I most definitely wasn't. The two of us had very different and complementary strengths as people, and in the sense that opposites attract, we became the best of friends in no time.

As Karl had told me, Roger had a second-hand Fender Bullet guitar for sale. It had arrived with some other bits and bobs in a job lot when he had bought himself a drum kit, on which he intended to learn. Despite being around music and musicians for most of his life, Roger had never been in a band, and although he had picked up some basics, he was at the start of his drumming career, and in fact had never really played with anybody else in any meaningful way.

The brothers' larger top bedroom had been chosen as the place that Roger would practise on his newly-acquired kit, and as such had been soundproofed in a rudimentary fashion with eggboxes and the odd mattress. I doubt that the neighbours thought that this helped much, but either way, the room had a good vibe to it. I had fallen in love with the guitar straight away, and definitely wanted it, despite not having the full asking price. I came up with a plan that suited us both, and after leaving a deposit of twenty pounds, we agreed that he would hold onto it and I would turn up every fortnight with a tenner each time I received my benefit payment. These occasions turned into jam sessions as I would want to have a go on my new guitar whenever I came round to pay the latest instalment. This led to Roger joining in, and before long, these sessions became longer and more coherent.

Playing with somebody so new to drumming proved to be the best thing that could have happened to me. I had songs to try out and was able to lead Roger into stylistic areas that suited the way that I was writing. Him being so inexperienced was a great plus as he hadn't learned any of the annoying clichés that other, more worldly drummers regularly fell back on, so I could steer him towards an economic approach that I really liked. The months went on, and as Roger got better, I brought Dave Rumney down too, guiding the two of them through some of the song ideas I had been working on. Things were going in the right direction. All we needed now was a bass player.

As luck would have it, one night I was in The White Horse pub in the centre of Charles Barry Crescent and I saw Cathy Brooks in there. I had met Cathy some years previously in the Moss Side flat that her band at the time, The Floating Adults, used to rehearse in. They were a nice bunch of people, and although, unlike me, they all seemed to have something of an academic background, they treated me well. I had hardly spoken to Cathy, apart from the odd 'hello', but I knew she played bass, and that piece of information had stuck with me. More recently she had caught my attention in a band called Horsehead, named, I believe, after the male singer's 'full can of hairspray' vertical gothic hairdo. We had a few friends in common, and I'd see her occasionally in The White Horse. I associated her with a small group of musicians, including Harry Stafford's Inca Babies, Big Ed and his Rockin' Rattlesnakes, Tools You Can Trust and the excellent, abrasive, politically charged Big Flame (or bIG fLAME as they seemed to prefer), who had been championed by John Peel. They were all jagged edges and unusual time signatures, with lyrics befitting a band named after a far left revolutionary feminist group.

I had seen Cathy playing bass for Horsehead on a float at the annual Hulme carnival, and was taken by her style of playing with her fingers rather than a plectrum and her severe demob haircut, shaven high at the nape of the neck, not unlike my own. I was feeling a bit full of myself that night in The White Horse so I rather rudely barged into a conversation she was having with two of her female friends and asked her if she was free the following day to play some music with me.

God only knows how I came across that day, all bluster and front, but to her eternal credit, Cathy must have seen through the rough and eccentric looking exterior and agreed for me to come round to her flat the following day in nearby John Nash Crescent. She could have said 'no' at any point, and many other people would have, but her lack of snobbery and her open-mindedness gave me a chance.

Cathy's room was tiny, with barely room for both of us plus our instruments. I showed her a few of the ideas I had been working on and she got her head round my unorthodox style in no time. Then, having broken the musical ice, we jammed for a while, with her bass taking the lead. Suddenly, the most wonderful bassline emerged as if from nowhere. A rumbling, insistent thing, musical at the top end but utilising the full extent of the instrument's potential, going as low as was possible, using the open E string to full effect. I was instantly energised and began to overlay some vocals, loosely based on a shocking experience I had the misfortune to witness some years before.

> Cut out and save
> Try and alter the pace
> What drained the colour away from your face
> When you came here to see me today
> I noticed the scenery change
> A loud scrape as he slammed on his brakes too late
> I tasted decay, in the second it takes
> To make a mess on the motorway...

In a matter of minutes we had written 'Kicking The Corpse Around'. I heard how powerful the sound of just a voice and bass could be. It had to be Cathy's bass, though, this I realised. It looked as though I had completed my search.

PART IV
And Here It Comes

Overleaf: Dub Sex at The Kitchen Studio
(L to R) Cathy Brooks, Roger Cadman, Dave Rumney (seated), MH
Photo by Todd Fath

19: Don't Trip On It

I gave Roger and Cathy a copy of the demo I had recorded with Dave at The Kitchen. Both had something of a 'the boy can sing!' moment when they heard the vocals. I'd had the same moment myself when I first heard them. It's hard to put my finger on what had changed in the few months leading up to making the demo, but things had improved in many ways. Better songs, better singing, more space within the music.

When we assembled as a fourpiece for the first time, I had the full confidence of the three of them as we began the process of getting to know each other, both as people and as musicians. We rehearsed at Roger and Andy's flat. My Giro-day instalments for the Fender Bullet meant that I had been going round regularly to have a play as Roger took his first steps on the green Pearl drum kit, but it was a different proposition with a full band in there. The biggest bedroom, the one repurposed into a music room, was just about big enough to fit the four of us in. Piles of magazines and records lay everywhere, waiting to trip us up if we veered from our positions. A large working men's club organ took up a huge amount of space against one wall, although I never heard or saw it working. Too heavy to move, I bumped my shins on it at least twice a week until I got used to the crowded terrain.

Cathy and Roger hit it off immediately, which is exactly what you would want a rhythm section to do. Being squeezed into a tiny space at rehearsals, coupled with the fact that Roger had never played with any other bass player before, meant that he never took his eyes off her, and an almost psychic understanding developed, based on the smallest of gestures or the slightest nod. Dave and I slotted into whatever space remained. I was further restricted by only being able to hear myself singing in one part of the room. Nevertheless, as soon as any music started, all these challenges were forgotten and the four of us got used to letting the sound wash over us.

The naive attempt to provide some rudimentary soundproofing on the two walls that were shared with neighbours was well-meaning but it had no real effect. Although we tried to keep rehearsals within reasonable hours, having a full band practising in a council flat was never going to be a popular move. This end of Hulme was a touch more civilised than the crescents, where noise from bands and parties were the norm. Many of our rehearsals ended with frenzied, out-of-time banging on the walls from Roger and Andy's neighbours, a sound we got to know well.

Rehearsing in such a residential area meant that we had to keep the flat windows closed for noise reasons, and this, coupled with the ad hoc soundproofing, turned the place into an oven. The heat was unbearable and the air unbreathable. We took to bringing a change of clothes as the ones we were playing in would become soaked with perspiration. Sweat dripped off my nose onto the neck of my guitar and hit my fellow band members as I flicked my hair out of my eyes while singing. Luxurious it most definitely wasn't, but none of us cared, such was the excitement of hearing our sound develop and improve.

We fell into a pattern of regular weekly rehearsals as a band. Roger and myself would still play together, just the two of us, whenever we could, and the same went for me and Dave. Thus began a productive time, with me working separately with the two of them on material in order for it to be ready to get cracking on in earnest at our 'official' practises.

The beginnings of a set started to emerge. 'Voice of Reason', 'Splintered', 'Play Street' and 'Kicking The Corpse Around' all came to fruition. The quality of the sound we were making took us all by surprise at first, a surprise that gave way to a deep sense of pride as we gradually came to understand how good this band could be. This feeling gave us something in common with each other. With renewed enthusiasm, song ideas, previously my department, started to come from everybody. This change in the way songs were written excited me. I could jump upon a drum riff, or a guitar sequence. I found myself writing differently shaped lyrics than I had done on my own.

One Saturday afternoon we were throwing a few ideas around that I had started a few months earlier. I had chanced upon a newspaper article concerning a terrible incident that had happened in a small town in the hills outside Oldham. It seemed that one nutcase resident, sick to the back teeth of teenagers disturbing the peace outside his house when scrambling on their noisy motorbikes, had erected a steel wire at neck height between two trees to teach the miscreants a lesson. The consequences were dire, as you would expect, and the story had stayed with me ever since.

I had started freestyling some lyrics over a beautiful three-note bassline of Cathy's when something quite magical happened. With a sense of economy I had rarely heard before, Cathy changed the entire direction of the song with the addition of just *one* note. Up to this point, I had been singing over a rumbling, but unchanging riff, somewhat reminiscent of Link Wray or Neal Hefti's theme tune from *Batman*, but in the space of a second, Cathy had made the most beautiful thing happen, mid-phrase. It was like seeing a brilliant chess player snatch victory from the jaws of defeat with a genius move that nobody saw coming, or witnessing a Brazilian footballer split open an unwitting defence with a seventy-yard diagonal pass. What I heard was so good it made me laugh out loud with joy. 'Tripwire' was born, and so was our band.

Over the first few months of getting to know one another, a sound had arrived. Roger and Cathy in particular found that their styles fitted together perfectly. Cathy, although a fine musician already, was drawn to simplicity, rather than showing off her proficiency, and this suited Roger down to the ground. Having never learnt any of the bad habits, he was mercifully free of clutter, and his deliberate lack of drumrolls and other crimes made him the ideal rhythm partner for Cathy. Their friendship shone through the music they were coming up with. Just listening to them mature, rehearsal by rehearsal, was inspiring beyond words, and led me to attempt to raise my own game, too. Cathy was inspirational in many ways; she had one foot in the world of music but she had a lot of other things going on in her life too. She was working towards her PhD in immunology and was highly regarded by her scientific community.

Roger and Cathy brought their 'real world' skills of organisation and handling money to the fore. I was useless at anything financial, but with a kitty set up, and Cathy and Roger involved, I was left to concentrate on more creative things. It was a real eye-opener to be respected and treated as an equal by people from what I perceived as straight society.

We would follow rehearsals with a trip to one of two local pubs, as a rule. The White Horse possessed all the 'dog on the roof' charm of a typical 1970s pub, but had become something of a magnet to people who had been drawn to the estate by the ease of life there, and the promise of free rehearsal space. Cathy knew many of these people, and gradually a kind of scene emerged, with bands swapping tips on where to play, and just generally getting to know each other.

At the other side of Hulme was the Salutation, in the shadow of the polytechnic. This was more student, although, being Manchester, it also had its share of musicians. Roger would often trash Simply Red's trumpet player, Tim Kellett, at pool. It felt like a metaphor for our war against bland music.

I had a plan of action. I had realised that John Peel had been quite taken by Dave Haslam's magazine, *Debris*, and had been giving airtime to some of the bands featured on the flexidiscs given away with each issue. Too Much Texas and Vee VV had been played on the show, and another band that we knew, Laugh, had ended up being offered a session after being brought to the attention of Peel and his producer, John Walters, by their appearance on a *Debris* flexidisc. I felt that if I could get a basic recording of how the band was starting to sound, then pass it to Dave, he would be so bowled over that we could be one of his featured bands. Peel would then offer us a session. I was so confident in this outcome that I could not even imagine that things could possibly go any other way.

I liked Dave, and I liked his magazine. Unlike other publications of the time, it was not afraid to feature more than just music, including articles on writers, artists and political thinking, too. Dave had lived around the corner from me in Moss Side, and when I visited him once, he was admiring a selection of 12-inch singles by The Woodentops, spreading them out next to each other on the floor, pointing out how the different sleeves related to each other. I loved that he was obsessive about music, and knew that he would understand where I was coming from, both as a person and as a musician. He had, of course, been the DJ at the Venue gig that exploded into a near riot, so I felt a kinship with him there, too, born out of this outrageous shared experience.

We booked ourselves into Jamie Nicholson's Kitchen studio. The studio itself was ingeniously constructed, using every nook and cranny of Jamie's four-bedroom flat. We played together live in what had been the upstairs living room, with Roger behind a padded partition screen to provide some degree of separation, while the bass amp and the two guitar amps were placed in storage cupboards and the downstairs toilet to avoid spillage onto the drum microphones.

A general headphone mix was achieved, the same for all four of us. It was a testament to Jamie's skill that he would get a workable sound and headphone mix quickly, without too much stopping and starting, which would have disrupted the flow of the session. Of course, we were well rehearsed, and not there to mess about. We worked fast, the four of us sweating buckets in Jamie's mattress-covered live room. We were now used to playing in extreme heat, so it was nothing to us.

Jamie enjoyed playing around with my voice, even creating weird psychological experiments to make me sing differently. He had me singing in complete darkness, and on one occasion I was put on his balcony with a mic and headphones to provide long falsetto notes. It had been snowing. Jamie said he wanted me to feel vulnerable and alone. He certainly achieved that, but it was beautiful to hear my voice break the peace and stillness of the white, snow-covered estate.

The finished tape featured versions of 'Splintered' and 'Kicking the Corpse Around'. These two songs taught us a lot about how we sounded, and what direction we could take. It was, however, the third track, 'Tripwire', that blew us all away. Confident and brash, it invoked early rockabilly and Motown, whilst most definitely being a child of the punk revolution that had so shaped me as a person. It played games with the listener via a series of false stops and starts, with unexplained nods towards a druggy, modern reality, without being brazen or obvious.

The song ended abruptly, in mid-flight, leaving my disembodied voice repeating over the stark silence. 'Don't trip, trip, trip, trip, trip, trip, trip, trip, trip!!' I knew the power of what we had created, and I had no doubt that Dave Haslam would not only accept it for *Debris*, but he'd push it up the schedules, such was my belief in what we had made.

Dave had started DJing at the Haçienda in a regular slot on Thursday nights. He called it 'Temperance Club'. His reputation had begun to grow a year before at a seedy basement club called Man Alive. Started by the highly abrasive and political Big Flame, The Wilde Club, as it was called, reflected the eclectic nature of fanzine culture, attracting bands of the stature of That Petrol Emotion and The June Brides. Dave would tap into this rich seam of independent UK music, mixing it with some class new soul and dance music, and it was this formula that was gathering strength now at the Haçienda, where numbers were gradually creeping up. I liked it, and ended up there a lot. Having worked there, I never had to pay in, likewise anybody who was with me, they just walked in alongside me. I went down one Thursday night and gave Dave a cassette featuring 'Tripwire' and the two other tracks. I believed that it was going to blow his head off.

The following week I went back to find out what he made of it. I felt a little nervous as I made my way down Medlock Street. I'd walked that path countless times but this time it felt different. I was on a mission. I'd staked everything on this, carrying my bandmates along in a flurry of self-belief. I could conceive of no other outcome, and now, as I climbed the metal steps to the DJ booth, I was about to come face to face with the first test of my plan.

'Hiya Dave, what do you think?'

Dave was between records and held a finger up as if to say 'I'll be with you in a minute', then went back to cueing up his next tune. The butterflies in my stomach flapped twice as hard as Dave took off his headphones and turned around.

He was smiling! He loved it! Not only was he prepared to put it out with *Debris*, but he wanted it to go out with the very next issue.

The deal was that Dave, us and the other band on the flexi (Two Thieves and A Liar) would each contribute £100 towards the manufacturing costs. We would receive loads of copies to send to agencies, press, and most importantly, John Peel. This was brilliant. Just for once, it felt as if I had got exactly what I wanted.

A gig at The Boardwalk was arranged for us by Chris Paul, a friend of Cathy's who had been involved in the International Youth Year Festival and was currently looking after the affairs of the Bhundu Boys, a Zimbabwean 'jit' group that John Peel had been giving airtime to. We were billed alongside Miaow, one of Factory's newer signings, and the subject of a great deal of interest from all directions. They contained Chris Fenner, who had played with Cathy in The Floating Adults, and were fronted by Cath Carroll, who had been on my radar for several years. Originally a member of 'Property Of...', who had been part of Manchester Musicians' Collective, she was involved with the much respected fanzine *City Fun* along with Liz Naylor, with whom she also performed. Factory had got behind Miaow, spending real money on studio time and photography by New Yorker, Robert Mapplethorpe. Mapplethorpe's photos of Patti Smith from some years before, stark black and white, were unforgettable. I certainly felt we were moving in the right circles.

Although we only had six songs ready, they were in good shape, and we hammered them again and again, rehearsing first in Roger and Andy's flat, and then moving to The Kitchen, where we hammered them some more, playing live through the studio's Fostex E16 desk. Jamie would be doing our live sound on the night, and had some good ideas to bring to the table as far as weird dubby effects were concerned. I took a lot of strength from the fact that Jamie had chosen to get involved, as a lot of the progress we were making was down to him and his inventiveness behind the desk. It felt as if we were assembling a team; we seemed to attract intelligent, creative people into our inner circle, which in turn made us believe in ourselves even more.

A combination of nerves and amphetamines meant that I was in a very trippy, sleep-deprived state by the time the gig came around, but this only added to our charm and overall sense of weirdness. Jamie's space echo tricks threw my yelps around the room, and, being overlaid onto a rock-solid rhythm section, the dub side of things never overpowered the driving punk assault that we had created. I was lost in the beautiful, swirling delays, duetting with myself as I screamed the refrain from 'Play Street', bouncing it against the back wall, like it was a living entity.

>I was as loud as an army!
>I was as loud as an army!
>I was as loud as an army!

Our first song seemed to have ended as soon as it had began, and the silence after we stopped playing was filled with the sound of an alien-sounding sweep of echoed voices, as Jamie stretched my vocals into a collage of barely human noises, nearer in spirit to the work of Adrian Sherwood or Jah Shaka than to The Boardwalk's usual indie fare.

The rest of the set went by in an instant, or so it seemed. The final song, 'Tripwire', caught people out with its stop/start introduction and brought things to a suitably confusing conclusion as my final advice rang around the building like a barked command.

>Don't trip!
>Don't trip!
>Don't trip!
>Don't trip!
>Don't trip!
>Don't trip!
>DON'T TRIP!!!

We exited the tiny stage, leaving our guitars against our amps to feed back, adding to the general mayhem. After a few seconds of stunned silence, I could hear people shouting for an encore. Flattering though this was, we had no more songs, having used up the six we had. The whole thing was a huge blast, and sent us proudly scurrying back to the lab to write more, full of a new energy and drive. I knew all along that we were on to something.

Next on our agenda was to get people interested in the demo tape we had recorded. We needed gigs and a record deal, and although the 'Tripwire' flexidisc was scheduled to be released with the next issue of *Debris*, we were still very much at the start of our journey. We had a batch of tapes made up at a commercial copying place, and started to think about where we wanted to send them.

I had designed an eye-catching case, featuring snarling dogs against a colourful backdrop, and had painstakingly worked on the lettering by hand, using Letraset transfers. I spent hours individualising them, making each one slightly different and, in doing so, hit upon a striking way of writing the group's name. Using Helvetica medium font in lower case, the 'd' and 'b' of 'dub sex' were equal in height and looked just great. I decided that this was the way I wanted the band name to be written every time. A brand was born! Ha ha!

We made a small list of potential recipients. Record companies, gig agencies, and journalists, mainly, although we wanted to give certain other people a chance to be in at the ground floor, so we made it our business to target individuals that we felt would get behind what we were doing.

Roger was on good terms with Mark E Smith away from music, and he arranged for the two of us to deliver a copy in person to his house in Prestwich. I was nervous as hell, and had ensured my pockets were full of goodies to make our visit go swimmingly. I'd been in the same place as Mark E Smith on many occasions, and had grunted 'Hello' once or twice, usually at Fall gigs, but turning up at his house and asking for a favour was a different proposition. He knew me as a friend of Karl's from a few years earlier. Roger, however, had more of a professional relationship with him, having sorted a car out for the group as part of his day job at Ryland Fleet Hire, so he took the lead on this one. Roger had organised it all in advance, so it wasn't as if we were cold calling or anything.

The door was opened by Mark's wife, Brix, who informed us that

Mark at the pub with some other mates and family members. We walked down to The George and joined them all briefly, handing over our tape in a low key manner. Mark couldn't have been friendlier, and looked happy to receive our gift of a tape with angry looking dogs on the cover. We didn't want to impose, so after getting a round in, we made our excuses and politely left after one pint and waited for Mark to contact us. The offer of a support slot or something. It was to be a very long wait.

Tapes went out to Rough Trade Records, Ron Johnson Records (home of Big Flame and other noisy stuff), In Tape Records (Membranes/Marc Riley and the Creepers) and a few radio stations. The *Manchester Evening News* had reviewed our gig with Miaow, so their music writer, Mick Middles, got one. John Peel was sent one, but presumably it joined the legendary twenty-foot high pile he would often mention. In the end, we got very little reaction from any of the agencies or record companies – save for the standard acknowledgement and quiet rejection letters – so we kept our heads down and got on with writing more songs and expanding our set. It was a fertile time, and led us to 'Man On The Inside', our first slow song. The vocals go from breathy to an all out scream in the course of the song. The songs 'Green' and 'Kristallnacht' started to fall into shape too.

I had stayed at Roger and Andy's flat after a particularly boisterous night. Roger and Andy were both at work, although I will never know how Andy could stand up and cut hair for eight hours after an extended pub session and three hours sleep. Autopilot, he called it. It was nice to be part of this surrogate family, trusted with a key and given the run of the place when nobody else was around. I was a model guest, tidying up, and putting records back in sleeves after the previous night's partying. This is what I was doing when the phone rang.

It was Roger. Dave Haslam had rang him at work saying that Issue 13 of *Debris* was back from the printers, complete with our flexidisc. He picked up about 30 copies, and having taken the rest of the afternoon off, hot-footed it to his flat where I was waiting in a highly excited state.

There it was. Our beautiful 'Tripwire' was at last a real record, with a catalogue number (Deb 5). I had done the artwork myself, a humorous-looking photo of quaint rural policemen on bicycles, with the band's name and the song title in hand-applied Letraset inside the back cover. Inside the magazine, Dave had printed a chart of his favourite records of 1986, and there we were at number 24, nestling away amongst the likes of Cameo and Tackhead.

We put our beloved creation on the record deck, and sat back as 'Tripwire' filled the room. I knew that the flexidisc would deteriorate after a few plays, but on this first hearing, it sounded every bit as fierce and in your face as it had at The Kitchen. No words were needed, or indeed possible. We just sat silently, pinned to our chairs by the sound that we ourselves had made, even more convinced that the future was bright and had already begun.

The *Debris* flexidisc won us quite a few new friends, just in time for our second gig. The idea was that we would play a full set for the first time, forty minutes or so, again at The Boardwalk, this time supporting Pop Will Eat Itself, a laddish, noisy group from the Midlands, very much the rising stars of the music press at the time. They were spirited enough, but came across as insincere to me, very much a case of style over content.

It was something of an eye opener to be treated the way a support band is often treated, after the civilised behaviour of Miaow, who, admittedly, were friends of ours. We were allowed hardly any time to soundcheck, and had to squash into a postage stamp-sized area of the stage to do our stuff. If anything, though, these trials worked in our favour, as our baptism into the real world served to weld us tighter together, a kind of 'us against the world' mentality.

The night's big revelation was a new song, 'Then and Now'. Even in my short life so far, I had lived through a number of heroin epidemics in several of the places I had lived. Langley, Rochdale, Hulme and Moss Side had all suffered from an influx of cheap and easily available smack. Hulme, with its thousands of flats in a small area, was in the grip of a huge crime wave, fuelled by an army of heroin addicted wastemen, taking full advantage of the easy access walkways and flimsy front doors to prey upon the estate's residents. The song came easily, invoking my experiences in Langley, Ashfield Valley in Rochdale, and Hulme itself.

> I used to live in this town
> Before things started spiralling down
> There's too much gear around
> And you're clamped by your necks to the ground
> And I never heard a dirtier sound
> No, I never heard a dirtier sound
> Then or now

This was as raw and as direct as I had ever been, lyrically, and every time I sang it, in practise or in front of an audience, I would re-live the experiences that led to it being written. The deceitfulness, the waste of talent, the tragic early deaths of friends that had barely reached their twenties, all of it. I painted a picture of what I knew, being woken in the middle of the night by the sound of a neighbour's door going through, as another flat was turned over...

> I heard them kick your door down
> Kick, kick, kick, kick, kick, kick
> Kick it all over this town

Roger's Northern soul-inspired backbeat linked in with every 'kick' I uttered, and my own staccato guitar harmonics reinforced his relentless snare, ringing around as a strangely musical counterpoint to the song's dark and dirty heart. This was unlike anything I had written before. Honest, fierce, and born from life experience. It was the highlight of the gig.

Our high volume practises were proving too loud and too frequent for the Cadman brothers' neighbours, so we were driven to change rehearsal rooms. It was the best thing we could have done. There was something about crossing town, and being in a workspace as opposed to somebody's living space, that suited us, and we would go there religiously, three times a week, and write.

Our new rehearsal room was a musty, dusty affair on Bury New Road in Higher Broughton, opposite a famously eccentric-looking pub called The House That Jack Built, which resembled something more akin to a fairground funhouse than a regular hostelry. Rooms jutted out seemingly at random, as an afterthought, and added to the weirdness of the whole area. The area didn't matter, though. We were there to play, and arrived and left together, Roger picked everybody up and dropped us all off afterwards. Roger loved driving and enjoyed contributing to the band like this. Just as well, really, as the rest of us were very much bus and cycle people.

The rooms were above a row of shops, and were run by a denim-clad, long-haired 1970's roadie-looking guy who himself lived in a flat above. He had his fingers in a lot of pies, and would rent amps to the various bands, although we were, by now, fully equipped. It was the time of the 'great' British Gas share sell off, which was being sold to the general public with an advertising campaign that had the catchphrase 'If you see Sid, tell him'. Share ownership was now a thing that the common folk could participate in, apparently. As the shares were limited to a certain amount per person, our landlord recruited Roger to buy a batch for him in exchange for several weeks free rent on the room. A real wheeler-dealer.

The Fall had rehearsed there previously, but during our time there it was mainly heavy metal and pub bands that throbbed through the wall between songs. The only way to combat this was to simply keep on playing, and these thin walls led us, perversely, to a very creative period as we went over things again and again in order to drown out 'Black Night' or 'Smoke On The Water' from our hairy neighbours.

The best thing about the room was that it was ours alone. We just turned up, switched on, and played. Within minutes of parking the car, we would be into our first song, all thoughts of everything else forgotten. And we'd play right up to the curfew hour, 10pm.

After one particularly loud and sweaty practise, the four of us were in the car at a few minutes after ten, which was the time that John Peel's weekday Radio 1 show started. It was something of a ritual to finish our rehearsal and then tune in to the Peel show on the drive back to Hulme, where we would debrief in The White Horse pub. Two records in, as we sped through Cheetham Hill, we heard a familiar voice.

> My stomach turned when I was told what you were told
> I was the last to know
> It stands to reason though
> Don't be surprised, it stands to reason…

'My God! It's "Tripwire"!'

And so it was! John Peel had blended my a cappella introduction into the record that preceded it, so there was no warning that we were going to be played. It was the second record on the programme. We sat listening in delighted silence and in some kind of a dream state as we coasted through Manchester. The song ended, my 'Trip, trip, trip…' repeating into the emptiness that followed the song's all out noise, and after what seemed like ages, John Peel's voice followed it.

'That was Dub Sex, from one of those flexidiscs given away with *Debris* magazine from Manchester, and I like that very much. We're trying to get them in for a session in the near future.'

Four joyous screams filled the car as we shared one of *the* great bonding moments of our life. Two gigs old, and we were to record a Peel session! I had arrogantly predicted that this would happen, but this was too good to be true.

I settled into my seat as the lights of inner-city Manchester twinkled below us. It would have been hard to wipe the stupid grin off my face, but I didn't particularly want to. For once, things had fallen right for me, and it felt magnificent.

20: Fire

With my musical adventures, it seemed like everything I wanted to happen was at last coming to pass, both in the rehearsal room and in the wider sense of organising the next stage of the band's life. The flexidisc release was treated as if it was a single, with prominent coverage on the singles' pages of the *NME* and *Sounds*. James Brown was full of praise, saying it was 'One hell of a tuneful but ratty racket.' Things were definitely on the up. For a change.

There was a change in my personal adventures too. Jane and I had been drifting apart for some months. After the Bonnie and Clyde intensity of the last year or so, things had simply run their course. There were no great rows or one big splitting up incident, and the hand-to-mouth way we had been living meant that there were no issues over shared tenancies or possessions or anything like that. Jane moved into another flat on the top floor of Charles Barry Crescent, just seven doors down from The Kitchen. We had been friends for years before we were a couple, and still had a lot of shared friends, so we slid naturally back into that way of being. I was always a welcome visitor at her flat, as she was at mine.

I returned one night from a particularly exhilarating midweek practise to find two fire engines busily about their work. On my flat! A firefighter grabbed me roughly and threw me to one side as I tried to explain that I lived there. They hadn't been there long, apparently, and didn't yet know the extent of the damage, or how many people were in danger.

'Have you got any children?' screamed the leader of the fire crew.

I answered in the negative.

'Pets?'

Once again, it was a 'no'.

These responses seemed to calm things down a little, but by now, the enormity of the situation was beginning to hit home. Jamie came out of The Kitchen studio and brought me to his flat. I was in shock, mainly at the thought of what could have happened if I had been at home asleep instead of out at practise.

Once everything had been extinguished and all was calm, the fire chief took me round the remains of my flat, explaining that the blaze had been caused by 'someone leaving a cigarette unattended in an ashtray on the bed'. I had a sudden memory of being roused from a catnap that afternoon. I lit a cigarette then rushed out of the flat as soon as I heard Roger's car horn, five floors below. The fire was undoubtedly my fault.

I felt about three inches tall as this absolute hero of a fireman showed me the twisted and melted residue of what had previously been my life. These Hulme crescent flats were insulated in such a way as to turn extreme heat in on itself so that it didn't spread to the rest of the block. Everything inside the flat had been subject to temperatures ranging from 100 degrees at floor level up to 1500 degrees at ceiling height. Wherever I looked, the grotesque shapes of my meagre possessions, melted beyond belief, looked back at me. My record player had almost liquefied, dripping over the table it stood on. I felt sick to the pit of my stomach.

I was back in a familiar place; alone and homeless. Many years earlier I was helped by some brilliant people acting selflessly when I was in this situation, I now found that same spirit of love and practicality in my new-found musical family. Andy and Roger took me in and looked after me until I was back on my feet and able to get a new place. They were there with meals, clothes and free haircuts, as well as treating me like an extra brother, tagging me on to the end of their massive, sprawling family.

It was a no-brainer for Andy and Roger to step in with practical help. I spent a lot of time there anyway. It was handled as if it wasn't a big deal. They had the space, they said, and I'd be doing them a favour, security-wise, by being there in the daytime, even if it was only for a week or so. Once again, these two brothers reminded me that there were decent people in the world, without making me feel like a charity case. Such unconditional help always touched me and I was determined to make sure that I didn't overstay my welcome.

It was time for me to make yet another visit to my old friends, Moss Side Housing Department. Previous tenancies in my name, dating back to the early 1980s, had ended with me just leaving, without tying up any loose ends, and I knew that they had then been run into the ground by the people who were left living there after I had jettisoned. I explained that I had only recently moved into the Charles Barry Crescent flat, and I wasn't the official name on the tenancy agreement. Furthermore, the flat had been razed to the ground on my watch. Jamie Nicholson, just a few doors down, was in an ongoing battle with the council just for knocking an internal wall through, and as I waited for my overworked Estate Management Officer to emerge, I fully expected to be laughed out of Moss Side Precinct for my sheer cheek. Of course, I couldn't have been more wrong, and left the Housing Office once more twirling a set of keys, this time for a three-bedroom flat on the top floor of John Nash Crescent. Not a bad result for an accidental arsonist.

I simply moved into another fifth-floor dwelling, which was in great condition. I had nothing, apart from a mattress, some frayed bits of off-cut carpet, and my guitar, which being stored in the rehearsal room had escaped my self-inflicted inferno. None of this mattered at all to me though, as in a matter of weeks I would be doing my first John Peel session. My entire life, it felt, had led to this, and I was ready.

January 1987 was the coldest, snowiest starts to a year that I could remember. The high buildings of Hulme served as a wind tunnel and freezing blasts of cold air attacked anyone walking through, throwing grit in their eyes and whipping every piece of exposed skin mercilessly. It was against this backdrop that we set out to London early one morning, pinching ourselves, scarcely able to believe what was about to happen. We'd been up all night, too excited to sleep, and after some early hours running around, we set off before sunrise for what would be the start of absolutely everything.

Roger, using his insider knowledge of the world of vehicle hire, had wangled a huge van and had constructed a way of pumping hot air into the back, where Dave, Andy and I were stacked amongst the band's equipment. The journey was only five hours or so, but we would have been frozen like aircraft stowaways without this extra modification.

We arrived in leafy Maida Vale mid-morning, to be greeted by BBC porters, whose job it was to help us carry our equipment. This was definitely uncharted territory, and as the wheeled trucks rumbled their way towards Studio 5, I knew we had to be brilliant. I owed it to every last person who had cared for me, and shielded me from the storm that had been my life so far.

The BBC's Maida Vale studios place in musical history is secured forever, and nobody was more acutely aware of this than me. Since I was a mixed-up teenager, John Peel had been my window on the world, and when it seemed like I didn't fit in anywhere on earth, I could always find solace in his avuncular voice. Much of my musical taste had been informed by listening to his show: every single, every album, every new genre, and most importantly, every session. The Peel session was a right of passage for anybody who was anybody as I was growing up. I firmly believe that the programme helped break down barriers of race, class and sex, simply by exposing us all to cultures and styles of music that we would never have heard otherwise. His love of reggae, in particular, led to him getting sent human excreta in the post, and made him the target of knuckle-dragging racists of every description. I knew whose side I was on, and here I was, to prove it.

Even in the twilight world before punk, artists of the stature of Led Zeppelin, Pink Floyd, Jimi Hendrix and Bob Marley had recorded here. From Bowie to Bing Crosby, the place echoed with the ghosts of the greats. Running through its labyrinthine subterranean corridors, I could imagine The Beatles being sneaked in under the noses of their screaming fans, or feel Winston Churchill giving his first wartime broadcast from here in 1939. The whole place was etched into UK history, and here was little old me, a Mancunian orphan, bringing my world to that world, on equal terms. I could scarcely believe it was all happening. I was, for once in my life, in exactly the right place at the right time.

I was introduced to our producer, Dale Griffin. This was a complete mindfuck to start with, as he had been a member of what was one of my favourite bands as I first dipped my toes into the world of music. Mott The Hoople had captured my imagination at the height of their success. They had been helped by David Bowie just like he helped Iggy Pop or Lou Reed in later years, and his gift to them, 'All The Young Dudes' (after they had turned down his first offer of 'Suffragette City') had been a worldwide hit, kick-starting a string of classic singles like 'Roll Away The Stone', 'All The Way From Memphis' and 'Honaloochie Boogie'. This Bowie connection meant the world to the ten-year-old me, and Mott The Hoople posters had looked down on me from my bedroom wall in many a foster home. Dale 'Buffin' Griffin nestled amongst his bandmates Ariel Bender and Ian Hunter, the very essence of glam rock, all feather-cut hair and silver trousers, peeking out from an untouchable world, like a visiting alien dignitary. It was hard to equate the diminutive figure that warmly shook my hand with the Rock God of fifteen years previously. Quiet and unassuming, wearing Cuban heeled cowboy boots and conservative blue jeans, Dale told me how much he was looking forward to recording us, and I felt ten-feet tall.

We had chosen our four strongest songs, which we had been rehearsing to within an inch of their lives. 'Then and Now' was the first song we recorded, and it couldn't have been more relevant, as Hulme was in the grip of what seemed like a never-ending smack epidemic.

I put down a guide vocal over the drum and bass takes, and Dave and I played the first of several guitar layers. Although we added to the basic sound, things were more or less true to the way we sounded live. As I sang the line 'I heard them kick your door down', I could almost hear the splintering wood. I was in the zone, singing about real events, real people who had stolen from me and let me down. This was absolutely true stuff, and you can tell that on the first listen.

Dale Griffin and his engineer, Mike Robinson, had spent some time getting a basic sound ready as we were setting up, and although I knew they were brilliant, experienced professionals, I was in no way prepared for what met our ears when, after a few run-throughs, Dale brought us back into the control room to hear how things were progressing. It was fucking amazing.

These guys knew exactly what they were doing. Beautifully equalised drums pounded relentlessly, meshing with the bass to make a firm foundation, and even at this early, unmixed stage, with just guide vocals and guitars, to hear what I had imagined in my head coming back at me through the BBC's Solid State Logic desk pinned me to the back wall, open-mouthed and blown away.

'Play Street' followed. A simple song that evoked childhood memories in many different deprived areas of Manchester. In the city that I grew up in, although two decades had passed by the time I arrived, the impact of the Second World War was still surprisingly real. Rubble and cleared bombsites served as unofficial playgrounds, and on the official side of things, there were 'Play Streets', normal thoroughfares, closed off to cars between certain hours so kids could play in them. I remember bouncing a ball against the Old Trafford terraced houses, and had always loved the natural flanged/chorus effect I heard.

'Kristallnacht' came next, and once again, Dale took my production ideas seriously. I wanted to pan a single word ('snap!'), making it cross from left to right in the stereo mix at the same speed as the drums, and he not only agreed but did it perfectly for me. Both Mike and Dale got more and more into things as the day went on, and it felt to me that they were enjoying themselves, too.

'Man On The Inside' was perhaps the biggest surprise of the session. Pulsing and slow, coming out of a mournful feedback storm, it dipped into the murky world of the people who surrounded the musicians – managers and agents and record company executives. I was thinking mainly about the sixties soul scene, and the song touches upon the sad end of Jackie Wilson's life, whilst referencing Chairmen of The Board's General Johnson by using his trademark 'rrrrrrrrrrrr' from the masterpiece that is 'Give Me Just A Little More Time'. Once again, my former Mott The Hoople idol understood me completely, adding length and shine to my extended falsetto notes.

With all four songs recorded, we hit the canteen in search of famous faces and subsidised snacks. Having known other bands that had recorded sessions at Maida Vale, we had heard about the rite of passage that was the BBC canteen. Several of our friends had come back with tales of beautiful, cheap, subsidised food, and well-known faces being filled with it. I fully expected to see Noel Edmonds cutting up Angela Rippon's minted lamb chop, or Maggie Philbin slurping a bowl of BBC soup, but no such luck. The food was cheap and good, as we had been promised, but with the exception of the nice Jamaican lady serving us, we were more or less the only people in there. No Barbara Windsor, no Basil Brush, just little old us, and a few serious-looking engineer types.

We rejoined Dale and Mike back in Studio 5. They had evidently got rid of us for a reason, and having had some time to work on the songs, they played them back to us as they stood at that moment. All four sounded magnificent, and we hadn't even started mixing in earnest yet. From afternoon until late into the evening, we listened as they shaped our sound into a fierce and textured thing, heavy at the bottom end, but containing real subtlety and beauty within the anger and pain. This couldn't have gone any better, and we all knew the kick start this would give to our cause.

The BBC had strict rules about letting bands have copies of their Peel sessions. They felt that if they let bands walk out of Maida Vale with a copy of their work, they could unofficially press it up and release it as a bootleg, thus negating the Beeb's exclusivity. They compensated for this by paying musicians well for the recording, and also for any repeats of the session in future, but it left me bereft. I would have to wait until the session was aired before I could hear it again.

We were contacted by Peel's people the following week, with the news that we were scheduled to debut on 4th February. I spent every night until the session was broadcast with the songs ringing around my head on a permanent loop.

In the meantime we turned our attention to the next big landmark in our brief lives as a band, our third show, and our first as headliner. It was a return to a place that had played an important part in my musical education. The Factory nights at the Russell Club had exposed me to Joy Division, The Gang of Four, Magazine and countless others. I had even headlined a Factory night myself, with Vibrant Thigh. Now, after being bought by the brothers Pinch and Sonny Burton, it had been renamed the PSV (Public Service Vehicle) Club and served mainly as a late-night hangout for Caribbean bus drivers, as well as inquisitive local music lovers. It was the perfect place, spiritually, for the first headlining Dub Sex show.

The Kitchen's trouble with the council rumbled on. Jamie's structural alteration of his flat to accommodate the studio had attracted the unwanted attention of the powers that be, and Jamie was looking at substantial costs. It was decided that we would put on a benefit gig at the PSV to raise money for the cause. The club could hold around 600 people, and it was beyond ambitious for us to think that we could fill it, having only done two support gigs before, but there was a buzz starting to happen around us, and I just knew that if we aimed high we would get what we wanted.

We were helped in our quest by our first major interview with a national music paper. I had been reading *Melody Maker* since I was a music-obsessed foster child, so it was wonderful for me to be told that, on the strength of the 'Tripwire' flexi, and the impact it had made, they were dispatching a reporter and photographer to the Hulme badlands to be the first amongst their rivals to interview us. The article wasn't due out until a few days after the gig, but the grapevine knew all about this interest so we filled the PSV on word of mouth alone.

Alongside our own progress, Lee and Karl had joined Martin Bramah to form Thirst, with Karl's girlfriend, Carrie Lawson, on second guitar. They too had become part of things at The Kitchen. Jamie let them use his studio to get their first set together, which featured Blue Orchids classics like 'Work', 'The Flood' and 'Agents of Change', as well as new songs by Martin such as 'The Unknown' and 'Riding The Times', which took Lee's bassline from the early Dub Sex song 'Kristallnacht' as its starting point. We were all still good friends away from music, and when Jamie organised the benefit gig to help with his current troubles, it seemed natural to invite Thirst onto the bill as well. It was to be their first gig. We had invited Dave Haslam to DJ too, and this gave the event another layer of credibility with the inquisitive hip audience.

Everything we did that night came off. From the thundering intro of 'Play Street' to the accusatory, finger-pointing 'Then and Now', we didn't put a foot wrong. In front of my neighbours and peers, who had been attracted to find out what all the buzz was about but wouldn't have known that the weird looking skinny kid they saw all the time was the singer, we turned in a tight performance. We had invited representatives from a Liverpool-based label called Skysaw Records, and we left the gig having been offered a one-off single deal with them.

Shortly after the gig, *Melody Maker* came out with our interview in it. Their writer Billy Smith had really been bitten. 'On record, the man's voice and guitar hammer like a pneumatic thunderbolt, but stood here, he's just another Bash Street kid ... Dub Sex certainly have the intelligence, the commitment and the sheer energy to succeed.' This was great stuff, and was accompanied by stark, moody photos of us taken in an eerie snow-covered Hulme. I felt validated. I had wanted to be part of this world for my entire life, and here it all was, Bowie on one page, me on the other, exactly as the ten-year old me had dreamed. Amazed as I was, I also knew that we were deserving of this attention.

We took a deep breath and waited for the transmission of our Peel session the following week. It was all that we'd hoped for. Peel was generous in his praise whilst introducing the songs, telling his vast national and international audience that we were 'my kind of a band, definitely'. Sprinkled throughout were superlatives like 'brilliant' and 'excellent'. Most impressively of all, the songs sounded fantastic.

21: The Art Of Surprise

Skysaw Records were the most enthusiastic of the small labels to show an interest in Dub Sex. They were one of the first, too, reacting to the first playing of the 'Tripwire' flexidisc within a short time of John Peel airing it. We sent them a copy of the three-track demo that we had given to *Debris* in the first place, and this got them even more interested. I talked to label boss Peter Leay on the phone, and his enthusiasm seemed genuine. His idea of releasing a four-track 12-inch single was exactly what I wanted to hear, so I invited him and his colleague, Barry, to our PSV gig. This was a test of how serious they were and they passed with flying colours, answering my questions about what they would be prepared to pay for, and agreeing with me that, even though we were a new band, it was worth investing in a decent studio for a decent length of time in order to capture what we all agreed was a new and unique sound. All this sounded good, and we arranged to drive over to Liverpool to visit the label's headquarters and see what they were all about.

With *Motown Chartbusters* on the cassette deck, we set off on a beautiful sunny afternoon towards Liverpool, and the next stage in our quest. We had gone through several bonding experiences as a band in the short time we had been together but this was a cut above. To be invited to make a record by a legitimate label was exactly what we had wanted, and for Roger and Dave, who had never had their name on a 'real' release, it was even more special. For Dave in particular. His experience of the music industry so far was as a sound engineer, always dealing with somebody else's music, and to have so much happening to him as a musician over the last few months had blown him away. He sat quietly in the back of the car, grinning nervously all the way up the M62. I took my place in the front next to Roger, in charge of skinning up, and ensuring that we never went short of uplifting music on the journey.

Skysaw Records was based in New Brighton, a seaside town that was popular in Victorian times but had gone to seed somewhat during the course of the twentieth century as resorts like Blackpool and Southport became more popular. Even though its days as a holiday destination were long gone, it retained a bruised and neglected charm.

The label was housed in a former railway station building, and seemed to us to be a hive of activity. 12-inch singles by KMFDM and Jegsy Dodd lay scattered around, ready to be posted out. Pete outlined his ideas for us sat amongst piles of posters and promotional materials. We had come armed with some ideas and questions of our own, especially Dave, who quizzed Pete and Barry about mechanical royalties in a somewhat paranoid fashion, as if he expected to be ripped off by somebody somewhere at some time. It was the music business after all! Cathy and I were more positive, and it transpired that this was to be the standard independent deal, with both parties splitting any profits 50/50 after the break-even point.

Even though we were a new band, only a few gigs old, I had absolute belief in what we were doing. Whoever was to put our records out would have to prove themselves by putting their hand in their pocket when it came to the recording budget. I wanted the option of full colour sleeve artwork, too, and total commitment to getting the records into the hands of reviewers, gig agents and radio stations. There was to be a week of recording at a studio of our choice, plus professional mastering at a decent mastering studio. We picked Suite 16 in Rochdale, formerly Cargo, which had been bought and transformed by New Order's Peter Hook and my old friend Shan Hira. The studio had been upgraded, but it retained the feel and mood that had brought out the best in many artists.

To be going into Suite 16 for a whole week seemed like an impossible luxury to me. When I had used the studio before, with Vibrant Thigh, we had recorded and mixed five songs in a single day. To have five whole days to record was hard to believe. I felt sure we'd have more than enough time to complete the job. We planned to record four songs. At this point, we had already recorded 'Man On The Inside' and 'Then and Now' at Maida Vale, and I had plans to replicate some of the delay tricks and general feel of the session. We had recorded 'Tripwire' with Jamie at The Kitchen, and I had some ideas for the vocals that had come from our time there. The fourth song, 'Green', was perhaps the most straightforward in construction, hanging itself onto a two-note bassline and leaving it to me to layer many guitar parts and panned vocal overdubs.

Shan was to engineer our session. As well as being the co-owner of the studio, he had been the drummer for Factory band Stockholm Monsters, as well as being Stephen Morris's drum roadie for many New Order tours. It would be fair to say that drums were 'his thing', and true enough, the first day was spent with Roger and Shan working together to achieve a good drum sound. Knowing we had some money coming in from the Peel session meant we were able to buy new strings and drumskins ready for the recording, and Roger's kit sounded amazing from the start. The three of us listened to Shan taking things even further, tweaking the top end for maximum attack, while still retaining the powerful sharp definition of his bass drum. We were enthralled.

With the drum sound sorted, it was time to add Cathy into the mix. She had been efficient when we had recorded at The Kitchen with Jamie, but was even more professional here, never missing a note as Shan blended bass and drums into a workable rhythm section, already listenable, even at this early, unmixed stage.

Dave took his first time in a 'proper' studio very seriously. Much to our amusement, he had invested in a tube of Fret Glide, a product sold by music shops to help heavy metal guitarists to 'shred' quicker when playing fast, overcomplicated lead guitar solos. Dave was mainly playing simple chords. His Kimbara Stratocaster copy was prone to going out of tune after each take, and the stopping and starting in the studio chipped away at his confidence. Eventually, the power of the music carried him through, and he turned in some good performances, even if they took a little longer than we might have liked.

By the time I did my main vocals, the other members of the band had finished their parts, packed away their equipment, and were visible through the studio window, a little audience of the people closest to the centre of the music, making me want to try even harder and sing even better. After a while, Roger came into the vocal booth with me, just to give me some spiritual support. Sitting silently behind me, taking in the atmosphere and hearing my vocals in isolation, he made an already special moment even more special, just by being there. Here, in this dimly-lit Rochdale studio, I was finding among my fellow musicians a sense of family that I had never known before, and it felt great.

Feeling that I had plenty of time meant that I could relax into the process and pick out hidden earworms within the wall of sound. I overdubbed extra vocals, reinforcing certain words. But the luxury of time suddenly disappeared. After getting the basic tracks down, we were left with only a day and a half to mix all four songs. This wasn't going to be enough. It meant that at the end of the five-day session our beautiful record was frustratingly lacking in bite. The bottom end that we were capable of producing live wasn't there, and all the instruments sounded strangely separate from each other where they needed to gel into a cohesive whole. For all my bullying of Skysaw into giving us enough money for a full week, even this had proved to be not enough time. They expected the tapes to be delivered as soon as we had finished, and would not be amenable to shelling out any more money, having been pushed to the limit of their budget already. To add to our predicament, Suite 16 was fully booked from then on, and we couldn't continue mixing there even if we had wanted to.

But, like others of late, this cloud had its silver lining. Dave knew Chris Nagle a little from his time working with Easterhouse, for whom Chris had produced an album and a single. I knew him as Martin Hannett's right-hand man and engineer of choice on piles of brilliant records, including most of the important Factory releases, like Joy Division's *Unknown Pleasures* album, and beautiful pieces of music by the likes of Durutti Column and Orchestral Manoeuvres In The Dark. When it was suggested that there was a chance that he could remix the four tracks we'd recorded in Rochdale, I was all ears.

With the Skysaw budget all used up, we put our hands in our pockets and chipped in as a band to pay Chris and hire a studio to do the remixing. I was as poor as a church mouse, and the rest were little better off, but somehow we raised enough for Chris's fee and an overnight 10-hour session at Yellow 2 in Stockport, Strawberry's sister studio across the road from the main building.

I liked Chris Nagle from the off. He was calm and quiet, and it was obvious that he was supremely skilled and knew the studio like the back of his hand. He had been given a cassette of where we were up to, but had only had a brief time to get acquainted with it, being so busy over the road at Strawberry. In fact, he could only spare the one night to mix all four songs.

It was an education watching Chris at work that night. We let him get on with it, as opposed to getting hung up on fiddly details and slowing the process down the way we had at Suite 16. Chris began by stripping the multitrack down to absolutely nothing, and then he re-built the songs from ground up. New tones emerged immediately. The rhythm section thundered like the way it did live. Chris had brought a few effects from Strawberry that created the most brilliant illusion of space around the trebly end, like my falsetto vocals and guitar harmonics. He widened the stereo field, making it seem as if we were coming at the listener from every direction at once, placing my voice high in the mix, giving a sense of urgency and authority.

Ten hours became twelve, and then fourteen, as Chris continued to work on the tunes, immersed in his meticulous checking and re-shaping as the cleaners came and went. With the single completed, he edited the ¼-inch master tape by hand, using a wooden block and razor blade in preparation for the mastering and pressing process. We lay draped across settees and on the plush carpeted floor, listening to what we had achieved. It sounded wonderful.

We were so new to the game that we had to leave the master tapes with the studio until our cheque had cleared. Chris, and Strawberry, had been 'bounced' on many occasions, and had no real proof of our honest nature. We piled into Roger's car and sped back to Manchester bleary-eyed and smiling from ear to ear as we blasted out the cassette copy Chris had given us secure in the knowledge that we had done ourselves, and the music, proud.

For such a brilliant record, we had to have an equally brilliant sleeve. Something that gripped you at first sight, while at the same time said something about the pace and ferocity of the music. Checking out several photography collections from Manchester Central Library, I found exactly what I wanted in a *Best of the Year* collection from 1973. In fact, two very similar photos had caught my eye. Both photographs featured snarling dogs in fierce competition at a greyhound race; muzzled with bulging eyes, the very embodiment of our sound. The images particularly suited 'Tripwire', the lead track.

We set about contacting the relevant photographers. The first one was amenable to us using his work, but wanted several hundred pounds up front for the privilege. This was several hundred pounds too much for little old us, so we cautiously contacted the creator of the other image, which was almost identical.

To our great surprise, he couldn't have been more helpful.

'Oh, that old thing!' he replied.

Having given up photography more than a decade earlier, he was amused and pleased by our request, saying that as long as his name ended up on the sleeve, then he was happy for us to use it for free. We duly added 'Photo by P. Hoare' to our Letraset-ed information, and all the components for our first single were in place.

It was going to look every bit as good as it sounded.

22: Coming Up On Your Blind Side

Our John Peel session was repeated just a few weeks after its original broadcast. This Radio 1 airplay lifted our profile across the country and led to us playing outside Manchester for the first time. We had been rehearsing loads, fired up by the attention that our session had generated, and had become a lot better in a very short time. The more we believed in ourselves, the more songs like 'Splintered' and 'Voice of Reason' became sharper and harder.

First off was Leeds, where John Keenan invited us to play at the Duchess of York. The gig felt like a big success. We recognised a young punky lad in the audience that we were sure lived in Hulme. He had been at the Pop Will Eat Itself gig and also our PSV show. Although we didn't know him properly, we did have a few friends in common. It turned out that he had made the journey on his own, and was rather bitten by the band's music. After much post-gig chatting, it seemed stupid to let him make his own way back to the very place that we were going to, so we bundled him into the van – he was as thin as a microphone stand anyway – and by the time we reached Manchester, our little crew had a new member. 'Rat', as he was known, joined us as a roadie.

I knew straight away that Rat was a beautiful soul. He was quiet most of the time, and spread a wonderful sense of calm that made you want to listen to what he had to say. We had a lot of shared musical tastes that the rest of the band didn't really go for, harder, more extreme bands like Poison Girls, Flux of Pink Indians, and other left-field artists often associated with the Crass label and commune at Dial House in Epping Forest. He had a taste for American hardcore too, and knew his way around the work of Black Flag and Dead Kennedys.

He'd left Scarborough in search of adventure, drawn to the inner city by the ever-expanding punk community, which was growing in numbers year on year, and found Dub Sex at just the right time.

Rat lived five doors down from Roger and Andy's flat, which by now was becoming something of a HQ for the band, and shared his Bonsall Street flat with another member of our inner circle, Stephen Bunn, who had become our live sound engineer. Stephen had been part of things some years before at Anthony Behrendt's Jerusalem studios. His band, My American Wife, were very much the 'band most likely to…' in 1985. They had attracted major label interest and a publishing deal, as well as playing some memorable gigs, notably supporting Fad Gadget at the Haçienda, a gig largely remembered for Fad Gadget's lead singer Frank Tovey's tendency towards self-harm.

Like many other people, Stephen had come to Manchester for the music, but in his case his entire band had relocated from Bolton with him in a quest for success and had never gone back. Stephen is one day older than me, leading to much mickey-taking of the 'What did you do in the war, Daddy?' variety. The two of us became close, a sub-unit within the band. His grasp of reggae-style dub effects was second to none, and before long, he became known as 'Dubmeister', a nickname that mutated to 'The Bunnmeister', and stuck. Gradually, an extended team was evolving.

Andy Cadman had a friend who had been around the flat a lot and would come with us to the pub after rehearsals. His name was Paul Humphreys. Paul was a little older than me, nearer to Andy's age. He had been involved with various bands in London some years before, managing an early version of The Monochrome Set, as well as knowing Wire, who I had a lot of time for. Being a person with a phone and time on his hands, Paul started helping us in small managerial ways, ringing agents and press, and generally helping with mailing things out.

Paul lived alone, and I think that being involved with the band helped him to get out and meet people. Either way, as things got busier, Paul ended up doing more, and in a very short time, he was being referred to as our 'manager' by people. It didn't hurt to look a bit more professional, and with Cathy and Roger working during office hours, and me being phoneless, it seemed like a good idea.

A strange and varied mixture of people started to turn up at our gigs.

Jamie Nicholson was a regular, Cathy's university friend, Anna, was another, and my friend Christina, who had been brought up as a child in the Hulme crescents before the real madness had started. Things were starting to grow.

We followed up the Leeds show with our London debut at The Sir George Robey on Seven Sisters Road. It had a reputation as a ska hangout, artists like Desmond Dekker, Madness and Bad Manners had graced its tiny stage in previous times. Excited as we were to be playing in the capital, the show was over as soon as it had begun. We found ourselves sandwiched between far too many bands, none of whom had anything in common with us. It was often the way for new bands trying to find their way. Reviewers from the national music press rarely left Camden, let alone London, and bands like ours would have to find London gigs of any description in order to be written about. This, and our next London appearance, at the notorious Bull and Gate in Kentish Town, taught us a valuable lesson about control. From now on, we would take an active hand in every aspect of a show. Wherever we could, we would pick the bands that played with us, making sure that they would share some common ground, and appeal in some way to the audience that we were starting to build. It was audacious for such a new band, and probably naive, but it helped us set out our stall and show who we were.

We knuckled down to a productive period of rehearsals. New songs emerged. 'The Big Freeze', 'The Underneath' and 'Push!' came through, along with the first stirrings of a song that I had started to get off the ground in Roger and Andy's flat the previous year, 'Turn Into A Blur'. We were in good shape for the release of our single, ready for the whirlwind of publicity and gigs.

Just as we'd hoped, and dreamed, the single was praised across the music press. James Brown wrote a feature for the *NME* and set the tone with his description of the band: 'Palpitating basslines with a dusty Manc drawl that's as gritty and piss-stained as the Hulme estate that houses the band.' I'd conducted a telephone interview with James and he let me speak for myself, the first time I had been quoted in the *NME*.

'I like directness and I don't like people bullshitting me. When we're up there playing, it's not just my voice, it's the whole band. It's important that the band has a lot of respect for each other.'

Very true, and perhaps the first stirrings of a sense of egalitarianism that would colour the way I wanted things to be run. For example, all songs were credited equally, to 'Dub Sex', and in any list of band members our names would appear alphabetically in an attempt to diffuse any kind of singling out of any particular person.

Other papers followed suit, notably *Record Mirror*, who sent correspondent John Slater to see what all the fuss was about. He caught me on an egalitarian mission too, quoting me on how I thought the music business needed to change: 'The people in power; programme controllers, pluggers, radio and the press. Even down to the people you pay to put up your posters (and don't) have got to change their attitudes. Put some honesty back into the business.' When asked about the demographic of our audience, I told John, 'In a lot of ways, I suppose we're making records for people who've stopped buying records. People who've lost faith.' No doubt that would have had the major record label bosses who were looking for the next big thing salivating at the prospect of picking us up.

With the big music papers on board, others followed, including *Underground*'s Craig Ferguson. He was a sucker, it seemed, for the 'Dub Sexy sound of claustrophobia and advanced neurosis'. Craig's early support meant a lot to us, and helped grease the wheels just that little bit more. The gigs we were getting offered were indicative of the progress we had been making, and it seemed that everything we had imagined was coming true in front of our eyes.

August started with a trip to Leeds again, this time to support Texas's Butthole Surfers at the city's polytechnic. It was part of a two gig thing, the other headliner being Steve Albini's Big Black, which I think would have been a more appropriate pairing for us.

We benefited from the larger venue and hip crowd. Stephen Bunn put in a great shift as our live sound engineer, dubbing the living daylights out of our ever-tightening sound. There was a strange and beautiful moment during the gig. As I sang 'so that anybody else can see' in the new song 'Believe', it was as if everything fell into place. My voice, Cathy's bass, Stephen's extreme live mixing, it was a real goosebumps moment. Stephen's live echo-drenched assault left the hall open mouthed and confused as my voice degenerated into the sound of a flock of furious birds, circling the hall and bouncing around the walls.

Butthole Surfers were something of an underground acquired taste, and were only playing a small number of European shows on this visit, so people had travelled from all over the country to catch the show. They were an all-out attack on the senses – filthy distorted guitars, demonic loudhailer vocals and an unrelenting double-drummer line-up pulverised the ears under a shocking and stomach-churning film collage. Added to this was the weirdness of naked dancer Kathleen Lynch, who kept in character for the whole night, emanating a studied and enigmatic strangeness both on and off the stage.

The gig got us another *NME* review, complete with a huge photo of me laying waste to my trusty Fender Bullet, captioned 'While my guitar frenziedly bleeds'. If a picture is worth a thousand words, this one left little doubt as to the extremist nature of what we did. Dark, mysterious and moody. Being associated with an interesting and uncompromising band like Butthole Surfers did us no end of good.

We followed that gig up a few days later with our first outdoor show, at the Manchester Show in Platt Fields Park. Headlined by press darlings Black Britain, it featured us and Happy Mondays, not long after releasing their *Squirrel and G-Man* album which had been produced by John Cale for Factory. This was an annual free event, put on by the city council, and previously been headlined by the likes of Simply Red.

It was my twenty-fifth birthday and I was blessed to have two gigs on the same day. Playing on your birthday is special enough for anybody, but to have *two* gigs really took the biscuit. For years, due to the way I had been living, I got used to treating the 7th August as just another day. I remember being alone on my twenty-first and it brought home the difference between my own life and the more 'normal' lives of other people. I visualised my former classmates in the bosom of their loving families for a rite of passage denied to me, receiving their first car, or the proverbial key of the door. Instead, penniless and downhearted, I wandered over to a nearby party in John Nash Crescent, thrown by some people that I hardly knew, and spent this supposedly special day with strangers. Today was the polar opposite of that.

First of all, I got a visit from Jamie. He had a session in his studio that day so couldn't come to the gigs, but had brought a card for me containing £25 in record tokens. It probably doesn't sound that remarkable an event, but this simple act of kindness got through to me, and was proof positive that music was leading me in a good direction, towards civilised, decent people. People that remembered birthdays.

I arrived at Roger and Andy's flat where we were all meeting up to get picked up by the van to set off for Platt Fields. Opening the living room door was the cue for a spirited rendition of 'Happy Birthday' from the rest of my band, plus Andy and Rat, who had assembled early, in order to spring the surprise. There were more cards and something even more special. The band had clubbed together to buy me my first ever Walkman. It was a yellow and green, non-Sony version, the most basic of machines, but for me, both the Walkman itself and the very fact of being thought about was priceless. I dabbed a happy tear from my eye, and turned towards the day ahead.

Filled with birthday chemicals, having been enjoying an extended party week leading up to this momentous weekend, we played a violently agitated set in the pouring Manchester rain. I was blinded by the deluge as water trickled down over my glasses and invaded our equipment. Fearful of electrocution, we stormed through our set at speed. I noticed that, despite being soaked to the skin, the audience not only stayed for all of it, but actually grew in size, as more and more wet punters drew near to listen. I felt like a soggy Mancunian pied piper.

We packed our equipment, plus Karl Burns, into our hired van and headed down the M62 to play show number two, at Planet X in Liverpool. We played everything twice as fast as normal, no doubt to the approval of the sparse crowd, who seemed to be drawn from the skater/punk community going from the t-shirts on display, celebrating bands like The Stupids and US hardcore acts like Black Flag and Flipper.

Karl, having assured us that his live mixing skills were second to none, proceeded to coax an eardrum-destroying wall of feedback that sent the few people there into a world of shock and pain. Luckily for them, he blew the entire PA up before we had a chance to get to the end of the set, which, although frustrating for us, probably saved the eardrums of many a Scouser. Happy birthday to me!

We were back in Liverpool the following week for another outdoor show at Earthbeat Festival, held over three days in Sefton Park. We were on a bill with a lot of upcoming bands, including Pulp and The La's. Also on the bill were The Stone Roses, fronted by Ian Brown. Ian had taken encouragement from Geno Washington at that party at Charles Barry Crescent thrown for his girlfriend Michelle's twenty-first birthday. Geno had told him that night that he should be a singer in a band.

The gig was a surreal experience. The stage was built in the park's Victorian bandstand, which looked out over a lake. The audience were on the other side of this lake, taking up residence on a hill. There were quite a lot of them, to be fair, but the distance between us and them meant that our 'in your face' all-out sonic assault went upwards, into the atmosphere, blown around by the wind on its way to the crowd. We gave it our all, to be rewarded by the sight of a family of ducks elegantly swimming past, furiously ignoring my wild man of rock antics, as the weirdness of the situation spurred us on to an angry performance. Weird though it was, it was rewarding to see quite a few Manchester fans there, a further sign that things were travelling in the right direction as far as building up an audience was concerned.

Riding the high, two days later we were back in BBC's Maida Vale studios to record our second John Peel session. It had only been a few months since out debut session, so we must have impressed somebody as were invited back quicker than most. We were more than ready to unveil some of our new material, which, in the wake of all that was happening, fizzed with an authority that had surprised even ourselves.

Once again, Dale Griffin was to produce the session, with the experienced Martin Colley as engineer. This time, though, things were not to go as smoothly as before. One of our new songs, 'Push!', was simply too extreme for Dale, featuring as it did some violent guitar mistreatment involving me scraping the fretboard against a metal microphone stand and randomly hitting my instrument to produce scratchy, atonal sounds. It was nothing that Jimi Hendrix hadn't done, even in the very same studio, but my Mott The Hoople buddy repeatedly stopped me in my tracks with a patronising 'Can you check your tuning, please, Mark?'

Excellent, never to be repeated takes were dismissed due to their perceived lack of musicality. The whole point of what I was doing was to subvert the traditional 'rock' format, but Dale was having none of it. It came to the point where he threatened to block the broadcasting of the song altogether, telling us that our session would go out with only three tracks. This was the last straw, and standing my ground, I proceeded to destroy my unfortunate guitar the way I set out to all along, perhaps a little less dramatically, but no less spiritedly.

Dale backed down, and the session went out on 24th August with 'Push!' as the first track, accompanying 'Splintered', 'Voice of Reason' and 'Kicking the Corpse Around'. It was disappointing that Dale hadn't got what we were doing this time, but it transpired that he was something of a reactionary when it came to the more extreme bands that passed through Maida Vale, definitely more at home with traditional guitar-based line-ups than with the likes of Test Department or Einsturzende Neubauten, although we were nearer to what he was used to than either of those two.

Great gigs were coming thick and fast. We played in a tent in Manchester's Castlefield basin as part of the Castlefield Festival, then back in Leeds to record a session for the BBC Radio Leeds *On the Rocks* programme, a very different experience from working at Maida Vale. On this one, we had to play absolutely live, inserting our tunes (six this time) into the show as it was going out. It was nerve-racking being cued in by a DJ knowing that there are no second chances, but we stormed it. If anything, the extra tension led to a fiercer, more extreme performance, and I took great pleasure in kicking seven shades out of my guitar during an extended version of 'Push!', which although only recently written, had already become a band favourite.

The session was followed by a live interview, which found me in a nervous and wired state, gibbering nineteen to the dozen. When asked about who our fanbase were, I told the good people of Yorkshire that it's 'basically people with ears'. I guess this was an upgrade in scale from 'people who've stopped buying records', in itself testimony to our summer of success.

Next up was our return to The Boardwalk, this time having built up enough of a following to headline on a prestigious Saturday night spot. The entire year had seen us growing in stature. It was a brilliant feeling to sell out a hometown venue, even though The Boardwalk was fairly small, and the rising profile of our support band, Inspiral Carpets, helped move a few tickets.

The gig felt great. We were called back for encore after encore, so we unveiled a new song. It wasn't quite ready, so we stretched and stretched the length of the middle 'freak out' section to a ridiculous length, destroying my last spare guitar in a frenzy of happiness and joy. 'The Underneath' dealt with my childhood, painting a gritty and often violent picture of the Langley estate and my time there. It was obvious, even from this first performance, that this song marked a turning point in our songwriting, and I knew in my heart of hearts that we had created an important thing. As my voice echoed the song's final words around the building – 'Get out and stay out' – I was transported back to my horrific early years, completely in the zone. Caught and mangled by Stephen Bunn's space echo trickery, the vocals seemed to go on forever, degenerating into an unholy and frightening parody of the human voice. This was real and terrifying, but also strangely beautiful. I knew we had a future single on our hands. This was the very opposite of the escapist, lightweight pop that seemed to be everywhere. It was fiercely non-fiction, and unafraid of the consequences, music that could only have been made by me, having lived through the storm alone.

23: Push!

We had sent a copy of the first single to Phil Korbel, hoping that he'd play it on *Meltdown*, his BBC Radio Manchester show, which was a sort of localised version of John Peel's show. Phil also operated as an activist, and one day while leafleting in central Manchester he was listening to his Walkman when 'Tripwire' came on in his headphones at the very moment that Cathy walked around the corner. Knowing her from seeing the band, the two got talking. Shortly after that they became a couple. Such is the power of music.

As a result, Phil drifted more into our orbit. As did Guy Lovelady, the man behind the football fanzine *Rodney Rodney*, and the label Ugly Man Records. Guy had started coming to our gigs, and it was becoming clear that he wanted to sign Dub Sex. Skysaw had done a job with our debut EP, but we had come a long way in a very short space of time, and we'd outgrown them already. Save for the pressing, almost all the action taking place around the release had everything to do with ourselves, as opposed to our record label, so we were keen to speak with Guy. We took him to The Church, a quiet pub in Longsight, empty apart from jobless cannabis dealers playing pool, and held a semi-formal meeting where we grilled him about what he could (and would) do for us.

Guy was quick-witted and funny with a soft Merseyside accent. I sensed he felt relaxed in our company. He didn't mind receiving the third degree from me and Roger, and seemed open to our plans to record at Strawberry, using Chris Nagle, which was expensive for a small label like Ugly Man, unsupported by any major backer. To his credit, he even talked about the promotion of the album, with Guy saying that he was prepared to pay for targeted adverts in the music press and the more switched on fanzines, as well as producing stickers and huge posters in central Manchester, where our fanbase, such as it was, would come to shop and be entertained.

For the sleeve, I said that I wanted silver outlines on the band's logo and album title, which would push up the costs, as would an insert featuring the lyrics to 'Push!'. I could have been saying anything though. Through a combination of listening to our first single and Peel session, as well as seeing us live, Guy had already made up his mind to release Dub Sex on his label.

Ugly Man Records had a distribution deal with Red Rhino, which ensured that our records would be in the right shops at the right time, an important factor, as people needed to be able to buy them the next day after hearing them on John Peel or wherever they heard them. The record-buying public is a notoriously fickle creature, and would give up on a release if it wasn't there for them exactly when they asked for it. A distribution deal ensured that from Aberdeen to Truro, and also in foreign parts, our beautiful records would be there when they needed to be. All we had to do now was to make the thing.

I woke up on the first day of recording at Roger and Andy's flat. The brothers had more or less adopted me by this time, feral creature that I was, and as most of the band planning and organising was done here, I felt like part of the furniture. It was a great little scene, with members of The Weeds and The Fall hanging around, and a steady stream of people turning up to have their hair cut in Andy's home salon. Although we had moved to a proper rehearsal room, there were guitars and other musical equipment in the room that we used to practise in, and I was encouraged to have a play whenever I felt like it.

Andy was a gifted guitarist himself and he was always ready for a jam upstairs, much to the delight of his neighbours. Time and time again he was there for me to bounce ideas off. Many songs started life in this way. These two brothers were the nearest thing to family I had known in my life, and it was perfectly appropriate that I was waking up in their flat on the day I had waited for since I was a music-obsessed kid.

All my life I had dreamed of making my first album. Every music fan has gazed out of the window at school, imagining artwork and titles, scribbling sleeve designs, and dreaming of who would produce their debut album, where it would be recorded, how it would be received. The day had finally come for me, and I bounced into the bathroom, splashed my face with water, and began the next big phase of the band's life.

As we waited for Dave to arrive, our morning was soundtracked by our new friend, Phil Korbel, on BBC Radio Manchester. He had been drafted in to cover the ultra-mainstream breakfast drivetime show. It was strangeness itself to hear Phil in such a normal 'radiophonic' environment. We were used to him bringing the likes of Swiss industrialists The Young Gods or French extremists Treponem Pal to an unsuspecting public via his *Meltdown* show. Here he was, giving out traffic updates in a decidedly BBC twang, as upbeat as 'Diddy' David Hamilton, Tony Blackburn, or any traditional breakfast show host. There was even a phone-in where Phil interacted with the public in a jovial and very DJ-like manner. This was surely to be no ordinary day.

After Dave arrived, the ride to the studio was quiet as far as conversation went, we hit a 'calm before the storm' kind of feeling, gladiatorial, almost. The importance of what we were about to do was not lost on anyone, and as we entered Stockport, with the smooth beauty of Smokey Robinson's 'Just My Soul Responding' washing us clean, we were linked as friends in a deep and real way. To an orphan like me, moments like this were important, humanising experiences. Music was giving me lessons in how to be part of the human race, lessons that had sadly passed me by earlier in life.

Our relationship with Chris Nagle had developed a lot since his rescue job on the first single. Roger and I had taken copies of the record to his house, and I'd been round since then as a friend. He lived in a small, newish house on Thompson Street in Stockport, just a ten minute walk from Strawberry. In the course of planning the record, I created a mock-up of the album we intended to record by collating various live and rehearsal versions of the songs. There was 'Push!' and 'Believe' from the Butthole Surfers support slot in Leeds, 'Play Street' and 'Kristallnacht' from the first Peel session, and rehearsal tapes of 'Voice of Reason', 'Kicking The Corpse Around' and 'Splintered'. Rough and ready though it was, Chris got it, and these home visits – which were more social occasions than pre-production meetings – went a long way towards bringing us together as friends, which in turn contributed to our work in the studio being natural and intuitive.

The first part of the recording was to take place at Strawberry's other studio, Yellow 2. Chris was a very hands-on producer, having already had years of experience as Strawberry's in-house engineer and having being part of 10cc's live setup more or less straight from school. He was already setting the desk up and readying the microphones by the time we arrived. He knew what he wanted.

The first day was spent with Roger and Chris working on the drums. There can be a lot of waiting around in studios, and it is quite an art to not be impatient and to be ready to spring into full action straight away when needed. For my part, I immersed myself in the process, taking notice of every subtle frequency change as Chris brought Roger's kit to life in front of my ears, turning percussive thuds into beautiful ringing notes. This was an education.

Next was Cathy, ever the professional, never putting a foot wrong as Chris expanded and thickened her sound. Roger and Cathy played together for a while to work on their headphone mixes, and then it was time for me and Dave. Our guitars at this point were guide guitars, we would be putting the real ones down later in Strawberry, having worked on the sound. Chris liked to use these ghost guitars as added texture, so it was important that we got them sounding right, and having done this, late into the evening of the first day, we started on the album's title track, 'Push!'. It sounded fierce.

Yellow 2 was an exciting enough place, but we were to be spending a large chunk of the recording time, and all of the mixing time, at Strawberry itself, which, to me, had a deep significance. To any music fan that had grown up during the seventies, the place had a fame and importance all of its own, and here I was, shortly to be singing in the very same room that 10cc's 'I'm Not In Love' was painstakingly constructed, to say nothing of all the wonderful records made by Chris himself here.

Entering Strawberry, the first person we met was Chris's wife, Julia, who was working on reception. She told Roger and me that Chris had been playing our monitor mixes to death at their home, and had been raving to her about our guitar sound and how he couldn't wait to work his magic on it. We felt ten feet tall.

Beyond reception was a short corridor, leading on the right to the mixing room where Chris had spent most of his adult life. He greeted us with warm handshakes, and we began the process of putting down our real guitars, with my vocals to follow after that.

The work went well from the start. We had been rehearsing and rehearsing until the songs were second nature, and I had worked out extra guitar parts to be overdubbed on top of my regular rhythm guitar lines. Chris had a whole bunch of tricks in store for us, and blew our minds with ambient microphone placements, giving depth and definition to things in a way that I couldn't have imagined before.

The finished parts, even in their raw, unmixed state, were astounding. Swarms of invisible locusts buzzed and swirled within the music, and surprising, unheard tones came at you from everywhere at once. Chris understood our music perfectly, he found things in it that even we hadn't expected to find. Songs like 'Splintered' and 'Push!' were built up, layer upon layer, into a fierce mesh of textured guitars and ghost sounds, surrounding the listener and tricking the ears into hearing sounds that weren't really there.

Chris had created an inspiring soundscape for me to sing over. Spending the largest part of the session on perfecting the drums, and multi-tracking differently treated basslines, he had inspired Dave and me to put our guitar parts down quickly and efficiently, and before too long it was time for me to be alone in the vocal booth, just me and my words.

I have always dealt in truth when it comes to writing songs. Cathartic though this may be, it meant putting myself in a dark and deep psychological place every time I sang them. Alone in the vocal booth, I revisited my fractured past, reliving the experiences that had led me here. Singing 'Play Street' took me back to my nightmare childhood and thoughts of how far I had come, and how sad it was that my mother was not around to know about it made it even more real to me.

Privately, in my own mind, I was dealing with issues of loss and abandonment for the first time, and in the most intense and harrowing way imaginable. I could never be satisfied with the trivial after having looked into the eye of the storm in such a direct and unflinching way. Songs of betrayal like 'Splintered', or the bleak horror stories contained within 'Kristallnacht' or 'Kicking The Corpse Around' were resolutely non-fiction, and the experience of singing them here, with the ghosts of the past stood next to me, changed me forever as a person, and as a singer. There was no turning back. I made a deal with myself. This was how I was going to write and perform forever.

The songs weren't all doom and gloom, I hasten to add, as euphoric, uplifting songs like 'Push!' and 'Believe' left me as proud and upful as I had ever been, and hopefully I passed some of that euphoria on to the listener, too.

Chris wasn't just a producer, he took our music to his heart, and went far beyond the call of duty in his quest for perfection. Using studio down time, as well as the time that we were supposed to have, his ear for detail and refusal to leave anything in less than a perfect state led to the *Push!* album sounding better than I could ever had imagined, and in doing so, created a bond between the two of us.

With the recordings in the bag, attention switched to artwork. We employed Todd Fath, a Hulme photographer. The idea was to carry on with the theme of movement that our snarling dogs had suggested so effectively on the first single. It was crucial to follow up such a well-received image with something equally striking.

Our good friend, the photogenic ex-Weeds drummer Simon Wolstencroft had volunteered to be our cover star, and spent a cold afternoon standing on one leg, running in fear from an unknown figure played by Paul Humphreys. Simon was drumming with The Fall by now, having taken over from Karl the year before. We understood that Mark E Smith was less than happy with extra-curricular activity by any members of his group, but Si was our pal so we didn't worry about it too much. We never heard any complaints from Mark, so I guess Si never told him.

We returned to live shows with renewed vigour. I was delighted to be told that we were to play with Wire, who had been one of my favourite bands since punk days. I had so much admiration for the oblique but believable way that they went about things. Playfully arty, but still masters of the dynamics of light and shade, Wire had conducted themselves with wit and dignity at every juncture of their career. Never bowing to commercial pressure, but still creating effortless pop masterpieces like 'Outdoor Miner' or 'Map Ref. 41°N 93°W', I was more than happy to be associated with them. They were only playing three UK dates, and we were invited to open for them in Glasgow and Manchester.

Glasgow Mayfair was a seven-hundred capacity former ballroom, situated on the city's famous Sauchiehall Street. Wire had always been a strange band, loved by those in the know, without ever translating that love into mainstream success. Their recent releases, in particular the amazing 'Drill', had seen them return to peak form after a fallow period in the early eighties, where the various members kept busy with worthy, but less commercially viable solo projects. Lead singer Colin Newman actually released an album called *Commercial Suicide* in 1986, which gives some insight into the band's distain for musical careerism. I had loved them since I was at school, when I proudly displayed my *Pink Flag* sticker on my homework folder, and I had seen them pull off several mind-blowing shows as an open-eared teenager.

I had a thing about presenting ourselves differently to the way that other bands did, and would experiment with stage positioning in a bid to look unusual. I resisted being singled out the way that most lead singers were in a bid to emphasise the equality within the band. I was sick of seeing bands lining up in the same old way: lead singer at the front, centre stage, drummer at the back. We would try to subvert this by setting up with the drums at the side, for instance. On this occasion, during our soundcheck, I decided to move my microphone stand to the extreme left of the stage, making the look of the band less regimented.

It certainly did look weird, having two members on one side, all bunched up, with the centre stage area empty. I felt quite the innovator.

The only problem was that, in my naivety, I had neglected to think about the monitor speakers at my feet. I had left the speaker wedge stage centre, like an idiot. In my new position, there was no way that I would be able to hear a thing that any of us were doing.

Suddenly, I noticed movement at my feet as a mysterious figure began to drag the speaker to where I was. Thinking it was a roadie, I gave him a grateful 'Thanks, mate'. A familiar voice answered me kindly, explaining the science behind monitor speakers in a Southern accent. It was Colin Newman himself! There was no need for him to go out of his way, dirtying his hands to help me out. This simple kindness by someone who had been an idol to me as a kid was a beautiful moment.

With any sense of impostor syndrome banished by the kindness of the man, we went on to storm the place, playing one of the most heartfelt and celebratory sets thus far. I sat perched on the side of the stage for Wire's own performance, which included a fifteen-minute version of 'Drill' and sparkling new material from their *A Bell Is A Cup (Until It Is Struck)* album. I knew I was in exactly the right place.

The day after, we played together again at Manchester International. On home turf, after such a successful first gig, the music was even better. People were getting to know us by now, and we were called back for two encores. Ending in a flurry of broken strings with an extended 'Snapper', I marvelled at the way the year had gone for us, scarcely able to believe our luck.

We had an album ready to release, a following that was growing little by little, and to cap it all, we had been invited to tour Germany in the New Year, where, largely due to John Peel, we had been gathering a small but loyal fanbase.

24: A Touch Of Evil

Drug dealers were springing up everywhere in Hulme, and not just the acceptable 'party' kind. Smack was all-pervasive so break-ins were rife, and now there were reports of muggings in the area. Several people near to me were involved with this filthy drug, including, it seemed, a member of my own band.

Dave had something of a background in the murkier side of the Mancunian drug world. Several years older than me, he had one foot in the Chorlton/Whalley Range scene, crossing paths with such opiate lovers as John Cooper Clarke and Nico, with whom Dave had been a sound engineer when Blue Orchids served as her backing band for a while. In fact, he had been introduced to me by Jane, my former girlfriend, who had something of an on/off relationship with the brown stuff herself.

Love is blind, and I was missing many tell-tale signs of recidivist behaviour in both of them. On one occasion, we had gone by coach to stay at Jane's family home in Otley, some 50 miles north of Manchester. The very next day she borrowed her mother's car and some money, and hot footed it to Dave's house on the pretext of finding some weed, with me in tow. Arriving at Dave's, I was told to stay in the car, which was suspicious enough. Thirty minutes later she emerged weedless and decidedly ambient, then it was back to Yorkshire in a hurry.

A council decorating grant cheque for £100 went missing. I began to hear reports of her being seen regularly in the seedier, smackier parts of South Manchester, a world that Dave also knew very well. I was hurt by all this, but understood that their friendship, like their shared love of opioids, pre-dated me by some considerable time.

Both of them knew my attitude to heroin. Dave in particular had stood on stage with me and played my anti-smack anthem 'Then and Now' many times, and understood the calamitous events in my own personal life story that had led to the scorn I felt about anything to do with it.

With reports coming in on the Hulme druggy grapevine that Dave had been dabbling again, all the signs were there. Dishonesty with money, pinned pupils from time to time, a lack of personal care, but most of all, a crushing need for cash that led to him selling certain items that I knew he didn't want to sell.

It was hard to spot at first. Dave's increasing sloppiness was covered up by the way the songs were arranged. The band worked from the bottom up, with fierce and precise drum and bass foundations keeping everything that went on top of that within strict parameters. Over this, it would be my voice and my own guitar playing that would be brought to the fore. Dave's guitar was largely textural, playing simple root chords to widen the sound, and with such a brilliant rhythm section, it sounded sharp and precise even if Dave's guitar fell outside the lines. So even if the clues were there, they went unseen. As usual, I turned to what was happening next, not seeing the writing on the wall.

I was in a strange position as a Hulme resident. On the one hand, I was a thriving musician, taking full advantage of the estate's demise to rehearse at full volume, live rent-free, and immerse myself in the community of artists, drop-outs and squatters that had taken root there. On the other hand, I had been born in the area, and sympathised greatly with the 'real' inhabitants of Hulme, disenfranchised and surrounded by what must have looked like the last days of the Roman Empire.

It was a period of great lawlessness. Instead of paying for electricity, for instance, it was not unusual for people to buy a stolen mains fuse (a fiver if you knew the right people) and simply reconnect the supply for the flat you had 'liberated'. These fuses were removed by the Electricity Board when they cut off the power, and official stickers over the mains box warned of the illegality of tampering with the electricity supply, and also of the very real danger of death by electrocution. What we did was remove this mains fuse when we were not at home, and hide it, so that if the authorities paid a surprise visit, we weren't caught red-handed. The electricity authorities were allowed to enter if they thought that something dangerous was afoot, and although in most cases they would have had trouble proving who lived where, at the very least they could leave you without power, which was a major pain in the arse.

One night I headed out to a party and, as usual, before setting off, I removed the mains fuse, plunging my humble abode into darkness until my return. I then made my way to Whalley Range where I was going to a have a bit of a session with some friends from Langley, one of whom, Jack, had taken to the South Manchester bohemian drug scene so thoroughly that he had moved across town in order to dive in. It was a great night and, as per usual, it carried on to the early hours.

At daybreak, I set off for home. I put on my Walkman, the birthday gift that had made me cry with happiness. I never took it off and would analyse rehearsals and gig recordings as I paced the city streets, lost in music. My choice that day was the desk recording of our recent show in Leeds with Butthole Surfers. Never before had we sounded so weird and powerful. Stephen Bunn's echo tricks were circling inside my head, every bit as aggressively strange as Dennis Bovell's best Pop Group work, and with this hallucinogenic soundtrack in my ears at full volume, I made my way back to Hulme.

Early morning was my time, definitely, walking through my city as it came alive. The first buses were crawling sleepily from the Princess Road depot, lights on as they braved the still dark day to pick up the first wave of shift working nurses and cleaners, letting them on free, following the unwritten code of the earlybird community. Passing Cornbrook Street, I thought of my mam, giving birth to me in the terraced house that was no longer there. Who was with her? What time of day was it? Questions that can never be answered invade my thoughts every time I walk past there.

I turned right at The Spinners pub and cut across the wasteland beside William Kent Crescent, a short cut to the adjoining block, John Nash, where I lived. There was always one lift out of order, and remembering which one it was, I called the other and listened to the untrustworthy noise of scraping metal as it made its weary way to the ground floor. I took a big deep breath and got in. It smelled of recent piss. The lift doors closed, but nothing happened at first. It felt like hours until this ancient machine began its laboured ascent to the top floor.

Emerging, blinking into the changing daylight, I turned the corner and started to make my way home along the walkway. In the distance, I could see the curved row of dwellings that contained my own. Something caught my attention. The floor outside my flat sparkled with broken glass. Lots of it. The broken glass was on the outside of the flat, as if somebody was breaking *out*, as opposed to in. I turned my Walkman off, and cautiously approached the scene.

As I got closer, I realised I was right. The broken glass covered the walkway outside my flat, and getting nearer still I saw blood on the floor, and smears of blood on what was left of the window frame. I had double-locked the front door on my way out, and it remained intact, but it made no difference, as whoever had been in had smashed their way out, splintering the wooden window frame of the downstairs front room in the process. Fuck. What had gone on here?

Unlocking the door, I entered a scene of total destruction. Posters had been viciously ripped from the walls, and some half-empty cans of paint that I had stored under the kitchen sink had been splattered across the walls. I nearly slipped on a further pool of drying blood and spotted a blood-soaked pair of tracksuit bottoms that I didn't recognise.

Whoever had been in had cut themselves badly enough to have to abandon what they were wearing and change into something of mine. Reeling with shock, I re-installed the mains fuse in the electricity cupboard and turned on the lights. The kitchen window was boarded up, and no light could get in there, so whatever had happened had taken place in complete darkness. With the flat illuminated, I took a deep breath and began to take a proper look around.

Every book in the house had been destroyed, ripped out pages littered the floor wherever you looked. Blood was everywhere, on the walls, on the floor, smeared on every surface I could see. A kitchen knife had been tied to the light fitting by a guitar lead and swung eerily over a mutilated potted plant. Other knives had been inserted into the flimsy inner walls, and the jagged remains of smashed milk bottles pointed threateningly upwards, sharp and dangerous, their former contents spilt everywhere.

Who had done this, and why? My brain struggled to process what I was seeing. Venturing further into the flat, I found that all my coats had been slashed as they hung in a cupboard-like recess. An atmosphere of real evil hung over the whole scene. This was personal.

In the downstairs room, where I slept, the entire window frame had been destroyed. My mattress had been thrown through the broken window, landing five storeys below. Flyers for upcoming gigs had been laboriously ripped up and lay scattered around. Was this the reason for all this destruction? Was this something to do with the band? We had been gaining ground rapidly over the year, and were becoming quite well known, in a limited and specialised way. Jealousy is a destructive emotion and Hulme was home to many bands who might have felt overlooked by our recent rise to prominence. I put it to the back of my mind and carried on looking around, feeling sick to the pit of my stomach as the wind howled through the place.

Upstairs, more devastation. A mirror had been smashed and my television screen had been put through. My settee and an armchair had been violently thrown through the living room window, which itself had been destroyed. Looking out, I could see my coffee table and cheap music centre in a pile five floors below. Whoever had done this could easily have killed someone, had they been passing as the contents of my flat rained down.

On the wall, a message, written in shaving foam that had dried. It was frustratingly unreadable as parts of the message had fallen off. More bloodied clothes lay near the window, none of them mine. Looking up, I saw three pairs of my trousers had been tied together by the ankles and attached to the central light fitting. They were stretched diagonally across the room to a nail that had previously held up a framed poster, and the crotch area of each pair had been painstakingly cut out. This was demonic.

Apart from the jealousy theory, I couldn't find any reason for all this hatred and mayhem. The symbolic removal of the genital area of my trousers worried me the most, but there was no reason for any of it. There were no aggrieved former girlfriends that would have done such a thing, and I didn't owe anybody any serious money for drugs or anything.

I sat on the stairs with my head in my hands when something occurred to me. I hadn't seen my guitar! Thank fuck for that. This was theft. Feeling slightly better, having forced myself to swallow this unlikely explanation, I went into the bathroom. My guitar lay submerged in the bath beneath a few inches of water, with the remains of the shaving foam emptied all over it.

This revelation hit me like an icy bucket of water to the face. This wasn't anything as normal as simple theft. We were in Manson Family territory here. All this devastation must have taken hours. Furthermore, the intruder or intruders must have gained access from the flat roof of John Nash Crescent itself, smashing through the glass doors, cutting themselves badly in the process.

It struck me that I was in great danger, and that anybody mad enough to do all this wouldn't think twice about inflicting real violence on me personally if they came back and found me here. Properly scared now, I came to my senses and got out of there as quickly as I could, heading for town where Andy Cadman was covering in a friend's barber shop. No way was I going to return to my flat alone.

We returned together at the end of Andy's working day. He'd cut my hair to calm me down, and kindly let me stay in the safe atmosphere of the well-lit shop for a few hours. If anything, I was more scared now, as things started to fully sink in. Together we stepped over the destroyed remains of my few possessions and began to survey the damage. An atmosphere of malevolence hung over the place. The determination involved in this orgy of destruction was unbelievable.

The dwelling next door in one direction was unoccupied, but on the other side, a group of university students shared a four-bedroom flat, and I called to ask them if they had heard anything. It turned out that they had heard all kinds of noise and disturbance in the early hours, and thinking it was a domestic incident, or just me on my own going crazy, they chose to ignore things.

Like many student residents, they had an inbuilt fear of Hulme's 'real' population, and stayed behind their doors, safely insulated from the life of the estate that they found themselves in. On this occasion, they were probably right. I can only imagine what would have happened if the intruders were to be disturbed in their work by a bunch of fresh-faced would-be vigilantes. They did say that all this destruction was carried out in the early hours of the morning, between two and about five o'clock, and therefore had happened in complete darkness. This, and the blood-soaked clothes, put a terrifying complexion on things.

As I left the flat, shaken up and scared, I knew that I would never set foot in there again. Andy boarded up the front windows, and put me up for a few days, after which I was taken in by Nicky and Tracey, some friends of mine that had a spare room in a different part of the same flatblock.

This was more than just a weird incident. I was profoundly affected by the sheer horror and hatred involved. Racking my brains to find an explanation, I returned again and again to the band. There was nothing else in my life that could possibly have attracted such unwanted attention. There were no Manchester gigs organised for a while, but I was convinced that I was in very real danger the next time I stepped out onto a stage. I carried my fear around with me in a constant state of paranoia, waiting for whatever was to happen next, rarely venturing out alone.

Difficult though it was, I tried to convince myself that the whole thing was a case of mistaken identity. I hadn't been living there very long, so I could make believe that it was the flat's previous tenants that were the real target of this demonic attack. It worked to some extent, but something had changed for me. Each day that went by without me getting murdered did serve to put distance between me and this terrifying ordeal, and although things were never to be the same, I forced myself to accelerate my mental recovery. Afraid or not, I had stuff to do, and people depending on me.

With *Push!* in the bag, and a German tour organised for the New Year, things were going right at last. Putting it all behind me, for the time being at least, I kept looking forward to the next exciting thing, which was mastering the album ready for pressing and eventual release. This was another first for me. I bought a cheap coach ticket to London, where studio time had been booked and the madness and violence of Hulme was far, far away, at least for now.

London has always been good to me. Sitting on the National Express coach, with the master tape for the album in a bag at my feet, I took time out to think about all the exciting stuff that'd happened to me in the capital. Apart from a very dim and distant memory of coming down on the train as a child with my mam, and losing a teddy bear, all my thoughts about the place were positive ones, and all of them related to music. Door-stepping John Peel and earning a session that I never did, seeing The Fall outside my Mancunian comfort zone, bringing Dub Sex to play our first London gigs, and recording the two Peel sessions that had led to all of this happening, all of these things had imprinted a deep love of the place in my mind.

Whilst I remain fiercely proud of my Northern roots, I have never been any kind of a separatist when it comes to the perceived North/South divide. I have always thought bigger than that, and, as a born outsider, have never bought into any kind of regional loyalties. After all, we were as separate from our contemporaries in Manchester as we were from anybody anywhere, both in the UK and further afield, and I was one excited bunny to be hitting London again for another brilliant musical reason.

I stayed at the North London flat of Skinhead Rob. He carefully unscrewed one of the plug sockets in his living room and removed a stealthily concealed lump of Lebanese hash which we proceeded to make short work of, staying up most of the night, reminiscing. Rob was an important character in early eighties Manchester. An unrepentant soulboy at heart, he was part of several scenes, and was one of the most enthusiastic and encouraging people I have ever met. He was close to The Fall – Karl Burns, especially – during the *Room To Live* period, close to Dub Sex at the start of our journey, and was part of the bunch of scooter enthusiasts that would frequent Berlin club with John Squire and Ian Brown in the lead up to them starting their band. Rob was at the Geno Washington party in William Kent Crescent alongside Ian and me, and had also been a welcome face at early Dub Sex rehearsals in Anthony Behrendt's studio when I was trying to get things off the ground with Lee and Guy Ainsworth.

There was something celebratory about my visit, as if the two of us were continuing a path that had been started years earlier. It was a good feeling to be at the flat of a good friend and ally on the night before mastering my first album. I eventually got a few hours sleep and set off for the studio spiritually uplifted, marvelling at the processes that had led me here.

Mastering the album was another milestone for me, another part of the mysterious process of making records that I had never been present for before. Chris Nagle's experience and brilliant production meant that everything was in fine shape, and the engineer was well into what he was hearing, boosting certain lower frequencies here and there, and making sure of a loud pressing.

I was packed off back to Manchester with a couple of acetates, true to the sound of the album but only capable of being played about five times. *Push!* was finished now, and the artwork was all in hand. I snoozed contentedly on the coach back, turning my mind to the next big thing. Germany.

25: Deutschland

The chance to tour Germany came about as a direct result of John Peel. As well as his regular Radio 1 shows, he was also a prolific broadcaster in other parts of Europe. He put together programmes for stations in the Netherlands and Finland, and his BBC World Service show reached into homes all over the world. It was in Germany, though, that he was perhaps loved the most, making shows for Radio Bremen, FSK Hamburg, and BFBS (British Forces Broadcasting Service), all packed with weird and wonderful records and session tracks. The youth behind the so-called iron curtain would cling to extremist music as a badge of anti-state sympathies, and with John Peel as their messenger, a dynamic underground scene had developed which regarded bands like ours as symbols of freedom.

It boggled my mind to think of the places that our music was reaching. We had been receiving letters from German fans for some time. They were full of questions about the UK music scene, quoting lyrics, and putting us into context with other left-field bands that they liked. I was struck with the attention to detail and genuine love on display, it was obvious that they had really listened to our music. For people in other countries to care about what was, in effect, stories from my life, was a massive thing for me. When news came through that a German agency called ARTLOS wanted to arrange a tour there, I was beside myself with happiness.

We were to play nine shows in ten days with a Welsh-speaking punk band called Anhrefn – Welsh for disorder. They too had risen to prominence due to the support of the Peel show, having recorded a well-received session.

I didn't have a passport when the invitation came in so I needed to get one sorted pronto. Officially, my address was still at the old flat, so I had to be there each day from about 7.30am to catch the post the moment it dropped through the letterbox. An atmosphere of real evil still hung over the place. Spending even the shortest time there filled me with dread, but I had to return day after day. It was starting to look like the resident evil was going to jinx the trip, but with just one day to spare my passport arrived. Game on.

On the morning of departure, I made my way from the crescents with the low January sun in my eyes. I could hardly wait to get started. I used to marvel at Karl when he would set off on one of The Fall's overseas jaunts, so nonchalant and last minute, but I supposed that the novelty had worn off for him. I was the total opposite. I had been washed, shaved and ready for action for hours already, waiting for this momentous day to break.

I was travelling light, even though I had packed everything decent that I owned, clothes-wise. I was the owner of one pair of boots and a pair of flimsy Kung-Fu slippers, and these were dutifully packed, along with a selection of mixtapes and vital albums on cassette. For my reading pleasure, I had taken out *Lost Highway* by Peter Guralnick from Hulme Library, an exhaustive look at the early days of American blues and country music, which I felt sure would come in handy on the longer sections of the journey.

We must have looked a strange bunch as Steve Hawkins arrived in the van to pick us up. Half of us were scruffy and punky-looking, with three of us (me, Roger and Cathy) sporting severe new haircuts. Stephen Bunn and Rat, along with the four band members, jumped in, and we set off on the adventure of a lifetime, stopping only to load the equipment and then onwards to Dover, where we were to meet our Welsh friends for the first time and catch the ferry. We were all finding it somewhat hard to believe that our music was taking us to another country. This was new ground for all of us, and as such, was a great leveller. None of us knew what was in store, and we were, each of us, equal in our joy.

People fell into certain behavioural patterns almost immediately. Dave was something of a sleeper, and seemed to always have his eyes closed for long journeys, which kind of fed into his growing distance from the rest of us. Cathy was a very self-contained person, and was often to be found deep in a book, but she was as wide-eyed as the rest of us, even though she was no stranger to foreign travel. Roger was a source of great amusement to us all. His day job in vehicle fleet hire meant that he spent most of his time behind the wheel of a car, and he was quite unprepared to be the passenger for once. He took up a position directly behind the driver, giving unwelcome driving advice, unable to switch off.

At Dover we met up with Anhrefn's van and decided to mix things up a little to ensure that we weren't totally divided into Manchester and Bangor camps. Two of us (Dave and Rat) would travel in Anhrefn's van while we took two of their number (Rhys and Sion) in ours. The idea was that we'd all get to know each other, but, due to shyness or some other reason, we all felt pretty separate at first, especially when our new buddies talked to each other exclusively in their native tongue. Things were not helped by the drug situation. We had been told by Dirk from ARTLOS that we shouldn't bring anything with us, as anything we needed would be given to us when we got over there. We were assured that speed and weed, our main drugs of choice, would be no problem to arrange, and it was better to not risk getting busted at one of the various borders we were to cross on the way. This was all well and good, but something inside me found this promise hard to believe so, in the early hours of the day before we were due to leave, I picked up a few grammes of amphetamine sulphate, just in case.

The sight of the customs at Dover brought me to my senses. I had told nobody about my emergency supplies, and realising that my stupidity could jeopardise the whole tour, I went to the little boy's room and ate the lot. Nothing had prepared our Welsh guests for this. Our poor, new-found friends had to endure an already excited Mancunian bending their ears. The only respite for these unfortunate souls came when we were on the ferry itself. They must have wondered what they had let themselves in for.

We were to land at Ostend, not far from Zeebrugge, where nine months earlier the *Herald of Free Enterprise* had taken in water through its open bow doors, killing 193 passengers and crew. Images of this massive ship lying on its side haunted my dreams in the run up to the tour, and Stephen Bunn and I made it our business to find the highest place on the vessel, then stay there until we had safely docked.

There on the top deck, the two of us marvelled at the very fact that we were taking something that had been born from my harsh upbringing and grown in a rough Manchester council estate, to a place so wildly different. Stephen and I were close already, but that night, high above the choppy waves of the English Channel, we bonded like brothers. Our belief in the power of music, up until then still something of a theory, was proved a thousandfold. As the harbour lights came into view, we toasted the future with our duty free whisky.

After docking, we hit a bar frequented by early morning drinkers, mainly sailors. We enthusiastically started putting promotional orange and black stickers everywhere, advertising our forthcoming *Push!* album. The sailors got excited by the word 'sex' in the band name and tried to force pornographic playing cards onto us.

On our drive to Germany we passed a sign for Heysel, site of another recent tragedy fresh in our minds. We didn't feel like hanging around anywhere near there and so hightailed it across the entire width of Belgium in record time. Clean as a whistle, as far as customs were concerned, our strange little convoy arrived in West Germany and made our way to Aachen, which was where ARTLOS were based. We were to stay one night there before setting off on a nine-day adventure, one gig each day, before finishing the tour in Wuppertal.

I had good friends in Aachen. There was Ulla Wilkin, a German girl who I had met in Manchester some years previously as part of Alan Wise's entourage. Her sister, Barbara, was one of Nico's best friends, and with Alan being Nico's manager, a kind of Deutsche-Mancunian alliance had sprung up between us all. Ulla was living near Aachen with Gina, an English girl who had worked at the Haçienda when I did, and was very close to my friend Mike Hutton. It was wonderful to meet them in a different country. As they whisked me away for a taste of German subculture, it felt that my life would never be the same again. My head was spinning.

Gig number one was at Cologne's Rose Club. It was a sobering and somewhat spooky experience to drive into this modern city, and think of the absolute devastation caused by the Allied saturation bombing of a little over four decades earlier. We passed Cologne Cathedral, which was left largely undamaged, and it was hard to work out what was so weird about it. The penny dropped eventually. It was the only recognisably 'old' building to be seen anywhere. The city suffered 262 separate bombing raids, but the Cathedral's twin towers had proved useful as a navigational tool so had been largely spared. The sight of its medieval splendour, juxtaposed against the backdrop of a city rebuilt after total annihilation, gave me goosebumps. Twenty thousand people had died here, in the very streets that we found ourselves walking around. I felt humbled and tiny.

Soundcheck was followed by an in-depth interview with a Cologne radio station, conducted in immaculate English by people who seemed to know everything about us and the context that we existed in. We talked to newspaper journalists, too, equally well briefed about our story so far.

The enthusiasm and musical knowledge of these German people came as a big surprise. Both Anhrefn and us were far from well known outside of specialist circles, and to be perfectly frank, we played much smaller venues in our native countries. But the power of John Peel meant that we were a much bigger deal in Europe than we were at home. We were to be paid two or three times what we were getting in the UK, with generous riders, decent hotels and restaurant meals provided as a matter of course. This was nothing like the struggle we were used to in England.

After the press junket, we were taken out for an Italian meal by the promoters. Nothing unusual about that, but to me, such civilised behaviour was a brand new experience. Eating out communally was a rarity for me, having only been to the odd Chinese restaurant or Manchester's Curry Mile in Rusholme, but here we were, getting treated with dignity and respect, and being given good food and wine. We were definitely not in England any more! I enjoyed the experience of us all eating together, and reflected that, once again, music had given me more of a family-type experience than all those years in care ever had.

The hotel, too, was many notches above what I had experienced in the UK. I had a room of my own in Cologne, and, even though we were in the most basic of establishments, the comfort level and the way we were treated beat my experiences in England hands down. There was clean sheets and fluffy towels! The hotel bar had further cultural surprises for us. Their method of being able to drink copiously, and then settle up at the end for everything was a display of trust that would never have worked in downtown Moss Side.

Wide-eyed though we may have been, we displayed a quiet dignity for the most part, and it was easy to get used to being treated that little bit better than we were treated at home, although, I for one would never take any such good fortune for granted.

The gig was a revelation. Bursting with pride, we bounced out onto the Rose Club stage, and even though I had temporarily lost the top end of my trademark falsetto due to being awake for the previous three days bending the unfortunate ears of my Welsh travelling companions, we still sounded great. The smart young audience lapped it up, and then cleaned us out of merchandise. We had made a small number of t-shirts with the words 'Dub Sex' on the breast and sleeve to help offset the costs of the tour. After the show, Rat popped his head round the dressing room door to ask 'How much for just the sleeve?' Apparently, the last person in the queue, so upset to have been robbed of an opportunity to own one of our shirts, had begged Rat to cut off a sleeve for him to wear as a headband! Truly, I was in my own version of Heaven.

I woke up in my hotel room with the previous night's encores still ringing around my head. I looked out of the window just to prove all of this was real. The breakfast buffet was a feast of exotic cheeses, sausage and black bread. Dave stocked up, making sandwiches for the long journey ahead, just for himself, naturally.

Today was special. We were going to Berlin. As something of an amateur history buff, I had read lots about Berlin, and the harrowing experiences of the civilian population at the end of the Second World War as they waited in the ruins of their city for Russian troops to arrive from the east, and Allied forces to arrive from the west. Around 35,000

Berliners had lost their lives in an onslaught of destruction by RAF Bomber Command, USAAF Eighth Air Force and the French Air Force. They were also targeted by the Red Air Force, as the Russians inched ever closer to Hitler's capital, hell-bent on revenge for the millions of their own citizens killed.

Having been born a mere seventeen years after the end of the Second World War, all this history was very real to me. The hangover from the war tainted all parts of British life for decades. I had played 'war' as a child, the same as practically every other young person growing up in the sixties. Films, books and popular songs were all steeped in a culture born out of the conflict, and now, as a young man of similar age to those who had fought here, I was to experience the place for myself.

The journey to Berlin from Cologne itself took about six hours. We were to join the famous autobahn constructed by Hitler as a means of transporting troops and equipment to the freshly conquered territories to the west of Germany. Hurtling along this artificially straight road, a mood of reflection came over us all. Enclosed on both sides by high banks of windbreaking concrete, we said little to each other, and thought lots. I commandeered the van's cassette player and inserted my copy of Kraftwerk's *Autobahn*. It seemed churlish not to.

Spiritually fortified by the simplicity and beauty of the music, I gazed out of the van window as we ate up the miles of motorway. My voice, so cruelly treated since we left England, had started to return after the previous night's exertions. I had always found it hard to hold back when singing, but I gave myself a shock when I lost the top end of my falsetto on the first gig, so I remained almost silent as we crept up on the divided former capital.

Darkness fell quickly. When we reached the border crossing, we were greeted by a vision of Cold War brutalism that served as a perfect introduction to Eastern Bloc living. For several miles, the land had been bulldozed flat and concreted over to form a kind of barrier area. Surrounded by intimidating high fences and guard towers, we slowed to a crawl, following the instructions mimed to us by a uniformed and heavily armed guard. Powerful blinding floodlights made the entire area as bright as an operating theatre, and wherever we looked, ridiculously young-looking soldiers stared back unflinchingly, steely eyed and wearing the vacant gaze that unites military personnel in every part of the world, a look that says 'Just try it'. Needless to say, nobody was going to try anything.

Waiting in line behind the other vehicles, we had time to take it all in. Just inside the main gate, a tank had been erected on a concrete plinth, pointing menacingly towards the West. Massive and intimidating, this was no relic from the Second World War, but a modern killing machine, and its placement was no accident.

We were halted by a spotty teenage member of the Deutsche Grenzpolizei, the specialist border force. Seeing a huge machine gun in the hands of a youth of about eighteen does wonders for one's powers of concentration. Our band of weird looking musicians adopted decidedly sensible 'Don't shoot me, please' expressions. Butter wouldn't melt.

Our young border guard explained to us, in a mixture of German and mime, that we were required to hand over our passports to his equally scary-looking associate, and with a heavy heart, we passed the only proof of our existence through the window. The second guard gathered them up, wheeled round in a parade ground manner, then marched away with them, double time, towards a spartan looking hut several hundred yards away, his gun swinging and banging into his side as he went.

I saw a wooden bucket, maybe a metre across, filled with concrete and housing a leafless, dead tree. The words 'Für Hunde' were written on a small sign attached to the side. I turned to Stephen Bunn in a vain attempt to lighten the mood.

'Shit, Stephen, the dogs in East Germany can READ!!'

My wisecrack went down like a lead lemming. Every single member of our travelling party remained stony-faced, or wore an unconvincing rictus grin.

The van was shepherded towards an iron structure, greeted by more armed guards.

'Who is Davvid Karmikkel?' a slightly older youth barked. Nobody said a word.

'Davvvid Karmikkel!!'

We looked at each other, confused. These words just didn't make sense. All we wanted to do was get out of this place. We were fairly spaced out from the previous night's gig and the travelling. Being barked at by a uniformed twenty-something was the last thing we needed. A shaky voice came from the depths of our van.

'That'll be me, mate.'

Turning around, we saw Rat offering his best smile to our impatient host. We had been working together for nearly two years now but none of us recognised his real name. I had been told it once and immediately buried it in the dark recesses of my mind. David Carmichael! Of course. Comparing Rat's passport photo to the real thing in a theatrical kind of way, our gatekeeper seemed satisfied that we were not about to bring about the downfall of the DDR and, returning our documents to us, he allowed us to continue unhindered through the remainder of no-man's land.

In no time at all, we had reached the next border crossing point, and with genuine relief etched into every face, entered West Berlin, where the highly organised and politicised punks of the squatted K.O.B. collective were waiting for us. Nine hundred miles away, Manchester was going about its business, but here, where East and West collided, I had a little business of my own.

Driving into divided Berlin was, of course, every bit as exciting as I had built it up to be. I had been steeped in the mythology of the place from watching a million Cold War movies, and had thrilled to Bowie's trilogy of albums recorded at Hansa studios by the Wall as well as his work there with Iggy Pop, which were a staple diet for any self-respecting punk.

Although the entire city had been levelled in the Second World War, as we travelled down West Berlin's wide streets, I felt as if I knew the place. Cylindrical advertising structures, about three metres high, were erected at regular distances on the pavements, just as I had seen in pre-war photos, but now informed Berliners of upcoming artistic events as opposed to the Nazi propaganda of previous times.

Once again, the lack of anything built before 1945 was startling. The Allied forces had all but wiped this elegant and historic city clean from the face of the earth, and the odd building that had survived the onslaught stood out a mile from its neighbours, which by their very nature, could not have been much more than about forty years old.

One such structure was the K.O.B. club, a legendary punk squat/cinema/political centre/ venue where we were going to be playing. Situated on Berlin's historic Potsdamer Straße, it stood several storeys high, very imposing and ornate, with its own off-street courtyard. It was run by a well organised group of punks who had resisted violent attempts by the Berlin authorities to evict them in a full-scale battle some years earlier. A huge, framed photograph dominated the main performance space, telling us all we needed to know of the building's more recent history. Taken from an upstairs window, it featured a club-wielding member of Berlin's riot squad, baton raised to strike, trying unsuccessfully to enter K.O.B. at the height of the siege. Hidden behind his crash helmet and blacked-out visor, he encapsulated perfectly the size and power of what this remarkable punk collective had been up against.

Our new friend, Armin, who had booked us, showed us round, detailing the various things that went on there. First thing in the morning they swept the pavement and put tables outside. The venue served as a café for people on their way to work, supplying vegetarian breakfasts to Berlin's hungry workforce. Inside, a cinema had been established, showing political and left-field films that were unlikely to be found anywhere else. A kind of unofficial help centre advised those in need on a variety of matters, all free of charge, and an energetic and cheerful collective of German youth ran the place as a bar during the rest of the day, until it became a gig venue at night.

I loved these people, and was bowled-over with what they had achieved here. They put us all to shame. Punk in the UK had degenerated into an inward-looking and fashion-obsessed beast. The early promise that had originally led kids like me in, had long since been replaced with a trivial, selfish frame of mind, far removed from the optimism that had fuelled our early rebellion. Additionally, several odious far-right groups had hijacked the whole scene, and the word 'punk' had come to mean something quite different from what it meant originally.

These Berlin punks were the perfect antidote to all that. Bright, and politically informed, they worked for each other and for the greater good of the collective at all times. We were to stay with them, in the once luxurious upper echelons of the building. Simply being amongst them, sharing vegetarian pizza and putting the world to rights, I felt proud to be included in what they were doing, even if it was only for one night. I resolved to blow their revolutionary minds in just a few hours time.

Berlin's subculture used John Peel as something of a barometer to check what was going on in other parts of the world. The hip Berlin radio stations and listings magazines had been trumpeting our arrival for several weeks now, and our hosts were well-informed about British music, plugging us for information about the most obscure and specialist artists imaginable. It was clear that both Dub Sex and Anhrefn had penetrated into these German's consciousness, thanks to John Peel's relentless support.

To simply be in Berlin was exciting enough, but after a brilliant soundcheck, as we waited for things to happen, hundreds of Berliners started to arrive at the K.O.B. club, milling around outside in ever growing numbers. We had decided to take it in turns as to which band opened and which one headlined. On this night Anhrefn played first and as their set progressed, it was obvious that there were many more people wanting to get in than could possibly fit in the 400-ish capacity club. The place got more and more crowded as we were due to take the stage, and the crowd swelled further as we watched from our elevated vantage point.

Storming into 'Then and Now', the entire place went crazy, and we proceeded to play everything faster and harder, spurred on by the mayhem unfolding in front of us. The venue had been seriously oversold, and as hundreds more people arrived, in the vain hope of being able to pay in at the door, a mini riot was beginning to break out. I looked out upon a scene of pure and beautiful chaos as irate punks smashed the huge windows at the front of the building, putting their heads through the damaged frame in an attempt to hear us. Ploughing through our set, we watched agog at the writhing mass of Berlin youth in front of us. Breathable air was in short supply up where I was, and it was all I could do to keep singing as everything kicked off.

The latter part of our set coincided with the arrival of all three emergency services – police, fire brigade and ambulance – as there were plenty of injured people, mainly superficial cuts caused by the broken windows at the front of the club. Never popular visitors, the police made several arrests. These guys meant business, and made the British police (no stranger to violence themselves) look like something from the *Dixon of Dock Green* era. This was brilliant. Scary, but absolutely brilliant.

The Berlin crowd would simply not let us finish. After a two-song encore, we were screamed back onto the stage where I broke three strings on my guitar playing 'Kristallnacht' in the very city that had inspired its writing. I threw it on the floor and we carried on, to the delight of our new German friends.

Still they wouldn't let us finish up, and as the only way out was through the massed audience in front of us, we had no choice but to carry on. Eventually, with me gripping the microphone stand for dear life, we played 'Green', leaving my howls to swirl around the venue as the song ended, caught as they were in a maelstrom of space echo and craziness. Chaos reigned everywhere as I explained to the crowd, 'That's it now! We've broken all the equipment, and we've run out of songs!'

Finally, they let us go, enervated.

Now it was time to explore Berlin. The temperature that January night had plummeted to an unimaginable -11 degrees so I was wearing every item of clothing that I possessed as we made our way to the Berlin Wall, a short distance away. We arrived there after a magical walk through the Potsdamer Straße district. Graffiti-covered and every bit as austere and imposing as I had imagined, the Wall had cut a major road in half where we were, making it stop in its tracks as it carried on into no-man's land.

On the East German side, a tower had been erected, housing armed guards who kept a watchful eye on the hundred-metre wide area of cleared land known as the 'Death Strip'. On the West side, where we were, a similar sized tower allowed us to climb to the same height, presumably just to wind up the guards stationed on the other side. We climbed the structure, close enough to look these young soldiers directly in their faces, and took it all in.

After the most profound and life-changing experience of my life so far, I gazed out over no-man's land. All was silent and the air was possessed of an alien coldness; a dry, barely breathable cold that I had never experienced before. Groups of rabbits emerged under the blinding spotlights illuminating the 'Death Strip' from the East German side. Nature always finds a way, and these rabbits owned this part of town, having been left to their own devices since the city was split in two more than two decades earlier.

I had something of a Damascene moment as I surveyed the scene I found myself in. Here I was, having climbed up from the very bottom of life's pile, in the company of intelligent, productive fellow human beings, having earned the right to be there as an equal. This validation, so late in my life, helped me find my own sense of self-worth, and confirmed to me that I was absolutely on the correct path. I had put my trust in music and it had not let me down. I have never felt as much at peace as I did at that moment in the silent January Berlin night, with only my band and some communist rabbits for company. Tomorrow we would advance deeper into (West) Germany, for now, though, I felt validated and as happy as I had ever been. Ever.

Riding high on a wave of enthusiasm after the first two shows, our little group settled into a thorough investigation of West Germany through our vehicle window. The van we were travelling in was by no means state-of-the-art, but was comfortable enough, and had a loud cassette player from which we could blast out an individualised soundtrack to accompany our adventures. We learned a lot about people's taste in music on the trip. I had spent ages making compilations, usually fairly upbeat and weird stuff. I remember PiL, Susan Cadogan, Chaka Khan, Ciccone Youth, Wire, and a whole smorgasbord of popular and less than popular artists. My copy of the soundtrack album for John

Carpenter's *Halloween* filled those silent moments of reflection as we ate up the miles.

It wasn't all left-field stuff though. Roger always had great taste in soul, and his Temptations and Smokey Robinson rarities were perfect for the longer journeys, as were Cathy's contributions, which included The Smiths' *Strangeways, Here We Come* album. As frenzied and angry as our own music was, we were all suckers for a well-crafted tune and criss-crossing Germany with 'Last Night I Dreamt That Somebody Loved Me' blaring out was a beautiful moment. By the middle of the tour, barriers had broken down between us and our Welsh companions. We were now getting on well, though we still felt a bit separate when our new buddies talked to each other in their native tongue, inserting English words like 'effects pedal' and 'wreckhead' into their own conversations.

The tour had been put together in a less than logical fashion, geographically speaking. After our Berlin date, we were to drive north west for another 300 miles to Wilhelmshaven, on Germany's North Sea coast. This was a fiercely maritime town, with a rich history of piracy and naval warfare.

On arriving, we were told that we were expected to play two sets. This would never do. Who did they think we were? The fucking Beatles? After much wrangling, we played our set in the usual way, wringing every ounce of emotional energy from our 45-minute onslaught, before disappearing into the damp sea air. Our audience was largely made up, it seemed, of hard-drinking sailors, curiously unbothered about the revolutionary nature of our music.

I provided the second set by myself after drinking a fine bottle of cherry brandy. Draping a bright yellow cagoule over the mike stand, I recited some barely understandable spoken word poetry over the *Halloween* soundtrack for about half an hour. I don't remember much after that, but I woke up with broken glasses after collapsing in a restaurant, and had urgent need of the German word for superglue.

Throughout these first few dates, it had been noticeable that Dave was growing ever more distant from the rest of us. Although none of us had ever experienced anything like this, we basically remained the same civilised people that we had always been. For Dave, it was different. Everything seemed to go straight to his head. It was very flattering to receive the attention we had been receiving from German fans, but Dave became a different person. He started playing the pop star in a frankly quite horrible way, treating our beloved roadie, Rat, for example, as an unimportant hireling, and behaving like a real primadonna with Stephen. He began to go missing when there was heavy lifting to be done, expecting his equipment to be set up for him. His attitude around female fans was creepy. In short, at the first sign of any success, he had let the side down, and we were all disappointed with him.

We continued criss-crossing divided Germany, collecting new life experiences all the time. In Mannheim's Café Vienna, despite getting a good reaction from most of the crowd, I had to duck as a bottle came flying towards my head. I had been spat at, heckled, and walked-out on before, but this was my first glassware, and choosing to treat it as a right of passage, I carried on regardless, playing harder and better. Out of fear, probably.

The tour schedule booklet given to us by Dirk from ARTLOS made for hilarious reading, the funniest parts being the distances between each show. 279 miles one day, 310 the next, 372 the day after that. The towns flew past as we made spider web patterns on the German map.

We followed the Rhine, passing the Lorelei rock. Legend tells of a beautiful maiden who threw herself into the river there after being cheated on by her faithless lover. She was transformed into a siren, and using her unearthly voice, would lure unsuspecting sailors to their death on the treacherous rocks. I didn't hear a thing, and our vanload of unsuspecting musicians lived to play another day. Phew.

In Germany's southernmost town, Sonthofen, we descended a steep mountainous road in the deepest, most silent snow I had ever seen in my life. This throwback of a place, hidden in the Bavarian Alps, was a million miles away from the cosmopolitan, urban cities we had played so far. Its population was a mere 20,000 souls, and gripping the tarmac like a mountain goat, we entered another world. Everywhere we looked,

German pensioners, the right age to be potential ex-Nazis, shuffled along the snow-filled streets wearing felt Alpine hats, complete with feathers.

I set out to investigate this weird little Christmas card of a town, taking Stephen with me for moral support. We asked a stern looking frau for directions to the nearest Post Office. She stared me malevolently in the eye, spat on the floor near my feet, and sped away without a word.

'Not a Dub Sex fan, then?' I thought, cursing my lack of German swearwords. It seemed to us both that after Argentina, this unfriendly place would be number one on any list of where to find ex-members of the Nazi party. How had we ended up here? Surely there couldn't be any fans of left-field UK music this deep in the Bavarian Alps?

How wrong I was. In the deepest part of the snow-filled valley, the grandchildren of these elderly Bavarians had made quite a scene for themselves. They had hired a medium-sized sports centre, and being the only fun in town, we attracted a weird crowd of snow-dwelling youth, big on drinking and English punk rock. John Peel, bless his cotton socks, had permeated even this frozen backwater, and our appreciative crowd of German music lovers proceeded to throw themselves wholeheartedly into things, bouncing, pogo-ing and slam dancing like there was no tomorrow. After the show, they were full of questions about the most obscure and strangest bands, from Bogshed to Big Flame and back again, and I left the mountains vowing never again to judge a town on first impressions. The next day's gig was another 300-mile drive away, and I for one, couldn't wait.

The tour continued to throw new experiences at us, and even the ever-growing chasm between Dave and the rest of us could not dampen our collective enthusiasm. In Saarbrücken, we played for a tri-lingual crowd in a glitzy club owned by a shady looking, but affable rogue, who seemed to control the whole town. He certainly ran the seedy, but legal, brothel across the road, which stayed busy long after we had packed up our equipment in the early hours of the morning. When engine failure hampered our exit early the next day, he came over with a bottle of rum for each of the vans in our convoy, making the sleepy journey to our next show that little bit weirder.

Our last show was in Wuppertal, a long drive up to the North Rhine-Westphalia region, several hundred miles away. It is famous for its Schwebebahn, or 'floating tram', a unique monorail system which the town's inhabitants are justifiably proud of. By the time our dishevelled bunch of travellers arrived, it was dark and we were seriously late for soundcheck, so sightseeing was out of the question. It looked good from what I could see, but we had to get a move on.

By now, we had become good friends with Anhrefn. We had even joined them on stage at the Rockfabrik club near Aachen, kicking seven shades out of some four-foot tall oil drums that served as tables in the industrial themed venue. Although they sang in Welsh, Rhys had taken to inserting the words 'Dub Sex' into one of their songs. To this day, I wonder what he was saying about us, but I reckon it wouldn't have been anything too bad. All things considered, putting both bands together had been an inspired idea. There is a certain harshness that binds the languages of German, Welsh and Mancunian English together, linguistically, and we all made a lot of friends, taking our music to every corner of this forward-looking country.

At Die Börse, the beautiful concert hall was quickly filled with inquisitive young Germans, and we played with joy and wild abandon, buzzing to have completed one of the experiences of our lives. We played every song we knew and treated the guitars like we hated them, having no gig the next day to worry about.

Entering the dressing room, drenched in sweat, a brilliant surprise awaited us, Jamie Nicholson had flown and hitch-hiked over to see us. His love of our band had brought him hundreds of miles. It completed a perfect circle, having Jamie there with us, at the hour of our greatest adventure. I threw my arms around him, amazed at his devotion and sense of mischief in keeping his surprise a secret.

Crossing the murky waters of the English Channel was a sad and moody experience for us. We had tasted something of a new way of being, and had been treated so well that it would be difficult to adjust to being treated like shit again in the UK. Customs officials singled out the van with me in for an exhaustive but fruitless search, and in no time at all we were hurtling back to our rainy home, with The Fall's 'Hit The North' blaring out one more time on the van's cassette player.

Touching down in Hulme, the flatblock lift was out of order, and skidding on a pool of dog shit, it was hard to believe that for the previous two weeks we had taken our thing to places that we could scarcely have imagined a short time ago. I shuffled up the endless stairs, and hitting my mattress, fell into a deep sleep, dreaming dreams of German motorways and the crashing waves of the huge black forbidding sea.

Being back in Hulme was a real shock to the system. I had never been so well looked after, spiritually or materially. The whole experience, and in many ways, the rise of the band in general, had given me a glimpse into a world that I felt at home with, perhaps for the very first time. All my life, I had been an outsider, but here was a world that I felt part of. Inclusion here was earned, and everything that was happening was down to the hard work that the group and I had put in.

Despite the life-changing nature of the German tour, things were not all well within the group. Dave's increasingly bad behaviour had driven a gap between him and the rest of us, and it was clear that things had to change. At the first sign of even limited success, Dave had turned into a complete big head, totally at odds with the egalitarian way that we ran things. In particular, his treatment of the people around the group was appalling. Rat and Stephen worked for us out of love for the music and frequently settled for very small wages. They were as much a part of our setup as the playing members, and it went against everything we believed in to operate a two-tier system when it came to our crew.

From the moment Dave started to act like a spoiled pop star, his days were numbered. I had not shared my worries about his drug choices to the rest of the band, but, as an avowed enemy of opiates and the world that surrounds them, I knew that these things never end well. Having spent the last few years in a relationship with an off and on user, I was still raw from all the disappointment, theft and dishonesty that I had to endure, and had no appetite to go through it all again.

Even taking my fears about Dave's drug use out of the equation, he had alienated himself from the rest of us musically. For some time now, his guitar parts had come to reflect the change in his personality. I wrote these songs, and had only decided to use a second guitarist to flesh out the overall sound, doubling up chords where a wall of sound was needed. Dave's vanity turned him into something of an old-fashioned lead guitarist, filling every available space with ego-driven fretwank, the opposite of what the songs needed.

We played one more gig with Dave, a homecoming headliner at Manchester's International club. Having played ten gigs in as many days in Germany, we were sharp and tight despite our internal problems. Dave's attitude away from the stage was as bad as ever and when in a fit of rage he stated 'I will never work with Rat again', we all knew that he was speaking the truth.

We went round to break the news in person, explaining our reasons. It was hard in some ways, but it was exactly the right thing to do. I had a batch of new songs to bring to the table that were deeper and more incisive than anything we had dealt with before. There was no way that I could risk them being bent out of shape by someone who put himself before the music. We holed up in our rehearsal room as a three-piece, and with the future ahead of us, we began the next phase of our great adventure.

PART V
Get This!

Overleaf: Dub Sex at The Boardwalk
MH and Cathy Brooks
Photo by Richard Davis

26: Funtime

A subtle change was in the air. A new, expensive drug was creating a bit of a stir within certain circles. Ecstasy was changing hands for £20-£25 per pill, which represented almost a week's money for somebody on unemployment benefit. Limited supplies of this novel new substance had emerged sporadically over the preceding year, and I had been lucky enough to be invited by Lee Pickering to one of the first and most exclusive nights based around ecstasy and acid house. It was called 'Naughty Neck' and was populated by various Happy Mondays and other inner-circle heads, like Matt and Pat Carroll from Central Station Design, and although I didn't partake on this particular occasion, it was obvious that something very unusual, and a lot of fun, was about to explode everywhere.

Jamie Nicholson was one person who got on at the ground floor as far as this new scene was concerned. He had already knocked one wall of his flat through to make a bigger recording space for his studio, but as acid culture grew, he turned his studio into an after-hours shebeen or blues-type hang out. Taxis would deliver confused and excited club goers to the Hulme crescents, all massive black pupils and twitching with MDMA. For them it was a huge adventure, but for us it was simply where we lived, and we took the anarchy and lawlessness in our stride, the same way that we did with all aspects of life in this weird little estate.

Our mini-album *Push!* was released in early 1988. It had been held up for what seemed like ages due to problems at the Red Rhino distribution company. All the major music papers got behind it – *NME*, *Sounds*, *Melody Maker*, *Record Mirror* – with my group taking up column inches next to the more expected rock luminaries. James Brown invoked The Cramps and Nick Cave in his review for the *NME*, and was especially kind about my vocals. Most of the music papers took my voice as a starting point. Like it or hate it, Chris Nagle had placed it firmly at the front of the mix, in your face and impossible to ignore. It was rewarding when Mick Middles, a writer who I had been following since punk days, used his *Manchester Evening News* column to spread the word. He had been instrumental in bringing both Joy Division and The Fall to the nation's attention, so it was satisfying to hear him enthuse about the album's dramatic opening.

Requests for interviews came thick and fast, and I started to enjoy them. John Robb was sent to meet us by *Sounds*. John, and his band The Membranes, had been on my radar for several years by the time we met up. They had been on the bill, along with ATV, when The Chameleons played Manchester's Free Trade Hall in 1985, a triumphant homecoming for them. I had missed The Membranes that night, but caught them supporting Pop Will Eat Itself shortly before we did, and had enjoyed their anarchic sense of surrealist fun. Their mayhem-loving followers were fond of sporadically throwing pre-prepared bits of ripped-up paper into the air, turning wherever they played into a kind of punky snow dome.

John himself had been drawn to Manchester from Blackpool, where he had been the brains behind the *Blackpool Rox!* fanzine. He'd become the go-to writer for the louder, more extreme bands coming through from America and the UK, and was commissioned by *Sounds* to write our first double-page spread. The article was one of the first to deal with issues outside music. Having more space meant that I could veer off from strictly musical subjects into the issues that had inspired the songs. When it was printed, they used a photo of the band taken when Dave Rumney was still a member. Dave had been blackened out, leaving a strange dark section where he used to be. History can be ruthless sometimes.

Being a three-piece had a strangely liberating effect. A friendlier atmosphere led to a period of creativity and I was able to really express myself on the guitar now without having to simplify things to accommodate Dave. Having said that, I still wanted to have the full force of a double guitar line-up, and we turned our minds to the question of who to recruit to flesh out our sound. I had a few ideas, but they had to be put on hold for the time being as we had an important gig to play.

We had been invited by the London magazine *Time Out* to play one of six nights they had arranged at The Greyhound in Fulham, a mini festival featuring the best new UK and American bands. We were in good company alongside such luminaries as World Domination Enterprises, Ut, the chart-bothering Roachford, and the wonderfully named Eight Track Cartridge Family. Our night was arguably the best billing of the whole event, featuring ourselves, Slab and The Shamen.

The Shamen's album *Drop* was a psychedelic-tinged affair, reflecting their love of sixties psych acts like Love and The 13th Floor Elevators, but having seen them several times live it was obvious that a major re-think had taken place after the arrival of Will Sinnott the previous October. He first appeared on the single 'Knature of a Girl', and it was apparent they were very much a group in transition, with one foot in the past while peeking into possible futures.

Stephen Bunn stepped in to play guitar for the gig. He was a fine, inventive guitarist, and knew our material backwards, having mixed our front of house sound since the early days. With little rehearsal, we turned in a blistering set on the night. Stephen's feedback howl opening on 'Man On The Inside' sent shivers down my spine. Having him there allowed me to run amok in the longer, freer sections.

We did an interview at the venue with *Melody Maker* and the gig was filmed by Factory Record's film arm, IKON. The IKON team of Malcolm Whitehead, Brian Nicholson and Howard Walmsley had been getting close to the band over the preceding year, and had been filming shows for a future release. The footage they got from this night is weird and eerie, lit in alien-looking greens and blues. It seemed like the troubles with Dave, although not very long ago, were ancient history.

At the end of the night, when the audience had filed out of the venue, leaving the bands to pack away the equipment and reflect on what had gone down, we found a black bin liner near the merchandise table. The Shamen had already left, and assuming it was a bag of their t-shirts, we rescued it for them and took it back to Manchester with us.

When we got back and checked the bag, it was not filled with Shamen merchandise at all but with several pairs of black army trousers and a few (non-band) t-shirts. Our manager Paul tried to find out who they belonged to, but had no success, and after a week or so, I gave them away to a particularly poverty-stricken Hulme neighbour. Waste not, want not.

The following Friday I received a visit from this neighbour, who arrived at my flat kitted out in the clothes that I had given him. At that time, Channel 4 put out a programme called *The Chart Show* which featured promotional videos but no presenter linking them up. Instead, information on the bands appeared in text form as the song was on. Having played with them so recently, it was exciting to see that The Shamen were to be one of the featured acts that night, and we settled down to watch them.

At the run out of their video, a box appeared on screen with the news that 'The Shamen have just finished their UK tour at London's Fulham Greyhound, where somebody stole the guitarist's washing!' I looked at my neighbour, unwittingly dressed head to toe in Shamen clothes, and spat out my tea. Ooops!

Despite all the action going on with the band, I dreaded the empty hours on my own. I was living something of a dual existence. I was flattered by the attention from people who liked the music we made which, on one level, was all I had ever wanted. I had withdrawn into a world of music when my mother was still alive, and all through my childhood I had dreamed of being part of a music scene as some kind of self-protection measure. Now, in my twenties, I saw myself in the very same music papers that had educated me and given me something to live for as a kid. My music was being played on the same programmes that I used to religiously listen to. All my dreams were made, yet when it came to my life outside the band, I was still desperately lonely. Somehow it felt like it was made even worse by the exciting times we were all enjoying as a band.

There were always projects on the go, so I could immerse myself in creative pursuits like making flyers for upcoming shows or writing songs alone in amphetamine-fuelled all-night sessions. I'd also spend time at the nearby PSV club, hitting Jamie's permanent party at The Kitchen afterwards, putting the world to rights as the sun came up. But even with all this going on, it was clear that something was missing from my life. Getting the band to this point had meant me interacting with people from 'normal' backgrounds, and deep down, a part of me must have subconsciously wanted what they had. After so long as a loner, insulated from the world, music was finding me a way back into the human race. Being around Roger, Andy and Cathy, for instance, had shown me another way of life, and I could feel the protective shell that I had built around myself start to break down.

I started to hang out with a photography student called Lisa. Born in Iran, her family had been forced to leave in a hurry when the previously exiled Ayatollah Khomeini returned to the country and established a hard-line Islamic republic. Although she was well into music, she seemed a million miles away from its druggy subculture, and after a short time as mates, we started to see each other as a couple.

We had first met when I had my flat destroyed a few months earlier. The first thing I did was call next door to see if the people living there knew anything about what had happened. Their flat was a four-bedroom monster-sized one, identical in size to Jamie Nicholson's Kitchen, and it was shared by four students, who kept their front windows boarded up and were so quiet that I wasn't sure that anybody actually lived there. Nevertheless, I knocked hard, still in shock from my brush with evil, and the door was opened by a petite, dark-haired, dark-eyed girl that I had seen before in The White Horse, where students and 'real' Hulme residents would mix a little. Bristling with nervous energy, I tried to explain what had happened, showing her the broken glass on the walkway. That was my first meeting with Lisa.

Over the next few weeks, I kept bumping into her as she cycled to the Manchester Polytechnic Fine Arts building, where she was in the last year of a photography degree. I began to join her and her friends in The White Horse, and got to know and like her. It felt good to be able to share some aspects of the band's success with somebody else. One perk was the fact that I didn't have to pay in anywhere, and I took full advantage of this. I had been invited to see Pixies and Throwing Muses at The International by Gareth Evans, who had taken over the job of managing The Stone Roses from my ex-Haçienda boss Howard (Ginger) Jones. This became our first date.

The Pixies were our contemporaries, and almost every interview we did with the major music papers ended up with us being asked our opinion on them. They had that 'quiet/loud' thing going on, similar to us, and as we veered towards the heavier side of things while still retaining a pop sensibility, comparisons were frequently drawn. I was slightly underwhelmed with them, to tell the truth. Something about them didn't ring true, with their third person approach. Having laid my soul out in songs, I mistrusted writers who used characters to get their point across. I saw Black Francis as belonging to a tradition of storytellers, as opposed to being a speaker of unembellished truth. It was Throwing Muses who seemed like the more interesting proposition, more fragile and human, somehow.

Lisa had her degree show on the horizon, and it did me a lot of good to care about something that somebody else was doing. She was a nervous kind of person and was going to bits with anxiety over it all, but I was able to guide her through this difficult period. Thinking of her and helping her made me feel more centred, giving me some perspective to my own, ever-maddening world. We definitely helped each other with our respective lives.

Lisa's flatmates kept themselves to themselves on the whole, although one of them, Catherine, was friendly and outgoing, and I would bump into her and her boyfriend, Chris Bridgett, at gigs and at The Venue. They were both from the North East, and talking to Chris, it seemed that we had a few things in common, music-wise. He had a soft spot for The Birthday Party, who I liked, and he had seen Dub Sex a couple of times, at the PSV and at The International. Spending time at Lisa's shared flat, I began to get to know him better. He had a good sense of humour, and was always ready for a little after-hours action at the nearby PSV club.

We had other friends in common, including Lee Broady and Danny Baxter, who lived on the ground floor of John Nash Crescent, and hearing Chris play guitar at their place one time after a night at the Haçienda, I began to realise that he might be suitable to take up the second guitarist vacancy created by Dave's exit. I showed him some of the more immediate, chord-based songs first, like 'Tripwire' and 'Push!', in order to help make things happen that little bit quicker. Chris was playing with Gary Terrell in a band called The Bogmen at the time, but increasingly I felt he might be what we were looking for.

I invited Chris to have a work out with us at the practise room in Salford. We were working fast, and although Roger and Cathy were rather cautious at first, I had good feelings about it all. After a few rehearsals, we all agreed that things were going well and we had ourselves a guitarist. We had a lot ahead of us, and it was good to get started on this 'post-Dave' period straight away.

27: Grip Of The Snarebeat

My friend Frankie from Langley was found dead on a bench next to Heaton Park lake. It was suicide. There is nothing that blows you completely out of the water like somebody you know taking their own life.

Frankie was part of a group of friends that I had met in the early eighties. I had always been attracted to the company of people older than me, and I had spent many hours with him and his friends. We stayed up all night listening to good soul music. He was a window cleaner by day, and his dirty blond hair and cheeky grin broke down many doors for him. Funny and popular, with all the confidence you would expect from someone who deals with the public day in, day out, Frankie was a lot of fun to be around, and him taking his own life was the kind of shock that made me examine everything I thought I knew.

Like all of us, Frankie was no stranger to recreational drug use, but, with hindsight, the clues were there that he had deep underlying psychological problems which couldn't have been helped by the lifestyle we were all living. He started to display signs of deep paranoia, convinced that he was being followed by unknown people intent on doing him harm. He had always kept himself clean and presentable, but this had gone out of the window as he spiraled down. He became scared and edgy. Poor Frankie. He took an overdose.

All the unanswerable questions flooded in. Could I have intervened? Were there signs that I had missed? A mixture of feelings, from anger to despair. I dealt with the shock the same way that I dealt with anything. Music.

Roger and I hardly talked on the way to our rehearsal room, both of us feeling the crushing heaviness of my grief. It was clear that some loud music could drown out these desperate, dark thoughts that I couldn't shake off. In the room, I strapped on Cathy's bass and laid it upside down on Roger's ride cymbal, with all four strings resting on the metal. Roger then started a violent cymbal roll, setting off the most wonderful, thundering cacophony, the two of us channelling something more than just music. Every sound on earth seemed to be in there. After silently mouthing 'One, two, three, four' as a strict hi-hat pattern and two note bass sequence rang around the room menacingly, I let it all come out, exorcising the bleak feelings, inventing lyrics on the spot that took me through my friend's last movements.

> No entry, by order
> It's locked
> I'll climb over
> And sit near the water
> There should be water

In my mind, I was there with Frankie, next to him on the park bench as the sun came up on his final day. Cornered and afraid in a place he would have loved as a child.

> Fifteen months later
> Same face, but older
> Eyes pierce into your shoulder
> Eyes pierce into your shoulder
> Your worries are over now

This was my gift to Frankie. I wasn't at his funeral, and the only thing I had to offer was my music and words, so this song became 'Instead of Flowers', to replace the bouquet that I would have brought.

> Instead of flowers
> Your worries are over now
> Over now

Shortly after the terrible news about Frankie, a phone call came in for me at Roger and Andy's flat. My old friend Mike Hutton had thrown himself under a train on a busy line close to his Didsbury flat.

Mike and I had spent hundreds of hours, weeks even, in each other's company, turning each other on to weird and wonderful music and hatching plans for strange artistic projects. The night was ours, or so we believed, and we would make full use of it, hitting Mike's Bonsall Street flat when the clubs had closed, invariably greeting the dawn in altered states, taking to the deserted streets in search of mischief.

Again, with hindsight the clues were there with Mike too. The two of us had slipped into a Catholic church one Sunday morning and hid at the back, soaking up the atmosphere. We were both of a Catholic background, but the whole experience seemed to affect Mike strongly, and he went off on something of a tangent from that point on.

Mike's mental state deteriorated quickly, but it didn't necessarily feel like a problem at first as he was such a strange cat anyway. His flat was a living artwork of its own, with mini-sculptures and strange paintings everywhere, and we were all used to his surrealist approach to life. Eventually, he began to hear voices and believe that he was being instructed by unknown forces to carry out instructions, often destructive in nature. He saw Letraset messages hanging in the air, telling him to kill people. That's when it became clear that this was real mental illness rather than simply eccentric artistic behaviour.

Mike's family eventually intervened, and he spent several months in a psychiatric ward at Withington Hospital. He came out a changed character. Weaned off street drugs, but filled with anti-psychotics and barbiturates, he became sluggish and slow-moving. He gained a lot of weight and was a different person to the Mike we once knew.

This was very upsetting to see. Of our group of friends, Mike was one of the brightest and funniest, and his future looked full and fascinating. I wonder what he would have contributed to the world had he lived. I know that it would have been brilliant, whichever path he chose.

The last time I saw Mike, he came to visit me at my flat.

'You've always had a lot of time for people, you, Mark.'

He had visited several of our friends at the same time, and none of us had thought anything of it. Replaying everything, it's clear that he was saying his goodbyes. He had been through the mincer that is the British psychiatric system, but at no point did I ever think he would take his own life. For one, there was his absolute devotion to his beautiful Dalmatian, Zero. Mike loved that dog, and was a brilliant dog owner.

Zero went everywhere with Mike, and wanted for nothing. After Mike's death, I spent a night sleeping on the floor with Zero, silently bonding over our missing friend, imagining that he was there with us. If Mike could leave Zero, then he was definitely beyond the point of no return.

Once again I dealt with this tragedy by immersing myself in music. Before too long, I had found the words I needed to express my feelings and was able to hang these words onto a beautiful bassline that Cathy had invented. It was hypnotic. I lost myself listening to Cathy and Roger running around this simple phrase, working out the details. It takes discipline and a distinct lack of ego to repeat a simple sequence endlessly for the good of a song. I could have listened to them for hours.

I noticed something very unusual. Cathy, having smaller hands, had developed a unique way of playing the phrase by snaking her thumb round the back of her bass and moving it up and down the neck of her instrument. I had never seen anybody else do that before. It sounded human and ghostly and utterly, utterly brilliant.

Isolated bass and voice had become one of our trademarks, but never had we used it to such devastating effect as on 'Caved In'. I spoke to my lost friend directly.

> Everybody's head caved in
> When they heard about what you did
> Can't sleep unassisted
> He went home to his kids…

This line refers to the poor train driver, having to return to his family after witnessing Mike's last act.

> I loved you, I really did
> Those days we used to change our shape
> And blend in with the landscape
> And have fun all day

I re-lived the whole experience every time I sang it, moved to tears.

Dog day in the rain
Many an old face
Super 8 film on your big day
It shakes and the colour's grained
No tears are going to wet my ears
I just grinned as they took you away
And that was some decision you made

Humanity was high on my agenda as 1988 progressed. Music was my path back to myself. I knew I had something unique to get across, and as the year advanced, opportunities to do exactly that were coming at me thick and fast. The departure of Dave had opened the floodgates when it came to new songs. I had been holding back on some of my better ideas, not wanting them to be sold short, but now I was able to start making them into songs. 'Every Secret (That I Ever Made)' and 'I Am Not Afraid' felt deeper and more inventive than what we'd done before.

This burst of creativity meant that we had something to get our teeth into with Chris now on board. We decided to concentrate our energies on recording, rather than overexpose ourselves playing small gigs. The thinking was that if we gained press attention by playing only big shows, it would, in conjunction with all the radio exposure we had been getting, make us seem 'bigger' than we actually were and would allow us to build a much higher profile.

So it followed that Chris's first proper engagement with the band was in the studio. Paul Humphreys had made arrangements for us to set up our own label. The troubles with Red Rhino had brought an end to our relationship with Ugly Man. Red Rhino's distribution network meant small labels like Ugly Man and others in 'The Cartel' could get their records into a series of independent record shops. The collapse of that coalition left them high and dry without a distributor.

Our guardian angels were SRD in London, both a label and distributor. Founded by the ideologically driven John Loder and his wife, Sue, the organisation was run from the rootsy Southern Studios, where great things had been created by the likes of Adrian Sherwood, who had recorded many brilliant On-U Sound records there. John Loder himself had been the engineer on many of the incendiary records released by Crass, and the anti-establishment nature of what they did appealed to me.

Seeing us as fellow travellers with much in common, and knowing the progress we had been making since our inception, John offered to help us. He wanted to finance our own label, paying for recording and production costs, and giving us a respectable budget for promotion, too. After the break-even point, profits were to be split 50/50 between ourselves and SRD. Cut Deep Records was born.

With a new line-up, and new, deeper and more emotionally incisive songs, we were chomping at the bit to get busy. We had knuckled down in the rehearsal room with Chris learning the new songs fast, and in no time at all we were bound to Bradford's Flexible Response Studios with Chris Nagle in the producer's chair.

Chris had picked this studio for its excellent live room, and after recording the bass and drum tracks, along with guide guitars and vocals, the idea was that we would continue at Strawberry, adding both guitars and my vocals, and mixing the record there, taking full advantage of the fact that Chris knew the place so well.

Malcolm Whitehead from IKON films also joined us. Malcolm had filmed several of our live shows and hours and hours of interviews with me for a documentary that IKON planned to make. We were all used to him and his colleagues by now, so they were invisible to us as they went about their work.

With everything in place, I was free to immerse myself fully in the making of our most hard-hitting record yet. Born from a place of tragedy that was still palpable, we had the two new songs that dealt directly with events that had only just happened. The lead song on the EP, 'The Underneath', was another new song. Writing it required me to stare in the face of my own pain and emptiness, alone and hurting, with a deep need to let my demons out. And out they came. It was the best piece of writing I'd put my name to up to that point.

The recording sessions had the effect of accelerating the speed of

Chris Bridgett's settling in period. In short, there simply wasn't one. Chris had to hit the ground running. He hadn't worked in a top flight studio before, so was plunged in at the deep end. His guitar playing complemented my own perfectly, and his enthusiasm and friendliness were a breath of fresh air after the negativity we had experienced at the end with Dave.

After recording the core elements in Bradford, we adjourned to finish the job at Strawberry. I really started to bond with Chris Nagle during these sessions. Bearing my soul in Strawberry's vocal booth, late into the night, I became a changed person, as the feelings that led me to write such songs were purged and made into something uplifting. My pursuit of truth and honesty as a writer were cemented during these sessions

In between trips to the studios, we had to fit in two gigs, including Chris Bridgett's live debut at our biggest Manchester show to date, headlining Manchester Polytechnic on Oxford Road. I had seen hundreds of bands there over the years. It was just a ten-minute walk from Hulme, so was a popular watering hole for many of my friends and neighbours. In particular, their Friday night socials were filled with Hulme-ites, attracted by the cheap alcohol and danceable soul tunes.

I decided to pop my head into the venue on the Friday before we were due to play there, just to get the vibe. I knew the place inside out, but now I was going to be playing there I saw it through different eyes. It was a good scene. Killing Joke and The Clash's 'Rock The Casbah' were the night's floor fillers, but I really enjoyed the extended Greensleeves 12-inch version of Dr. Alimantado's 'Born For A Purpose/Reason For Living', a record of great beauty.

Having got myself all excited to be playing a hometown gig in such a vibrant place, I found a quiet corner and made a large spliff. Most of the pubs that we frequented turned a blind eye to the smoking of weed, and I had spent many stoned nights in this very establishment before now. Unfortunately though, on this particular Friday, my luck was out, and two huge doormen pounced on me, gripping me firmly and confiscating my small lump of Afghani black, doubtless to be sold again later or used for their own recreational purposes. I was escorted roughly to the door and ejected with the news that I was henceforth barred from the establishment. This was hilarious. In six days time, these black-suited bullies would in effect be working for me.

Gig day came, and sure enough, the bouncer in question tried to stop me from coming into my own show. I've never been one to pull rank, but it was sweet to sail on past him into the rapidly filling hall. I stopped short of asking him for my draw back, but the helpless look on his face more than made up for that. The show was filmed by IKON. Chris Bridgett was nervous, and quite rightly so, having been forced to undergo a real baptism of fire, but he did brilliantly.

Two days later we were playing in London. We had played entry level gigs before, crammed onto bills with too many other bands at pub venues like The Sir George Robey and Bull and Gate, but, with all the attention we'd been getting, our bookings moved up a level. This one was at Dingwalls in Camden Lock, a venue that had played its part in the punk explosion, hosting early shows by the likes of the Sex Pistols, The Clash, The Stranglers, The Ramones, and just about anybody who was anybody. Fast forward to 1988, and the venue was still at the centre of everything, hosting a club night called Panic Station in conjunction with the music paper *Sounds*.

We were booked as the support act to a band that I had a lot of respect for, World Domination Enterprises. I had been thrilled by their 'Asbestos Lead Asbestos' single, and even felt that both our bands shared some common ground, which was rare enough in itself. We both employed gut-wrenching low bass frequencies, and Keith Dobson's approach to guitar demolition mirrored my own slabs of sharp, shrill punctuation over a rock-solid rhythm section. In a world of careerists and frauds, our two bands exemplified honesty and an understanding of punk's true meaning. We made new friends amongst the World Domination Enterprises fans that night.

The new songs that we had recorded for 'The Underneath' EP developed a life of their own that night. It was a great way to kick off the next stage of the band's life, and served to knit us all together. Chris and I were already spending a lot of time together, at parties or at The Kitchen, which was becoming more and more lawless as the ecstasy scene grew in size and importance. I, for one, could hardly wait for what was coming next.

28: Two Eights Clash

The start of summer saw us invited back to Maida Vale Studios to record our third session for John Peel. We were starting to feel like regulars on the most important and influential radio show on the UK airwaves. It was quite a buzz, so imagine the horror when on our way to the studio the hired van came grinding to a halt shortly after Birmingham. The engine gave up the ghost. Nothing could have been worse. When we rang the studio to break the bad news, we all thought that the session would be cancelled. Instead, we were told to come down as soon as the repairs were done, and we could have not one, but two days to complete the session – today and the following week too. It was an amazing stroke of luck.

We arrived in London in the early afternoon and spent the rest of the day recording. Although I was getting to know my way around the labyrinthine sprawl of underground corridors at Maida Vale, I never lost my child-like sense of wonder at simply being there. Dale Griffin was our producer once again. Safe in the knowledge that we'd been granted extra time, we didn't suffer from the sense of working against the clock that had plagued our second session, so were able to add extra 'shimmering' guitar parts.

With Mike Hutton's death still raw and fresh in the mind, we turned in an emotionally charged performance of 'Caved In'. When I was putting the vocals down, it was as if it was just me and Mike in that vocal booth. I emerged tearful and drained, but at the same time I was pleased to have done such a good version. Mike, like me, was brought up on John Peel, and we would frequently listen to tapes from the show at his flat, so singing a song about him here at the BBC Maida Vale complex felt perfect and the first step towards some sort of closure.

We included 'The Big Freeze' and 'I Am Not Afraid' on the session, too. Both of these songs had been started when Dave was in the band but had come to life after the arrival of Chris Bridgett. Our two guitars went well together, and both of these tunes sparkled with energy and verve. Chris and I were having a ball by this point, wringing every last drop of pleasure from the Hulme scene. It was a great time to be alive, and you can hear that in every note.

The big revelation of the session for me was 'Snapper'. Lyrically, it deals with my experience of being beaten up very badly as a fifteen-year old by three drunken thugs when I had dyed my already bleached blonde hair a fetching shade of blue and it ended up a filthy shade of green. This was enough to make myself a sitting target in the violent, punk-hating backwater that I lived in. Here in the vocal booth of BBC Maida Vale Studio 5, I re-lived every blow as I sang.

> Bury my head in my knees
> Arms at my face for a shield
> Red on the floor beneath my feet
> I can breathe but I can't see
> Line up for the way out!

Closing my eyes, I was back in Middleton, curled in a ball, expecting to die from the kicks and blows raining down on me. The track is one of the most accurate and satisfying of this whole period. After a tense start, the dual guitar parts spiral and circle around each other in ascending and descending patterns. It is a powerful piece of work that showed a new way forward for the band. I had been trying for years to express how things were that night. Now 'Snapper' existed, I felt cleansed.

This was the best produced of our sessions so far, with very good reason. Normally a band would have one day to record and mix all four tracks but due to our misfortune turned good fortune, we were back the following week for an entire day of mixing on some of the best equipment in the world. With more time to spare, we saw a different side of my former childhood Mott The Hoople hero. Of all the sessions he produced for us, this is by far the meatiest. I could tell that Dale enjoyed it, too.

It was probably a side effect from getting slightly better known as a band, but all of sudden, the visual side of what we did started to have much more importance than it had in the past. Opportunities to get on television were presenting themselves, and it was a blessing to have been taken under the wing of Malcolm and his IKON team. Flattering, too, as I had cut my teeth on his work as a teenager, and had got to know him, pre-band, when I worked at the Haçienda in the early eighties. I held both him, and the bands that he worked with, in high regard.

IKON were probably best known for the 'Love Will Tear Us Apart' video, filmed at Tony Davidson's rehearsal rooms on Little Peter Street where I'd rehearsed with Vibrant Thigh. Apart from producing promotional videos for Factory and other left-field bands, IKON were tasked with the job of filming whoever played at the Haçienda. This was projected live on the two large screens on either side of the stage, at eye level to the balcony, and was quite the novelty during the club's early days. It also meant that a permanent record of concerts was being built up by Malcolm and his team, usually capturing these bands at the peak of their strength and creativity. Sales of the popular releases like Joy Division, New Order and The Fall would help to finance more left-field artists, including us. I will always love Malcolm for that. To be taken seriously by such an experienced and creative man helped me believe in myself and the musical mission I was on.

IKON were booked in to make a promotional video for 'The Underneath' single. The filming took place over two days at the Chorlton rehearsal rooms used by The Stone Roses, with Malcolm and his team arriving the day before to set everything up. I, of course, joined them for these preparations. Malcolm, along with his colleagues, Brian Nicholson and Howard Walmsley, had spent a lot of time planning what we were going to do. Much fun was had assembling scaled-down train tracks in a circle for the band to perform inside the following day. The idea behind the video concerned itself with movement, Malcolm envisioned lots of fast edits and sharp, moving sequences.

We performed the song again and again for two days, as the cameras flew past us, following a carefully plotted curve mapped out by the mini railway beneath our feet. The trust and friendship between me and Malcolm meant that I would be up for trying out his ideas without question. I knew that however unusual some of his requests might have sounded, they would have been born out of the purest artistic intentions. Likewise, I had no problem with being filmed in absolute close up, it was easy to forget that he and his team were there. Filmed from inches away in some places, the film captures the very essence of the song. Beads of sweat are flicked all over, and with each explosive 'p' sound, spittle is expelled towards the camera, and by extension, the unsuspecting viewer.

The film is enhanced by another of IKON's trademark stylistic tricks, one that had caught my eye on several of Malcolm's earlier videos for Factory bands. It echoes Joy Division's *Granada Reports* version of 'Shadowplay', with moving cars and atmospheric traffic footage adding to the motorik nature of their performance. Malcolm had his own take on this, and at a certain point, after I have sung the first two verses, the whole screen explodes in a confusion of fast-moving abstract colours. Malcolm had driven around Hulme and Manchester's neighbouring inner-city areas with the camera jammed into a little space at the top of the car window. Hours of footage was boiled down to the most exciting bits and then fed into the Chorlton material, with us encircled by the camera's eye. Tension builds until everything kicks off in a riot of visual feedback with split screen images of us at full throttle. The stuttering images and fast-paced editing suit the song beautifully.

The crescents were the place to be that summer, full of strange characters and unusual lives. I weaved in and out of it all – on the one hand mixing with the great and the good of the current UK independent music scene, while all the time feeling equally comfortable with those on society's bottom rung.

John Nash Crescent itself was a kind of snapshot of the wide range of people that, for one reason or another, had found their way to Hulme. Just on the top floor where I lived, we had teachers, fashion students, 'professional' shoplifters (who would relieve Waterstones of any book you cared to name and deliver it to your door for half of its retail price) and overly noisy sex workers, whose Academy Award-winning moans of ecstasy would bounce around the concrete structures, fooling nobody.

Two doors down lived Piggy, immortalised in an unforgettable graffiti campaign stating that 'Piggy Nuts Bricks For Beer', something that was very believable. The walkway around his flat was strewn with stickers given away with *Class War*, a revolutionary publication with a weekly 'Hospitalised Copper Of The Week' pin-up that featured some luckless frontline police officer with blood streaming down his face. Extreme though it all sounds, Piggy and his heavily-pierced girlfriend were the very model of politeness to their neighbours, and had a love of dogs matched only by their hatred of mainstream society and its laws.

The stairways and walkways of Hulme's crescents were something of a hotbed for political education. May 1988 had seen the introduction of Clause 28, which banned the promotion of homosexuality as a 'pretended family relationship'. The stairwells of our estate served as a Soviet-style news noticeboard on the subject, a vital component in the growing resistance to Thatcher's hated bill.

It was on the Hulme walkways that I first realised how big a rubber bullet was, as a series of Republican posters printed an actual-sized picture of one. The word 'rubber' in this context brings to mind a small, bouncy thing, designed to deter, not maim, and to see this hard plastic, dildo-type object's actual size was a sobering experience.

The biggest and most localised issue on Hulme's unofficial political noticeboard had been gathering momentum for some time by now, but 1988 was very much the year of Viraj Mendis. Mendis, a Sri Lankan national, had come to the UK to study in 1973 but had overstayed his 12 month student visa. As a member of the Revolutionary Communist Group and a supporter of the Tamils, he claimed to be in danger of death if he was returned to Sri Lanka. In December 1986 he ran into the Church of the Ascension (next to the PSV club and Charles Barry Crescent) and, supported by the resident priest, Father John Methuen, invoked the centuries-old right of sanctuary.

The next two years saw Mendis holed up in the church, as the residents of Hulme set up the Viraj Mendis Defence Campaign and organised regular protests. The summer of 1988 saw the biggest rally yet, in the (un)natural amphitheatre of Charles Barry Crescent. There was an afternoon of earnest speeches and a set by lesbian activist group, The Friends of Dorothy.

Anticipation was high as we waited for Viraj himself to speak from his place of sanctuary. Hundreds waited with bated breath when suddenly, a loud female Yorkshire voice rang out over the estate.

'Reg! Reg! Come on, Reg!'

It was my ex-girlfriend, Jane, in a chemical world of her own, oblivious to the mini-Woodstock taking place five floors below, calling her dog at the top of her voice. Half the audience collapsed with laughter, and the other half tutted in disgust. So funny.

I was spending a lot of time at The Kitchen. I was always welcome to just go round in the daytime as recording sessions were going on. I could just hang out on my own downstairs. It felt good to be trusted by Jamie in the same way that the Cadman brothers trusted me. The weekend raves there were becoming more and more extreme, and all this action attracted a lot of people into Jamie's life. As he (somewhat naively) always thought the best in people, it was left to me to keep a more streetwise eye on the various chancers and hustlers who circled interestedly.

One person that we both liked a lot was Marcel King. Apart from everything else, the summer of 1988 was the summer of Marcel within our circle. Marcel was known to all of us as the teenage lead singer of Sweet Sensation, a Manchester soul band that had appeared on the television talent show *New Faces* in the 1970s, and had chart hits with 'Purely By Coincidence' and 'Sad Sweet Dreamer', which had actually made number one in 1974.

Success had, in many ways, chewed up and spat Marcel out. He turned up at Jamie's having lived a hard life since the heady days of his youth, and he bore the scars both physically and mentally. One thing he still had, however, was an absolutely beautiful voice, and before too long, he was making new music with Jamie. I ended up providing backing vocals on 'Fatal Attraction', a pulsing house track written by Marcel and Jamie. Singing with Marcel, and hearing him sing close-up, was an unforgettable experience.

It looked as though things were starting to happen again for Marcel, as *The Face* magazine included him in an article by John McCready on the new soul scene in Manchester, alongside Chapter and The Verse and Factory's 52nd Street. I kept him company on his photoshoot, looking moodily over the balcony of Charles Barry Crescent. Me, and someone that I'd watched on *Top of The Pops* when I was in care. The surreal experiences were coming thick and fast from every direction now.

A few doors down from Nicky and Tracey's flat, where I was staying, lived an eccentric, but driven character called Richard Roberts. He was very handy, in practical terms, and had a sideline making and fitting elegant looking burglar-proof wooden shutters on the outside of people's flats. He cultivated an image quite at odds with his bleak concrete surroundings, wearing a suit and tie, and acting like some displaced English gentleman, throwing dinner parties and being noticed in the bright blue taxi that he drove around the estate. He was also something of a person collector, and as my profile as a musician was rising, in a localised way, I ended up at one of his soirees. It was weird to collide with so-called 'normal' people, and I spent a pleasant afternoon chatting to the sister of Richard's friend, John.

None of the people there had anything to do with music, and John's sister, Bev, had even brought her one-year old daughter to the party. Her husband was drunk and asleep in Richard's spare bedroom, apparently. I had absolutely no experience with children, and had no idea how to even talk to someone so young. It didn't matter, though, as one-year old Ellis proceeded to throw up all over my favourite grey suit, breaking the ice. Messy though this was, it felt good to be around normal people, far away from the druggy chaos of my world of music.

Nicky and Tracey, who had so kindly taken me in when my flat was destroyed, were becoming closer to each other as a couple, and moved into another flat together. In the space of an afternoon, I found another flat, just eight doors down on the lively top floor of John Nash. Chris Bridgett decided to move in too, and although we had no real possessions, and did little more than stay there, it did no harm to the running of the band to have us in the same place like this, right in the middle of everything that was going on.

29: Turn Into A Blur

Dub Sex were invited to contribute to a compilation album released by new label SCAM. The label took its name from the initials of its two founders: Sarah Champion, an *NME* writer who had written early articles about us, and Alison Martin from Red Alert music publicity. They asked us to join the likes of James and Inspiral Carpets on *Manchester, North of England*, a tape and vinyl release. Given the short amount of time we had to get something together, rather than record something new the decision was taken to offer up a remix.

Using downtime at Strawberry Studios, Chris Nagle deconstructed 'Instead of Flowers' in such a revolutionary way that I was moved to tears when I heard the results. Ordinarily, I would have been involved in any remixing of any of my songs, but on this occasion Chris worked alone, and as such, took the song to places that I could never have imagined. Slowing the beat down to a funereal pace, and bravely losing the insistent hi-hat pattern that the song is built on, a new, oppressive mood was established from the start. Ghostly new synth lines pan from left to right and disembodied voices that are not really there whisper and hiss as slabs of subsonic bass weave in and out of the mix, low enough to be felt as much as heard. My voice, taken down in pitch by the song's new tempo, seems far away, frightening and afraid at the same time. Buzzing guitars punctuate the piece, sounding like swarms of ghostly bees.

In an echo of the first time we heard John Peel play 'Tripwire', we were all in Roger's car on the way to rehearsal when we first heard it. Hardly recognising it as ourselves at first, we were stunned into silence from the opening howls until the song's end, in which Chris unplugs the tape machine, making the listener feel as if they have been washed down life's bathplug as the whole thing swirls backwards to an uncomfortable conclusion.

The track was placed last in the album's running order, and it is as if time itself has stopped when 'Instead of Flowers' has finished with you.

Cleansed by the experience, and psychologically closer to Chris Nagle than ever before, I prepared to go deeper still on our next single, the recording of which was just around the corner.

Phil Korbel had organised a live radio broadcast from one of our favourite venues, The International, which had passed from Roger Eagle to Stone Roses manager, Gareth Evans. This was actually as live as you could get, going out in real time from the stage to our local BBC network – so live in fact that we were warned about swearing.

We were joined on the bill by Man From Delmonte and Inspiral Carpets, plus 808 State who were the 'between the bands' act. They featured (A Guy Called) Gerald Simpson whose groundbreaking 'Voodoo Ray' single had been released earlier in the year. Its staccato, minimalist pulse, extended for 15 minutes or more on the night. It was unforgettably special, like change was afoot. As I watched the International go apeshit over our new song, 'Swerve', I knew that the future looked bright, warped and interesting.

We were to take our heavily-rehearsed show on the road with a national tour. With our usual one-off gigs, we'd travel back home after the show every time, but this time we had consecutive nights of gigs so the whole team were booked into hotels. With the exception of the German tour, I had never had much experience of hotels. The tour schedule contained parts of the UK that I had never been to before, and I was beside myself with excitement once again.

We were mainly booked into university/polytechnic venues, and I had high hopes of a good reception in these centres of learning, after all, we had been getting played loads on John Peel and had enjoyed prominent coverage in all the music papers. My imagination was confident that 'our people' were out there somewhere, subliminally beginning to love us as they revised with late-night radio on.

Real life conspired to stop my dreaming in its tracks at the first show. Arriving at Teeside Polytechnic, in Middlesbrough, we were herded into what looked like a school canteen, notable for a distinct lack of any advertising for our gig. A motley collection of students were taking advantage of the cheap drink prices as we arrived, but none of them looked as if they cared about music anyway.

Exclusively male, and veering towards the sport-loving 'jock' type, they had started on the piss-weak lager well before our arrival. I could see them sticking their fingers in their ears as we soundchecked, guffawing in their rugby shirts and branded college clothing. By the time we were due on, they were pissed. Our soundman for the tour, Jem Noble, ensured that we were as loud as we could possibly be, and being ignored by most of the half-full audience brought out the best in us. Keeping the gaps between songs really short in an attempt to cover up the drunken heckling, we turned in an angry and aggressive set.

The songs went by in a flash until about three numbers from the end when a viscous globule of spit hit me in the face. The dirty, dirty bastards! Not since Deeply Vale festival had this happened to me, and that was in the bad old days at the hands of glue-sniffing punks, not supposedly educated people. These rugger boys had made me so angry I was microseconds away from taking my guitar off and wrapping it around this privileged little loser's head. I am, however, a man of peace, and refusing to dignify the idiot's actions with any kind of response, we continued to the end of the set at about twice the normal speed. If anyone wanted an encore, they could go fuck themselves, I thought. I needn't have. The silence as we walked off was deafening. As we packed up our gear, I prayed that the people of Sunderland, where we were heading next, had better manners.

Back at the hotel, I found myself in an introspective mood. Everybody else was in party mode, drinking brandy and larking around, but the experience of being ignored for forty minutes and then spat upon had wobbled my perch somewhat. Retreating to my room, I constructed a response to the night's events in the only way I knew how. I wrote a song.

'North By North East' arrived more or less fully formed that night. As well as the demoralising events that had happened only a few hours previously, the song's lyric embraced loneliness, drug use and my love of soul music. In the space of a few hours, I managed to turn myself around and give myself a good talking to. What right had anyone to rattle my resolve? Why should I let myself be affected by anything, ever? I believed one hundred percent in what I was doing, and from the depths of despair came one of the most joyous and uplifting songs I ever put my name to.

> We went north by north east
> That's when it occurred to me
> That we're stronger than negativity
> And we're stronger than we seem

It had the effect of levelling my dark thoughts after a pretty rough psychological mauling. I woke up the next day bright-eyed and bushy-tailed, as they say, and ready for whatever was coming next, which was Sunderland.

The first gigs of the tour were sensibly near to each other, meaning that we didn't have to spend hours and hours travelling between towns. We even had time for Chris Bridgett to call at the family home, where we were supplied with sandwiches by his lovely mam, as our collection of shady-looking miscreants waited outside, parked precariously on a forty-five degree slope. All thoughts of the previous night's insults had been banished. There was a freshness and sense of determination about us, and I, in particular, was ready for anything. We hit Sunderland and got a nice surprise.

The scene there could not have been more different from the demoralising events of the night before. We were playing in a large hall, with a decent PA, and being well advertised we were confronted with a hall relatively full of inquisitive music lovers. We played well, probably out of sheer relief, and it was a blast seeing the audience come to life as our set progressed.

After about four songs, a voice was heard from the darkness.

'Tripwire. Play Tripwire'.

We had started the set that night with 'Tripwire', and this shouted request threw me a little. Why was this person shouting for a song that we had played only a few minutes earlier? Weren't they paying attention?

I was harsher than I had any right to be as I snapped back into the dark hall.

'We've just played it, you dick!'

It felt out of character for me even as I was saying it. I was clearly punishing this poor guy for the crimes of my previous night's audience.

After the show, in the college bar, an unhappy young man approached me for a word.

'I've been into your band since your first Peel session. I saw you in Leeds some time ago, and have never shut up about you ever since. I've brought four of my friends down to turn them onto Dub Sex. Why did you have to show me up like that in front of everybody?'

It turned out that he and his friends had arrived late and had missed the first few songs. Wrapped up in my own headspace, I had not even considered this possibility. Here was somebody who was actively on our side, and I had behaved like some idiotic, self-obsessed rock star. I was deeply ashamed, and vowed that I'd never do anything remotely like it ever again.

The tour continued apace, with visits to Middlesex, Norwich and all kinds of new places for me. It was a time of growing belief within our ranks, and saw us get better as the gigs went on. At the Leadmill in Sheffield, a venue that I had always wanted to play, we turned in a brilliant performance to a sold-out crowd, despite me suffering from the effects of a particularly aggressive batch of bathtub amphetamine which turned the whites of my eyes a fetching shade of neon pink.

Melody Maker sent Cathi Unsworth to review our show at Dingwalls, where we were supported by Inspiral Carpets, and she enthused that we were 'dark, savage and defiant'. Jacqueline Harte told her readers in *NME* that we were 'one of the best live bands in Manchester right now'. I wasn't about to disagree, but it is always good to read such stuff.

Coming back to Hulme after all this action was brilliant for me and Chris Bridgett. When not staying in hotels, we'd be dropped off after gigs in the seriously early hours of the morning, and dive straight round to The Kitchen where Jamie had scaled up his acid house shebeen to a ridiculous degree. Word had been getting round for the whole year now, and as the acid house scene grew in size and importance, and the relevant drugs became cheaper and more available, we were assured of dangerous and edgy fun at any old time.

Although our music was rock-based, we were always accepted as fellow extremists by the dance world, and it became a regular thing for us to come straight from one of our own shows in another part of the country and party like animals until morning in a haze of windowpane acid (red or clear) or its tiny black microdot cousin.

We were ready to record our next single. From the start, we approached this one in a different way to our previous ones. Our label, Cut Deep, was to all extents and purposes our own, although we left the day-to-day business to Paul Humphreys. Strawberry gave us some office space above the studio, so as part of their setup, we were able to negotiate a favourable deal on recording time.

In preparation for recording, Chris Nagle had been down to rehearsals with us, sitting silently as a maelstrom of noise wrapped itself around him. Having him there, and seeing him so committed to what we were doing, made us all raise our game. This period of pre-production gave him a chance to absorb the overtones that surrounded our music. The intense volume we were so fond of playing at would lead to random happy tonal accidents, as if the song itself was joining in with us. Chris would be tasked with re-creating all this weirdness in the studio, and as he sat there, eyes closed, listening, I knew that this record was going to be special.

We had decided upon two main tracks to take into the studio: 'The Big Freeze' and 'I Am Not Afraid'. I had come up with both of these songs with Dave in the group, and had tried to make progress with them at The Kitchen where Jamie let us rehearse going through his mixing desk. The recordings of the rehearsals made it clear to me that Dave was not really getting these songs, so I shelved them for a time.

In both cases, the songs are carried along by the repetition of simple motifs on one guitar, while I would reinforce this groundwork and add overdubbed slabs of crazier stuff. The trick is to stay true to the simplicity of the riff that the song is based on, and in this respect, Chris Bridgett proved to be ideal for the job. It is no easy thing to keep the same guitar pattern going for long periods of time without losing timing or intensity, but Chris rose to the occasion. I felt strong and free to project my personality onto the songs guitar-wise, feeling a confidence that simply wasn't there with Dave.

At this stage, I felt that 'I Am Not Afraid' would be the single's A-side, but Mr Nagle had other ideas. His pre-production visits to the rehearsal room had seen him exposed to another new song which was based on ideas I had been trying to get across since the early days in Bonsall Street. In those days I had called it 'Turn Into A Blur', and it touched upon some different lyrical issues to the song that it became. I had included references to one of my favourite soul singers, Jackie Wilson, who had died some years earlier. The lyric originally lamented his passing with 'I get the sweetest feeling/but the feeling died', but the song evolved to focus upon its parallel themes of survival, and the need to communicate.

The song's central hook served well as a simple summing up of everything I am about as a singer and maker of music.

> Search for the right words
> Search for the missing words

Since my first stirrings as a teenager, this is all I had ever been trying to do. I would occasionally fall in love with a particular word, and in some cases, I knew that I would be using this word as the title of a future song. 'Push!' had started life like this, and I knew that I would write an uplifting and intriguing song of that name as soon as I had decided on the title. This new song was just like that.

On the wall of my flat was a piece of paper bearing one word: Swerve. I had become mesmerised by it. It had elegance and movement, and although only six letters long, it had a mystery all of its own. For months, I lived with it stuck on my living room wall, unsure of how I would use it, until a flash of inspiration made me insert it into this new 'Turn Into A Blur' tune, mainly as texture. Never before had such a simple decision had such a massive effect on a song that I was writing. It was a beautiful moment. Freshly inspired, I was able to finish it.

> Swerve or get hurt
> The choice is yours
> Grown up in the dirt you learned what I learned
> And in this battle of nerves
> They can hurt but never come first
> Search for the right words
> Search for the missing words
> Swerve

Even in its unfinished state, Chris Nagle saw its importance, and his enthusiasm for it led to us prioritising it over the other two candidate songs as we went into Strawberry to record the single.

Song-wise, I had some clear thoughts about how I wanted things to go. 'The Big Freeze' was born during the UK's fierce 1986 winter. It was a time of iced-up water pipes and farm animals frozen into grotesque shapes on the evening news. As always, Britain was unprepared for this extreme cold snap, and the entire country was brought to a standstill.

Musically, it mimics the structure of a Northern soul stomper, with Cathy's bass calling to mind the driving beauty of the Spencer Davis Group's 'Keep on Running', making a solid foundation for me to wig out over on guitar. The changes between verses were originally intended to have Motown-like sampled horn parts over them, a technique that I had also tried on 'Caved In', but in both cases they simply didn't sound right, so we opted for a full and multi-layered wall of guitars to hammer home our point. It features me saying my own name in my own accent, or to be more precise, the word 'Mark' in a different context. The Mancunian accent, for me, is a thing of great beauty and speaks to me of the people that have shown me so much love throughout my life.

'I Am Not Afraid' marries bleak lyrics, written in Hulme at a very lonely point, to a sparkling and uplifting tune. It finds me gazing out from my window at a brutalist scene.

> It was dark when I opened my eyes today, again
> Wind and hail, trace the letters of my name
> I am not afraid
> And I will never be afraid again

The song is based on a guitar motif that echoes The Kinks' 'Tired of Waiting for You', or Blue Oyster Cult's '(Don't Fear) The Reaper', but these are just reference points. Chris Nagle made me focus on the musical side of things rather than the all-out energy I was known for, and when he asked me to add 'some of that lovely shimmering stuff you do', I was flattered and gave my all to do just that.

Chris knew how to get the best out of me vocally, too. The song concludes looping around my passionate 'be brave' hook line. In any other world, this would be a worthy A-side were it not for 'Swerve'.

It was exciting to go into Strawberry with such a new song. We had been playing it for a while, but it still had a little growing up to do. It was built on the drumbeat that Roger had used for one of our first songs, 'Later'. We had played 'Later' at our first gig, and it was a mainstay of our early sets, although it had never been recorded. Over this simple and powerful beat, I inserted a vocal introduction, so that for the first part of the song it is just voice and drums, isolated and designed to grab the listener's attention from the start.

> Get this! Both our telepathy works
> Just let me say something first
> You and yours deserve
> Everything you ever had in reserve

A double snare cracks and the rest of the band come in. I play staccato chords choked by my right hand, complemented by Chris Bridgett playing one-note harmonics which follow exactly the double-time hi-hat pattern. From the very second that the song starts in earnest, everything meshes together into an irresistible groove. Metronomic, but human, each beat emphasised by all of us at once, doing to the ears what a stroboscope does to the eyes.

Turn into a blur
So everybody wonders where you are
Jump over the kerb and escape unhurt

Chris Nagle brought so much to the creation of 'Swerve'. He suggested a genius chord change to lead into the 'search for the right words' strapline, transforming the song into a twisting and turning thing, with real movement within its rigid structure. At one end of the sonic spectrum, the song features my trademark fake tremolo. Born out of poverty, and not having a guitar with a tremolo arm, I developed a way of playing single harmonic notes pressing on the 'dead' area between the guitar's nut and the tuning apparatus. Chris loved this, and made it a feature of the song.

At the other end of things, Chris paid extra special attention to Cathy's bass, layering many takes into a cohesive whole. Some low, some higher, some clean, some distorted. The very nature of the performance meant that even 'identical' takes would differ slightly, leading to a thicker and wider sound.

'Swerve' was a joy to make and, in particular, was a joy to sing. Chris's gut feeling about the song was spot on.

With all three tracks in the bag, and people actually interested in what we would do next, I took a deep breath and waited for the coming year to arrive.

30: The Ecstasy And The Agony

Jamie Nicholson had unleashed a real beast when he turned his flat into a rave space. For many people, The Kitchen was now the centre of the known universe. Ecstasy was starting to become more popular with more people, and, although the price remained high, it was becoming less and less rare. I had been around the early movers and shakers, but I was relatively late to the drug itself. The reason for this was largely financial. For the price of one pill, I could afford enough speed to keep me bouncing around for days, and as a die-hard enthusiast, I would always plump for the devil I knew.

I was no stranger to far-out electronic music, of course. The foundations of house music had been laid years before when I worked at the Haçienda. For me, this particular winter was the winter of 'Newbuild' by 808 State, the last full recording by the group that features Gerald Simpson. Gerald was a product of these very flats, and you could hear the Hulme-ness of it all seeping through every groove.

It was only a matter of time before ecstasy and I became better acquainted. My introduction to the chemical side of it took place in decidedly undancelike circumstances. Although I was not a dealer of recreational substances, I would pick the odd thing up now and again for friends, more as a favour than as a money-making exercise, and it was one of these 'mercy missions' that led to my first MDMA experience. The Fall were playing at The Ritz, eleven days before Christmas, and I was tasked with helping the occasion go with a festive bang. I had been asked to pick up an amount of the same pink speed that had turned the whites of my eyes such an alarming colour when Dub Sex had played Sheffield, and drop it off with a member of the group's entourage at soundcheck time. I was going to the gig anyway, and I was happy enough to help. I must have been in the good books of the person that I was picking this speed up from, or perhaps he was just overcome with Christmas spirit, either way, he packed me off with a small red capsule of ecstasy with the brand name Dynasty, saying, 'There ya go, Mark. Season's greetings!'

I called in The Ritz in the late afternoon, did the business, said hello to Funky Simon and the rest of the band – minus Mark E Smith, whom I was led to understand was often elsewhere while the soundcheck went on. I had decided to wait until shortly before The Fall were due to go on before sampling what I had been given. Ecstasy had always been seen as intrinsically linked to dance music, and apart from people like me, with a foot in many different worlds, it was yet to make inroads in the world of 'rock'. I never was one to do things the regular way, though, and on this night, my beloved Fall soundtracked my introduction to a whole new experience.

Immersing myself deeper than ever before into the labyrinthine complexity of the group's sound, I was surrounded and enveloped by a truly great performance. 'Big New Prinz' and 'Bremen Nacht' turned me inside out with sheer force, they seemed to stretch to impossible lengths. Mark E's vocals materialised inside my head as well as assaulting me from every possible angle. I was curiously lacking in the 'loved up' feeling that I had been led to expect, but this had probably been kicked out of me by The Fall's relentless display of power. They really had been in peak form.

With the anthemic 'Hit The North' ringing round my head, I eventually made my way back to Hulme. I felt energised, and although I had enjoyed my first flirtation with this new wonder drug, it wasn't the religious experience others had reported. No longer a MDMA virgin, I went back to mine alone and lost myself in music of many kinds, eventually sleeping a dream-filled sleep with alien sounds and an abstract collage of moving light behind my closed eyes.

We made a new video with Malcolm Whitehead and the IKON team for 'Swerve'. This time we used our own rehearsal room in Higher Broughton, and over the course of a day, played along to the track hundreds of times, or so it seemed. Malcolm had strong feelings about the song and wanted to frame us in a harsh, austere setting, focussing not on gimmicks of any kind, but on an honest portrayal of what we really looked like when we were doing our thing.

I had been given a 'sawn off' guitar by a friend, and it was a real piece of work. It looked and felt as if it had been fashioned from the heaviest, most densely solid kitchen table on earth. It weighed a ton with half of it missing, so God only knows how heavy it was before it had been so roughly customised.

I loved it, mainly because, in my eyes, it was a direct reference to Pete Shelley's guitar that he butchered in similar fashion in the early days of Buzzcocks. It has to be said, however, that Pete's was at least playable, unlike my own. It was a good day when it stayed in tune for a whole song, and, apart from looking brilliant in the video, was about as much use to me as the slab of wood that spawned it. In a fit of punk fundamentalism one night, I had printed the slogan Work Harder onto the scratch plate. Malcolm was well in favour.

Malcolm saw me as a purist, beyond vanity in many ways. He thought that I was true to the spirit of rebellion that punk had kick-started several years earlier. I loved him for that. Here was someone who had helped shape the world as I knew it, had witnessed performers like Lydon and Curtis at the height of their dangerous early powers, and he would make me feel that I was every bit as important as those who had come before me.

The 'Swerve' video is a statement of intent. Its grey/black minimalism and lack of personal vanity puts it in complete opposition with the way that independent music was going at the time. In particular, Manchester was beginning to be tarred with the 'baggy' brush, and as the lurid colours and fake bonhomie of a thousand Mondays and Roses copyists began to burn retinas everywhere, I was proud to stand against the trivial, superficial world.

The musical side of my life put me in touch with a world that I had hardly ever seen. In this world, people were kind to me and interested in what I thought. Although we were on the lowest rung of music's ladder, and far from making money from what we were doing in any real way, days when we had Dub Sex stuff to do would find us well looked after for the basic necessities. There would be enough to eat and drink, and between us all, we would find a way to ensure that there were enough substances to go round. It was easy then, to ostrich my head away from my own personal circumstances, which, in contrast to the accelerated progress of the group, left a lot to be desired.

My relationship with Lisa had ended, amicably enough, when she returned to Camden where her family had settled after being ejected from Iran. I found myself alone a lot. Even when I shared the John Nash Crescent flat with Chris Bridgett, he was spending most of his time elsewhere.

I took over another flat, this time in Charles Barry Crescent, on the same walkway as The Kitchen studio/shebeen. This flat was handed over to me by John Kennedy, who had employed me years earlier at Berlin. He had been living there with his boyfriend, Gary, a lovely, friendly man who did some background technical jobs on behalf of Factory Records. I could physically feel the pulse of the bass-end of the tunes pumping out of The Kitchen as I lay in my bed. It made more sense for me to be there rather than trying to get to sleep with the relentless throb of the Jam MCs shaking the whole block.

I never settled in this flat, and for a while I became feral. All band business was routed through the Cadman's place and, as I always behaved well, I was more than welcome there. The truth was that I would rather be at Andy's, at Jamie's Kitchen studio, or anywhere else in the world than go back to my new flat. Even with so many friends living nearby, I felt lonely as soon as I got home, shutting my front door to a different, better world outside. As far as money went, I was living on the breadline. What little I had went on amphetamines. The contrast between my music life and my real life was huge, and only I knew about it. In the big picture, something had to give.

Christmas was approaching, and with it came ghosts from my distant past. For all the progress of recent years, I was hit with a very real sense of desolation. My mother, of course, had died at Christmas, and even with so much to be upful about, it was hard not to get caught up in thoughts of how life might have been in some imagined parallel universe where she had never left and I had a better start in life.

The estate emptied out considerably at Christmas. Students returned to their hometowns, and it seemed that even the most drug-fuelled and wilfully eccentric residents had somewhere to go. It was the opposite for me, and I had no choice but to brazen it out, hitting The White Horse and the PSV every night, smiling on the outside to mask my underlying emptiness.

Not everybody was fooled. Several doors down from The Kitchen lived a girl called Bridget. She shared a flat with my friend Boz, who had just started to make music with Dub Sex roadie, Rat, under the name Flea. Bridget had moved from Hull to study and was a popular face in Manchester's rapidly growing electronic music/acid house scene. We had become close friends and I would go round to hers for long afternoons. She had a background in art history, and introduced me to the work of Gustav Klimt and Wassily Kandinsky, all in a natural and non-patronising way.

Bridget, knowing me that little bit better, saw through my 'life of the party' mask. She also knew that I was desperately poor, existing on a Giro that was gone the minute I received it. I was at her flat the week before Christmas. The place was full of visitors, but Bridget took me to one side in her kitchen, away from everybody.

'Now, don't be embarrassed, but I know you're going to be at a loose end this Christmas.'

This was true, but I hadn't expected anyone else to know or care about such things.

'Well… you're not the only one. Me and Boz are staying here, and I'm going to do Christmas dinner for us and a few other friends. We're all chipping in a few quid towards the food, and you're more than welcome.'

I was touched, and although this simple gesture really got through to me, something made me turn it down. Maybe it was the 'few other friends' part, but more likely it was my ingrained discomfort with what

I, in my oversensitive state, perceived as charity. I was always welcome at Roger and Andy's flat, too, but something stopped me from going there. I had become a regular fixture in recent times, and worried about overstaying my welcome, although nothing could have been further from the truth. Christmas did that to me. I overthought everything and projected feelings onto people that simply weren't there. Turning down Bridget's kind offer, I resolved to spend yet another Christmas alone. It would be over in no time anyway.

I went to the PSV on Christmas Eve, stretching the little money I had as far as I could, staying as late as possible before eventually being ejected with the pool playing diehards that frequented the upstairs games room. My plan, as much as there was one, was to sleep through as much of Christmas Day as I could, waiting until the world started up again. Exhausted, I did just that, drifting off as the sun was rising.

Suddenly, I was aware of some very loud banging. Still in my sleeping dream state, I could hear noises and a familiar voice.

'Mark! Mark!'

The banging continued.

'Mark! Mark! It's Nicky!'

Nicky Carroll, who had so kindly taken me in when my flat was destroyed, was almost smashing my front door down in his attempts to rouse me.

'Right... No arguments! You're coming to my mam's with me! Get your shit together.'

In an echo of Dave Fielding's family years earlier, Nicky simply could not take the fact that I would be on my own at Christmas. Blurry eyed though I was, I managed to put one foot in front of the other all the way to the Fallowfield council estate where Nicky had grown up.

I knew a little about Nicky's Dad, Joe Smythe. He was a lifelong socialist and railway worker. He had published a collection of poetry called *Liberation Soldier*. It was full of anti-Thatcher, pro-working-class verse, including a brilliant poem about a family doing a 'midnight flit' from Longsight's notorious Anson Road estate. I had read this collection, and it was a genuine honour to meet the man himself.

After a hearty meal and half of Steve Martin's *Three Amigos* movie, most of Nicky's family had fallen asleep in their armchairs. It was hard for me to keep my own eyes open, but out of manners, I did.

Sitting in this unfamiliar room, listening to a least three different people snoring, I reflected on the kindness that I had received from families like this at various times throughout my life. No doubt, the feelings of loneliness would return when the festive period was over, but for now, I was amongst good people.

31: TV Eye

SRD encouraged us to use a professional designer, Paul Khera, for the sleeve of 'Swerve'. Paul had a strong connection with Mute Records, a label that I had a lot of time for, and his work for Erasure had put him in the slightly bigger league of mainstream chart return shops. This was all well and good, but it was probably the fact that he had worked with Rough Trade's AR Kane that had swung it for me.

Paul's sleeve for 'Swerve' was a departure from our other records. Our previous sleeve for 'The Underneath' featured my junior school in Langley alongside more scenes from my childhood and other visuals that had a great deal of personal meaning for me. Zero, my late friend Mike Hutton's Dalmatian, graced the back cover. It had a DIY feel to it, with its Letraset song titles and deliberately amateurish look. Paul went the other way, wrapping the 12-inch single in a luxurious blue-green matt effect. Even the label itself proclaimed a new-found professionalism, with the band's name repeated faintly underneath the main information, like a sweet wrapper. Photographs of an abandoned puppet adorned both sides. Although I had only minimal input into the project, I was happy to see the final results, every bit the equal of the major label releases it was designed to share window space with.

As our profile grew, so did Paul Humphreys's role as manager. He certainly looked and acted as a band manager was supposed to. Fashionably dressed, in expensive boots and leather jacket, usually sporting a t-shirt from some credible band or other, he cut quite a dash in certain circles. He was easy going and very forward with strangers. I often found him a little too tactile for my liking, he had a habit of putting his arm around you when he talked, which I sometimes found overfamiliar, although these displays of bonhomie seemed to be well-received by other people. Each to their own, I suppose.

Paul definitely filled a gap for us, and it was left to him to liaise with John Loder and SRD while we as a band got on with writing, playing and recording. The first Cut Deep release, 'The Underneath', had gone out in both 7-inch and 12-inch versions, and had received Radio 1 airplay on the more commercial Janice Long programme as well as the usual John Peel plays. This led to SRD looking more favourably on the whole operation. Having the office at Strawberry, and the studio as the label contact address, gave Paul and Cut Deep another layer of credibility. It meant they were more inclined to listen when Paul suggested releasing other music from the weird little scene that was springing up around this well-known and historic studio.

Chris Nagle was part of the furniture at Strawberry, and, as such, had access to the studio in a way that nobody else did. Chris had been using 'dead' studio time to make his own music, along with his wife, Julia, and singer/guitarist, Tim Harris. The results had taken everybody by surprise. Sampler-driven, moody and multilayered, it nodded towards the deep, expansive sounds that Chris had brought to his work with Martin Hannett and Factory, but welded to a crisp, European dance sensibility. It was hard-hitting and drenched in Strawberry's unique array of effects, which Chris himself had done so much to refine over the previous decade.

Chris and Julia had called their new project What? Noise, and their first EP, 'Vein', became the second Cut Deep release (CUT 12002). It was a triumph, receiving 'Single of the Week' in both *NME* and *Melody Maker* in the same week! Such a coup was highly unusual, and it seemed that at last some well-deserved praise was coming Chris Nagle's way after so much time of having his brilliant work overlooked.

What? Noise began to join Dub Sex as support on certain dates. Both groups worked well with each other, sound-wise, and with Chris having played such a large part in creating our records, it was natural and obvious for such a pairing to happen.

Talk turned to a projected new Dub Sex release, a special mini-album of remixes by a host of worthy producers, all of whom had become interested in what we were doing over the last year or so. Paul had been spreading the word far and wide and the time had certainly come to start thinking about our next album in earnest.

This remix album idea never came to fruition, which is a shame, as Paul had got the likes of Flood, Vini Reilly and Jim (Foetus) Thirlwell interested, as well as Martin Hannett, a person I had wanted to work with since I first started making music. Chris Nagle's deconstruction of 'Instead of Flowers' had got us all thinking outside the box, and I was keen to take our sound into 'dubbier' areas.

IKON's 'Swerve' video was taken up by MTV. Even though they had hours of time to fill with their 24-hour format, we were mainly relegated to the specialist, middle of the night shows like *Music Box*. One side effect of the video was that it led us to another televisual opportunity – we were invited to make our first television appearance on a Granada arts programme called *The Other Side of Midnight*, conceived and presented by Factory Records head honcho, Tony Wilson.

Tony Wilson had been a re-occurring figure through all of my musical and personal life. I had first met him at the filming of one of his *So It Goes* programmes as a teenage punk, and had of course played at The Factory with Vibrant Thigh in July 1980. Later, when I worked at the Haçienda, Tony and the other Factory higher-ups were always nice to me, but there was always a sense of employer/employee about our relationship. Things were different now, and the headway that I had been making with the band meant that I was starting to be taken more seriously.

Being on TV was a pretty big deal and it was important we got it right. With only four channels on UK television, viewer numbers for each channel were high. On the eve of the recording I stayed up all night, ironing an unworn white shirt and polishing my red Fender Bullet to within an inch of its life. As dawn broke over Hulme, I had the closest shave that I think I ever had in a bid to look as baby faced as possible for the Granada cameras.

Arriving at Granada, we were shepherded into the all-white studio area, where we set up and ran through 'Swerve' and 'I Am Not Afraid', the two numbers we were going to be dealing with. We did about six versions of each, although we knew that only one song was to be featured on the programme.

New camera operator, Ernie Budd, explained his plan to me as the whole studio shuddered with the noise that we were making getting our levels right. He was to use just one camera, approaching the band from some distance away and focussing on each of us in turn during the song's long guitar introduction, finally arriving on my face as I started to sing. We looked sharp and squeaky-clean against the spartan, white studio.

Halfway through the day, we were relaxing in our dressing room, soaked in sweat after a series of energetic run-throughs. We were sharing a sneaky spliff when the door opened and a tour guide ushered in a party of a dozen old ladies, evidently part of a 'behind the scenes' tour.

'And here you can see a local band, in here to record some songs for an arts programme presented by Tony Wilson...'

We scattered in all directions, wafting the air in a vain attempt to dilute the cannabis-filled atmosphere, but we were caught red-handed by the blue rinse brigade.

'Oooh, I like him!' said one of their number. Tony was something of a household name with this age group, due to his high profile as a newsreader over the years, and he certainly seemed to bring out their mothering instinct on this occasion. They came and went without commenting on the exotic smell, and as they were herded over to the set of *Coronation Street* or something similar, we collapsed into a pile, laughing our faces off, each and every one of us.

The week after the recording I met Ian Brown on an 86 bus into town. The Stone Roses had recorded 'Waterfall' for the show the week before us. Ian was modest and philosophical.

'Well, Mark, we'll see if we're all any good on telly now, won't we?'

The Other Side of Midnight was broadcast across the North West, the Midlands and Scotland late on Friday night, just in time for those coming in from the pub. When the Roses show aired, their slot helped catapult them into the nation's consciousness. Our own appearance, excellent though it was, was cut drastically short by the show's producers, bringing the credits up hurriedly before I had even had time to get to the song's 'I used to believe in you...' hook line.

We were soon invited back on to TV though, and this time it was to be primetime. BBC 2, no less! The show was *Snub TV*. We had been on the radar of the show's creators, Pete Fowler and Brenda Kelly, for some time, as they had featured our earlier releases in their magazine, *The Catalogue*. When they were given the chance to create a TV show featuring the same left-field bands, our IKON connection counted for a lot. They loved Malcolm's work, and just working with him reflected well on us.

The show was syndicated to the pan-European Super Channel, as well as reaching USA, Russia, Portugal, Denmark and Greece, and quite simply was the best programme around, sprinkling smaller bands like ourselves and World Domination Enterprises amongst better known acts like The KLF, New Order and Björk.

It was a fertile time for independent music, both at home and in the United States, and *Snub TV*, despite operating on a budget of just £700 per episode, was able to attract the hottest and most relevant bands around. Pete and Brenda worked as a pair, and would be coming up to Manchester for a packed weekend filming 808 State and MC Tunes, amongst others, in the basement underneath Eastern Bloc Records.

For our slot, it was decided that we would organise a gig at The Boardwalk, with up-and-coming noise merchants King of the Slums as support. Everything tied in nicely with the release of 'Swerve', and I was more than happy to be appearing on national TV for the second time in a few short months, in each case with different songs.

Little by little over the preceding years, we had been building up a following in small steps. It seemed to be the best way of going about things, although it was frustrating sometimes when we saw our contemporaries and former support acts being lionised by a music industry hungry for a foothold in the burgeoning Manchester scene. The Boardwalk was not the largest of venues, but tickets had sold out well in advance, and the sight of a queue of bright young things snaking around the venue before the doors had even opened filled me with happiness.

We were to unleash something of a surprise. I had decided to enlist another guitarist, Tim Costigan, to learn and play my parts, leaving me freer to project vocally and make the most of myself as a performer.

Tim was a brilliant mimic, guitar-wise, and we worked together to make things flawless, so that it came to pass that I could play at the biggest and most important gig in my life so far without the luxury of even having a guitar to hide behind. It was a revelation. Staring each and every audience member in the eye at once and discovering a new way of moving, I was in my element. The thought of the millions of primetime, international viewers made us turn in one of the best shows ever. A groundswell of love hit us in the face.

On the night that the *Snub TV* episode went out, I was publicly berated by a fierce and drunken Hulme political activist in The White Horse pub, of all places. She had taken umbrage after seeing my admittedly 'wired' interview, which followed the 'Swerve' footage.

'When you speak on TV, you're not just representing yourself, you're representing your class, your estate, the people you came from!' No pressure, then.

All of this served to teach me a valuable lesson about how quick people are to judge. There was much more to know about my *Snub TV* interview than was apparent by watching the portion that was aired on BBC2 that night. I had been grabbed by interviewer, Brenda Kelly, the very second I left the stage after the encore, so I was dripping in sweat and breathless. Although clearly in a euphoric state, I actually touched upon some intelligent stuff, but as I leaned forward to make my points, I unveiled the dressing room wall behind me, covered in obscene and shocking graffiti that would have given the viewers of *Right to Reply* a collective heart attack. The words, 'Fuck', 'Shit' and 'Piss' screamed loudly and colourfully above my head, and to protect the morals of a BBC teatime audience, my words of wisdom were chopped to pieces. This had the effect of making me seem impassioned and worthy, but at the same time, stutteringly inarticulate.

Passing through foster families and children's homes for most of my life meant that I was very rarely photographed. It was strange then, to see the way that I moved and looked on film, especially in an interview situation. MTV's *Music Box* had taken an interest in us, and I ended up doing several interviews, usually with either Roger or Cathy, in their

London headquarters. I seem nervous, animated and serious on the footage, but you can tell, I think, that I am sincere in what I am saying.

When 'Swerve' was released, I headed into Manchester city centre to meet Andrew Berry's sister, Cath. She worked at Red or Dead in Affleck's Palace, and on our way past the nearby Eastern Bloc record shop, it was there in the window. Cath went inside and bought one while I stayed outside, embarrassed and proud at the same time. It was hardly chart rigging, after all.

I was at The Kitchen with my friend, Devon Shaw. He had been making some cutting edge dance music there under the name Devious D, and was amongst the first to react to the new sounds coming in from Chicago and Detroit. Creative people always seem to find each other, and The Kitchen was a magnet for so many one-off and unique talents. Devon, like Marcel King, was certainly that. He was also drop dead funny, and even liked my dancing, which made him one of the good guys in my book.

I had been invited to a party in town that looked pretty tasty. The listings magazine *City Life* had been set up in 1983 by Andy Spinoza, Ed Glinert and Chris Paul (who had given Dub Sex our first gig, supporting Miaow). It had been recently bought by *The Guardian* group, who published *Manchester Evening News*, and although there were many who resented what they saw as a corporate takeover of a rootsy and independent magazine, they were throwing a celebratory bash at South, a subterranean haunt known to veterans of Manchester club life as 'Bernard's Bar' and 'Stuffed Olives', and was one of the city's best known gay bars.

Midnight came and went, and Devon and I decided to catch the last hour of this celebration (or wake, depending on your opinion of *The Guardian* takeover). It was only a ten-minute brisk walk away. Things were jumping by the time we arrived. The party was about five hours in, and groups of lightweight journalists were drunkenly falling around the dancefloor to popular tunes by the likes of Chaka Khan and Prince.

I knew a lot of the *City Life* staff, Sarah Champion in particular. I was talking to a group of writers when I noticed a face that I was sure I'd seen before, but couldn't quite remember when or where. Suddenly, it came to me, this was Bev who I'd met at the afternoon party thrown by Richard Roberts in his John Nash Crescent flat a few months earlier. Her tiny daughter had been sick all over me that day, but I found it hilarious, and we'd ended up in deep conversation. I remember saying 'One day… all this will be yours!' indicating the grey wasteland of Hulme with a sweep of my hand, as we caught some air on Richard's balcony.

I went over to her group of friends, and hardly had time to say hello when she cut me off mid-syllable.

'I'm not married now!'

It wasn't as if I had asked or anything, but this exchange put a different slant on things, and after talking exclusively to each other for the rest of the party, we ended up at her terraced house in Longsight. Not something that was planned, but an unexpected surprise that kind of blindsided me.

I awoke to an empty house. Bev had to pick up her daughter, so I made a coffee and waited for her to return so I could say my goodbyes properly. Before too long, she returned with her daughter, Ellis, a tiny thing, barely up to my knee, dressed in a bright yellow dress, burbling baby talk to me as if I'd known her for ages. A few minutes later, unsteady on her feet, she grabbed me around the leg to balance herself, pointing to a sponge ball that she couldn't quite reach, asking me in pre-language noises to get it for her.

After so much time in my harsh urban world, such a direct, trusting, innocent gesture was a breath of fresh air. I was charmed.

32: Overground

The BBC invited us back to their Maida Vale studios once again, to record what would be our fourth session for John Peel. Over the course of the preceding two years, I had gone from being overwhelmed by the sheer sense of history that hits you as soon as you enter the complex, to feeling a solid and worthy part of it all myself. By now, all traces of impostor syndrome had been eradicated from my mind. Working with Dale Griffin each time had led us to understanding each other better, and our earlier confrontations had been put behind us. The songs we planned to record were a taste of how far we had come, and I really felt as if I belonged there.

The session was recorded on a Sunday, and with only a skeleton staff in the building our motley crew had the run of the entire complex. It did not take much to imagine the previous goings-on in this magical place. Formerly the Maida Vale Roller Skating Palace and Club, it was heralded as 'the largest broadcast studio yet constructed in this country' when it opened in 1934. We had used Studios 4 and 5 – previously used by the likes of Jimi Hendrix, The Beatles, Bowie – on our first three sessions. This time was to be different, as we were led into the huge, cavernous expanse of Studio 3. This space could accommodate a hundred-and-fifty-piece orchestra and a hundred voice choir.

The session hinted towards a new direction with an extended dubby work out on 'Swerve'. Along with 'North By North East' and 'Kumina', we also debuted the freshly written 'Time of Life', albeit in an embryonic form.

I had laid down all four guide vocals with the band, but when doing the main vocals this amazing space belonged to me alone. The band stayed in the control room, and I had the lights turned down. It was just me and producer, Mike Robinson. I always preferred a complete take when recording vocals, as opposed to dropping in individual words or phrases, so after a few run throughs, I took a short break and returned to the vocal booth.

It was a weird and spooky experience doing my vocals in this warehouse of a recording room, all alone, with the lights down. Directly in front of me was a plaque informing me that Bing Crosby had recorded his last ever vocal there (eight songs with the Gordon Rose Orchestra, three days before dying on the golf course at La Moraleja in Spain). Being reminded of the room's rich past certainly focussed my mind for the job ahead.

I checked that Mike was ready for me, and with no further ado, set about 'Swerve'. It had an extended dubby front piece that was still new and surprising to me as we'd constructed it especially for the session, inserting the harmonic string bending at the song's start as a kind of 'prequel'. It sounded great. The music stripped itself back to Roger's opening drum phrase, and I was in the zone as I took a deep breath of BBC air and spat out my first line, elated and elevated.

'Get this!'

It felt magnificent.

When I came out of the vocal booth, I was drained, emotionally and physically. Barefoot, and drenched in sweat, I went for a wander on my own through Maida Vale's endless network of corridors in search of a drinks machine and a place to recover. I wanted to be on my own, but turning a corner, I came across a relaxation area where an intriguing looking woman sat with her eyes closed. She didn't look asleep, merely having a moment. Sensing the presence of another person in the room, her eyes sprung open.

'Hiya, I'm Mark. I've just been recording in that massive orchestral studio room. Have you seen that place?'

She stared at me as if I was speaking in tongues. Surrounded by people who were used to the way I speak, I had forgotten how thick and impenetrable my Mancunian accent could seem at first hearing.

I stuck out my hand.

'I'm Mary.' She was smiling. 'I'm recording a session for the Kid Jensen show. It's my first time here.'

This was Mary Margaret O'Hara, a Canadian singer. The Kid Jensen show that she was recording for was earlier in the evening schedules than Peel. I chose to take this as a sign that we ourselves were moving closer to a breakthrough of sorts. I'd never met any other musicians while recording at Maida Vale, and I'd forgotten that a whole world of entertainment was being created here, classical, jazz, drama and everything in between.

We chatted for a while and I was captivated. Just sitting here with this sophisticated, exotic singer from across the Atlantic spoke volumes to me about how far we'd come in such a short time. I could get used to this.

The door swung open, breaking the spell. It was Roger.

'C'mon, Mark, are you coming for a listen to that?'

I certainly was, and shaking Mary Margaret O'Hara's dainty hand again, we said our goodbyes as we headed off in different directions, back to different studios and different worlds.

With the session in the bag, we piled up the van and headed back to Manchester. The songs in my head repeated themselves in a sleep defying loop as the miles ticked away at the end of another life-affirming day. In less than a fortnight, the fruit of our labours would be aired on Radio 1 and would lead us into the next stage of our adventure.

We were invited by The Stone Roses to support them at two sold-out shows, one at Queen's Hall in Widness on Friday 5th May, and the other on the following day at Manchester's International 2.

It was strange to see the meteoric rise of The Stone Roses, having known them since before they had even got their band together. Early on, in scooter run days, when my girlfriend Catherine and Ian Brown's girlfriend Michelle had been good friends and next-door neighbours, I had spent many an hour with Ian and Skinhead Rob, all of us graduates of the punk wars, although Ian and his friends had something of a soft spot for the very laddish side of things, like Slaughter and the Dogs and The Angelic Upstarts, which I was less than keen on. They also had a reverence for The Clash that I found baffling, to the extent of following them around on tour, even camping out outside Manchester's Pluto

Studios when the band recorded 'Bankrobber' with Mikey Dread. In my eyes, punk was meant to sweep away such adoration, levelling the playing field for a brave new world without heroes.

I was very exclusive about the music I liked, snobbish even, and second wave bands like Sham 69 and their ilk did nothing for me. It was a combination of the football hooligan posturing and the backwards-looking, speeded-up rock approach that turned me off. I was being educated by forward-looking innovators like The Fall and The Pop Group, and delving into the world of reggae and soul music, so I was amused more than anything by Ian and his mate's love of these pretenders to the punk throne. That said, we had more in common than not, and I look back upon those times as character-shaping and important for both Ian and me in planning what would come next with our respective groups.

Fast forward to 1989, and Dub Sex were part of a wave of groups gathering momentum and starting to pick up interest from the national press. It was for this reason, rather than us all knowing each other from years ago, that led to us playing with The Stone Roses. Little old Dub Sex had something to bring to the table, according to their manager, Gareth Evans. For all their progress, The Stone Roses were not liked much by John Peel. He pronounced himself 'slightly mystified by the great appeal of The Stone Roses' and they were never invited to record a session for the programme. He mistrusted what he felt was 'their late sixties whimsy'. Were it not for the Festive 50, which was calculated by listener's votes, their music wouldn't have been heard on Peel's show. He felt they smelled strongly of hype, and it was to counteract this feeling that we, as long-standing Peel favourites, were invited to do these shows in an attempt to bring some indie credibility to the proceedings. Other rising bands, such as Kit and Inspiral Carpets, were picked as support bands around the same time, and for the same reason.

So it was that a mere three days after the release of *The Stone Roses* album on Silvertone records, The Stone Roses were to be accompanied by Dub Sex for two celebratory and life-affirming shows. For all my reservations about the music, and the management techniques that surrounded the band, it was wonderful to see friends doing so well, and, to be fair, the band were very good and their fans knew they were in at the start of something special.

The Widnes gig was something of an awayday for the rapidly growing group of Mancunians that had been following the Roses since their earlier days, when Pete Garner and Andy Couzens were part of things. These were, on the whole, real hardcore music fans, record shop workers and regular gig goers. I felt we were among friends.

I spent a lot of the afternoon with Ian Brown and Ste Cressa, the Roses' talismanic extra member. In the old days of scooter runs and Berlin nightclub, Cressa was arguably the most recognisable member of their crew. He was first off the block with the flared trousers thing and had featured in a pre-Roses article on this weird 'casual' fashion that was starting to get noticed in Manchester. They called Ste and his cohorts 'The Baldricks' which amused us greatly at the time.

Ste added more to the Roses ambience than just looking stylish. He would place himself behind John Squire's guitar amp, operating John's delays and other effects at certain, pre-rehearsed times in the set. Shaven headed and sealed in his own bubble, Ste would colour the set with the funkiest double-time dancing imaginable, becoming a fan favourite, and frequently appearing as a fifth member in publicity shots.

Our set was sharp and precise, played to a rammed to capacity hall, but there was no question as to who the bright young things in front of me had come to see. This was the start of something massive. Beatlesque, even.

Backstage, the Roses plus Cressa turned in to face one another. They resembled a football team, seconds before a big game, receiving a pep talk from Ian.

'Right...'

He was slightly too far away for me to hear in detail exactly what he was saying to ready his people for what was to come, but it ended with just one word, accompanied by universal high-fiving.

'Showtime!'

And then they were gone.

I climbed a rickety ladder with Roger up to a platform high above the stage to take it all in. Situated directly above Reni, we got a taste of the adoration that surrounded the band.

The Roses had played things very smart when it came to the satellite towns around Manchester and Merseyside. Having taken the trouble to play places like Warrington, St Helens and Widnes on their way up, they had earned the undying loyalty of the kids from these parts. The sheer cheek and self-belief of them, and in particular Gareth Evans, paid off big-time, propelling them into the big league from the off.

The following day, we were to open up for the Roses at their most important Manchester gig so far, at Manchester International 2. It had sold out immediately, and even in the afternoon, people had started to gravitate towards the venue. We were frustrated by the length of time that the Roses took to soundcheck, but, hey, it was their big night after all.

We waited patiently as Ian allowed some local kids to beatbox and rap during their soundcheck, having got into the building through the loading area doors. The International 2 was well-known for local youth offering to 'mind your car, mister?' (roughly translated as 'give me a pound or we'll trash your car'). It was sweet of Ian to be so civic-minded and encouraging to these apprentice bad boys, but time was pressing on, and by the time we got our equipment on stage it was about ten minutes before the doors were due to open.

After the briefest of level checks, we started 'Swerve' to see how it all sounded together. The door staff decided that they could wait no longer and hundreds of Roses fans spilled into the venue, making a mad dash for the front of the stage. In the space of one verse, the club was almost full to capacity. A little of our mystery had been sacrificed, sure, but this was shaping up to be something special. We made a retreat to our dressing room and waited for showtime.

Eight o'clock came around fast. The venue was so full that there was no way that we could get through the crowd in the normal manner. We had to leave the dressing room via a rickety fire escape and, protected by huge security staff, were smuggled through the car park and into a side door, and from there onto the stage. This was like something out of *A Hard Day's Night*!

All those times with Michelle, Ian and Catherine in the Hulme crescents came flooding back to me, plotting to make a dent on the world of music, steeped in punk idealism. Even in our wildest dreams we couldn't have imagined this kind of action. The Roses were seriously breaking through, and it seemed as though we were to be right behind them.

Our gig went by in something of a flash. We knew that the night was all about The Stone Roses and their triumphant homecoming show, so we kept things concise, a half hour or so of our best stuff, ending with an extended, dubby 'Swerve', in the manner of the version we had recently unveiled on John Peel's show. There were shouts for an encore, but less, as they say, is more, and as the band left the stage, leaving me to reinforce the song's title into everybody's brain, I knew we had won ourselves a lot of new friends.

After the two Roses gigs, there was only one day to recuperate before we were to play with Happy Mondays at the Haçienda in a hastily arranged benefit show for the victims of the Hillsborough disaster, which had taken place just three weeks earlier. The nation was in a state of shock at what unfolded in front of their eyes that fateful Saturday. I had spent the day with Ellis, who was then not even two years old. It was just the two of us that afternoon, and we had been having a fine time messing about in the garden and reading her collection of Mr. Men and Meg and Mog books as the radio burbled with the familiar sound of the Saturday football round up. It was FA Cup day, and although City had been embarrassingly knocked out 3-1 in the fourth round by lowly Brentford, I still kept an ear out for what was happening in the two semi-final games, featuring Everton v Norwich from Villa Park, and Liverpool v Nottingham Forest from Sheffield Wednesday's Hillsborough ground.

Nobody who saw footage of the disaster could remain unmoved. As fans tried in vain to help their trapped fellow supporters by passing them upwards into the stands above, it was clear that a major humanitarian incident was taking place. Ninety-four people died that day, and one more a few days later. Some 766 were injured.

Within weeks, the Hillsborough disaster fund had begun to receive money from thousands of people in the UK and around the world. I wanted to help in some way, having been so affected by the tragedy, when we got a call asking if we could play with Happy Mondays at the Haçienda. The event was to be compèred by Wah! Heat's Pete Wylie. All profits would be going to the disaster appeal. I was proud to be a part of it.

There were a lot of psychic forces at work that night. The nature of the horrific tragedy at Hillsborough had been amplified by the gathering knowledge of ineptitude and fatally flawed decision-making by South Yorkshire Police. The people who were lost should never have been lost. We were gathered to remember them, as well as raise money and awareness, and a ghostly atmosphere hung over the Haçienda.

I knew that this would be an emotional day for me. I had spent years in the Haçienda, working there or just hanging out, and so much of that time had been spent in the company of my great friend, and co-worker, Mike Hutton. It had been less than a year since Mike took his own life. I would be singing 'Caved In' directly in front of the alcove that we used to sit in, waiting for people to turn up, with spring daylight coming through the glass roof panels. Ghosts lurked everywhere.

The venue was seriously oversold, and there wasn't the slightest bit of spare air to be had anywhere. The sight of hundreds of young people crushed up against a barrier, struggling for air, at a benefit show for Hillsborough, was irony itself, and with the events in Sheffield so fresh in everybody's minds, a palpable sense of danger infected everything. Every song we played was harder, truer, and more intense than ever before, and I underwent something of a personal exorcism, staring at the alcove in which Mike and I would shirk our glass collecting duties, saying my goodbye and moving on.

From the hi-hat introduction of 'Instead of Flowers', to the last notes of 'Swerve', I was thoroughly in the zone. Water dripped down the walls, and the crowd, packed together like sardines, were really getting into it. I stared out at the crowd during the extended middle section of 'The Underneath', when suddenly I was gripped by real fear. Ever since my flat was trashed, and my clothes mutilated in such a demonic and scary fashion, I had been half expecting some real trouble at one of our gigs. The fear had almost receded by now, as we had played several headliners since with no trouble, but there, as I gazed out, lost in the swirling mesh of guitars, somebody was pointing a gun at me! My whole life flashed in front of my eyes in a few seconds and I felt sick to the pit of my stomach. Was this it? Was I going to die here, of all places, halfway through a song?

A stream of cool, beautiful water hit me in the face. My would-be assassin had been aiming for me, but with a water pistol. I could have kissed him, and everybody else in the building. Filled with the born-again joy of someone who had been excused certain death, I completed the rest of the set six inches above the ground. Today was not to be my day to die after all.

I was greeted in the downstairs dressing room by Mondays' talisman, Bez, who told me 'I loved it. Don't know what the fuck you're on about, like, but I loved it!' Ace. For the third time in a week, we had knocked it out of the park.

We had been short of a babysitter for Ellis for the night, but a friend of ours had recommended a young lad called Finley who had looked after their two kids recently. This unfortunate 15-year-old had recently moved down to Manchester from Edinburgh after the death of his mother in tragic circumstances. Aware of his tender years, we were all on our best behaviour, keeping weed out of his way, for instance, and trying to set something of a good example. Arriving home after the show, our new babysitter was crashed out on the settee, surrounded by records, in and out of their sleeves. Hip hop and reggae, mainly.

There was scarcely time to recover from the Roses and Mondays shows when it was time to crown a brilliant week with a trip to London for another sold-out show. The gig came about when I was having an innocent drink in Dry, a bar set up by Factory Records on Oldham Street, when an unfamiliar voice called my name. Turning around, I saw

Mike Edwards, lead singer of chart bothering Jesus Jones, surrounded by an adoring bunch of acolytes, hanging on every word he said.

'This is Mark Hoyle,' he proclaimed to his followers, 'and if it wasn't for him and World Domination Enterprises, there wouldn't be a Jesus Jones!'

Apparently, our shared bill with World Domination Enterprises at Dingwalls the year before had been one of the defining moments of his gig-going life, and having watched entranced from the side of the stage while both bands did the business, proceeded to go right out there and start a band of his own. I was by no means the world's biggest Jesus Jones fan, but it is always gratifying to be told such things. In practical terms, too, Mr Edwards settled his debt nicely, giving us a support slot at London's ULU at the height of their chart success, and speaking well of us everywhere, which helped oil the wheels a little.

The venue held about a thousand people, and was respectably full as we went about our business. We were on top form after the exciting week we'd been having, and it was a celebratory show. In spite of Mike Edward's good intentions, we were stopped in our tracks by ULU's notoriously heavy-handed stage crew the minute we reached the time our set was meant to finish, but even this couldn't put a dampener on the proceedings.

There had been a good turn out from Food Records, Jesus Jones' label, and we ended up drinking late with members of Voice of The Beehive and The Shamen, amongst other London luminaries. There was talk of us getting involved with Food at one point, according to our manager, Paul. He had sent the first single their way on its release, but it seemed we were not to the label's taste. Close one, I thought, independence suited us best.

Our six-day flurry of action was complete. With all this action behind us, it was time to turn our minds towards recording again, and an exciting development had come about. Martin Hannett, fresh from producing Happy Mondays' *Bummed* album, wanted to produce Dub Sex! Martin had been at the helm for so many of the records that had shaped me, as a musician and as a person, and knowing the strength of our new songs, the album we were going to make together had the potential to be incredible. I told Paul to set up a meeting, and gazed out of the van window all the way back to Manchester, dreaming dreams that were starting to now come true.

33: Martin Hannett And Me

I was still in council care when I first heard the work of Martin Hannett. I was staying over at my dad's, he was in the pub as usual and I was glued to the radio when I heard *Spiral Scratch* for the first time. I'll never forget the bus ride home that time with the effortlessly cool Shane, daughter of one of the children's home staff, after she'd been shopping at Virgin Records on Lever Street and bought the record. I held it in my hand and saw 'Martin Zero' credited on the back, Martin Hannett's best known pseudonym.

Throughout my late teens, I was thrilled by his productions. Martin's output during the 1979/80/81 period was breathtaking. Joy Division, Basement 5, Magazine, A Certain Ratio, Section 25, Durutti Column, as well as Martin's major label productions for John Cooper Clarke and Pauline Murray and the Invisible Girls (on which he also played bass) were all part of the soundtrack to my life. I could wax lyrical about a great many of the records that Martin made, usually with Chris Nagle engineering.

Martin belonged to the musical generation that preceded punk. His involvement with Tosh Ryan and the Music Force organisation, which was all about taking control out of the hands of London agencies, had a real effect on the Manchester music scene, clearing the way for punk to blossom and building confidence in Manchester as the musical heavyweight that it undoubtedly was.

Martin had approached Paul Humphreys with a proposition for us. It wasn't just an enquiry, he had things all sorted out in his mind. He had been listening to our previous releases and Peel sessions for some time, having always kept an ear on what Chris Nagle was up to. He had recently worked with Happy Mondays at The Slaughterhouse studios in Driffield, Yorkshire and felt that the studio would suit Dub Sex brilliantly.

This completed a circle for me that had begun at the dawn of punk, which, of course, was the very thing that had saved my life back in the bleak days of my shattered childhood. All roads led here.

I was lucky that Martin wanted to meet up the following week. I was beside myself with excitement and having to wait for any length of time would have caused my little head to explode. I didn't need to, but found myself revisiting his back catalogue, especially the earliest Factory productions, usually recorded at Cargo/Suite 16 in Rochdale. From Martin's first Joy Division session there through to his later, better funded work for larger labels, you can hear the sounds that he heard in his head go from conception to reality. Bands would often preview new tracks on John Peel sessions, and it was an education to follow a song from its earlier, sketchy version and then compare it to what it became after Martin had got his hands (and ears) on it.

The meeting was to take place at Jamal's wine bar in Fallowfield. It was important for us all to be in the right frame of mind so I made sure there was enough speed and weed about my person to make things go swimmingly. Paul and guitarist Tim Costigan accompanied me, but it soon became clear that Martin had limited interest in talking to anybody but me. To be isolated like this, by a producer that I had so much respect for, was extremely flattering but I had heard from other people who had worked with him that he would pay special attention to vocalists, separating them from the rest of the band, making them feel special in order to bring out the best in them.

Martin had been brought up in Hanbury Street in Miles Platting, a few streets away from where I had lived with my dad all those years ago. The area, known as The Tripe Colony, was a mesh of terraced houses and pre-war walk-up flats. When I told Martin about my past in nearby Lymouth Road, we found that we had a great deal in common. I had followed a parallel path to him in a lot of ways. I knew the junior school and church (Corpus Christi) that he had attended very well. We were both Catholic lads who had passed the eleven-plus examination, making us eligible for a grammar school education – me at Cardinal Langley in Middleton, Martin at Xaverian in Rusholme – and we both knew what it was to be from a poor area and go to a 'posh' school. The feeling of being different had brought out similar character traits in us both, a sense of resilience, and a knowledge that we would have to try that little bit harder and go that little bit further in order to equalise the unseen barrier that definitely existed between classes, especially in the seventies.

Martin, unlike me, was, a gifted academic, and had been drawn towards the scientific from an early age, eventually getting a chemistry degree from UMIST. His formative years were spent immersed in the world of amateur electronics. Miles Platting borders the city centre, and the Oldham Road area was a hotbed of electronics shops, which Martin would frequent in search of components, building his dream hi-fi from scratch, bit by bit.

That day in Jamal's was a revelation. We talked for hours, about reggae, Northern soul, Krautrock, and I was happy to be able to thank Martin for the joy he had given me since I was a teenager. I was keen to let Martin know that I had got inside some of his lesser celebrated productions, such as the Pauline Murray and the Invisible Girls album, and The Durutti Column's sublime contribution to *A Factory Quartet*, featuring Donald Johnson on drums.

Martin had already made up his mind about me, it seemed. He loved 'Caved In' and 'Swerve' in particular, but he delighted me by telling me of the effect that I had on him as a person, before we had even met. My basic honesty as a performer had been remarked upon before, but it was quite another thing altogether to hear your favourite producer tell you such things.

'We're both Em Aitches, Mark!' he told me, making a meal of the fact that we had the same initials. 'You're doing it for all of us,' he said as the afternoon progressed into more of a serious session.

Drinking was Martin's thing and Paul Humphreys, keen to impress on behalf of the band, had kept them flowing. Things got predictably messy, but by the time we said our goodbyes, I knew that I totally wanted Martin to produce our next batch of material, and we arranged for him to come down to out rehearsal room to hear things for real.

At this point, we had been rehearsing at The Boardwalk for quite some time, and had become pretty well embedded in the scene there. I had first visited the place when it was a left-field theatre that had been taken over by Colin Sinclair with the help and backing of his father. I had only come to drop something off for Karl, who, along with the rest of The Fall, was rehearsing on the club's stage, but I was struck by the building's potential and its geographical location, near the Haçienda, at the Hulme end of town. Mark Smith hated visitors to practises and soundchecks, and I made it my business to not hang around too much, but before too long, we had taken on one of the rehearsal rooms beneath the club, and had become part of the furniture ourselves. We were in interesting company, too. Bands like Inspiral Carpets, New Fast Automatic Daffodils, D.Tox, and A Certain Ratio could be heard throbbing through the inadequately soundproofed walls, and we would sharpen up our skills against them on the subterranean pool table that Colin had installed.

The Boardwalk was, during this period, one of the most important gig venues in the city. Chumbawamba, The Verve, Hole, Rage Against The Machine and Sonic Youth all played there on their way up, and our first two live appearances had taken place there. We were given honorary free life membership, and would arrange to rehearse when there was somebody good on upstairs.

All in all, Dub Sex felt at home there, and it felt good to be inviting Martin into our world, for what we hoped was the beginning of a fruitful working relationship. The idea was to record a single first, and then book a month in The Slaughterhouse to get the album down, taking it to Strawberry to mix, a combination that Martin had used to great effect on Happy Mondays' *Bummed* album.

At this point, we shared our rehearsal space with a band called Laugh, who we had a good relationship with. We could leave the equipment set up, all ready to go, so it was a case of just plug in and play, which was exactly what we did. We were well prepared for Martin's visit, having made sure that we were stocked-up on spare strings, pharmaceuticals and weed. We had spent time getting the songs that we would potentially be recording with Martin into good shape, although they had been growing in maturity in our set over recent months anyway.

Two of the songs that we had chosen for the single, 'Time of Life' and 'Kumina', had been part of our latest Peel session, and I had some ideas of how to proceed, having already had the experience of recording them with Dale Griffin. The third song, 'Over and Over', was newer and less worked out, but saw me moving in new areas, lyrically, and I was keen to see what Martin would make of it.

Everything went well that night. It was as if having Martin there brought out another level of intensity. We treated him to a full set first, at breakneck speed and righteous volume. It was in our rehearsal space that we felt free. We soon forgot about our special visitor and got lost in the beautiful overtones circling in the air, invisible sounds, different every time, formed by the juxtaposition of all the instruments colliding with each other.

Chris Bridgett and I had meshed into a fine guitar partnership. All those hours in Strawberry and Maida Vale, and playing gigs up and down the country had paid off. When in full flight I could hear locust swarms and the murmuration of half a million birds weaving in and out of the music, a random factor that led the brain into areas it didn't know it wanted to be led into. Beautiful.

I knew all about Martin's unique sense of hearing, and that he would catch these 'ghost' tones that haunted the songs when they were set free, and sure enough, his head was bobbing the minute our secret weapon was let loose. This relaxed all of us, and I knew then we were right to involve Martin so closely.

After playing the set through, with particular attention to 'Time of Life', which Martin loved, Cathy left the room to go to the toilet. Martin wasted no time in grabbing her bass and starting a jam with Roger and Chris, loosely based on the song's chord structure. Martin played sitting down and seemed to get lost in what he was doing, head down, no eye contact, nothing. I was taken back to his appearance with John Cooper Clarke on BBC's *Old Grey Whistle Test*, the head Invisible Girl being almost invisible himself as his instrument talked for him.

The focus of what we were playing shifted as we went along, and adding falsetto vocals, drenched in reverb, I realised that we were in the process of writing something entirely new. I wish we had recorded that day, but the entire rehearsal only exists in the memory of the people involved, and there is something ephemeral and right about that, too.

When Cathy came back from her toilet break I would have expected us to continue with what we had been doing, but Martin had other ideas. Head down in intense concentration, he had no intention at all of letting Cathy have her bass back any time soon. We carried on with our improvisation for what seemed like ages, but was probably only about 15 minutes until eventually Martin relinquished control of her instrument and the spell was broken.

Roger and I took Martin back to Chorlton, planning and plotting our overthrow of the entire world as we cruised South Manchester after dropping him off. Sharing a spliff and blasting Chaka Khan at full volume, we took stock of things and decided that, yes, today was one of the better days.

Almost straight away, Martin was on the phone at all hours of the day and night, filled with enthusiasm for the project. He was a charismatic and persuasive man. He seemed to be diving in with both feet as far as Dub Sex was concerned, and having allowed himself to get inside the music, he had some radical ideas about how to go about making this album.

'I've had it in Notator, Mark. Been playing around with it.'

Martin once again focused upon me, away from the rest of the group, building up a relationship between the two of us outside of the band dynamics. He seemed to be oblivious to the very deep loyalty and love that we had for each other. The phone calls increased in regularity and intensity, with Martin at one point suggesting that we replace Roger with a programmed Linn drum pattern, which horrified me. Alarm bells should have started ringing, but I dismissed his suggestion and we moved on to the next thing, with Martin's overstepping of the mark never mentioned again. This was him testing the water, seeing how far he could go with me. I like to think I gained a further level of respect for standing my ground. Maybe not, but at least he knew where I stood.

Martin had some other ideas, too. He suggested that we have a look at another studio, Axis in Sheffield. The plan would be to record three tracks there over two days and bring them back to his beloved Strawberry for mixing. His trademark AMS delay-driven sound could not have been achieved anywhere else.

The trip to Sheffield to check out the studio demanded an early start, but this was no problem at all. There was nothing I enjoyed more than being in top class studios, and choosing somewhere to record with Martin was something I had rehearsed in a dream. Getting picked up by Roger in the morning, we had something of a moment together, realising that this was the start of the next phase of our band's journey, and just one more life experience that we could hardly have imagined a few short years before. Today was a humdinger.

Martin lived in a semi-detached house on Nicolas Road in Chorlton. It looked like all the other houses on the street, with its small, unkempt front garden and dusty bay window. Martin's wife, Wendy, opened the door to us and led us into the front room where Martin was waiting. The room seemed somewhat neglected at first sight, bare floorboards and piles of stuff everywhere, with a light covering of dust. Martin's young son, James, had overturned a two litre can of paint in one corner of the room, and it remained untouched, hardening fast, but Martin didn't seem bothered in the slightest by the chaos surrounding him, greeting us warmly and ushering us in to his lair.

He had already started drinking by the time we arrived, and, with this in mind, we chopped out a few lines of speed to balance things out. It wouldn't do to have Martin drunk on the job when we got to Sheffield, and, while it was hardly sophisticated chemistry, one aspect of amphetamine use is that it negates the effects of alcohol. The idea was that it would have slowed Martin's drinking down a bit, but as the day progressed, it became clear that he was now able to drink even more.

Either way, the start of our adventure saw us bright-eyed and bushy-tailed for at least the first part of the journey, and before too long, we were on our way over the Snake Pass to Sheffield, where studio owner and ex-Comsat Angel, Kevin Bacon, was waiting to give us the hard sell.

The Comsat Angels, although never having recorded with Martin, had placed themselves musically in the sonic world that Martin had brought into existence. Their *Waiting For A Miracle* and *Sleep No More* albums had got my attention on release, but owed much to their interpretation of Martin's Strawberry sound. Kevin Bacon, being the band's bass player, was perhaps the Comsat Angel that had been listening the hardest to the spaces inside Martin's work, and it was clear from the off that he was impressed with the idea of having him record at his studio. It was weird, and kind of amusing to see Martin's charisma at work with such a willing victim. He couldn't do enough for us, he really wanted this project to happen.

Axis itself reminded me of some of the BBC studios that I had spent time in, with a large, wooden floored, gymnasium-type live room. Martin put the studio staff through their paces with a detailed and rather unfriendly question and answer session, and it soon became apparent that Martin had changed his mind about recording there. We retreated to a nearby pub. Martin expressed his dislike of the 'vibe' at Axis, and that he now wanted to use Strawberry for recording as well as mixing. Fine by me, I thought.

The session was about two weeks away, and with Cut Deep's office being above the studio, and having strong links with the studio's owners, we were able to wangle a week's recording time on tick, as it were. Nothing is free, though, and it would be the group that would ultimately pick up the tab, which would be thousands.

The day came and as we waited for Martin to turn up we diligently set up our instruments with the help of engineer Jonathan Barrett, who we knew well as a friend. Hours went by, with Dub Sex raring to go and Martin's phone ringing off the hook. After he finally answered, Roger hightailed it over to Chorlton to pick him up. On arrival at Strawberry he barely said a word to anyone. Instead, he hit Paul up for some money and installed himself in The Waterloo pub across the road for a liquid breakfast.

This was not what I wanted at all. Martin seemed like a different person to the mischievous, enthusiastic guy that had won me over at our previous meetings. We were all aware of Martin's eccentricities and reputation, but this was a wasted day and it was all I could do to keep everybody's spirits up. Eventually, Martin ran out of money and finally joined us, only to make Jonathan start again with his setting up.

Gazing at Martin, slumped on the Strawberry settee, it was clear that nothing was getting recorded today. I had been beside myself with excitement to be working with the man that had been at the helm for some of my favourite pieces of music, but the man snoring loudly in the control room was not that man. Hoping for a better day tomorrow, we reluctantly called it a day and arranged for Martin to be picked up by Roger on his way in, at least that way he would be in the right place at the right time.

For the next few days, Martin's behaviour continued in pretty much the same fashion. He would arrive with Roger or in a taxi, and disappear for hours into the Waterloo while we waited for him to join us and start working. Luckily, Jonathan Barrett was an experienced and competent engineer in his own right, so we were able to carry on regardless, and managed to get basic versions of the three songs down, with guide guitars and vocals. Martin contributed very little to the proceedings, apart from agreeing that we sounded great just as we were, and that it was always his intention to capture our sound in as natural and realistic a way as possible. I had been told about this hands-off approach before by various people with experience of making records with him.

Martin would always work with a brilliant engineer, who knew exactly how to get the best out of whichever studio they were working in. They would be his 'hands', leaving him to the more cerebral side of things. Chris Nagle, for instance, engineered countless records with Martin as credited producer, and found himself in a kind of translator role, channelling Martin's more esoteric ideas into reality by knowing how to achieve the things he wanted fast and efficiently.

Towards the end of the week, Martin began to engage a bit more, but he was far from the sharp, brilliant force of nature that I knew he had been. As something of a perfectionist myself, I was taken aback by Martin's sloppy attitude at times. I was unhappy with my vocals, for instance, and wanted to do them properly, but Martin insisted that the guide vocal take was fine. It was as if he just couldn't be bothered. He would come to the studio for a short while, make a few comments and give Jonathan a few jobs to do, then disappear again, returning pissed and confrontational a few hours later.

All kinds of mayhem broke loose at various moments during the week. Martin drunkenly erased some 'never to be repeated' guitar parts. Without Jonathan Barrett, I don't think anything would have got finished at all. The absolute low point came when I had to go across to the pub and physically snatch Martin's pint from the table in front of him, telling him, 'If you want to finish this, it'll be in the control room.' He followed almost immediately, and we had his attention for a while at least, but, by this time, our faith and trust in Martin was seriously dented.

Martin mixed what we did on his own, with none of the group there, eventually presenting us with a reverb-drenched mess that we considered unreleasable. The drums sounded like cardboard boxes, and all semblance of power and discipline had been blurred by needless effects. There was no way that we could release this as a follow-up to 'Swerve'. Reluctantly, we were forced to drop Martin from the project and abandon our plans to record with him. It was a huge disappointment to me that things had turned out this way, but it was totally the right thing to do.

Martin, having been informed about our change of plan, began a barrage of phone calls at all times of day and night, pleading, almost, to be re-instated as producer. He would wax lyrical about my talent and how he could take what I was doing to the next level, reiterating that I didn't need the rest of the band, and that the American market was ready for a harder edged, impassioned sound, and I was the man for the job. The sheer sense of desperation in his voice, and his Machiavellian scheming with regard to my band made it perfectly clear that our relationship was over.

Martin continued his telephone campaign, switching from me to my girlfriend, Bev, who hadn't been going out with me long enough to have to put up with this kind of nonsense. Aggressive calls started to happen in the early hours of the morning, demanding that she talk me into changing my mind, again saying that with him at the controls, the lucrative US market was ours for the taking. He would go from calm and nice, painting a picture of future success and financial security, to threatening her ('You'd better fucking make sure Mark changes his mind').

It seems obvious to me now, with the benefit of hindsight, that Paul Humphreys and Martin had struck up some kind of a deal away from, and behind the backs of, the band. His need for money, for whatever reason, had led him, in my opinion, to behave in ways that he never would have before, and, having been the keenest on this project, it was me who felt it the hardest. Whilst I believe that Martin's love of what we did was real, and his enthusiasm for working with us was genuine, we had simply met up at the wrong end of Martin's working life, and with his problems being so huge, it was never going to work. I was upset, of course, but we still had a record to make, and at least we didn't have to jettison a whole album the way that The Stone Roses did after being disappointed by Martin's production (again at Strawberry) a few years earlier.

I knew exactly what to do next. I had felt a tiny bit disloyal to Chris Nagle in wanting Martin to produce our next batch of work, but this was simply the way that things were. Chris knew that I had always wanted to work with Martin, or rather, the Martin that had impressed me so much in the past.

We were all professionals, and bands tried out different producers all the time, for all sorts of reasons. I contacted Chris, and he, being the gentleman that he is, refrained from telling me that 'I could have told you things would be like this', and listened to what I had to say.

Nobody had been closer to Martin than Chris, and nobody had as much first-hand experience of the way his life had gone in recent years. The two of them were not as close by this point, but Chris had seen the way Martin's life had developed, with all its implications. Chris had long outgrown the position of 'engineer' to anybody, and was a highly successful producer in his own right. He loved Dub Sex, and had been a huge part of the music we had made since our first single, so it was the most natural thing in the world for Chris to come back on board. Truth to tell, he had never really been away.

Our experience with Martin made us even more determined to make 'Time of Life' as brilliant as it could possibly be. We'd had two trial runs at it by now, and learnt a lot about the song and how to approach recording it. Chris had the inspired idea of repeating the 'chorus' section twice at the end of the song, and as soon as we heard it, we couldn't imagine it any other way. It makes the song's hook line burrow into the listener's head, creating a tidy earworm.

The sessions, at Out of the Blue and Strawberry, were a revelation. After the frustrations of our experience with Martin, we were in no mood to waste any time, and, being on top of our game, got stuck right in, recording blistering versions of 'Time of Life' and 'Kumina'. Chris was similarly energised, and unexpectedly created the beautiful 'Time of Dub'. In a similar manner to his radical 'Instead of Flowers' remix, Chris had stripped the song to the very bones, slowing things down and surrounding the tune with ghostly keyboards by his wife, Julia. The guitar-driven original mix was turned on its head, leaving drums and vocals to dominate, with clipped interjections of sub-bass and gated synth patterns. Beautiful.

I only met Martin once more after our Strawberry adventure. We had both turned up at a private party in the Factory-owned Dry bar on Oldham Street. He was fine, and there were absolutely no hard feelings. I bought him a pint and it was as if the trials and tribulations of recording together had never happened. We said goodbye and left on good terms. It was such a pity. I wish things had turned out differently.

PART VI
I Want

Overleaf: On stage with Dub Sex, Manchester Poly
Still from IKON video
Filmed by Malcolm Whitehead

34: Time Of Life

Things were changing for me during the early part of 1989. I was enjoying the first wave of my new relationship, and after so long in the austere surroundings of Hulme it was good to have a different kind of backdrop. For all the benefits of life on a doomed estate, it was hard not to be affected by the sheer uniformity of everything. Longsight, on the other hand, displayed a different type of individualism to Hulme's graffiti. People here had more of a long-term outlook, and looked after their area more. The houses I would visit were different in construction from each other, and people had gardens, which they used and decorated to reflect their personalities. I began to meet other, older musicians, part of Manchester's massive underground Irish music scene, and would be welcomed at outdoor Irish music sessions, raucous affairs, swarming with kids.

I still had two flats in Hulme. As the estate's final days approached, the powers that be cared less and less about such details. I would receive Giro cheques at one address, and store what few possessions I had in the other. Gradually, I began to spend more time in Longsight, taking Ellis to the local parks with her mother, finding pleasure in simple things, a world away from the edgy, druggy atmosphere. I had the best of both worlds, on the one hand loving the humanising effect of being around a young family, while always being welcomed by my extremist friends in the crescents. This time, though, I had a choice. I started to feel part of this small family and, after a while, it didn't even seem strange anymore.

As the band picked up new followers, it was important to us that new fans could get hold of a record in order to catch up on the story so far. We thought it might be a good idea to compile all the singles and the *Push!* mini-album together on one release via Cut Deep. It was also a way of creating a bit of breathing space for us, having something out while writing and building up songs for the next real album.

Chris Nagle had booked one night at Strawberry to put the tracks in order and make a master. After all the dramas and emotional experiences we had gone through recording there, this was a very simple task; celebratory, even. I sat next to Chris as he worked. We had decided the running order democratically as a band earlier in the week, and for me it was like a speeded-up journey through my life. The album starts with my voice, disembodied, almost speaking…

> My stomach turned when I was told what you were told
> I was the last to know. It stands to reason, though
> Don't be surprised, it stands to reason

There is a slight gap before everything explodes and I am hearing myself, screaming in the dark in Rochdale, what seemed like a lifetime ago. The songs came thick and fast, one after the other. 'The Underneath', 'Swerve', 'Push!', every tune released so far, ending with a jubilant and uplifting 'Believe'. It was a white-knuckle ride of an album, that's for sure, and although it contains different singles and EPs made at different times, it sounds fluent and cohesive, as if it had been recorded all at once. I sat there drained and grinning. It felt like I was somebody else listening to this music for the first time and I loved it.

The sleeve was to be designed once again by Paul Khera. It featured doctored photographs of religious statues, which had nothing to do with me. I had used photos of the crucifixion statues outside my junior school on the cover of 'The Underneath', but that was because of my personal connection to these particular statues. I suspect Paul Khera thought I was something of a gory religious statue fan. Still, it looked good.

Splintered Faith was to be our last release on Cut Deep. Though this was to all intents and purposes our own label, Paul Humphreys was running it and things had been going downhill with Paul for some time. When we first started to break through, we assigned managerial duties to him almost by default. It was not something that we had planned. The trouble began in earnest when SRD encouraged us to set up Cut Deep Records, which was, at first, nothing more than a way to release music by ourselves. We were so busy holding things together and writing new material (and then touring it) that we stepped back a little, allowing Paul to take a more active role in the label. This was a classic example of us taking our eye off the ball, and left Paul with far too much involvement.

He talked SRD into letting him expand the label, signing other artists, like a revitalised Biting Tongues. Paul then wasted no time in becoming a cartoon version of a record label boss. The explosion of The Stone Roses and Happy Mondays meant there was a great deal of interest in Manchester music, and Paul spent countless hours living as a bon viveur, a permanent fixture in Factory's Dry bar, drinking like a fish and lording it up with whoever would give him the time of day.

We saw the writing on the wall when he was trusted to attend the mastering session for 'The Underneath'. The band was playing somewhere, and his role was mainly to deliver the tape to be mastered, ready for pressing. In this situation, the band are sometimes asked if they want anything scratched into the run-out groove of the record. We hadn't specified anything on this occasion, but when the finished product arrived, we were all horrified to see that Paul had inserted a dedication to his then girlfriend. For us to have sweated blood over a release, only to have our heartfelt, deepest feelings used as a glorified Valentine's Day card was too much.

Although the label had come about directly because of Dub Sex's music, and the buck stopped with us in real terms, Paul was arranging studio time on credit from Strawberry for all and sundry, acting like some poundshop Brian Epstein. Coupled with his deluded behaviour and disastrous business style, we decided that it was impossible to continue working with him. I had long suspected financial irregularities, and all of us had felt the dishonesty in the air with Paul's behind-the-scenes wangling with Martin Hannett. He had been overstepping the mark for some time now, and although it was our own fault for letting him, things had to stop right there. We cut Paul off, leaving him with Cut Deep and going our separate ways.

This meant we were without a manager or a label with 'Time of Life' ready to go. We turned to SCAM, who had included us on their *Manchester, North of England* compilation. To be involved with a female-driven label was a breath of fresh air after the toxic masculinity on show almost everywhere else in the music industry. We were civilised people and, having a female bass player, had been exposed first-hand to lazy, casual sexism that we all found abhorrent. It was certainly time for a change.

SCAM was very much driven by Sarah Champion and Alison Martin, who we felt were a good addition to our team as both were very strong with promotion. Sarah and Alison introduced us to Penny Anderson. Penny was a writer for *City Life* magazine, alongside Sarah, and lived in India House in Manchester town centre, where Alison also lived. We took her on to assist with management duties.

A new label and manager weren't the only changes to take place. We had been on the books of a London-based agency called Miracle, who would arrange gigs for us and take a commission from our fee. We had thought that they would be useful for getting gigs in London, which would help when it came to getting reviewed in the main music papers, but it soon became apparent that we were in no way a priority for them. As we got better known, we would be approached directly by venues, and many of our southern gigs were organised that way.

We changed to an agency run by an old friend. Out of Dave Haslam's *Debris* fanzine had sprung a record label called Play Hard, and from that sprung an agency called Blast Hard. Dave worked together with Nathan McGough, stepson of Mersey poet Roger McGough, from an office in Princess Street. It was a lively little place, and even before becoming involved with the agency I would call in sometimes on my jaunts to the city centre, just as a friend to say hello.

It made sense for us to become part of the Blast Hard roster. Sarah and Alison were part of the same world as Dave, and it seemed to me that we were dealing with friends, as opposed to being just another band on a faraway agency. The focus of the music industry had shifted over the last year, and all eyes were on Manchester now anyway. Dave invited me in for a *Debris* interview, one of the more incisive and considered ones we had done, looking at how far we had come since we had first crossed paths in the mid-eighties.

Brian Turner worked on the gig arranging side for Blast Hard. I had known Brian since the days of the Manchester Musicians' Collective when he was the bass player for Mick Hucknall's Frantic Elevators, and would tease him about the huge pile of unsold 7-inch copies of their 'Holding Back The Years' single, which a common friend, Aidan Cartwright, had stored under his bed, gathering dust. We were in good company, as the likes of Happy Mondays, MC Buzz B and King of the Slums were also on the books, as well as Factory band The Train Set. Brian set up some dates for us around the country with New Fast Automatic Daffodils in support.

First up we had a new single to get ready. Penny introduced me to a word processor. I went to her flat on a few occasions to write press releases and discuss band matters, getting ready for the release of 'Time of Life'. Although Paul Khera's recent sleeve artwork had served us well, I felt little connection to it in the way that I had with our other releases. 'The Underneath' 'Push!' and 'Tripwire' sleeves had hands-on involvement from me and the rest of the band. I was keen to get us back to this state of affairs. I designed the sleeve for this release in conjunction with Mick Peek, whose work had graced recent releases by 808 State.

I had found a 1950s book called *Volkswagen: A Week at the Factory* in Mick's office, and, using an enlarged and abstracted close up of VW side panels on a production line, the two of us created my favourite Dub Sex sleeve. Simple and repetitive, coloured in bold maroon and blue with white lettering, the sleeve would look great in record shop windows. It made for stark and vivid t-shirts, too. All we needed now was a mind-blowing video.

We were approached by Edward Barton, who, as well as being an inhabitant of the Hulme crescents, had struck up a working relationship with IKON. The idea was that Edward would direct and IKON would be involved with post-production duties, alongside a company called 'DAT2DAT'.

Edward's very existence was an art statement in itself. He presented himself, entirely straight-faced, as some eccentric country gentleman figure, always in character, dressed in anachronistic tweeds, sporting a huge, flowing beard of the type favoured by Victorians. Against the background of inner-city Manchester, he stood out a mile. He was one strange cat.

He had grown up in a military family in Libya and was educated privately, before turning up in Manchester where he studied History of Art at Manchester University and got fully involved with the city's art scene. He signed to Cherry Red records in the early eighties and released a weird little record called 'It's a Fine Day' (credited to Jane and Barton). It was a female-voiced, a capella version of one of Edward's poems. Its pure, innocent vocal had elements of pastoral England about it and, like a lot of his work, put people in mind of a childhood that may never have actually existed outside their own flawed memories.

We were invited to his flat in Charles Barry Crescent, one floor below The Kitchen studio. His flat, in keeping with just about everything else about this fascinating man, did not disappoint. Being under a death sentence by now, the flats were not subject to regular, or indeed any kind of inspection from the relevant authorities. Many residents were now expressing themselves by modifying their living spaces: walls were sliced in half, doors were blocked up and replaced by entry and exit holes, murals and graffiti art abounded. It was apparent that the whole estate would be coming down before too long, and we would probably never have another chance to use a whole housing estate as a canvas in this way. People surpassed themselves, ripping down walls and creating art that they could live in.

Edward's flat, of course, was the weirdest of the lot. He had 're-purposed' the place as a permanent Edward Barton art exhibition, containing areas devoted to his artistic obsessions. It was a crazy, disorientating experience. In one part of the flat a wall was devoted to a huge collection of dishevelled and sinister looking teddy bears, abandoned-looking and unsettling. Another part of his living space housed a collection of children's shoes, just piled high, leaving it to the observer to make sense of. Childhood in all its forms was a recurring theme in Edward's work.

I gingerly sat on the edge of the settee, trying to avoid the glassy-eyed stare of a stuffed dog (just head and paws!) that inhabited a kennel facing me, and listened to what he had to say. Edward had recently directed the 'Sit Down' video for James, but what he proposed for us was darker and deeper, weirder and scarier. He saw us, quite correctly, as being separate and at odds with the UK music industry, and had invented a fictitious 'Band Burial Department' that would bury us as we performed the song.

We did stand apart from the recently lionised Manchester bands; we mined a harder, darker seam. Edward loved us for that, and had come up with a plan that would see me gagged and stopped from singing as we gradually became buried deeper and deeper, until only our singing and dancing heads remained, echoing more extreme productions of Samuel Beckett's *Endgame* or the horrific decapitation machine in the 1979 film *Caligula*. The message was that whatever you did to us, we would keep on until the very end, and it was a message that I wholeheartedly approved of. I was totally won over, and we shook on it there and then.

As well as being a filmmaker and something of a living work of art, Edward was a man possessed of a great deal of self-confidence. As introspective as his poetry often was, he was well-connected and loved by a wide range of musicians. Something about the man's vulnerability made you want to do things for him. He was like some creature from another artistic world, like Ivor Cutler or Viv Stanshall, and his eccentric persona brought out the protective side in people, me included.

Edward had come up with the idea for a compilation album featuring his songs and poems, performed by his friends, famous and non-famous. The cast list was impressive. Alongside ourselves, it included Inspiral Carpets, A Guy Called Gerald, 808 State, Fatima Mansions and Ruthless Rap Assassins amongst others. It was especially good to see Manchester's black musical community getting behind such a project. We were delighted to be involved.

Edward had paid for one day at Out of the Blue studio so we had set aside a day to prepare and rehearse one of his poems the week before. We had picked 'Barber Barber', Edward's ode to the elderly barber who cut Cathy's and my own hair, as well as Edward's. He was like a relic from another age, tucked away deep inside an aging building on Portland Street, pumping out immaculate wartime-looking severe crops, year in, year out for as long as anybody could remember. A real part of Manchester history.

It was good to be in Out of the Blue, and to see Adam Lesser, who had started Studio Lustrette in the Hulme crescents way back when I first moved there. I was pleased that this hard-working and driven guy had done well enough to scale things up and move the studio to Ancoats, where things were looking up for him. It was clear though from the minute that we walked in that we had been getting a little too used to the good life in the studios we'd been using. Things were different at this end of the food chain. Chris Bridgett picked up a phone in Adam's office to make a personal call, and was told bluntly that such a thing was not allowed. Money was tight. It was cold in the control room and we had to supply our own milk and coffee. It felt like a dose of realism after Strawberry and Maida Vale.

We tried to make things different for Edward's compilation. Roger had constructed a drum machine pattern instead of traditional drums, and I played percussion as well as providing a different style of vocal, one that was breathy and disembodied at first, rising to a scream at the end of the song. Delayed guitars bounced dubbily around the parameters, nailed down by a deep, simple bass motif. We had risen to the one-day challenge.

Before making the video with Edward, we had some gigs to play. A show at Dingwalls in Camden Lock promoted by *Sounds* proved to be Chris Bridgett's last gig with us. Chris had started to become somewhat estranged from the band of late, keeping different company and being less interested in practical things like rehearsal room rent and future band plans. Chris had joined in the wake of Dave Rumney's sacking, and to his credit, had hit the ground running, stepping in at short notice, but he had very much been my appointment, and Cathy and Roger weren't as close to him, friend-wise, as I was.

Chris had been moving in a different direction to the rest of us for some time. He had embraced the Madchester thing with open arms, and felt drawn to the dance/rock hybrid that was evolving as ecstasy culture made inroads in the wider independent musical community. I think Chris saw us as being left behind by the way that music was heading, and wanted to be a part of this indie/dance crossover, whereas our inclination was to become even fiercer and rockier, as a response to what we perceived to be a trivial and escapist way of being, lacking emotional depth. We felt that it would prove to be a passing fad, and while enjoying the scene immensely on a social level, held no desire to jump on that or any other bandwagon.

After the Dingwalls gig, Chris stayed in London with some of his friends as opposed to coming back in the van with us. It became clear that our time together had run its course. We parted company in a civilised fashion. He formed a new band called Hypodelic, featuring Gavan Whelan on drums, with Chris taking on singing duties as well as guitar. I was pleased to see Chris doing what he wanted to do with the indie/dance crossover, but it wasn't what I wanted to be doing. Dub Sex was once again boiled down to the three core members. In many ways it was always thus.

Back in Manchester our attention turned to the 'Time of Life' video. The first job in hand was finding somewhere to shoot this complicated film. Edward had the idea of using the Hulme crescents themselves, as they could be used to do the same job as an expensive scaffolding platform. If cameras were set up on the first, third and fifth floor, then we could achieve some brilliant shots, akin to using a cherry-picker extending ladder of the type used by fire departments. The trouble came when we had to dig the holes to place the band in. These needed to be deep enough to house a person. Try as we might, we could not find anywhere in the entire central Manchester area that would let us dig down to a depth of more than a few inches. It was a sobering experience to think that just a short way below our feet lay the remains of thousands of people's lives. Manchester (and Hulme in particular) is built on the rubble of the terraced housing that stood there throughout most of the twentieth century, my own birthplace included, and it didn't take much to reach the next layer down. Like some warped pastiche of the unearthing of the city of Troy by Heinrich Schliemann in the 1800s, the collective past of all who had lived there before lay beneath our feet. It led to deep feelings, but no chance at all of any digging.

Luckily, the ever-resourceful Mr Barton knew of the perfect place; a quarry on the outskirts of Glossop. Overlooked by huge cliffs, it gave us height, muddy earth to dig in, and a sense of abandoned desolation that would add to the mood of the video. It was going to be a real guerrilla job. The plan was to break in one Sunday, when the quarry was closed, and film from the crack of dawn until darkness sent us home.

Vans were hired and teams of helpers assembled; a motley crew of diggers, helpers, film people and one small child. We had hired spades, wheelbarrows, pickaxes and other useful items and were good to go, despite the incredulous looks on the faces of the plant hire people who thought we were weapons-grade idiots. Our suspicious-looking convoy of two transit vans sped towards Derbyshire's High Peak, leaving the orange glowing city behind us.

Edward was no stranger to unorthodox filmmaking techniques, he had broken into forbidden places before. Using his own bolt cutters, he removed two hefty padlocks from the main gates.

'Throw these, as far away as you can,' Edward instructed us. Apparently, he had fallen foul of the law on a previous video shoot by being found in possession of broken locks.

Pushing open the access gates, we were in. The quarry itself towered over us. Day was starting to break now, illuminating a savage, unforgiving terrain of ugly grey rock and sandy earth. The lip of the quarry dominated everything, standing several hundred feet above us, looking as if it was just about to collapse. Blocks of scree and small rocks sporadically rained down from the upper slopes just behind us. It would be hard to imagine a harsher, more forbidding place. It looked for all the world like some barren, dangerous alien landscape, and I was going to be buried in it.

First things first, though. If a band were to be buried, then five holes would have to be dug to put them in. If anybody ever thought that the music industry was an attractive, even glamorous career choice, then this video shoot would have served as an education, if not an outright deterrent. Our loyal team of assistants were each given a shovel and a cup of tea from a flask. As the morning sun illuminated the unyielding rocky landscape, the back breaking toil began.

Although the video needed to see us disappear into the cold Derbyshire earth up to our temples, we could do that by kneeling down so the holes needed only to be three-feet deep. Even this was a Herculean task in the freezing wet Glossop drizzle, but our determined team dug for all they were worth, topping each hole with a board containing a guillotine-style space for our necks to go through, which was then covered with mud.

It was one of the coldest and vilest days ever, but we followed Edward's direction, running through 'Time of Life' again and again until we turned fetching shades of blue. Being the singer, I was subjected to the most abuse. I had to repeat my vocals many times, sinking deeper into the ground each time, until only my dancing eyebrows remained, stubbornly refusing to give in to my tormentors. The cliff started to disintegrate just behind me, sending a small avalanche of malevolent sharp rocks in my direction. The fear caught on my face is very real indeed.

Edward, despite having turned his living space into what was effectively a museum of childhood, was curiously unused to the real thing. He had devised a storyboard utilising the skills of Ellis, aged two-and-half. The idea was that she would try to stop me singing as I sank deeper and deeper into the earth. She was to insert her fist into my mouth, clap me hard around the ears, throw mud into my face, that sort of thing, and had proved an enthusiastic torturer when we had rehearsed a few moves at home. The trouble began when it came for her time to shoot. A Derbyshire quarry at six in the morning is no place for a pre-school infant in the first place, and the freezing sleet made things even less child-friendly. Emerging from one of the lorries with a brightly coloured beach ball, Edward threw it towards Ellis in a misguided attempt to strike up a game of catch and get her in a playful mood. Unfortunately, it hit the poor girl square in the face, causing a screaming fit that seemed to last for hours. Running into the arms of her chaperoning mother, she refused to take any further part in the scripted pieces so the whole video had to be rewritten on the spot.

Our soundman, Jem Noble, along with Edward himself, took over Ellis's jobs, pulling hair and throwing mud, as well as chasing escapee guitarist Tim over the quarry's edge. Ellis appears only fleetingly in the finished video, as it explodes from black and white into moody colour at the song's conclusion.

We also inserted my good friend Nicky Carroll upsidedown in one of the holes to represent the recently departed Chris Bridgett, and it is his trainers that can be seen over my shoulder as I bring the song to its end, reinforcing the cynical hook line. Whatever the chorus said, we were a million miles away from 'having the time of our lives', and this can be seen in all of our faces.

During the final bit of filming, I had to be rescued from my hole by two burly helpers, having lost the use of my legs through cramp and temporary paralysis. I believe that the very real danger we were in is one of the main reasons that the film exudes such a believable air of menace. I, for one, was definitely bricking it.

The 'Time of Life' single was released when Manchester was in the grip of a period of worldwide interest, and served as a beacon of hope to those people who found the media's creation of a scene around Happy Mondays, The Stone Roses and their ilk a little unconvincing. Although we were busy partying hard with the movers and shakers of these 'baggy' groups, and were invited to support by the bands themselves, we were perceived as having a harder edge and a less trivial outlook. We were driven not by a desire to lose oneself in music, but to immerse yourself within it, staring that which frightens you square in the face. Our strict, linear rock sound was at odds with the escapism on offer almost everywhere else. I for one took a lot of pride in that.

The hook line of 'Time of Life' was seen by some as being directed at the good time groups that had followed in the Roses and Mondays wake, although it had its roots in something far more personal. Not everybody got it, of course, one snidey *NME* review missed the point entirely, writing, 'Tarted up with new tech, they growlingly enquire: "Are you having the time of your life?" To which one can but reply: "Not while I'm listening to you, Squire!"' Hilarious.

Another who didn't fully get it was the one charged with promoting us, Penny. Being a *City Life* music reviewer, she was exposed first-hand to the successes of other groups. It became clear after a fairly short time that she saw us very differently to the way that we saw ourselves. Penny wanted to shape us into something that we most decidedly weren't. She suggested the addition of a female keyboard player, and wanted me to wear contact lenses on stage. She wanted me to be more of a 'traditional' kind of frontman and for the band to adopt a brighter, funkier way of dressing, and embrace a dancier, poppier style of music. This was happening everywhere you looked in Manchester and further afield, and we as a band were proud to not be a part of it.

Penny never properly gelled with us as people. There was no big falling out, but as soon as the 'Time of Life' release had run its course, we were on our own again. We handled management duties, such as they were, between ourselves. Cathy and Roger, being the most practical members, took the lion's share of the work.

I always maintained that a person's reaction to our music said more about the listener themselves than it did about us. Of all our singles, 'Time of Life' made it a lot easier to see those who understood us, and those who let the point sail gleefully over their heads. Thankfully, at ground level, where it mattered, our small but loyal following took it to their hearts, ensuring that 'Time of Life' entered the independent charts as soon as it came out, despite a minimum of radio play.

Having a weird and wonderful video for people to show meant that we were invited onto interview shows to talk about the single. The video was so different to anything else that it ended up getting lots of airtime on shows like MTV's *Music Box*, where it nestled amongst bigger artists with money behind them, unlike little old us. We travelled to London to be interviewed for ITV's *Transmission*, and shone like a beacon of honesty when compared to the careerist go-getters that populated the rest of the show.

One of our new supporters was Clive Selwood of Beechwood Music. Clive had a long-term association and friendship with John Peel, which dated back to 1969 when he ran the commercial side of Dandelion Records. They released such varied artists as John's beloved Gene Vincent, as well as alternative English bands like Medicine Head and Tractor. Their association was just as strong in the 1980s when the pair combined again to release selected sessions recorded for John's Radio 1 show. These releases proved popular, and eventually led to Selwood releasing compilations featuring records that had done well in the independent charts on his Beechwood label.

'Time of Life' was included on *Indie Top 20: Volume VIII*, alongside such luminaries as Depeche Mode, The KLF and Wire, and, perhaps more importantly, ended up on the parallel video release, which got it seen by many more people than just those who watch music television in the early hours of the morning. Peel drew the nation's attention to it in a column he wrote for *The Daily Telegraph*. We were all highly amused to sneak uninvited into the very mouthpiece of the Tory heartlands.

We embarked upon a tour to support the single's release, and the changes we were going through made things interesting for both our audience and ourselves. We started with a dual guitar line-up of me and Tim Costigan, with Tim bringing his mate Gaz in for one memorable show at Hulme's highly politicised Bonfire Night Party, held in the grounds of Birley High School. The residents of Hulme kicked against the Thatcher government as only they could, with revolutionary music and the ritualistic burning of a pirate ship lovingly built just to be destroyed. Thatcher herself was burned in effigy to the noisy delight of all present, every one of whom would have been affected by her government's all out war on the working class. I felt proud to have been involved, but have sweeter memories of the event to add to my political ones. Looking down from the stage, shielded from the increasingly rowdy crowd, sat Ellis, transfixed by it all. She had never seen me do my stuff in real life.

The tour continued, taking in such far flung and infrequently visited places as Aberystwyth University and Lancaster Sugarhouse, gaining us new supporters as we went. Not many, it has to be said, but these people were seriously into it. At one of the last tour dates, at The Citadel in St Helens, we turned the place inside out, receiving a loud and positive reaction. Following a few encores, I lay slumped and sweaty in the dressing room when a confident sounding voice cut through the post gig chatter.

'You know what your group needs, don't you, mate?'

I was, of course, all ears.

'Go on then, I'm sure you're going to tell me, aren't you?'

'Me.'

This was Chris Cookson. Something made me take what he was saying seriously, and I invited him to Manchester for a try-out. It turned out that he was right.

35: Human

Chris Cookson put himself forward just as a vacancy appeared in the band. Tim Costigan had become homesick and decided to leave us. It was a sad moment for all of us. As well as being an inventive and accomplished guitarist, Tim was a beautiful person, with a calm and patient manner.

Tim had come to us via his cousin, Guy Lovelady of Ugly Man Records. Guy assured us that Tim was a skilled and technically proficient guitarist, and had followed the band since Guy had released our mini-album *Push!*. Tim had only been involved in a few short-term projects before, mainly around his hometown of Warrington, but Guy told us that this was one opportunity he didn't want to miss out on. He was prepared to uproot himself to move to Manchester in order to throw himself into what we were doing. We arranged for him to come down to a rehearsal where he demonstrated that he'd done his homework. He had learned all the songs in detail, even replicating Chris Nagle's digital delay tricks with absolute accuracy.

Guy arranged for Tim to move into Mike West's house, not too far from Bev's place in Longsight where I was spending most of my time. Mike West was the singer in the band Man From Delmonte who were on Guy's label. He lived in a three-bedroom terrace house with his tiny but insanely loud Yorkshire terrier, Roger, and an intriguing Scottish artist called Catriona Ross. Mike's band were managed by Jon Ronson, another writer for *City Life* magazine who had recently moved from London to Manchester. Jon was a frequent visitor to the house, so it seemed that Tim's great upheaval would be tempered in part by the prospect of some interesting company at least.

Tim moved in, and I made it my business to make him feel at home. Naturally shy and softly spoken, it must have been weird for him to be surrounded by these larger-than-life personalities. I would have him over for meals and to play music together at Bev's house. The two of us would go down to our Boardwalk rehearsal room in the daytimes, writing new material and becoming friends.

Tim, to his credit, really tried to make a go of things in Manchester, but the shock of relocating was simply too much for him. It may have been down to his shyness, but he never became part of the household at Mike's, and I was the only person that he got to know in any real way. I think he began to feel that he was imposing somewhat by spending so much time at Bev's, although in reality nothing could have been further from the truth. These were exciting times for everyone, and Tim being so warmly welcomed was an extension of the welcome that I had received myself.

Eventually, after a few months of feeling lonely in his tiny room at Mike's, Tim could take no more and told us that he couldn't carry on this way. He had relatives and a girlfriend in Warrington, and had been masking his true feelings for quite some time. I understood completely, although this news was a bit of a blow for me. He really was the one that got away.

Chris Cookson was also from a different background to me and the rest of the band. He came from Newton-le-Willows, a smallish, semi-rural market town roughly half-way between Manchester and Liverpool, where a very different kind of music scene existed. As in any small place, the local musicians had all eventually found each other and a great deal of cross-pollination had taken place. Chris used to say that he had played with everybody in Newton-le-Willows, and this included, to our great amusement, Rick Astley.

The quiff-headed, grandma-friendly 'nice guy of pop' had taken Stock, Aitken and Waterman's 'Never Gonna Give You Up' to number one in 25 countries, bagging Best Single award at the 1988 Brits, but could be seen some years before plying his wares in the Merseyside pubs and clubs with Chris behind him. How could we resist somebody with such a weird back story?

At the other end of Chris's spectrum of influences lay a far more appropriate scene. He had been involved for some time with a producer called Gerry Kenny, aka The Minister of Noise. Gerry – along with partner, Brenda – had set up a recording facility called NAAFI in the fields around Newton. The studio proved to be a massive hit with Northern European black metal bands like Darkthrone, whose metallic worldview incorporated a love of the extreme dub/metal assaults which Gerry produced under his 'Sir Freddie Viaduct' alter ego. Chris learned a lot about electronic extremism by getting involved. All of this was great preparation for joining us.

It was an ear-opener to be exposed to Chris's skilful, effects-based style of playing, featuring meticulous digital delay settings and such oddities as the much-maligned 'e-bow', which he would use to fill the air with twisted cello-like string sounds and what sounded like the crying of distant seagulls. Chris's more measured approach worked well with my frantic style, and I liked what he brought to the newer songs. It felt like the beginning of a new phase in the band's life.

I found that as my personal circumstances changed, so too did my songs. The positivity of living in a family began to filter through to my lyrics. These newer songs, while still firmly rooted in the realities of where I had come from, started to show themes of redemption and celebrated the bravery of choosing love over cynicism. One such song was 'Until Now'.

> Until Now
> I must have had my head in a hole in the ground
> Until now
> Everybody else was slow
> And I know what I know
> But it kept on letting me down

Culminating in an uplifting affirmation of the way I felt:

> Completely
> Completely needed!

Other new songs rode on a similar wave of optimism, 'Slipstream' in particular, which had been one of the first songs I had written since becoming part of a family unit. The writing showed love arriving in the life of a person who previously knew nothing of such a thing.

> I heard you'd chop down trees
> To be with me
> And sneak down dark and dangerous streets
> Frightened of every creak
> So pick up the receiver and speak
> I've come to need
> And don't be afraid
> Of sounding naive
> And don't say that life is cheap

This was a million miles away from songs like 'Splintered' or 'Kicking the Corpse Around'. I was proud to be able to express myself in such clear and honest terms. After all, if I could come through everything that had been thrown at me, then maybe the songs that came out of it could help and inspire others who found themselves, through no fault of their own, at the bottom of life's pile.

I had struck up a friendship with Man From Delmonte's manager, Jon Ronson. The band were a quirky, jangly concern, slightly too twee for my taste, but I liked them all as people well enough. Jon was a witty individual who I had met a couple of times when he was social secretary at Central London Polytechnic and had booked us to play there.

We played a brilliant headline show at the venue supported by Factory hopefuls, The Train Set, but it was at our first gig there that Jon first clicked with me, and vice versa. On that occasion, Jon had booked us as support for The Flatmates, a band who frequently shared bills with fellow Bristolians The Brilliant Corners and Blue Aeroplanes, but were best known as part of the lo-fi, *NME*-championed C86 scene. They touted a limp, female-fronted insipid pop which left me less than impressed. Jon had broken his leg the week before so, rooted to the spot by the weight of his plaster cast, had no escape from my relentless piss-taking. Ripping into the headline band, life in general, and everything in between, I found a ready audience for my somewhat twisted sense of humour. Not only that, but I found that this diminutive, bespectacled social secretary to be a pretty amusing cat in his own right. In the shadow of the Post Office Tower, I made a mental note to mark Jon down as one of the good guys, and thought no more of it, until he showed up in Manchester the following year with his finger in a variety of different pies.

One of these pies was his involvement with a small, Stockport-based radio station called KFM. Jon cut his teeth at the station working alongside Terry Christian before being given his own show. His programme went out in the early hours of the morning to a small but loyal group of insomniacs, who would form part of the show's content themselves, phoning in to talk to Jon directly on a wide range of off-the-wall subjects. Jon had a keen interest in the weirder side of life and his radio show delved into such dark areas, punctuated, of course, by some seriously good music. Jon invited me on to his show and we struck up quite a rapport. Gradually, we would begin to see more of him socially, and he became closer and closer to the group.

Jon shared a flat in Dickinson Road with John Bramwell. Mr Bramwell performed as Johnny Dangerously, although, after once turning down my offer of a joint, would forever be known in Dub Sex circles as 'Johnny Carefully'. On one of my visits to the flat, I had brought Ellis with me. She had become fascinated with a small model motorcycle that she had found on Jon's windowsill. Walking straight up to him, she stared deep into his eyes from just a few inches away, and said, 'I used to have a motorbike, but then I crashed it, and now I'm a little girl.'

Both of us stopped dead in our tracks, open-mouthed. I had heard accounts of such things before, where memories of past lives lived on in very young children, disappearing gradually as the child got older. Frustratingly, Ellis could not be encouraged to elaborate and moved on to asking for a drink of juice and talking about her pets while the two of us picked up our jaws from the floor, wierded-out completely.

I appeared on Jon's show many times, perhaps none so memorable as the time I would talk about a life-changing experience in the countryside between Liverpool and Manchester, when Dub Sex played at a secure prison which housed some of the most high-profile child offenders in the country.

The gig had come about because Chris Cookson had started work there as a teacher of music and recording technology. Even though these young people had committed some of the most horrific crimes imaginable, they were still children, and their punishment was to be taken away from the rest of society, both for the protection of the public at large, and to effect some form of rehabilitation.

From the outside, there were few clues to the nature of the establishment, or the tragic histories of those who lived there. As someone who had spent many years in the British care system, the place reminded me of many other children's homes, all unbreakable security glass and doors that were immediately locked the minute you passed through them. This place was undeniably different, though. It may have been our knowledge of the crimes of the young people housed here, but it was hard to shake off the uneasy feelings that crept in as we drove through the high security fencing that surrounded the unit. We had arrived at Red Bank.

Chris, in his capacity as teacher/enabler, enjoyed a good relationship with those prisoners who had opted to involve themselves in music. The unit was well funded, so when several of them wanted to form a band, there was sufficient available resources to kit them out. The philosophy behind Red Bank meant that simply being incarcerated, away from family and friends, was punishment enough, and nothing was spared when it came to educational pursuits like this. So it came to pass that we were greeted by what is perhaps the most unusual support band we had ever encountered. This shy-looking four piece were dressed in new, rather expensive looking casual wear of the type favoured by the 'baggier' end of Mancunian youth, box-fresh trainers and fashionable haircuts. None of them would have seemed out of place at the Haçienda or any of our usual haunts, apart from the fact that some of them looked far too young to even get in. These were just kids, for God's sake, and it was almost impossible to believe that each of the baby-faced boys setting up their gear had taken another human life.

In theory, we were not supposed to know the details of who had committed what, but we got to know anyway, and heartbreaking stuff it was, too. One member had killed his next-door neighbour at the age of twelve after she initiated and then finished an affair. Another member had been convicted of a stabbing at a school very close to where I lived, after being driven to the end of his tether by repeated bullying. Either way, these kids (and kids they were) had crossed the uncrossable line, in most cases before they had fully got through puberty. It was a seriously fucked up state of affairs, and one that made you count your own blessings, big time.

The band's equipment was far better than our own. Our gaffer tape-covered amplifiers had been through hell over the last few years, and my own mistreatment of guitars was legendary. It was strange borrowing a gleaming Fender Stratocaster from one of our new, homicidal friends, to use as a spare in case of breakages. This was no ordinary gig day.

The audience was led in by prison officers and teaching staff, all dressed in their civilian clothes, and were seated with each row of young offenders being broken up by an adult staff member every three seats or so. Some of them looked painfully young, and all of them were on their best behaviour for the whole of the gig.

I have very few memories of the musical side of that night in Red Bank, probably because the whole situation was so weird. I can shut my eyes and see the support band, dressed to the nines in their Joe Bloggs gear, and bring to mind a vague, jangly wash of guitars, but the substance of what went down evades me. Even our own set is hard to recall in detail, as if the enormity of it all has washed my memory clean. What I do know is that I was tremendously moved, and triggered back to my own experience of institutionalised childhood.

It was a sobering experience to think how different things could have been for these boys if things had gone in another direction for them. In many cases, they had simply reacted in the heat of the moment to a situation they had no control over, and had made a terrible, terrible decision. A minute or two either side and things would have been different. Very different.

I returned to Manchester a changed person, knowing for sure that with very little change in circumstances it could have been me or one of any number of children I had been in care with that had to remain behind that 20-foot fence as we drove away. The thought that life could have been so different for these kids continued to haunt me, which is probably why I babbled about it on Jon's radio show. A story of such a weird experience would have attracted little resistance from Jon.

For my part, I wrote a song called 'I Want'. Swathes of synth-like guitar punctuated an almost military drum pattern. I sang without my guitar, as exposed emotionally as I had ever been. A changed person. The lyrics tell of a life wasted after making a split-second mistake.

> A child's mind
> Is a scrambled landscape most of the time
> But that's when I committed my crime
> And that's when I kissed my sister goodbye
> These days since I made the fear subside
> I don't cry
> Cause I want my life to be dignified
> And I want to forget the worst day in my life
> And breathe in deep at the seaside
> While I still have time
> And even in the bad dream night
> I don't cry
> Cause I want my life to be dignified
> Write it in bold type

I felt it. Felt it bad.

We got our heads down and entered a seriously productive phase of songwriting. Something in me had changed for the better. Having the influence of Ellis in my life was to be the making of me as a human being. Here was a chance for me to reverse a lifetime of pain, and have a hand in constructing a childhood for Ellis that was the polar opposite of my own. It wasn't even something that I had to think consciously about, each new day brought new wonders. Watching her master the art of walking and language, little by little, opened me up to what life was really all about, and somewhere inside I made a silent vow to not fuck this up, under any circumstances.

Whilst never leaving behind the events and real-life trials I have had to get over, I found myself with more positive things to say in songs. I had always been an optimistic person, but such thoughts had previously been based on blind belief in the human race. Now, here was positive proof that I had been right all along to think the best of people. New songs flowed, uplifting and full of unashamedly joyous celebration as I embraced my new lifestyle with great vigour, throwing myself into looking after Ellis and enjoying the experience of being part of a family.

Songs like 'Glee' found me expressing the deep satisfaction I experienced teaching Ellis to speak, an honour that was new to me. It must have seemed surprising for people who knew me, as Ellis started to accompany me everywhere. She spent countless days riding on my back in a steel backpack, chunnering into my ear, her baby talk gradually evolving into English as she began to understand the world around her. I had never been as happy in my life.

'The Rescuers' and 'Untouchable' sound like songs written by somebody with something to live for. They fizz with life, and the very pace they are played at reinforce the celebratory mood.

It was time to get into a decent studio and capture the sound of the band that we had become, but first of all, after a series of dates up and down the country, mainly in the north, we were to unveil the new line-up at a prestigious headline gig at the Haçienda.

The psychic significance of this was lost on nobody who knew me. I had, in the space of a few short years, gone from collecting glasses and working behind the bar, to headlining the place. There was something beautifully symmetrical about this, and I resolved to give our rapidly growing fan base an unforgettable show.

It felt good to be unveiling a markedly different line-up. I had enjoyed being a stand-alone vocalist, but there was something weird about teaching songs I had written to other guitarists, and not playing them myself. My style had developed on its own and as such is impossible to replicate. It was a joy, then, to let loose and hear things the way I had intended them to sound in the first place. Whilst enjoying the sound of the band over the last year or so, I felt that we had been missing my wilder approach, which gave us an edge and bite that these songs needed. Having not played my guitar live for some time, I threw myself into it with passion.

With new songs, and an inventive new backdrop – stark red and black, constructed in three pieces so it could be used in every size of venue – we were chomping at the bit. We attracted a decent crowd consisting of inquisitive newcomers, fans that had followed us since the start, and a healthy smattering of the city's movers and shakers who had come to see what all the fuss was about.

IKON were on hand to record everything, and their video pans through the crowd, revealing a rarely glimpsed Chris Nagle, threatening to break out into a shuffle, and various Inca Babies and New Fads members. We made new friends and provided our longer term supporters with a glimpse into the next stage of our adventure, debuting new material that they would come to know and love well before it was released. I used to love that when I was a young punk, knowing a band's songs from seeing them live, and then hearing them come of age as they made it onto record. It made me feel a part of everything, and these people in front of me had earned the right to experience the same feeling as I'd had in the early days of The Adverts or Buzzcocks, standing proudly as TV Smith or Pete Shelley announced 'This one is a new one...' when my friends and I already knew it backwards.

Drenched in sweat after the show, I was approached by some expensively dressed young music lovers, one of whom insisted that I sign his coat. I was no stranger to being asked for an autograph, but this was about a hundred pounds worth of Italian designer bubble jacket. After trying unsuccessfully to talk him out of it, I gave in. The kid had brought along his own permanent marker, which suggests a degree of premeditation, so he must have known what he was doing.

Bez was among the first to crash the dressing room, offering hugs and congratulations, and 808 State's master of ceremonies, Eric Barker, made a point of telling me the same thing Bez had a year earlier. 'I love it. I haven't got a fucking clue what you're singing about, but I love it!'

It was time to get these new songs on tape. We had booked Out of the Blue Studios, reuniting with my old friend Adam Lesser. The location of the studio gave me a spooky feeling in a lot of ways, revisiting the streets that I knew as a child, and being so close to Ancoats Hospital where my mother had died. Experiences like this turned bad memories good, and I was able to replace the horror with new, positive thoughts where previously only chaos and sadness had existed.

In the producer's chair, working alongside Adam, we recruited Isabella Brunner, an enthusiastic Austrian producer. The session was filmed by Cathy's partner, Phil Korbel. We had picked three new songs to record: 'Slipstream', 'I Want' and 'Until Now'. All had been getting better each time we played them and had been well received when we previewed them at recent gigs, especially the Haçienda show. They marked a new approach for us, with instrumental passages that had the capacity to stretch in size, depending on how we felt.

There was something very exciting about having the power to change the nature and length of a certain passage, as opposed to having a rigid, set number of bars that stays the same each time. The band had to keep alert and look out for my cues, often thrown out at the last moment, accompanied by the smallest of gestures to let them know when and where to change direction. Playing this way had taught us lots about the new songs, and all three, whilst remaining short enough to keep the listener fascinated, were expanded beyond the traditional three-minute pop song format, especially 'Slipstream', which featured every trick in Chris Cookson's considerable toolbag, swirling in and out of my own guitar histrionics before snapping back with perfect control into the voice, bass and drum outro.

The real revelation of the session was 'Until Now'. We focussed on this as the main track and spent an entire day creating a series of dub versions, some slowed down to half speed and featuring terrifying distorted and bent out of shape vocals, making me sound like the disguised voice of a pitch-adjusted criminal on a television crime documentary.

Isabella and Chris Cookson had formed something of a mutual appreciation society which led them to try and impress the other with a fiercely competitive dub-off as each pulled new tricks from their armoury, mixing-wise. The rest of us sat back and took it all in. This kind of thing could only make things better, we thought, and we were right.

36: Endgame

Cathy had some huge news to break. Having been involved with Friends of the Earth and supporting green charities for several years, Cathy and Phil had decided that a more extreme course of action was required to highlight the existential threat facing the world's rainforest regions and galvanise people into paying attention to the very real dangers of climate change and environmental destruction. They were going to embark on a 16,986km tandem ride from Sydney to Manchester. They would follow a route through rainforest areas on the whole, stopping to engage with local radio, newspapers and television news programmes to bring attention to their cause. With short hops by plane over war zones and oceans, the whole journey would take at least eighteen months. It meant that Cathy's involvement with the band would be coming to an end.

It was difficult to process the information. This was the biggest thing to happen to the band since we had started in earnest with Cathy and Roger back in 1986. It wasn't in any way comparable to the departure of Chris Bridgett, or the sacking of Dave Rumney. Ever since that fateful first rehearsal, writing 'Kicking The Corpse Around' in her tiny bedroom in John Nash Crescent, Cathy had been the key to everything: her unique bass sound; the way we learned to construct songs leaving space for each other to fill, taking turns to be the focal point of the group's dynamic; and, most of all, the sense of calm organisation that she brought to everything she did. I had come a long way as a human being in the last four years, changing from a feral lost boy into a person capable of love and talking about difficult personal subjects in my songs. So much of who I had become was down to the band, and Cathy was a massive part of that.

At a get-together for Cathy and Phil at Chorlton Irish Centre, I was taken for a spin around the car park on the tandem that was to be their home for the next year and a half. This really brought things home to me. I kept my true feelings in check as I was fully behind what they were trying to do. I had a great deal of respect for Cathy's beliefs and the way she conducted her life. She was the type of person who taught by example, rather than loudly pontificating about the way other people lived. I wished her well.

We organised a big farewell gig at The Boardwalk, a full circle closure: we'd debuted there as support to Miaow and had created some of our finest songs in the venue's subterranean rehearsal rooms. News of the way things were changing had spread amongst those who knew us, and there was a real end-of-an-era feel about the gig. Friends and fans of the band had travelled from London, Leeds and Scotland, knowing that it was their last chance to see Dub Sex with Cathy. Many of the people who had been important to us along the way were there.

I put my feelings of unease about the future to one side for the time being in order to get through it. Looking sharp under the striking red and black backdrop made for us by Catriona Ross, we were fierce and celebratory. It was good to play new songs about new subjects, songs like 'Glee' and 'Untouchable', but it was the better-known songs, like 'Swerve' and 'Time of Life' that took the roof off. Considering the massive changes that were just around the corner, it was an uplifting, raucous gig.

When the day came for Cathy and Phil to leave for Australia, a small group of us went along to Manchester Airport to see them off. Roger, out of all of us, seemed most affected. The bond between him and Cathy had grown over the preceding years into something akin to a brother/sister thing, and they as a rhythm section had linked to each other in a deep and real way, experiencing many life-changing experiences together. If Roger's eyes were filling up, mine were even wetter. I had no desire to make Cathy sad, but warm, salty tears were starting to drip down my face. I wiped them clean before she could see how affected I was.

Our sound engineer, Jem Noble, and Cathy's friend Val had come along to say their farewells, but it was left to tiny Ellis to take the edge off things, riding a metal trolley with screams of delight and requests to go faster, blissfully unaware of the importance of the occasion. Our motley crew reached the departure area and I picked up Ellis from her seat on the trolley and hid behind her, using her as an emotional shield as I waved to Cathy and Phil for the final time. They turned the corner and with one last wave, disappeared from view.

Cathy's departure was broadcast by Paul King on MTV's *120 Minutes* programme. The magnificently mulleted Mr King also advised any potential future bass players to contact us. Nothing came from this, but it mattered not as I had been pointed in the direction of an excellent candidate: a young, enthusiastic all-out music-lover currently working in a science-fiction book shop. This was Jay Taylor. He worked alongside Mike Noon, a freelance writer who had reviewed us a couple of times in the *NME* and his own, *Moral Sense* fanzine. Jay was already a bit of a Dub Sex fan, having been present at several of our recent shows, and had his feet firmly planted in the right place as far as new music was concerned.

Jay and Mike were part of a real underground scene, reviewing and seeking out the very best of American, European and UK music wherever it could be found. They had created a free fanzine called *Hungry and Homeless*, one sheet of double-sided A4 folded into quarters and left on the counters of record shops and clubs all over the city. They were in the dead centre of an international fanzine network that brought music to my attention that I simply would have never heard. St. Johnny, Come, Codeine, The Archers of Loaf! US rock obscurities nestled along more celebrated noisemakers like Ministry or John Zorn's Painkiller on a series of lovingly constructed mix cassettes. It was like having a spare John Peel around.

Jay became a regular fixture at Bev's house in Slade Grove, Longsight. When we began rehearsing with him in earnest, he proved to be a fine bass player, but was also much more than that. His love and total immersion in music of all kinds made him a skilled writer. Jay had prepared well with the songs that he knew, learning Cathy's basslines note for note. He was enthusiastic and eager to impress. Although Jay's bass style was very different to Cathy's, he had studied her settings and made a good attempt to replicate her sound, although, to be fair, she was a totally unique bass player, and copying her exactly was more or less impossible. There were various newer, unrecorded songs to be woven into the set, and it was on these that Jay did especially well, having more leeway to be himself. Songs like 'Untouchable' and 'Slipstream' had been aired at Cathy's farewell show, but they were still fairly unfamiliar to those that knew us, so Jay felt more comfortable with these.

Jay's first outing as a member of Dub Sex was at the newly-launched Soundgarden. The combination of new songs, a new member, and a venue that was new to almost all of the audience meant that the novelty factory was high, and led to a sell out gig. All eyes were on us and what we did next.

The Soundgarden was dead central, a stone's throw from Piccadilly Gardens and in view of the former Woolworths building, which I could not pass without thinking of the dreadful fire there over a decade earlier. I had been going to see live music in Manchester for most of my adult life, but had never known this space used before. We were playing on a metal grille-type framework with retina-burning lights pointing up into our eyes. Aesthetically it looked stark and interesting, but being blinded every thirty seconds made it hard to communicate with Jay and Chris Cookson, leading to something of an insular performance from me. The metal lattice-style stage bounced and wobbled with every step I took, so it was an intense and curiously static gig, with us standing stock-still, trying to keep our balance.

We had brought some new songs to the set, like 'Otis Blue', built upon the last bassline Cathy had come up with before going away. Named after the Otis Redding album, it once again celebrates my love of soul music, ending in an impassioned howl and the repeated phrase 'Just listening / just listening to you' all accompanied by some brilliant distorted slide guitar from Chris Cookson. On a recording of the gig, Julia Nagle can be heard in the audience enthusing about 'Otis Blue'.

Despite the odd highlight, and the birthing of new songs, I came off stage thinking that Dub Sex might have run its course. Jay as a person was a fine acquisition, but our music without Cathy simply didn't feel right, and her absence as a band member greatly affected the group's dynamic. Roger was moving into another phase of his life, too, with a new relationship and new priorities, and decided that he couldn't give as much time to music as he previously had. I had come a long way in my life too. Perhaps this was the time to stop. We left the equipment at the venue overnight, and when Roger and I arrived to move it the next day, we decided that things should end there.

I was spending more time with Chris and Julia Nagle at their house in Stockport. The singer in their band What? Noise, Tim Harris, had left and there was a space in what they were doing that I could fill perfectly. Chris was always an understated type of person, very much a man of few words, but talk of combining forces was always in the air.

Chris and Julia had a young son, of similar age to Ellis, and I would bring Ellis to play with him as we would plan our next musical move. Chris was frequently pulled away to work on records at Strawberry, and while he worked with the likes of Cud, The Wedding Present and Strangelove, Julia and I would use the time gainfully, creating backing tracks to use when Chris could engage fully with what we were doing.

Chris had recently produced *Some Friendly* by The Charlatans, which went straight to number one in the UK album charts, just reward for this brilliant and unassuming man, who had, truth be told, deserved a full producer's credit for many albums on which he is simply listed as 'engineer'. From leaving school up until now, his unique sense of space and discipline had turned the good into the great, and as Strawberry house engineer, it was him that turned the vaguer ideas of the people that worked with him – Martin Hannett in particular – into hard scientific reality. It was brilliant, then, when Chris's Charlatans album went to number one. Although the goalposts had shifted somewhat since I was small, in my mind, such a feat still belonged to the likes of Slade or Bowie, or some other music industry heavyweights whose world would never touch my own.

I had, of course, been one step removed from real chart success on several occasions. The rise of The Smiths, featuring Mike Joyce of Manchester Musicians' Collective colleagues, The Hoax, had been very close to my world, and The Chameleons had shown me that even a North Manchester council estate background was in itself no barrier to breaking through. These two bands were a pointer to what was starting to happen now. The Fall, for instance, were enjoying a purple patch in their third decade, with a major label deal and tunesmith Martin Bramah part of the band again. The Stone Roses, Happy Mondays and Inspiral Carpets were all mainstream *Top of the Pops* bands now, and it felt that it was very possibly my turn. Chris Nagle and I had linked psychically over the last few years of making records together, and him getting a number one album had felt like a personal victory for all of us, and the key to a bright, shared future.

The end of Dub Sex opened up new possibilities. As well as the opportunity to work with Chris in What? Noise, Jay and I were starting to write new songs, with Jay on guitar now, as opposed to bass. Roger stayed just as close a friend as he ever was. Chris Cookson returned to Newton-le-Willows and the musical life that he had there, teaching at Red Bank and starting a new project called Frantico, to which Jay and I were invited to contribute to.

I was seeing more and more of my young friend, Finley. Despite an eleven year age gap, we had much in common. Ever since he had come into my life as a babysitter when Dub Sex played the Hillsborough benefit gig at the Haçienda, he had become something of a fixture at Slade Grove, messing about on our upright piano, playing New Order and Pet Shop Boys basslines. He was soaking up the soul and reggae tunes in my collection as well as more obscure stuff recorded from John Peel, like Nine Inch Nails and Muslimgauze's incendiary 'United States of Islam'.

Away from music, the two of us shared the experience of a disastrous childhood. Finley had lost his mother in heartbreakingly sad circumstances, and had been shunted around relatives in Scotland before ending up in Manchester with one of his late mother's former partners. His story was an intriguing one. He was the son of Ghanaian jazz musician Cab Kaye (Anglicised from the original 'Quaye'), who had worked with such luminaries as Dizzy Gillespie, Charlie Parker and

Shirley Bassey in a long career. Finley would boast of his musical heritage to anyone within earshot, but almost nobody in our circle of friends believed him. They pitied him, putting things down to the overactive imagination of a damaged young man. It was, though, all true.

Finley, like myself, had bypassed the 'normal' way of growing up, and consequently had no social boundaries, feeling the equal of anybody he encountered and engaging with his elders and so-called 'betters' in a way that reminded me of myself at the start of my own musical journey with the Manchester Musicians' Collective. For all his problems, Finley possessed a huge deal of self-confidence, and would frequently comment on the work of other musicians, saying 'I could do better than that'.

Chris Cookson had organised a gig at The Citadel in St Helens. He was to play backing tracks from behind the mixing desk, and wanted me to contribute 'made up on the spot' vocals that he would dub up and throw around the venue, in the manner of a Jah Shaka or On U Sound event. I was to get a lift to the gig from Bev's brother, John. Shortly before setting off, Finley called round, so we bundled him into the car and brought him along.

Our set was exciting, and very much unknown territory, as I stretched my voice into new and weird areas, mangled beyond belief by Chris's space echo trickery. Finley stood behind the mixing desk with us wearing a pink bubble coat and a happy grin. I decided to put his bravado to the test, passing him the microphone.

'Go on then, Finley!'

He didn't need telling twice. Although his delight at finding his voice made him fill up the sparse backing track up a little too much, there was no doubt about it, the boy could sing.

I arranged to meet up with Chris Nagle at the launch of Sarah Champion's new book *And God Created Manchester*, an exhaustive look at Manchester music. Coming as it did, during the height of Madchester and all that surrounded it, the book was something of a big deal. The launch took place in the Victorian splendour of Manchester Town Hall's Great Hall, beneath Ford Madox Brown's twelve magnificent pre-Raphaelite murals depicting such momentous events as 'The Baptism of Edwin' and 'The Expulsion of the Danes from Manchester'.

Sarah had written an informed account of Manchester's musical landscape. As an *NME* writer, she was exposed to the best (and worst!) of everything across a wide range of genres, and her book reflected this, featuring the often unspoken worlds of the hip hop, acid house and dance music communities, as well as the guitar-based fare that was the staple diet of her day job. Sarah had started writing at a ridiculously young age (mid-teens) and approached it with the verve and enthusiasm of a true fan. She was knowledgeable, too. Being the main music writer at the *Manchester Evening News* put her in the right place at the right time, ideally positioned to see the ascent of the new music from its first early stirrings.

Sarah devoted the best part of a chapter to the Hulme scene, filled with pearls of wisdom from me, speaking with the relaxed honesty of someone who is talking to a trusted friend rather than a journalist. I knew that she understood and cared very much about what I was trying to do.

> Here comes the kings of these slums. Like Mark Hoyle. He enthuses, 'Hulme is full of people who have escaped the poor, overspill estates like Wythenshawe and Langley. Hulme is poor, but it's far better. There's a cosmopolitan-ness here. It's full of personalities and cultures, it's near the city centre and there's lots going on...' [...] Hulme smells. Stinks of piss and beer and decay and just plain *fear*. Fear like hospital disinfectant. Fear like sweaty police cells. Fear like a knife pulled in a back alley. Fear that leaves you screaming in your sleep. Fear that has you digging your nails into your palms until they bleed. Fear like Dub Sex. Dogs grow like their masters and bands sound like their homeland. Dub Sex sound like Hulme. Hulme is huge, bleak, dark, eerie, most of all *frightening*. So are Dub Sex.

She clearly wasn't looking for work from the Hulme Tourist Board. Of all the writers that had got behind us thus far, Sarah got it the most, and she took the trouble to delve that little bit deeper into my own part in it all, focussing on the words, something other writers didn't understand, perhaps due to my strong accent and unorthodox delivery.

'Mark wrote lyrics so awesome that you just wanted to snatch them from the air and hug them tight,' she wrote, leaving it to me to expand on our best-known tune in my own words.

> 'Swerve' is about not giving in. It's about having the nerve, believing in yourself, not getting dragged down, keeping out of trouble. Dub Sex saved me personally. I've spent my whole life since I left care trying to set up Dub Sex. I was going totally off the rails. Now at least I know where the rails are. The rails are my belief.

And here I found myself at the book launch with Chris Nagle, the UK's number one producer. In the ornate, immaculately tiled Town Hall toilets, I stood in the urinal next to Charlatan's front man Tim Burgess, pondering how far we all had come. We had been sharing Chris Nagle to some extent; he had been working on their 'Indian Rope' single while we had been deep into our stuff with Chris at Strawberry. Never having met before, but each being aware of the other from Chris and the music scene in general, we said our hellos without shaking hands.

I disappeared into the night full of excitement and hope for the future. That future would be a very different beast to all that had gone before, I knew that much, and it felt natural and right to draw a line under Dub Sex. It was an emotional realisation for me to come to. It was like starting from scratch, which, in many ways, was exactly what I was doing.

Chris was a busy bunny for the following few months. It would be some time before he could give himself completely to our new project, so, not wanting to waste a second, I rented a rehearsal room at The Boardwalk and began to write with Julia in preparation for when Chris could join us. Julia and I hung out together, appearing on Jon Ronson's KFM radio show, and getting the word around about the new project. Slowly, I began to feel a part of things, and when Chris's work commitments were over, the three of us started work on the new What? Noise in earnest.

It was a new decade, and I was starting out in a new band, with new people, drawing a natural line under all that had gone before. Everything was in front of me, and the life I had lived up to this point had more than equipped me for anything that could possibly be thrown my way.

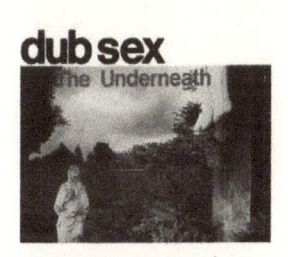

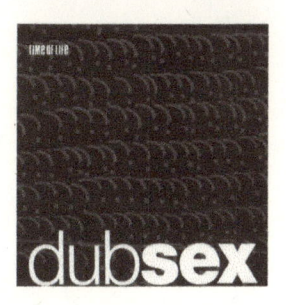

APPENDIX I
Discography

A discography of released music that was made during the span of this book (1979-1990)

Vibrant Thigh

'Wooden Gangsters' on *A Manchester Collection* (Object Music 1979)

'Walking Away' on *Unzipping The Abstract* (MMC Records 1980)

'Wooden Gangsters' on *Teenage Treats Vol 1* (Xerox Records 1998)

'Walking Away' on *The Deeply Vale Box Set* (Ozit Records 2015)

'Wooden Gangsters' on *Greater Manchester Punk Two Now We Are Heroes 1978-82* (Vinyl Revival 2017)

'Walking Away' on *Plastic Dance 2* (Finders Keepers Records 2019)

'Walking Away' on *Keeping Control* (3 CD compilation) (Cherry Red Records 2023)

Dub Sex

'Yonkers' on *Two Points To Tonka* (cassette) (Son of Inevitable Records 1985)

'Tripwire!' Flexidisc free with issue 13 of *Debris* magazine (Debris 1986)

Dub Sex 12 inch 4-track single (Skysaw Records 1987)

Push! 7-track mini album (Ugly Man Records 1988)

The Underneath 12-inch 4-track single (Cut Deep Records 1988)

'The Underneath' 7-inch single (Cut Deep Records 1988)

Swerve 12-inch 3-track single (Cut Deep Records 1989)

'Voice of Reason' on *Bananas* (compilation album) (Ugly Man Records 1989)

'Instead of Flowers (remix) on *Manchester, North of England* (compilation album/ cassette) (Bop/Scam Records 1988)

Splintered Faith compilation album (Cut Deep Records 1989)

Time of Life 12-inch 3-track single (Bop/Scam Records 1989)

'Barber, Barber' on *Edward Not Edward* (compilation album) (Wooden Records 1989)

'Swerve' (John Peel session version) on *Manchester, So Much To Answer For* (compilation album) (Strange Fruit 1990)

'Time of Life' on *Indie Top 20: Volume VIII*, (compilation album) (Beechwood Music 1990)

'Instead of Flowers remix/ Time of Dub' on *Subculture* fanzine free CD (Subculture 2000)

'Over and Over/Time of Life' (Martin Hannett versions) 7-inch single (O Genesis Records 2014)

'North by North East' on *21 Songs For John* (compilation album/ download) (Unwashed Territories 2014)

'Swerve' on *Manchester, North of England* (7 CD compilation box set) (Cherry Red Records 2017)

Search For The Right Words (compilation CD) (Optic Nerve Records 2019)

The Manchester Mekon
'The Idle Gnome Expedition' on *No Forgetting* album (Discos Transgénero 2017) (Mark Hoyle guest vocal from 1980)

APPENDIX II
Then...

Overleaf: Midland Hotel, Manchester, 1992
(L to R) Arthur Brooks, Rat, Cathy Brooks, Bev (with Stefan Hoyle in baby carrier), MH, Finley McGowan holding Ellis Cain, Jem Noble
Photo by Phil Korbel

Jay Taylor joined me and the Nagles in What? Noise, and we recorded many tunes at Strawberry, as well as a session for Mark Radcliffe and Marc Riley's BBC Radio 5 show, *Hit The North*. Julia Nagle would subsequently join The Fall.

Chris Cookson, Jay Taylor and I started to make music as Frantico, recording 'Too Many Guns' at NAAFI in Newton-le-Willows.

In 1992, my son Stefan was born, a brother to Ellis. The two of them are my world.

After cycling from Sydney to Manchester, Cathy formed Dumb with me, Jay Taylor and Jonny Hankins, soon to be joined by Jay's sister Beth on drums. We recorded two albums (*Thirsty* and *King Tubby Meets Max Wall Uptown*) and three singles 'Always Liverpool', 'Stephen' and 'Do One' as well as a John Peel session (January 1997). Jay later left to join John Robb in Gold Blade.

Finley McGowan took ownership of his father's name and, as Finley Quaye, released the double-platinum selling *Maverick A Strike* album in 1997, winning the 1997 MOBO award for Best Reggae Artist, and a BRIT award in 1998 for British Male Solo Artist. I played on his follow-up album, *Vanguard*, and Finley released his version of Frantico's 'Too Many Guns' on his 'Ultra Stimulation' single which entered the UK charts in 1998.

With Chris Cookson and Cathy Brooks, I started Ninebar, an electronic, sample-based dub band, featuring me and Cathy on stage, and Chris mixing live. We supported Finley on his first major tour, playing to thousands at the height of his chart success, and recording sessions for Manchester-based radio stations Radio Space and Radio Sonic. Chris Cookson went on to join Jah Wobble's band as guitarist, playing all over the world.

After a period working for Stockport MBC and Manchester Adventure Playground Association, as a youth/play worker, I began working on a series of spoken word/prose pieces, which would eventually become *Angel Meadow Story*, performed at Manchester's Whitworth Art Gallery by SPIRIT:level, an electronic/film partnership with my colleague, Wark. These pieces were published in very limited editions by Paper Piano publications of Manchester.

In 2013, Dub Sex reformed for a series of shows and festival appearances. Cathy, Chris Bridgett and I were joined by Kev Clark on drums, and my son Stefan Hoyle on guitar. The following year saw the release of two songs originally recorded at Strawberry with Martin Hannett ('Over and Over'/'Time of Life') as a 7-inch single on Tim Burgess's O Genesis label. This was followed in 2019 by the release of *Search For The Right Words* on Optic Nerve Records, a Dub Sex compilation album.

In 2015, I appeared live with Heath Common, playing bass at *Still Howling*, an event to mark the 60th anniversary of the first reading of 'Howl' by Allen Ginsberg. I also appeared on the eponymous Heath Common album in 2017, contributing guitar and vocals to 'Satori In The Sky' and 'Basquiat and Warhol', which also featured on his *Beatsbox* EP.

In 2019, I provided vocals for a one-off track by Funferall called 'Beach Virus'. The lyrics I used were taken from a postcard sent to me by Mike Hutton shortly before his death in 1988. The track was written by me and collaborator, Wark, and released on the Mad Pride benefit album, *Enragés Fou Noix*.

SPIRIT:level released the 7-inch single 'Orgreave/F.U.C.K.E.R.Y!' in June 2024 on Paper Piano Records.

Acknowledgements

For help in writing this book, Mark Hoyle would like to thank Tony McHale, Kathy Moore, Brian Logan, Martin Coogan, Mark Iveson, Lee Pickering, Terry Egan, Jacqui Carroll, Cathy Brooks, Chris Nagle, Todd Graft, Rat, Roger Cadman, Ian Atkinson, Howard Morrison, Bill Byford, Dave Haslam, Richard Davis, Richard Wills, Jon Ronson, Ginette Carpenter and Dave Norman, Beth Taylor, Steve Hanley, Mark Burgess, Ian Daley and Isabel Galán at Route.

For more on Dub Sex:
www.dubsex.net

For more on this book and for Route's book list:
www.route-online.com